William A. Schram

10—

D1483380

Road to
Reformation

BOEHMER

MARTIN LUTHER

1483-1546

2160542A

NCMC
BR
325
.B57

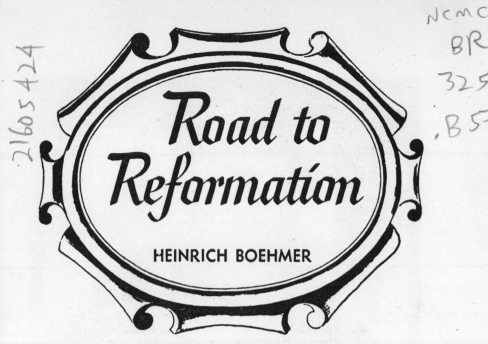

Road to Reformation

HEINRICH BOEHMER

Martin Luther to the Year 1521

Translated from the German by

JOHN W. DOBERSTEIN

and

THEODORE G. TAPPERT

*Published and Distributed in the Public Interest
by authority of the Alien Property Custodian
under License No. A-1013 issued to
The United Lutheran Publication House*

MUHLENBERG PRESS PHILADELPHIA, PA.

1946

COPYRIGHT, 1946, BY MUHLENBERG PRESS

COPYRIGHT OF ORIGINAL GERMAN WORK VESTED
IN THE ALIEN PROPERTY CUSTODIAN, 1945,
PURSUANT TO LAW

3rd Printing

This is a translation, with minor revisions to
bring it up to date, from the second German
edition of Heinrich Boehmer's *Der junge Luther*

PRINTED IN U.S.A.

TABLE OF CONTENTS

FOREWORD

In the sixteenth century, anyone who set out to give a scientific explanation of a man's character and destiny first sought to determine the constellation of the stars at his natal hour. This method was formerly used with respect to Luther also. Melanchthon cast the horoscope of the Reformer several times, and his example was often imitated by the astrologers of his and later ages, despite the fact that Luther's ridicule of "that scabby art *astrologia*" was familiar to them. There is hardly anyone today who believes that the problem of Luther's life can be solved by such fantasies. Today, if one wished to explain the physical and psychical constitution of a man, one would not search the stars, but would rather examine the environment in which the man developed and investigate whether and in how far his physical and psychical peculiarities might be demonstrated to be due to the influences about him or to heredity.

The biological investigation of heredity, which concerns itself solely with the bodily structure of living beings, has already reached a few positive results, but the psychological investigation of heredity is still in its beginnings. Biologists and psychologists are agreed, however, that the problem of heredity can be studied only in those indviduals whose antecedents are accurately known, and for whose development one possesses an unbroken chain of precise observations from earliest infancy to ripe old age. For just as the conformation of the skull and the color of the eyes and hair change in the course of years, as everyone knows, so the character of a person also changes. The youth is different from the child, and the man is different from the youth. Therefore, if one's knowledge is limited to either youth or adulthood, one can never distinguish between the transient and the permanent peculiarities of character and endowment.

Unfortunately, on the basis of contemporary accounts,

we can trace Luther's development only from his thirtieth year. For the time preceding, we have at our disposal only a few *casual* utterances of the Reformer, concerning *isolated* events and facts which appeared to him *later* to be especially important for some reason or other; but in many instances we can no longer determine with certainty whether they were actually important in his development. As far as his antecedents on the paternal and maternal sides are concerned, we are informed in regard to his father alone, and then only to a degree. But, after all, how little we know even of him! As for his mother, of whom, according to Spalatin, he was supposed to have been "the spit and image," we have only a very shadowy conception. Only the names of the paternal grandfather and grandmother have come down to us, while of the maternal grandmother, on whose hereditary influence we should place an especially high estimate according to the opinion of some scholars, we have not even the name. We can maintain with some degree of certainty only that she came from Smalcald and hence was of urban extraction. From this it is evident that, even if the principles of psychical heredity, for which we have been searching so long, should finally be discovered, the psychologist would never be in a position to explain the personality of the Reformer genetically by means of these principles.

But the biological investigation of heredity is in no better position to solve this problem. When we hear that Luther's parents were both "small, short people, a swarthy folk," it no longer appears at all unusual that he himself attained only medium height and had brown eyes and brown hair. But having established this simple fact, with which the biologists cannot do very much, we are again at the end of our knowledge. If we were to compare the portraits of the parents, done by Lucas Cranach the Elder in 1527 (now hanging in the Luther Room of the Wartburg), with the few genuine portraits of Luther by the same Cranach, we could not even answer with certainty the apparently easy question as to whether the Reformer took after his father more than he took after his mother, despite Spalatin's opinion quoted above.

It is consequently mere humbuggery to keep on trying to deduce certain real, or supposed, peculiarities of Luther from certain real, or supposed, peculiarities of his antecedents. It is claimed, for example, that because his father occasionally drank somewhat beyond the requirements of thirst, he himself was therefore hereditarily cursed with the inclination to dipsomania. We are also reminded that Luther's uncle, Klein-Hans Luder, was sentenced by law in Mansfeld no less than eleven times between 1499 and 1513 for assault, battery, and calumny and also that the Luders of Möhra, according to the evidence in the criminal record of the Salzungen court-treasury, extending from the second half of the sixteenth to the first half of the seventeenth century, had a very decided tendency toward violence. [1] The conclusion has been drawn from this that there is some truth in the old legend that Hans Luder fled from Möhra because of a murder, and that it is also to be taken for granted that the Reformer himself had a similar hereditary predisposition toward rowdyism, or at least toward rash outbursts of passion. The violent deeds of the Luders in Möhra would indeed be of interest to the psychiatrist if the Luder family had differed in this respect from the other peasants of Möhra. But this is not at all the case. Other peasants of Möhra, according to the evidence of the Salzungen criminal record, were just as much given to rowdyism, or, more correctly, just as much inclined as the Luders to settle their larger and smaller affairs by way of the old German custom of the "vehmic court" or feud; that is, by taking the law into their own hands. What is more, in this tendency they were not at all exceptional among the peasants of western Germany or, for that matter, of all Germany in that time. When things were going reasonably well, all the peasants of that time were given to physical violence. As

[1] So H. Brückner, *Archiv für sächsische Geschichte*, II. Boehmer's own later investigations, however, have not confirmed these statements. Cf. Boehmer, *Allgemeine Ev.-Luth. Kirchenzeitung*, 1926, pp. 1060 ff.

Adam Moser has conclusively proved, it was not until after the Thirty Years' War that this tendency toward violence and taking the law into their own hands gradually disappeared among the German peasantry.

The fact that Klein-Hans Luder was a brawler and a "cut-throat" is certainly not to be denied. But from the conduct of this one and apparently only misguided member of the Luder family in Möhra one certainly cannot draw any conclusions as to the psychical constitution of the brother or even of the nephew, especially since we have no idea whether this conduct was conditioned by a psychical defect or only by the conditions under which Klein-Hans Luder lived. The same is true concerning the tendency toward drunkenness so arbitrarily ascribed to the Reformer. That this tendency can be transmitted and that it can produce very grave consequences in the physical and psychical constitution of descendants was known in the sixteenth century. As an example of this Luther later pointed warningly to the case of his nephew, Hans Polner, who, as he said, was the son of his drunkard brother-in-law, Hans Polner of Mansfeld, who begot him when he was "in his cups." But in this same much-quoted passage of the *Table Talk* he mentions this hereditarily cursed nephew expressly as an example opposite from that of his own father—a man who was physically and mentally sound, for whom wine was not "poison," even if he did occasionally drink a glass too much. That Luther was not mistaken in this is confirmed by the whole life story of the elder Hans. If the latter had been a "tippler," he would certainly never have been able to rise from the status of a common laborer to that of a prosperous small businessman, and he would never have succeeded in finding anyone among the Mansfeld capitalists to advance what was for those times a very considerable capital for the establishment and expansion of his business.

We must conclude, therefore, that the problem of Luther cannot be solved either wholly or in part by the methods of the hereditary theory. The modern investigation of personality, however, employs not only the watchword "heredity," but takes into consideration the formative influences of "environment" as well. In fact, there are still some few today who place more importance on the establishment of these influences than on the investigation of ancestry. There probably is no one today who denies the significance of the environmental factors in the psychical processes of life. Only one difficulty remains, and that is the question whether it will ever be possible to ascertain fully and exactly what is the great mass of influences which the word "environment" embraces. And the answer to this question is simply, No.

What is impossible in a living person is naturally ruled out as a matter of course in a person who is no longer living. The only thing that can be known with certainty about the environment of a man of the past is a mass of unrelated fragments, out of which only the constructive imagination of the historian can fashion some sort of coherence. The portraits which are made after this manner often have a great aesthetic appeal, but one must never forget, in the pleasure which one experiences in their contemplation, that they are all more or less reconstructions, and that they never reveal clearly whether or in how far the person whom they reflect has actually been influenced by the fortuitously transmitted events and facts therein employed, which are arbitrarily labeled "environment." For like a plant, a person takes from his environment only what is compatible with his nature. Which of these environmental factors have influenced him, therefore, is never to be taken for granted, but must always be examined point by point. It is consequently impossible to reconstruct, as fully and exactly as the environment theory requires, Luther's environment in Mansfeld, Magdeburg, Eisenach, or even in Wittenberg. It is impossible to determine what were the general and specific environmental "pulls" which contributed either to the promoting or retarding of his development. It is, therefore, advisable to avoid this fruitless

attempt from the very outset and to limit oneself solely to
the ascertainment of *those* facts and events which have been
demonstrated to be significant for his inner and outward
development.

Thus it becomes evident that neither of these two theories
which rule the modern investigation of personality is work-
able in practice, and consequently neither can be applied to
Luther. Does it follow, then, that the task we have set ourselves is utterly impossible? If what we call personality were a
product only of heredity and environment, it would be impossible, and we would in fact have to abandon the task without
going any further. But personality is not merely a collective
name for the physical and psychical characteristics which
happen to appear in an individual. Nor is it simply the sum
or product of these characteristics, hence an aggregate which
cannot even be explained by the analytical method. But it
is rather that "something" which cannot be analyzed further,
which is always found in motion and flux, which is mysterious and yet clearly perceptible, and which works in, with,
and under the above-mentioned characteristics. The real task
of the biographer is to grasp that "something" and describe
its workings. Everything else he has to do, such as the gathering and criticism of the sources, the establishment of specific dates and events which comprise the external history
of the person concerned, and the ascertainment of the original relationship between these facts—all this is merely preliminary to his real task. The biographer will be able to
accomplish such a task only if, in all his analysis and deduction (which have played the leading role in the positivistic
scientific scholarship of the last decade), he has not wholly
lost the capacity for allowing a personality to work on him
in its living wholeness and if this personality is clearly
reflected *in its wholeness* in the sources which are at his
disposal.

The fact that the sources for the biography of Luther are
so abundant—the Weimar edition already includes ninety

quarto volumes and the Ludwig Enders edition of the letters
almost 4,000 numbers—does not in itself prove that a biography of Luther is possible in the sense just indicated, for
there are scholars who have written almost as much as
Luther but who have so completely blotted out their real
selves that one does not find so much as a trace of it in their
works. But Luther could never have done this. On the contrary, he always spoke out frankly, freely, and without undue
discretion or caution, saying just what he felt and thought.
Even his most scholarly books are "fragments of one great
continuing confession." That is to say, they were revelations
of his powerful personality which were the product of the
strongest inner commitment and shot through with the feeling of the moment. Therefore, if we would learn to know
him, we do not have to begin by taking precautions of any
sort, nor do we have to start by feeling ourselves laboriously
into his mind and spirit, nor first carefully weigh and suspiciously turn all his words about in order to get out of them
some possibly intended secondary or concealed meaning. It
is enough to hear him. And for that reason, he shall be made
to speak in his own words as often as at all possible in the
pages which follow.

Yet, in the course of time, they would all have sunk to the level of the cottager if they had not regularly married only among themselves and invariably bequeathed their possessions, without division, to the youngest son. The elder sons had to seek employment outside the village, unless they married into another estate or worked all their lives as hired men for the youngest son (in the latter case giving up all hope of having their own families). So it was that the number of farms capable of providing a span of horses for service to the lords, and the number of families belonging to the ruling community, remained quite constant for centuries. This had very serious consequences for the families themselves. They seldom died out completely, but after several generations they usually lost their inherited property and disappeared from the village forever.

Nevertheless, one of these old "quit-rent" families succeeded in maintaining itself to the twentieth century in its ancestral village and in its own class, the class of the modest landowner. This is the family of Luder, or Lüder, of Möhra, located about an hour's journey north of Salzungen. In 1536 the family owned all of five farms in Möhra. But even at that date the members of this family had spread out so much into the neighboring villages that Martin Luther, when he went from Eisenach along the border of the Thuringian forest in May, 1521, had the impression that they took in "almost the whole neighborhood." From this we are justified in concluding that the Luders had been living in this old border territory between Thuringia and Franconia for centuries. However, there is specific evidence for the existence in Möhra before the year 1500 of only one branch of the family. This is the branch of which the Reformer's grandfather, Heine Luder (who died about 1510), was the head around 1480. The records show that this Heine Luder had four sons—Gross-Hans, Klein-Hans, Veit, and Heinz—by his wife Margaret, nee Lindemann, who died in ripe old age at Mansfeld in 1521. Heinz, as the youngest, had the claim to the

CHAPTER I

EARLY YEARS AT HOME (1483-96)

In the fifteenth century the population of the electoral villages on the western edge of the Thuringian forest included an uncommonly large number of prosperous people who occupied a legally favored position. They were the so-called "quit-rent folk." As their name suggests, all these "quit-renters" were still under obligation to pay rent to the petty secular and spiritual lords of the valley of the Werra. But the rent which they had to pay was levied not on their persons, but on the land which their ancestors had received from the lords as hereditary fiefs. Nor did the obligation to pay rent prevent them from selling or bequeathing their possessions at their own discretion. As a consequence they had come, by the late Middle Ages, to comprise a body of free landowners, and they had only one lord, the Elector. Previous to the promulgation of the law of 1513, the Elector very seldom interfered with the village self-government. So the people could exercise all the rights of a ruling community with practically no interference. They could choose the mayor and other village officers, pass local ordinances, impose fines, and administer the community treasury. But what was most important, with the exception of the backwoods settlers (the so-called "cottagers," who were not free, had no rights whatsoever, and at most occupied only a house and garden), they had the right to share the use of community forests, fields, meadows, and water.

In the light of all this, it is easy to understand that these people experienced no hardship, as a rule, when the Elector placed a tax of one gulden on every span of oxen they owned. Nor is it difficult to understand that they were often in a position to own a pair of horses and keep several hired men.

3

PART ONE

THE REFORMER IN THE MAKING

paternal farm. Veit married into another farm. Gross-Hans, however, decided, not later than the fall of 1483, to leave his fatherland and friends forever. Together with his young wife Margaret (nee Ziegler, of Möhra[1]) and his first-born infant son, he sought his fortune as a miner in the copper mines of the county of Mansfeld, to which he had probably been directed by the miners in the recently opened copper mines near Möhra. He first migrated to Eisleben, the chief city of the county. Here it was that, toward midnight on November 10, 1483, a second son was born to him on *Lange Gasse* where the Luther school stands today. The very next morning, after the custom of the time, he had the infant baptized in the tower room of the neighboring Church of St. Peter by the parish priest, Bartholomew Rennebecher. The boy was named Martin after the saint of the day.

It appears that Hans Luder did not prosper in Eisleben. On this account he moved to Mansfeld with his little family in the early summer of 1484. Here he probably began as a common laborer in the mines. But before 1491 he found opportunity to enter, as a shareholder, one of the many little associations which were formed to mine copper. At the same time he leased a little foundry in partnership with another Mansfelder. It appears that the necessary capital was advanced to him by one of the Mansfeld copper merchants. This was often done in Mansfeld at that time. But it also happened very often that the new operator sank back again into the class of wage laborer because he was unable to satisfy the capitalist. If Hans Luder wished to escape this fate, he had to bestir himself. In the very year in which his family was increasing most rapidly—at the beginning of 1505 there were four sons and the same number of daughters, and at least one child had already died—he had to watch his pennies carefully. As an example of the poverty in his parents' home at this time, Luther tells us that his mother, like other

[1] So Boehmer, in the *Allgemeine Ev.-Luth. Kirchenzeitung*, 1926, pp. 1062 f.

poor women, had to gather the necessary firewood in the forest and drag it home. It was only at the beginning of the sixteenth century that Hans Luder had paid off his debts to such an extent that he could lay by several guldens each year for expenditures which were not absolutely necessary. It is characteristic of him, however, that he continued to exert himself to enlarge his business. By 1511 he was part-owner of at least six shafts and two foundries, and one of these must have been a very considerable enterprise, for that day. But he did not get to be a rich man, even in his old age, if the 1250 guldens which his heirs divided on July 10, 1534, actually represented his whole fortune.

Was he just as successful in rearing children as he was in his business during his early years? If we listen to Luther, who surely was not inclined to judge too severely, we cannot answer this question in the affirmative. Neither of the parents understood that every child must be handled differently. They cut them all to the same pattern. Furthermore, both of them were convinced that a child cannot thrive without thrashing any more than without eating and drinking. Accordingly they did not fail to reach for the switch even for very minor offenses. For stealing a nut, Luther was once beaten by his mother until the blood flowed. Another time, for a similar misdeed, his father "flogged him so severely that he ran away from him and bore him a grudge for it." But the fact that his father later made such an effort to "win back to himself" the estranged little fellow shows that it was not out of brutality, but from a mistaken sense of duty, that he treated his own flesh and blood so severely. Like the mother, he "meant heartily well by" his little ones.

For this very reason, although it must have been very hard for him to scrape together the necessary groschen, Hans Luder sent his little Martin to the town school. And he did this as early as possible, probably on St. Gregory's Day (March 12) of the year 1488. From this time on, Martin may be presumed to have plodded to school practically every day for eight whole years—for there were no holidays in those days.

What could the youngster learn in this school? Properly speaking, only four things: reading, writing, singing, and Latin. Latin was the most important subject. Even reading was taught from a Latin primer. He also learned to write from Latin texts. At the same time he had to memorize several Latin words every day, and occasionally longer passages from the primer as, for example, the Ten Commandments, the Creed, the Lord's Prayer, the Ave Maria, and so on. But since the teacher could not give his attention exclusively to the primarians (he had to drill the "Donatists" and "Alexandrians" of the higher classes at the same time and in the same room), he had to content himself for the most part with a mechanical hammering of these venerable passages into the little ones' heads and a brief explanation of the Latin vocabulary appearing in the texts. Hence Luther could hardly have received any religious stimulation in these courses, the only courses in religion that he ever had in his life.

When a pupil had completed the requirements of the first class, he passed on to the second class. Here he learned to conjugate and decline from Donatus, and if, after much practice, no misfortune befell him, he was also initiated into the mysteries of Latin syntax by way of the *Doctrinale* of Alexander de Villedieu. But it is certain that Luther never got that far in Mansfeld. There is every reason to believe that he never got beyond the second class. For, on account of the mechanical method of teaching at that time, even gifted students usually had to spend many years learning merely to read and write. And as a rule it was even longer before they finished the study of Donatus.

Why, then, did they torment these poor youngsters, as Luther later affirmed, for as long as twenty and more years with Donatus and Alexander de Villedieu? The answer is that knowledge of Latin was still the requirement for entrance into the clergy and all the other higher professions.

And why did they put so much emphasis—next to Latin—
upon singing? Because by tradition the students had to take
part as singers in all church services. Thus, on principle, they
learned only what they could sooner or later make use of.
But it is at first somewhat astonishing to find that they always
had to memorize verbatim the meaningless mnemonic verses
of the so-called "Cisiojanus," which was used to reckon the
days of the church calendar, while they were taught no arithmetic at all, or just a very little in the course in singing. Perhaps, being guided in the selection of the material of instruction only by considerations of utility, it was believed that
arithmetic was unnecessary, since most of the students later
became clergymen and therefore could go through life without a thorough knowledge of mathematics. From all appearances Luther never had any real instruction in arithmetic in
his whole life. It is possible that the curious weakness in
figures, which we observe in him later, was due to this. At
all events, nothing was done in the schools which he attended
to remedy the weakness.

To determine the value of an educational system, one
must ascertain not only *what* the instructors teach, but also
how they do their teaching. As far as the latter is concerned,
little can be said in praise of any of the schools which Luther
attended. The instruction in all of them consisted for the
most part in a mechanical cramming and hammering of facts
into the pupils' heads. In justice one must add that the
schoolmaster of that day could hardly have discharged his
duties in any other way, for he had to teach a foreign language to children of the most varied ages (at the same time
and in the same room) and simultaneously impart the art of
reading and writing to the little tots. It was necessarily inherent in this method of dull drilling, moreover, that the
schoolmaster could not get along without resort to the rod.
For when one drills, one cannot, in the long run, hold the
attention of boys and girls except by force. It is not surprising, therefore, to find that there was a great deal of thrashing

going on in the Mansfeld school, and that it was sometimes quite unreasonable. So Luther, when he was in the primary class, was flogged not less than fifteen times on a single morning (by a novice teacher, it would appear, who had not yet learned to know the children), because he could not decline and conjugate—a thing which could not properly have been required of him at the time, for declension began only in the second grade.

In consideration of all this, it is easy to understand why Luther passed such very unfavorable judgment on the schools "under the papacy." What the lower school in the late Middle Ages offered by way of pabulum to the youthful mind was really very insufficient. Nor was the complaint without foundation that its pedagogical method was not at all adapted to "first-rate talents" and that its discipline had "something of the hangman's art" about it. But, of course it does not follow from this that Luther, like many another student who had spent twenty or more years "on Donatus and Alexander," had "learned nothing" in this school. Two things he learned very thoroughly there: Latin and singing. It is true that he was later dissatisfied with the Latin which he had been taught, for it was not classical Latin but the "corrupt" Latin, so sharply criticized by the humanists, which was employed in churches, schools, and trade during the late Middle Ages. Yet his own example shows what power, richness, and preciseness even this somewhat less polished Latin was capable of in the hands of a great writer.

As far as the "singing" is concerned, there is no doubt that his musical talent was awakened and wonderfully developed as a result of the instruction. Most of the very significant knowledge and skill of which he later gave evidence was gained in the lower school. He could hardly have learned much in addition during his years as a student and monk.

In addition to Latin and music, to his great regret he was taught "no history at all" in the school. But he did receive

instruction in some few of the "poets." In all probability
these were simply the three commonly used textbooks of
Pseudo-Cato, Aesop, and Terence. Because they were limited, he "learned" them so thoroughly that he still knew large
parts of them by heart and could quote them on the spur of
the moment when he was an older man. And he not only
"learned" them, but he learned really to love them, despite
the fact that they were used mostly for practicing declension,
conjugation, and rules of Latin syntax. Even as an old man
he continued to treasure the moral maxims of Pseudo-Cato
(which he had studied as a primer-boy) and the fables of
Aesop (which he had studied in the second grade) so highly
that he called them the best books next to the Bible itself.
In fact, he once began (1530) to rewrite the fables for the
use of the German people. With regard to Terence, whom
he liked particularly, he later expressed the opinion that one
page of his comedies is worth more than all the dialogues
and colloquies of Erasmus of Rotterdam. He was quite as
appreciative afterward of the two dreaded tormentors of the
schoolboy in that day, Donatus and Alexander. So he evidently developed a taste in his early school days for these
dry-as-dust authors, probably because they stimulated him
to reflection—for he was particularly susceptible by nature
to such stimulation.

Accordingly, Luther owed the much abused lower school
something more than his expressions of disapproval would
lead one to expect. The little that it intended to teach, it
taught him very thoroughly. And although it concerned
itself only with the memory, and consciously trained only
the memory, it nevertheless awakened and helped to develop
his other mental faculties as well—for instance, a linguistic,
dialectic, and musical talent. He must certainly have found
some pleasure even in the instruction he received in Mansfeld, particularly in his singing classes. This appears from
the fact that the awakening of mental powers and the emer-
gence of new intellectual interests release a flood of happiness

in the soul which allows one to forget all one's sorrow, at least for the moment.

But there is something else that was working upon Luther's soul in these years and that was making an even deeper impression. This was the memory of an injustice that had been suffered. There is nothing remarkable about the fact that the Reformer apparently remembered most vividly those events of his childhood—in themselves not uncommon —through which his belief in the justice of parents and teachers was first shaken. Such experiences always make an indelible impression upon a sensitive child. In fact, they often become the cause of serious inner conflict because they stand in such sharp contrast to the authority which parents and teachers claim. Because this is a common and normal experience, we must not allow ourselves to be misled into representing Luther's youth as a kind of martyrdom. Even if his parents did not understand the fine art, so often praised by Luther, of mixing earnestness with kindness in such a way that earnestness never degenerates into harshness or kindness into weakness, he could see by their attitude, even at that time, that they "meant heartily well by him." And though it was often exceedingly difficult in those years for his parents to provide sufficient bread and milk for the constantly growing troop of children, yet, as far as we know, he never had to suffer real hunger, for he surely would not have forgotten to mention it later if this had been so. In spite of all their cares, his parents did not behave at home as if the wolf were at the door. On the contrary, as the Reformer once explicitly declared, Father Hans was by nature a jovial companion, always ready for fun and pastimes. Mother Margaret, too, although she was of a more phlegmatic temperament, could on occasion rise to such high spirits that she broke out in her favorite melancholy ditty:

Mir und dir ist keiner hold,
das ist unser beider Schuld.

Martin had contacts at home other than those with his parents. He had many brothers and sisters, and thus there was always someone with whom he could amuse himself, after the fashion of children, without being called to order on every occasion by his strict mother; the more the children took care of themselves, the freer the careworn mother was to carry on her domestic duties. And then, too, in the long run the harsh treatment he received in school scarcely dampened his spirits as much as a soft-hearted and sensitive later generation might be inclined to think. If thrashings are a daily occurrence, it is only when healthy youngsters are flogged with unusual severity or without just cause that it makes a deep impression. Besides, when he was a primer-boy, as he relates later, he found friends among the older pupils who treated him kindly and even carried him to school. He found comrades among his classmates too. And with these he must have had all sorts of adventures in his free time, for how could growing boys be together for five minutes without hatching out something to afford sport and fun for themselves, if not for their parents and teachers? One such occasion was his appearance with a school chum as a *Wurstsänger* at the happy time of the festival of pig-slaughtering in Mansfeld. The fact that in later days he happened to mention only this one harmless boyish prank does not, of course, mean that he always slunk timidly home like a whipped cur, or that he only ventured out when such "nice" diversions tempted him. It simply means that he had no reason to parade before the world such boyhood memories no longer interesting even to himself.

Can we say that there were incidental impressions at that time which might have muddled or, perhaps, even tainted his youthful temperament? At the close of the fifteenth century Klein-Hans Luder, a younger brother of his father, appeared in Mansfeld, and there he behaved so badly that, as already mentioned, he was haled into court no less than eleven times between 1499 and 1513 for assault and battery. But from all appearances Martin did not come into close contact with this uncle. At all events, he never mentioned him later. He was probably no longer at home when the bad man descended upon Mansfeld.

Martin himself relates, furthermore, that his father got a little tipsy now and then, and that on such occasions he was especially cheerful and jolly. It is not impossible, and yet scarcely very probable, that this happened during the time when Martin was still at home, for at that time his father still had to struggle so hard for an existence that he could hardly afford such excesses. In any case, the good foundry-master had himself under such control in these weak hours that he did not become the laughing-stock of his children. This is sufficiently proved by the fact that even as a mature man Luther respected no one so highly and obeyed no one so willingly as his venerable father. Moreover, Martin was by no means the only one who had this feeling toward his father. Hans Luder also enjoyed such esteem among his fellow-citizens that before 1491, when he was still a young beginner, they elected him as one of the so-called *Vierherren* who looked after the interests of the community in the city council. If he had been a confirmed drunkard, as has been rashly inferred from the above statement of Luther, certainly no one would ever have thought of entrusting such an office to him or, for that matter, of advancing him money, as already noted, for the establishment and expansion of his business. For even at that time businessmen had no use for drunkards. Consequently we have no reason whatever for doubting Luther's assertion that his parents were pious people, that is, thoroughly honest and upright.

Can we also say that Luther's parents were "pious" in the sense in which that word is used today? Our chief source of information, Luther himself, does not mention the matter at all. Why not? We may assume that he was silent because he had nothing special to say about it. Like all good

citizens, his parents conscientiously observed the precepts
and usages of the traditional religion, but in this respect they
hardly distinguished themselves from their fellow-citizens
by any unusual zeal. The fact that Hans Luder, together
with some other men of Mansfeld, tried in 1497 to procure
an episcopal indulgence for St. George's Church only demonstrates that he was already counted at that time among the
little town's upper class, and not that he was any more concerned than other people about the salvation of his soul.
There is just as little ground, however, for concluding from
the fact that in a grave illness he once refused to make a
gift to the church and thereby neglect his children, or from
the fact that he was indignant about his son's entrance into a
monastery, that he was critically opposed, if not to the
church as such, at least to certain churchly practices and
teachings.

It is said that Luther's mother devoted herself diligently
to prayer in her old age. But it is quite possible that, as often
happens, she acquired her zeal with increasing years. At any
rate, Luther never suggests that she taught him to pray or
that she tried to exert a religious influence on him in any
other way. Neither does he mention anything of the kind
with reference to his father. But he does frequently tell of
the queer things he learned from both parents concerning
the activity of the devil, of witches, and of other demonic
powers. When one of his little brothers died, his mother
wailed, "That wicked witch, our neighbor, has murdered
my poor child." Later, when a priest was denouncing witches
in general and soon afterward became ill and died, she
immediately blamed it on the neighbor woman. And then
she gossiped about how the wicked woman had accomplished it. On another occasion his father came home in a
thoughtful mood; he was returning from a visit to a dying
man who had shown him his back, which had been frightfully lacerated by the evil spirits in the mines. Luther's
father himself almost died; so low had the dreadful sight

brought him. The fact of the matter is that the mischievous pranks which the devil was supposed to have played on the miners and the deeds and misdeeds of the brownies, wights, nymphs, and ghosts were frequent topics of conversation in the Luder home. Every thunder and hail storm immediately called forth the statement, "The devil is loose." Every unusual instance of illness and death evoked the question, "What witch is responsible for this?"

Of course, when they related such stories, the parents also invariably discussed the means of protection against such bogeys. In addition to the rather uncouth popular methods of warding off evil, they mentioned particularly the countless means of grace which the church had created and commended to the faithful for this purpose. Thus the horror which gripped the children, as they listened breathlessly to such recountals, was changed to a comfortable sense of security and a relieved wonder at the marvelous power of the holy Mother Church which is superior to all hostile powers. But the parents were certainly not satisfied simply to talk of these things. There is no reason to doubt that they made diligent use of these means of grace. Not a few of the ancient rites, designed to avert evil, which had come to be given a Christian stamp (the Reformer later called them "ungodly errors"), were already familiar to Luther in his home. Such rites were the spreading of consecrated palm branches over a fire in the shape of a cross to protect from hail and thunder storms, the use of consecrated herbs as a protection against witchcraft, and the sprinkling of hearth, home, beds, and so forth with holy water. In all likelihood he was encouraged by his parents in early youth to call upon the mighty patron saints (as, for example, St. Anna, who was a favorite of the miners), to cross himself on every occasion, and to sprinkle himself with holy water. The deeper he fell into that gloomy world of superstition, the more inward, conscious, and personal his relation to the faith of the church became. His interest in all that he saw and heard in the church became much keener.

If there is anything characteristic of the first thirteen years of the Reformer's life, therefore, it is the absence of any striking events or experiences. But this very absence demonstrates that he was to develop in an entirely normal way under quite normal conditions. He himself later called repeated attention to only one particularly fortunate circumstance—that he had upright people for parents. We may add, as another fortunate circumstance, the fact that he sprang from a rising family, a family which was gradually fighting its way upward in the hard struggle for existence. Children of such families are accustomed from youth to take life seriously, to spare themselves no pains, and to make full use of every opportunity for development and advancement. Something extraordinary can always be expected of such children.

CHAPTER II

AT SCHOOL IN MAGDEBURG AND EISENACH
(1496-1501)

In the spring of 1496 Peter Reinecker, a Mansfeld foundry-master, decided to send his son Hans to the "then famous school" at Magdeburg. Since young Reinecker was a good friend of Martin Luther and of about the same age, Hans Luder thought it would be a good thing to allow his son to go with him to the distant city on the Elbe. Besides traveling expenses, he probably gave the boy an introduction to the archiepiscopal official, Paul Mosshauer, a native of Mansfeld, who was good enough to take the little fellow-countryman into his house. But Martin had to earn his board by attaching himself to one of the little school choirs which strolled from door to door, singing and begging for alms. This was done at that time without incurring any disgrace, even by the children of respectable and well-to-do people, if they were attending a school away from home. Begging was not considered disgraceful and the giving of alms was considered to be a meritorious act, even if alms were given to one who was unworthy.

Martin went to the school of the *"Nullbrüder,"* the Brethren of the Common Life. It does not appear that he was strongly influenced in any way by the Brethren. In any case, a more lasting impression was the sight of the devout Prince William of Anhalt, who had entered the Franciscan Order in 1473 as a common monk, and who, in spite of his frailty, still went through the city at times with a sack on his back begging for "bread in God's name." Luther wrote in 1533, recalling his coming upon the noble penitent on the *Breiter Weg*, which at that time was already the main street of the city: "He had so fasted, kept vigils, and mortified his flesh

17

that he looked like the picture of death, mere skin and bones.
Whoever looked at him gasped with reverence and must
needs have been ashamed of his own [worldly] calling."
Martin did not say that he himself experienced such shame,
and it is not very probable. Thirteen-year-old boys are not
yet accustomed to reflecting upon their own position in life.
If anyone makes such a striking impression upon them that
they are involuntarily and irresistibly moved to imitate him,
they are generally content for a time to copy him outwardly.
It is nothing more than play, even if the image of the
admired personality has impressed itself indelibly upon
their memory.

About Easter, 1497, Martin returned to Mansfeld. We do
not know why. Apparently it had occurred to the parents in
the meantime that they had relatives in Eisenach, where
things would be better for him than in Magdeburg. In any
case, they sent him on at once to Eisenach. The relatives
there, Conrad Hutter, sexton of St. Nicholas, and his wife
Margaret, of Smalcald, an aunt of Martin's mother, received him kindly. But it appears they could not even furnish
him with free quarters. He probably lodged at first in one of
the hospices or in a school, for these places often provided
rooms for poor students. What he needed in addition he had
to beg for as a "crumb-seeker," or singing student, just as he
had done in Magdeburg. Since he was already accustomed
to this mode of life, he hardly considered this a misfortune.
He was also very well pleased with the parish school of St.
George. Later he spoke to Melanchthon of the headmaster,
John Trebonius, praising him as a gifted man, and he
struck up a friendship with the assistant teacher, Wiegand
Güldennapf, of Fritzlar, that lasted long after his student
years.

So from all appearances he was well satisfied with his
lot when, one day, a "matron," or distinguished lady, who
had noticed his earnest singing and praying in church,
offered him free board in her house. Not even Mathesius,

who was the first (1562) to report this incident, knew the matron's name. But since Luther himself expressly designates the well-to-do merchant, Henry Schalbe, as his host in Eisenach, we must take it for granted that it was the wife (otherwise unknown to us) of this Henry Schalbe who thus befriended him. But this kindness was not bestowed upon him without some recompense. In return for being allowed to come to the Schalbes' every day to eat, he was required to take little Henry Schalbe to school. In other words, he had to watch out for him on the way to school and in school and oversee his school work. This was a condition of service that was common in well-to-do homes then, as it is today, in which, as a rule, both parties were benefited. Whether he also lived with the Schalbes cannot be determined. At any rate, the word "Wirt" does not include this. It is therefore not impossible that there is some truth in the statement of the otherwise very untrustworthy Dr. Matthew Ratzeberger that in Eisenach he received "his board and room" at "Kunz Kotta's," whose wife Ursula was by birth a Schalbe. In other words, it is possible that he had his room at Kotta's and his board at Schalbe's since it is certain that he was very well acquainted with the Kottas at that time, as we gather from the later relations between himself and this family.

The Schalbe house was probably the most pious home in Eisenach. The head of the house was so devoted to the Franciscans of the little cloister at the foot of the Wartburg that Luther later actually referred to him as a "servant and captive" of these monks. That his wife also took religion seriously, we may well conclude from the often-quoted words which Luther once heard from her lips: "There is no dearer thing on earth than the love of woman if it is enjoyed by one who fears God." Luther found the same earnestness also among the friends of the family, Vicar John Braun of St. Mary's and the Franciscans from the Wartburg, who, during the next few years, gave him the benefit of their pastoral advice and encouragement. As far as we know, it was here in the Schalbe household that he became acquainted with a circle of people for whom religion was the foremost interest in life.

In such a group as this one cannot remain neutral, no matter how hard one tries. One must either join in with it or, at least inwardly, remain aloof. Young people are more inclined to do the latter. As a rule they rebel against the opinions which are considered to be the only valid opinions in their environment and, in obstinate self-reliance, decide in favor of the opposite course. Young Luther was of a different stamp. We know that he acquiesced with a receptive spirit in the views which were so strongly represented in the Schalbe circle. Thus he unconsciously came to a sort of decision with regard to his future, for the convictions to which a person comes at that age are usually espoused with all the ardor of youth; if they are renounced later, it can be only after severe conflicts. Therefore, we hardly go amiss if we declare that he had begun at this time to become familiar with those attitudes and views which later led him into the monastery.

But this Eisenach period was also especially significant in the development of Luther's mental faculties. To be sure, the parish school of St. George was a lower school of the usual type, but as a student of the highest class he now had abundant opportunity to practice the speaking, writing, and versification of Latin. It is conceivable that this practice gave him far greater satisfaction than the mechanical method of teaching in the lower classes. He therefore threw himself into his studies with such eagerness that, as Melanchthon reported, he soon left all his classmates behind.

The place in which a person awakes to full consciousness of himself always holds a special charm for him. So his "good city Eisenach" always remained especially dear to the Reformer. Meanwhile, the timid boy had become an alert and happy youth, and the Latin tyro had become a perfect Latinist who could learn nothing more from Master Trebonius. The father was now confronted with the question whether he should send his talented son to a university for further education. Since he still had to provide for at least seven children, he had to ponder this question carefully. His business had prospered so well in the last years, however, that he believed he would be able to provide Martin's expenses for a fairly long stay at a university. But which of the already very numerous universities of Germany should Martin choose? Leipzig was closest to Mansfeld and many boys from the Harz region attended it. Erfurt was not nearly so conveniently reached from Mansfeld, but it enjoyed a better reputation at that time than the university at Leipzig. It is possible that this decided the father in favor of Erfurt. If he had chosen Leipzig, Luther's whole subsequent development would undoubtedly have been different. He might have become a monk—certainly not an Augustinian, but perhaps a Dominican or a Franciscan. And who knows whether in that event he would ever have found his way out of the monastery? Even the lives of men who are destined by their activities to guide the history of mankind into other courses are apparently composed of sheer fortuities. It is by such chance incidents that they are generally forced into their proper career and are often prompted to do the deeds in which a later generation finds the characteristic revelation of their inner nature and the necessary consequence of the conflict of their personal individuality with the incongruous circumstances of their environment.

CHAPTER III

IN THE UNIVERSITY AT ERFURT (1501-05)

For the modern German, the transition from school to university has meant the substitution of freedom for slavery. For the German of Luther's day, as still in some measure for the Englishman and American of today, the transition was from relatively loose to very strict regulation. This was rather emphatically brought to the attention of the young student *"Martinus Ludher de Mansfeld"* immediately upon his matriculation at the end of April, 1501, when the rector or dean of the arts faculty asked him which *bursa* (college or hostel) he had selected. For the old *bursae* still maintained their sway in Erfurt. Every student had to join a *bursa* and be able, when asked, to name the one to which he belonged. If he happened to be such a black sheep that no *bursa* would accept him, he was not permitted to continue in attendance at the university, and under some circumstances he even had to leave town.

We are not told why Luther chose the *bursa* of St. George at Lehmann's Bridge, although it enjoyed a good reputation at that time (the students had given it the curious nickname *Biertasche*). We know only that this *bursa*, like all the others at Erfurt, was a hospice with strict monastic household regulations. On the whole its members were allowed even less freedom of movement than the seminarians of Roman Catholic or Protestant theological schools enjoy today. As a student, Luther could not go out or eat or study or sleep when he wanted to. As long as he was a member of the *bursa*, day and night, whether he was in the house or outside, he was constantly under the regulations and under the strict oversight of the rector and master of the *bursa* as well as of the instructors and proctors of the university. Moreover, he

22

could not even dress as he pleased, but after the fashion of
some American, English, and Russian students of today, he
had to wear some sort of uniform which immediately distinguished him, wherever he might be, as subject to the
regulations.

Nor could he study what he wanted or how he wanted.
Like all other students, Luther had first to complete the
course leading to the master's examination, which was prescribed by the arts faculty. For this purpose he was placed
under the guidance of the rector of the *bursa* and the *magister* belonging to it. He was permitted to attend lectures
outside the prescribed course only when the rector of the
bursa had no objection. But he had little time for such extras
anyway. The required lectures and recitations, the daily
reviews conducted by the master of the *bursa,* and the weekly
disputations took up so much of his time that he could
indulge in such additional pleasures only occasionally. So
Luther was never a "student" in the sense in which this word
is understood today in central or northern Germany. To get
an idea of the kind of life he lived, one must look into a
present-day seminary for the training of priests, for the spirit
which prevailed in the *bursae* of that day still survives in
modern seminaries. Even the clerical atmosphere which
today distinguishes these church institutions was not wanting in the *bursae.* Although the *bursa* of St. George did not,
as it appears, have a chapel of its own, the regular day's work
nevertheless began as a matter of course with prayer and
devotions and was accompanied to its very close by more
prayer and devotions.

According to the practice of all students in the arts faculty, Luther first satisfied the requirements—both lectures
and recitations in languages, logic, and philosophy—for the
bachelor's examination. After he had passed this examination at the earliest time permitted (St. Michael's Day,
1502), he immediately entered the course leading to the
master's examination. This was also the usual procedure.

Beginning in the fall of 1502, therefore, he took the prescribed courses, applying himself especially to the works of Aristotle on natural philosophy, metaphysics, and moral philosophy, and the sciences of the old *quadrivium*—geometry according to Euclid, arithmetic and music according to John de Meurs, planetary astronomy and perspective. He succeeded in disposing of this good-sized task in less than two and a quarter years, and again he passed the master's examination at the earliest time permitted (presumably January 7, 1505), this time standing second in a class of seventeen. Hence it cannot be denied that he used his time to good advantage and applied himself diligently to his studies during these four years.

But were the pains he took worth while? Like most superior men, Luther later spoke very disparagingly of what he had gained from these studies. One distinction of the contemporaneous academic instruction, however, he always recognized with unreserved appreciation in later years. This was the effectiveness with which the students were trained and guided in methodical thinking. This end was served not only by the courses of instruction in the old and new logic, but also by the grammatical and rhetorical exercises, and above all by the weekly disputations, which were usually valued more highly than the lectures. It is true that Luther later expressed the opinion that the disputations were a futile threshing of straw. But he maintained throughout his life that disputation was in itself the best method for the development of the logical faculties. In his own case, at all events, this method was eminently successful. The fact that he had already gained a reputation among his fellow-students as a sharp dialectician and ready disputant, and had on this account been nicknamed the "philosopher," clearly demonstrates that his youthful mind had not received four years of such training in vain.

What fault, then, did Luther have to find with the method of teaching at Erfurt? It was not the form and method of presentation—the general practice of dictation, for example, or the exclusive use of Latin—for he himself afterward used this method when he occupied the professor's chair. Nor does he ever complain about the professors whose lectures he attended. He continued to think highly of two of them, Jodocus Trutvetter of Eisenach and Bartholomew Arnold of Usingen, after 1517. What he found fault with was the content of the instruction, the material on which these men lectured, or, rather, had to lecture. There was no academic freedom in Erfurt; nor did it exist elsewhere. All the professors were bound by oath to expound the works of Aristotle in their lectures, and they were obliged to interpret Aristotle according to the *via moderna,* the scholasticism of the English Franciscan, William of Occam, whose teaching was officially recognized in Erfurt. The "Modernists," or Occamists, differed from the Thomists and Scotists chiefly in their flat denial that human reason can attain certain knowledge of the supersensuous realities of faith. But they denied this only to emphasize more strongly that in its dogmas the church possesses an absolutely infallible knowledge of these realities and that it is consequently necessary, not only on moral and religious but also on scientific grounds, implicitly to accept and obediently to believe these dogmas, no matter how absurd or contradictory they might appear.

Were these teachings offensive to Luther? Yes and no. In later years, of course, he would have nothing to do with such an absolute submission to the dogmas of the church. But he always clung to the conviction that reason is incapable of discerning the mysteries of faith which are affirmed in the plain and distinct words of the Holy Scriptures, that to human reason these mysteries always remain absurd, foolish, and hidden, and that on this account they must be believed in spite of reason. As far as the world of sensuous and inner experience is concerned the Occamists did not dispute its accessibility to the human faculty of perception. But when they refused to attribute the character of evidence or science to the perceptions which man can gain in this way, they did so only because they recognized logic as the sole science in the strict sense of the word, and not because they believed that correct perceptions were impossible in this sphere of experience. On the basis of Aristotle, therefore, they taught these second-class sciences just as thoroughly as they did logic. Yet they did not follow the Stagirite slavishly. In the first place, they improved upon him *in maiorem gloriam ecclesiae*—that is to say, they tried to bring his teachings into harmony with the dogmas of the church—and, in the second place, they always conscientiously noted those perceptions which went beyond Aristotle.

So it happened that Luther's instructors at Erfurt were already teaching him the proofs for the belief that the earth is not a disk but a sphere and that the moon produces the tides. They told him, too, that storms are generally, but not always, caused by natural forces. He also learned that alchemy is a very questionable science and that there is nothing in astrology to boast of. To be sure, he heard that the starry heavens influence the human sense-organs, and through these react upon the emotions. But man is capable of resisting this influence, he was told, and consequently the astrologer can at most predict how man *can* act, not how he actually *will* and *must* act. Luther's later decisive pronouncements against these pseudo-sciences are, therefore, in the final analysis a result of the critical attitudes which Trutvetter's lectures on natural philosophy had awakened in him at the university. It is quite true that these lectures strike a modern reader as very naive. But it was not the so-called "naive cosmography," but the scientific cosmography of the time, which Luther learned from them and adopted.

The Modernists of Erfurt used the books of Aristotle as guides for ethics and politics as well as for natural philosophy. But they admitted this pagan teacher as a serviceable guide only in the narrowly limited sphere of earthly and natural human activity. They insisted that he could not have

known anything of the Ultimate Cause, of supernatural purposes, or of eternal bliss; hence what Aristotle had to say
about the activity of natural reason and about the natural
earthly community (the state) was only of relative value.
Just as the Modernists placed revelation above reason, so
they consistently regarded the lay ethic of natural reason as
inferior to the supernatural ethic of the monk, and they
placed the earthly community under the supernaturally
established empire of the pope which embraces all peoples.
For they recognized the pope, and not the general council,
as the head of the church, differing in this respect from their
master, Occam. And it was in this very part of the course for
the master's degree that the ecclesiastical cast of Erfurt Aris-
totelianism cropped out most noticeably.

It cannot be said, therefore, that the Erfurt Modernists
were blind to the "blindness" of the great pagan master. Yet
they were sufficiently blind to use, as the basis of their
instruction, not only Aristotle's works on rhetoric and logic
and his *Poetics* (which appealed to Luther throughout his
life), but also his works on natural and moral philosophy,
from which, according to Luther's later opinion, one could
learn nothing in regard to either natural or spiritual matters.
And the Modernists were still blind enough, in the exposition
of these books, to lecture on the Occamistic doctrine of the
unlimited potentiality of the human will (which Luther com-
batted with such vehemence after 1513), and the doctrine
of the purely ornamental character of divine grace. That is
why almost all the teaching in the arts faculty seemed to
Luther to be a waste of time and mental energy.

Does it follow, then, that the preoccupation with Aristotle, as interpreted by the Erfurt Modernists, was no more
than a waste of time and mental energy as far as Luther was
concerned? It does not. For not only did Luther acquire a
mass of worthwhile bits of information—by an arduous process, it is true—but he also learned to make the scientific
method and the scientific *Weltanschauung* of the time his

own. It is quite understandable that, when he entered his years of struggle and conflict, he regarded this as a rather dubious gain. Yet after he had cast off what he deemed altogether untenable, much of what he had pored and sweated over when he was a student remained to be utilized for the construction of his new views. That is why, in his old age, he began again to express appreciation of the ethics and politics of the great pagan master. But even in the years of conflict, the basic principles of Aristotelian physics were never questioned. They were a permanent part of his *Weltanschauung* all through his life.

However, Luther did not confine himself as an arts student at Erfurt to the prescribed scholastic books. Alongside the ponderous tomes of Master Occam and other scholastics which lay on his study table in the *bursa* of St. George, there sometimes appeared one of the slender volumes of the "Poets." Who had called his attention to these books? It was the Erfurt Modernists, Trutvetter and Usingen, for these scholastics were modern in this respect, too, that they familiarized themselves to a certain extent with the humanistic culture of their day. The first poet Luther happened upon (or, rather, was permitted by the rector of the *bursa* to read, since this official had to sanction all such extras) was the so-called new Vergil. This was the work of the pious Franciscan, Battista Spagnuolo, of Mantua, in whose eclogues not even the eagle eye of an inquisitor could very well find anything blameworthy. Later on he also read Ovid's *Heroides,* Vergil, Plautus, and perhaps also Horace and Juvenal.

More than this Luther's "scholastic studies"—and possibly the *dominus rector*—did not permit. But this estimable gentleman could hardly have objected when Luther attended a short lecture, delivered during the summer semester of 1504 by one of the traveling humanists who occasionally appeared as special lecturers even in the rather "unenlightened" town of Erfurt. This humanist was Jerome Emser, of Ulm, later Duke George of Saxony's favorite man of letters, and the subject of the lecture was Reuchlin's drama, *Sergius*. It appears that neither the person of the lecturer nor the wretched brain-child about which he spoke made any impression at all on young Luther. At any rate, he never mentions either of them afterward. Hence he became acquainted with humanism just about as much as the present-day student for the priesthood becomes acquainted with contemporaneous belles-lettres. This conclusion is not altered by the observation that several of the young men with whom he associated at that time—for example, John Jäger of Dornheim, called Crotus Rubeanus—later reappear in the so-called "poets' circle" of Canon Conrad Mut, of Gotha, called Mutianus. And this is so because we know that the poets' circle was not formed until the doors of the monastery had already closed behind Luther. Superficial though this first acquaintance with the new cultural movement was, it was not wholly without significance for him. He was stimulated by it to read some, if not many, of the Latin classics which had not been familiar to him before, even by name. He read them with such application, in fact, that he could later quote them from memory. In itself this would suggest that he found pleasure in reading them. But he gained no more from this reading than an enrichment of his knowledge of classical and new Latin literature and a refinement of his linguistic skills. He never became a humanist, then or afterward.

Not even the most diligent student can forever stifle the need for recreation and friendly exchange of ideas with his contemporaries and schoolmates. In the *bursae,* as in all student hostels, however much the rules might breathe the spirit of the monastery, there was a gay and rollicking common life. There was also a lively intercourse among the various *bursae.* Accordingly it is hardly necessary to mention that Luther, too, had his associates and intimates among the *bursa* students. We know only one of the members of this *consortium,* however—the aforementioned John Jäger, of Dornheim, near Arnstadt, who later, in his *Letters of*

Obscure Men, railed so amusingly and yet so maliciously at
the medieval spirit of the Erfurt *bursa.* We do not know
what the nature of the fellowship was. The only thing that
is certain is that they used to sing and play the lute. We also
know that Luther often went on trips to Mansfeld during his
holidays. These journeys always took at least three days. It
was on one of these walking trips at Eastertide that, a half-
mile from Erfurt, he accidentally cut the artery of his thigh
with the sword that he was carrying, for no one made such
a journey unarmed in those days. The blood flowed so copiously that he had to press the blood vessels together with all
his might. In his distress he prayed fervently, "O Mary,
help!" Meanwhile his traveling companion had hurried back
to the city to secure a surgeon. But it was a long time before
the physician arrived and could bandage his leg, which, as
we can imagine, had become quite swollen. Then both of
them combined their strength to get Luther back to the St.
George *bursa.* During the night the wound broke open
again. He bled so much that he lost consciousness. How he
was delivered from this peril he does not say. He relates
only that in his terror he again called upon Mary, and that
he employed the weeks, in which he had to lie still, teaching
himself to play the lute. As is usual with young people, it
appears that he soon overcame the fright he experienced in
this incident. He does not even intimate that in the moment
of danger he felt any anxiety for the salvation of his soul.

The truth of the matter is that we know almost nothing
about Luther's inner life during this time. He himself says
only that when he was twenty years old (about 1503 or 1504)
he happened upon a complete Bible for the first time in his
life. It was in the university library, into which one of the
professors probably took him. He opened the volume at the
story of Hannah, the mother of Samuel, but had to close it
again shortly when the bell called him to a lecture. Then he
thought to himself, "How fortunate I would be if I owned
such a book," and soon after he bought himself a Postil, or

book of sermons. He tells us, further, that hitherto he had
known only the Sunday Gospels and was astonished to find
such entirely unfamiliar stories in the Bible.

It has been said that Luther could not possibly have
reached his twentieth year without having seen a Bible. But
inasmuch as he asserts this so positively, and inasmuch as
the Bible did not figure either in the instruction of the lower
schools or in the curriculum of the arts course, we have no
reason for doubting his statements. The episode shows that,
even as a bachelor of arts, Luther had a very lively interest
in religion, an interest which was not fully satisfied by regular participation in the customary services of the church. It
also suggests that he felt occasional impulses to provide
means for his own private edification. But we cannot now
determine what were the thoughts and moods out of which
such interests and impulses grew.

CHAPTER IV

FROM STUDENT TO FRIAR (July 2-17, 1505)

"Oh, what a majestic and glorious thing it was when the master's degrees were granted and torches were carried before them and they were honored! I hold that there is no temporal, worldly joy equal to it." One can still feel in these words of the Reformer something of the elation which he felt when, at the beginning of February, 1505, he received the brown master's hat and then ascended to the lecture desk to deliver the customary formal master's address before the assembled university. But this event provoked even greater joy in the Luther home in Mansfeld. Henceforth Father Hans looked upon his son as a kind of higher being whom he could no longer address as "thou" (*Du*), but only with the more respectful "you" (*Ihr*), and he surely insisted that the mother and brothers and sisters also should not withhold this address of respect properly belonging to the newly fledged Master of Arts. But what was to become of this higher being? In any case Martin was bound to serve the university for two more years, lecturing in the faculty of arts. It was, therefore, almost to be taken for granted that he would make use of these two years in pursuing further study in one of the so-called higher faculties, for as a mere *magister artium* he could never make very much of himself.

But in which of the three higher faculties should he enroll? The medical faculty was rejected as a matter of course, for at Erfurt, as elsewhere at that time, it really existed only in name. The theological faculty was not considered, for as a theologue he would have had to take the vow of celibacy, and Father Hans was already contemplating a bride from an honorable and wealthy family for the young *magister*.

Thus only the faculty of law was left. To be sure, that profession did not offer the prospects that it does today. But if Martin succeeded in winning the confidence of a prince, he could, as *doctor juris*, acquire wealth and honor in abundance and perhaps attain to nobility. So it was decided that Martin should be a lawyer.

The lectures in the arts faculty began on April 23, but those in law not until May 20. For the first time in his life, Martin had a whole month for introspection. The observation that "during that time he wandered about sadly" shows how it affected his spirits. What made him feel so sad? It has been supposed that the sudden death of a fellow-student who had been especially intimate with him made him sad, and great pains have been taken in the attempt to ascertain the name of this friend. But Luther himself gives another reason for his sadness. It was *tentatio tristitiae*, anxiety over his sins and fear of the Last Judgment. In this state of mind, on April 23 he began the lectures which had been assigned to him in the arts faculty, and on May 20 he began his legal studies in St. Mary's *bursa* near the cathedral. But it appears that not even his preoccupation in the entirely new sphere which opened itself to him in the *Codex Juris Civilis* and the *Gloss* of Accursius was capable of helping him out of the anxiety into which he was plunged. As early as June 20, which was in the middle of the semester, he took a leave of absence in order to visit his parents in Mansfeld. Unfortunately he has not told us why he went to Mansfeld. He says only that this time, too, he made the long journey on foot. About June 30 he again set out for Erfurt. On July 2 he had come as near the city as Stotternheim and he had only a few more hours to travel when a heavy storm suddenly broke above him. A thunderbolt struck immediately in front of him in such a way that he was hurled to the ground by the air pressure. Overcome by sudden panic, he invoked St. Anna, who was regarded as the most efficacious helper in such an extremity. But to render his prayer even more effective, he added the vow: "I will become a monk."

Was this vow only the impulse of a moment of stress and strain? Luther never expressed himself on the question. But we are not apt to go wrong if we assume that a resolution which had long been prepared for in the inner struggles of the last month, but which had been repressed until now by doubts and scruples of one kind or another, suddenly came to expression in that moment of extreme nervous tension. For Luther was one of those men who make decisions only after long and tenacious struggles but whose decisions are crystallized abruptly in a moment of tempestuous activity. We may even conclude that, inwardly, he was already on the way to the monastery before the lightning flashed down on him at Stotternheim. The convulsive fear which seized him in that moment only hastened the decision but did not call forth the mood from which it sprang.

But just because it was extorted from him, as it were, by such an external event, Luther did not afterward experience that feeling of relief which usually accompanies a spontaneous release from an inner tension of long duration. On the contrary, he felt a decided disillusionment, even regret. When he had reached the city safe and sound, therefore, he did not feel that he had to fulfill his vow immediately, but first consulted his friends and acquaintances as to what he should do. Many of them advised him not to enter the monastery. Many, but not all. Several of his friends and teachers were of the opinion that morally he had already bound himself irrevocably. And in all conscience he had to admit that these few serious-minded ones were right. After he had obtained a dismissal from the university authorities and had sold all his books—except his Plautus and Vergil, which he could not part with—he invited his acquaintances and friends to a farewell supper in his "master's quarters." On the morning of the following day his friends accompanied him through the Komturgasse to the gate of the Black Cloister. "Today you see me, and henceforth nevermore." That was the burden of the conversation he carried on with his weeping friends. One sees from this that he had now quite made up his mind. He was firmly resolved to forsake the world forever.

CHAPTER V

IN THE BLACK CLOISTER AT ERFURT (1505-08)

Besides the Augustinian chapter house at the Augustan Gate there were no less than five monasteries in Erfurt in the year 1505. These were the Benedictine abbey on Peter's Hill, the Carthusian in the southern part of the city, the convent of the Dominicans on the left bank of the Broad Creek, the Franciscan on the right bank, and the little cloister of the Servites, or "Servants of the Holy Virgin," at the Krämpfer Gate. The "Black Cloister," the monastery of the Augustinian Hermits, was not far from Lehmann's Bridge, in the northeastern part of the city. Why did Luther choose this one? He does not tell us, but we may suppose that it was because in this monastery he could hope soonest to reach the goal of "evangelical perfection," toward which he was striving. Since its entrance into the Saxon Congregation of the Observance (1473), this monastery was commonly considered the foremost center in the town for the cultivation of the ascetic ideal, and had therefore enjoyed for years the greatest prestige.

Consequently the chapter was very careful in admitting new brothers. When Luther applied for admission on July 17, he was not immediately received into the monastery, but he was first relegated to the monastic hostelry for observation of the state of his soul. For before the authorities went any further with him, they had to be assured that "his spirit was of God," and he had to be given the opportunity, as a guest of the monastery, of earnestly examining himself to see whether he could endure the "harshness" of the Order and abide in his purpose.

According to the prevailing law, Luther was not bound to procure his father's consent for his entrance into the Order.

But it seemed utterly impossible for him to take this important step without the knowledge and approbation of his family. So even before July 17 doubtless he had informed his parents of his intentions and asked for their blessing. Nevertheless, the answer that he received from Mansfeld shortly after July 17 exceeded even his worst apprehensions. His father acted like a madman. This time he not only addressed him with the less respectful *Du,* but he also cut him off completely from "all paternal grace and favor." His mother and the rest of his relatives also let him know that they would have nothing more to do with him. Thus he was now suddenly confronted with the difficult choice either of breaking with his family forever or going back into the world again. Then, unexpectedly, a second letter from Mansfeld relieved him of the painful necessity of making such a choice. His father had given in at the last moment. Two younger sons had died suddenly of the plague, and at the same time a rumor had come to him that Martin, too, had been stricken by the disease. When this news turned out to be false, friends and acquaintances had told the hot-tempered father that he was in duty bound to "offer something holy to God," meaning that he must allow his son Martin to become a monk. He still had many misgivings but he finally gave in, though "with reluctance and sadness."

Now at last, about the beginning of September, 1505, Luther's reception took place in the monastery church with the customary formalities. During the hymn, "Great Father Augustine," he received the tonsure and the black Augustinian habit with the large cowl and the so-called scapular— a sleeveless cloth vestment falling to the feet before and behind, which from now on he had to wear constantly, even while sleeping. At the conclusion he was ceremoniously conducted into the convent where he was received into the monastery community as a novice by all the brothers with the kiss of peace.

The Order of Augustinian Hermits was a mendicant

order. The Erfurt monastery, however, was so wealthy that
its inmates had long since ceased to beg for a living and
hence they were no longer recruited from the lower classes
but rather from the middle and higher ranks of the population. Illiterates were admitted only as monks of the second
class—that is, as *fratres,* or lay-brothers—those who had to
perform the menial tasks in the monastery hostelry. Only the
monks of the first class were entitled to a vote. These *patres*
were without exception educated men and clerics, and in so
far as they were not studying or teaching or holding an office
in the Order or the monastery, they occupied themselves
solely with singing, praying, and other ascetic practices conducive to the sanctification of the self.

These exercises also made up the chief element in the
training of Martin Luther as a clerical novice. Like all novices he was first instructed by the master of novices in the
prescribed acts of reverence and all the other external observances peculiar to the monastic life. He had to learn how,
where, when, and before whom to bend the knee and throw
himself to the ground. He had to accustom himself to go
about constantly with his head slightly bowed and his eyes
downcast, never to speak or eat except at the designated
times, never to drink while standing, never to forget the
prescribed saying of grace at the partaking of a piece of
bread or a goblet of water. He had to learn to suppress
every inclination to laughter and to learn how to make himself understood by means of the carefully inculcated sign
language of the monastery, not only in the church and the
cloisters, but in the refectory and the dormitory as well. At
the same time he was drilled by the preceptor in the special
liturgical observances of the Congregation and in the use of
the breviary of the Order which contained the necessary
directions for these observances. In addition to these external exercises, the master of novices did not fail to impose
upon him various little tests of character. Thus, for example,
probably from the very first day, he had to clean and scrub

his own cell. This was by no means a severe task, for the room was only about three yards long and two yards wide and contained only one chair, a table, a candlestick, and a bedstead furnished with a straw mattress and several woolen blankets. He often had to help in the kitchen and he probably had to go along with others on several occasions to beg from door to door in the city.

But greater stress was laid on two other means of spiritual education: confession and the reading and study of the Holy Scriptures. It is probable that the first book that came into Luther's hands in the monastery was a red leather-bound copy of the Latin Bible, which he now "read eagerly and learned devoutly and zealously" day after day, according to the prescription of the Rule. During this quiet study he also had time to reflect upon the state of his soul so that he might be in a condition "to confess aloud, discreetly, and humbly" to the preceptor at least once a week as required by the Rule. In this way his day's work was regulated and "rationalized" down to the minutest detail from early morning till night. Nothing was left to his own judgment. Nothing escaped the command of the master. Thus he could not even mortify his flesh as much as he might wish. As long as he was a novice he had to adhere strictly to the direction of the preceptor on this point. What the Order required of him in the way of ascetic practices was not excessive. He probably accustomed himself very soon to eating only twice a day—after Mass and in the evening before Compline—and only once a day, in the evening, on the more than a hundred fast days. It appears that it was a greater trial to him that his cell was not heated. But in this regard no more was demanded of him than of other brothers. For, as far as we know, they, too, had no stoves in their cells. If they became too cold, they had to seek out the *vaporarium*, or common warming room.

Nothing is so tranquilizing to a troubled spirit as to be set down in a new environment and to be forced to adapt oneself inwardly and outwardly to its mode of life. And the assignment of many little new duties is not prejudicial to this calming influence, provided that the spirit is thereby diverted from constant preoccupation with the self. But in the monastery all these numerous new duties were primarily intended to serve toward the perfection of the individual self. And even if every little violation of the rules of the Order was not considered a sin, yet a monk was in far greater danger of falling into sin and guilt than a man of the world. It is no wonder, then, that young Luther very soon fell again into anxiety over the salvation of his soul and that he now suffered more than ever from this anxiety. But this was a phenomenon that had long been well known to the old monastic spiritual directors. And the "fine old man" to whom the soul of the novice Luther was entrusted—he is probably identical with the *institutor*, John von Grefenstein or Grebenstein, of whom he spoke on one occasion with reverence—was not perplexed about it. When Luther wanted to unbosom himself completely and confess every sin he could remember, even though he had already made a general confession at his reception, the director curtly and sharply refused to allow him to do it. He treated him the same way when Luther brought up "foolish" (that is, probably only imaginary) sins. But when it seemed necessary to him, he discussed Martin's doubts and misgivings in a kindly spirit. On one occasion, for instance, when Martin was complaining to him how much he feared the wrath of God, the director comforted him "wonderfully" with the casual remark: "God is not angry with you; you are angry with Him," and another time with the reproachful question: "Do you not know that the Lord has commanded us to hope?" He was finally able to ease the mind of the young brother again and again in this way. But this consolation never lasted very long. Luther would tell him repeatedly that absolution did not console him, even though he was fully convinced of its power to forgive sins.

The spiritual director therefore sought to assist him in

still other ways. Besides the Bible, he put into his hands various old monastic devotional books which were the stock contents of monastery libraries, such as the *Vitae Patrum* (legends of the Fathers), and the *Collations* of Cassian of Marseilles. He also permitted him to study other books which had nothing to do with monastic life itself. One day he brought Martin a copy of the *Dialogues* of Vigilius of Thapsus against Arius, Sabellius, and Photius, ascribed to Athanasius, which he himself had copied, and in the end he discussed with him all sorts of topics which were the concern of his own inner life. On one occasion he told him about the difficult confessional cases he had to deal with. Another time they were talking about John Huss, and the director did not hesitate to confide in him that it was his opinion that Huss "was executed without instruction, without evidence, and without confutation." In this opinion he was not alone in the Order. So this "truly excellent man, who was without a doubt a true Christian even under the cursed cowl," knew how to help his pupil calm himself again and again and win back the conviction that in the monastery his poor soul had found its rightful place. Meanwhile Prior Winand von Diedenhofen and the others in authority in the monastery had gained the same impression concerning the young brother. Indeed, the influential Father John Nathin was at that time so taken with him that he enthusiastically praised him to the nuns of Mühlhausen as a new Paul miraculously called by Christ.

When the anniversary of Luther's reception arrived, the motion to permit him to make his profession met no opposition in the monastery. The ceremony took place in the monastery church with the usual formalities, probably as early as September, 1506. It consisted mainly in formal taking of the three vows of obedience, poverty, and chastity. At the end of the ceremony, as was customary, he was congratulated by the whole monastery on the fact that "now he was like an innocent child who had just been baptized." This expression was used because the Augustinian Order attributed the same impartation of regeneration to the taking of vows as to Baptism. They actually defined it, therefore, as second Baptism. In fact, in the monastery of the Barefoot Friars at Arnstadt, Luther once heard to his great edification that a monk could acquire this great blessing repeatedly; for this purpose he needed only to renew his resolution to keep the vows faithfully.

Probably on the same day that he made his profession the new *pater* was instructed to prepare himself without delay for a second change of position — entrance into the priesthood—and for this purpose to study the massive tome on the Canon of the Mass by the Tübingen professor Gabriel Biel. As he said later, he read the book with a bleeding heart, meaning that he read it with the strongest inner concern. It is probable that he was ordained a subdeacon by Prior Winand on December 19; a deacon by the suffragan bishop of Erfurt, John von Laasphe, on February 27, 1507; and finally a priest on April 4 by the same prelate in the Erfurt cathedral. He thereby acquired not only the mystical ability, but also the right, to celebrate the mass. At that time it was already customary to celebrate the day when a young priest first exercised this right with some special festivity. Even the monastic priests who had renounced the world were wont to allow the world to take part in this celebration, at least in the persons of their nearest male relatives and friends.

And so Luther, too, was instructed by his superiors to inform his father that he was now a priest and to invite him to his first mass. This was probably the first time since his reception into the Order that he had had any correspondence with his family. His letter was well received. Father Hans promised to come if the monastery chose a day for the celebration which would be suitable to him. The prior was kind enough to acquiesce in this request. So the first mass took place in the monastery church on Cantate Sunday, May 2, 1507, in the presence of the sturdy foundry-master and a

number of other Mansfelders who had ridden with him to
Erfurt, twenty horses strong, for this express purpose. That
Luther ascended the steps of the altar with some trepidation
is altogether possible. The Mass is such a complicated action
that a young priest reciting it for the first time can very
easily make a mistake. But when he came without mishap
to the solemn prayer, *Te igitur clementissime pater*, with
which the silent mass begins, then all these minor anxieties
were swallowed up in the staggering consciousness in the
profoundest depths of his soul that he was now preparing,
in all his frailty and unworthiness, to appear before the awful
majesty of God. It is quite possible that this feeling so over-
whelmed him for a moment that he would gladly have fled
from the altar, but there is no truth in the story that he had
already turned his back to run away and was only held at
the altar by a word from the prior or the master of novices.

After the mass a little feast was held in the monastery
refectory at which the relatives and friends of the new priest
were present as guests of the monastery. Since the father
had risen to the occasion with such extraordinary nobleness
and generosity (he had donated fully twenty guldens to the
monastery kitchen, for that time a little fortune, as a contribution to the celebration), Luther concluded that his father
was now fully reconciled to his taking monastic vows and
he began quite candidly to tell how he had come to make
this decision. But when he came to speak about the storm at
Stotternheim, his father interrupted him with the remark:
"But what if it [the storm] were only a ghost?" that is, a
devilish delusion. And when he went on nevertheless to
justify himself the father became almost rude, and without
paying any attention to the Fathers on all sides who could
not help overhear, he said, "Have you never heard the commandment, 'Honor thy father and thy mother'?" Whereupon
the son fell silent, not because he felt hurt, but rather because in his spiritual pride he now believed he had one more
reason for despising such a worldly-minded father. Yet it

irritated him that he could not honestly do this and that he could consequently never escape the memory of this painful incident.

After the celebration of the first mass the daily routine began again. But for Luther it now had a new aspect. Instead of working in silence toward the perfection of his own soul, he had to return to the school bench. At the command of the prior, he now had to study theology in the Order's school of advanced study (*Studium Generale*), which was connected with the monastery. This school, notwithstanding its high-sounding name, had only a few professors. The chief professor, or regent, was the previously mentioned Father John Nathin, a pupil and follower of the famous Tübingen Occamist, Gabriel Biel. He gave the important lectures on the *Sentences* of Peter Lombard which was still the chief textbook in the study of theology throughout the West. Besides these lectures, Luther doubtless attended several minor courses of lectures in exegesis up to the fall of 1508. On the days when he had lectures he did not have to take part, from beginning to end, in all seven of the daily monastic services in the monastery church. But the choir still occupied him so much that he had to apply himself diligently to study in the time that was left.

We still have all the large volumes that he studied, either in whole or in part, during the months from May, 1507, to October, 1508. He used the *Glossa Ordinaria* as an exegetical guide. As a commentary on the *Sentences* he used the *Collectorium* of Biel, the *Quaestiones* of d'Ailly and Occam, and probably one or another of the shorter writings of the latter author. We do not know whether he had time and opportunity to study the *Summa* of Thomas Aquinas and Scotus' commentary on the third book of the *Sentences*. At any rate, the commentaries of Biel, d'Ailly, and Occam gave him enough to do. These three works look forbidding enough even from the outside, but their contents are still more so, even to one accustomed to difficult reading. Even one who is fairly well read in the scholastics can follow them only with difficulty at first. But, as Melanchthon testifies, Luther studied them with pleasure. In fact, he studied them so thoroughly that in later years he was still able to quote Biel and d'Ailly. Evidently he took them in with great ease. Why? Because they were all "Moderns" and therefore did not oblige him to unlearn what he had learned before. As a student of theology, therefore, he remained under the influence of Occamism.

One might ask: Were his eyes now being gradually opened by this renewed intensive concentration on the fundamental principles of the *via moderna* to the deficiencies and weaknesses which were being pointed out so energetically at this time by Peter Tartaret, Cajetan, and others? This was not the case. On the contrary, he became even more of an Occamist. This does not mean that he found himself in complete inner accord with this theology on every point. Young people often swallow a philosophical or theological system hook, line, and sinker, if it is praised by their teachers as the last word in wisdom and if it seems reasonable to their intellect, even though it leaves their deepest spiritual needs unsatisfied and stands in direct contradiction to their own experience. The fact that at the end of 1510 Occamism was still for him the only possible theology and philosophy does not prove positively that he had found in the Invincible Doctor or his greater and lesser prophets an answer, or even a kind of answer, to the questions which were tormenting him, for if that had been the case, he would hardly have felt the urge to break with Occam. Nor does it follow that there was even a temporary repression of these questions by the subtle problems of scholastic theology which now claimed all the powers of his mind. It was precisely in this study of the scholastics that he was repeatedly meeting the very problems that were personally so interesting to him—such questions as whether man can achieve the perfect love of God and earn the grace of God; whether sins are actually done away completely by absolution; what is to be done about predestination, and so forth.

Inwardly he stood at exactly the same point at which he had been at the end of his novitiate, when, in the fall of 1508, he suddenly received orders to take the place of Father Wolfgang Ostermayr in the chair of moral philosophy which had been entrusted to the Augustinians in the arts faculty of the University of Wittenberg.

CHAPTER VI

ON THE OUTSKIRTS OF CIVILIZATION (1508-09)

"A poor, unsightly town with small, old, ugly, squat wooden houses, more like an old village than a town"—this was the impression which Wittenberg still made on people, twenty years after, when they came to pay due honor to the place which had since become so famous. "It is a poor, wretched, filthy town, hardly worth a red cent in comparison with Prague. Indeed, it is not worthy of being called a town in Germany. It is a town with an unhealthy and disagreeable climate, without vineyards, orchards, or fruit-bearing trees, with an atmosphere like that of a beer-cellar, altogether uncouth and made unpleasant by smoke and frost. What would Wittenberg be if it were not for the castle, the chapter house, and the university? Without these one would see nothing but Lutheran—that is to say, filthy—houses, dirty streets, and all the roads, paths, and alleys filled with slop. One would find a barbarous people which trades only in beer and catchpenny merchandise. Its market is not peopled. Its town has no citizenry. The people wear small-town clothing, and there is great want and poverty among the inhabitants." It was Cochlaeus, the impassioned foe of Luther, who uttered these words in 1524. He was just as eager to have this "stinking hole, this barbaric underworld, this heretical new Rome" wiped from the face of the earth as he was to have the "infamous, blaspheming, heretical scamp," Luther, exterminated.

But the scholars from other parts who settled permanently in this town on the Elbe expressed quite similar opinions. Valentine Polich of Mellerstadt substantiates these opinions when he says tersely and pointedly that "in Wittenberg one dwells as if in a carrion-pit." And Luther was still

47

wondering in his older days how Elector Frederick could
have conceived the idea of establishing a university in this
spot, which was hardly a town and was obviously not apt to
become one, despite all the efforts of the princes. He also
calls particular attention to the fact that "the market-place
in Wittenberg is a dung-heap." And to the unattractive
environs of the city he dedicates the sprightly lines,

> *Sändicken, Sändicken, du bist ein Ländicken!*
> *Wenn ick di arbeit, bist du licht,*
> *Wenn ick di meye, so finde ick nicht.* [1]

Opinions concerning the inhabitants were just as unfavorable as those about the town. Of course the abuse of Cochlaeus is not to be taken too seriously. But the distinguished
Christopher Scheurl, of Nuremberg, summarily characterizes
his new fellow-townspeople as crude, besotted, and glutton-
ous. And when Luther fails to find culture and courtesy, a
sense of honesty and decency, hospitality and religion, not
only among the burghers and peasants but also among the
nobility in the circle of the Elector, and when he says, as late
as 1532, that "the Wittenbergers dwell on the outskirts of
civilization," he means practically the same thing.

Nevertheless, interesting though these opinions are, we
may not overlook the fact that they are invariably based
on very limited and isolated observations and experiences
which, in themselves, do not permit the deduction of any
general conclusion in regard to the character of the Wittenbergers. It must be remembered, moreover, that those who
expressed these opinions were all South or Middle Germans
and that they were consequently men of an entirely different
stamp from the Wittenbergers, whose blood was a cross of
Flemish and North German and who were on this account
a people of a considerably cooler temperament. In order
not to draw any false conclusions, it is necessary to supple-

---

[1] What a land! Nothing but sand! You're easy to plow, but when harvest-time
comes, nothing is there!

ment these very subjective and colored opinions with a number of objectively established facts which will enable us to form a balanced judgment.

According to the Wittenberg town register, during the year 1513 there were only 172 *Brauerben* (that is, burghers entitled to the privilege of brewing) and 184 *Budelinge* (that is, small home-owners) in the town and 26 residents in the suburbs. Exclusive of the 56 cottagers in the *ville neuve* beyond the Apollo or Castle Gate, the town accordingly had only 382 taxable persons. The total population was 2,000 at the very most. Like all the colonial towns, Wittenberg had been planned on an ample scale. But apart from the castle, the collegiate chapter house of All Saints connected with the castle, the lecture hall of the university, and the parish church of St. Mary's, the town had very few prominent buildings. Probably all the inhabitants, as was the case in other towns of this kind, were still engaged in agriculture. The chief industry was brewing. Crafts were represented by the guilds of bakers, butchers, shoemakers, tailors, and clothmakers. In addition we find a guild of wagoners. Trade was not insignificant. Especially lucrative was the privilege granted to the town by that great patron of towns, Frederick the Mild—a monopoly in supplying the whole region with salt.

As far as the government of the town is concerned, Wittenberg enjoyed special privileges as the capital of the old electorate. As early as 1441, it had possessed full jurisdiction within its precincts, which included five villages. The office of mayor changed hands every year, and the mayor was judge. Together with eight *Ratsfreunde*, or councilors, he administered the affairs of the town. The magistrate who represented the Elector merely had the right of confirming the election of the "Commission of Six," which was chosen annually, before the councilors went out of office, for the purpose of auditing their accounts. It is clear from this that the town had such a measure of independence that it was able, when the religious question first arose, to pursue a policy different from that of the Elector.

Ample provision was made for the religious needs of the inhabitants of Wittenberg, just as such provision was made in all the German towns of that age. In addition to the spacious parish church, there were at least three chapels, a chapter house, and two monasteries—the Gray Cloister of the Franciscans in the northwestern, and the Black Cloister of the Augustinian Hermits in the eastern part of the town. The most powerful religious corporation of the whole electoral district was the chapter of All Saints, which also had jurisdiction over the town parish. It owned the Castle Church, which had been renovated by Elector Frederick and whose large treasure of relics attracted spiritually needy souls from far and wide. Among these 5,005 relics were some very curious articles—for instance, a piece of the Burning Bush of Moses, nine thorns from the Crown of Thorns, thirty-five fragments of Christ's Cross, and some stalks of the hay and straw upon which the Christ Child lay. There were a few remnants from the manger, the cradle, and the swaddling-clothes of Jesus, bits of the hair, camisole, coat, girdle, veil, and milk of the Blessed Virgin, and not less than 204 parts of bodies and one whole body of the innocent babes of Bethlehem. But it was not the singularity of these relics which attracted so many people on Misericordias Domini Sunday, when they were exhibited on the narrow galleries of the Castle Church. It was rather the indulgence of more than 1443 years which could be secured by adoring the relics, and the additional Portiuncula Indulgence, granted to the church in 1398, with the promise of "remission of punishment and guilt for all repented sins."

Closely connected with the chapter was the university, which had been called into existence by Elector Frederick in 1502 to rival the university in the neighboring ducal town of Leipzig. The connection with the chapter grew out of the fact that the wise prince tried to avoid making too heavy drafts upon his purse. Like all the princes who established universities, he founded his school, as far as it was at all possible, on ecclesiastical benefices. No less than twelve of the twenty-two professorships were combined with the benefices of the chapter, the number of which had been considerably increased. He added three more chairs in a very simple way, by charging the two Wittenberg monasteries with the responsibility of furnishing and maintaining three professors. This arrangement left only seven professorships to be supported from his own pocket.

Frederick did not depart from the usual practice in the internal and external organization of the new institution of learning any more than he did in the arrangements for its founding. The *"Leucorea"* [1] was, therefore, a university just like the others of that time. And the fact that it had so little to distinguish it prevented it from being really successful despite the unabashed advertising of the rectors, Mellerstadt and Scheurl. The influx of students from the outside had already begun to fall off alarmingly as early as the winter of 1505. When Luther made his first appearance there, in the winter of 1508, there could hardly have been more than three hundred students in the town.

According to the arrangement which had been made, the Augustinian Hermits had to fill two professorships. These were the *lectura in Biblia* in the theological faculty and the chair of moral philosophy in the arts faculty. The first of these had been occupied since 1502 by John von Staupitz, the vicar-general of the Saxon Congregation of the Augustinian Order. His work as vicar-general made such demands upon his time, however, that he lectured very infrequently. He was elected dean of the theological faculty for the winter semester of 1508 and 1509. He was still in Munich when the semester began (October 18), and we do not know whether he returned to Wittenberg during the months which followed. It is quite possible that he did not appear in the

---

[1] Wittenbergian (University), in Greek, "white hill."

town at all during his deanship, or that he was there only
for brief visits.

The Order's chair in the arts faculty was provisionally
assigned to Father Luther in October, 1508, before he had
reached his twenty-fifth year. The honor was not without
its responsibilities. The young instructor had to buckle down
at once, and he felt like a student facing the terrible ordeal
of hazing. In the first place, he had to lecture on Aristotle's
Nicomachean Ethics for a full hour, at two o'clock, four
times a week, and he had to lead the student disputations
three evenings a week. At the same time he had to continue his own studies in the theological faculty, attending at
least two hours of lectures on each of the first four days of
the week. In addition, he had to take part in the recitations
and disputations of the theologues. His load probably became even heavier during the summer semester. For after
he had been made *baccalaureus biblicus* on March 9, 1509,
he was obliged to undertake another course of lectures in
addition to the one in the arts faculty. This additional lecture series was on a number of chapters of the Bible, assigned
to him by the theological faculty. Meanwhile he was undoubtedly required to attend the recitations and disputations under both faculties just as he had before. He succeeded in finishing his theological study in the fall by passing his examinations on the *Sentences*. Before delivering the
required inaugural lecture, however, he was suddenly called
back to Erfurt.

This first year at Wittenberg was, therefore, a year of
unusual industry for Brother Martin. In a letter to John
Braun in Eisenach, dated March 17, 1509, he complained
about the grind, particularly in philosophy. He found little
pleasure in philosophy anyway. He would have preferred
trading it for theology from the very start—for the Occamistic theology which "delves into the kernel of the nut, the
core of the wheat, and the marrow of the bones." For in
Wittenberg Luther had again encountered the great ex-

ponent of this theology, Jodocus Trutvetter, who had fallen into disfavor among the Erfurters. When Luther wrote this letter, he was burdened with so many tasks of one kind or another that he actually had to steal time to write it.

It is not very probable, as we must gather from all this, that the intimacy between Luther and Staupitz, to which the former often alluded in later years, can be traced back as far as the winter of 1508-09. It cannot be shown, as we have observed, that Staupitz stayed in Wittenberg for any length of time during this year. And during the summer semester of 1509 he was constantly occupied, as far as we can determine, with affairs out of town. More important than these deductions, however, is the fact that the marginal notes which Luther added to the *Sentences* of Peter Lombard in 1509-10 contain no trace of Staupitz' influence. This is significant especially with regard to the section treating of predestination, for it was on this article, as he himself confessed, that he received instruction from Staupitz. Moreover, his attitude toward Staupitz during the controversy in the Congregation (which had already begun at this time) would not suggest that his personal relations with the vicar-general were as close as his own account of their mutual friendship would imply. The earliest evidence for such intimacy between the two brother Augustinians dates from the period after the summer of 1511, when Luther was again transferred to Wittenberg. As far as can be determined, he returned to his monastery in Erfurt in October, 1509, with the same spiritual outlook with which he had left it a year before.

CHAPTER VII

LAST YEAR IN ERFURT (1509-10)

Luther received a very cold welcome in Erfurt when he returned from the new university of Electoral Saxony, which was still held in scant respect. The theological faculty obstinately refused to recognize his Wittenberg examinations and grant him the degree of *Sententiarius*. It was only the energetic recommendations of Dr. Nathin (who apparently brought about the recall of the gifted student in order that he himself might be somewhat relieved), that prompted the faculty finally to grant him the right to give lectures as a *Sententiarius*. He delivered a formal inaugural lecture in the so-called "heavenly auditorium" above the transept of the cathedral. On the very next day he exchanged this heavenly place for the more modest auditorium of his monastery. Here he apparently lectured three or four times a week until October, 1510, exclusively on the *Sentences* of Peter Lombard, to the little group of student monks assigned to him by the prior.

We still possess the monastery library's copy of this famous book which he used for the lectures, and also the volume of St. Augustine (likewise borrowed from the monastery library), with which he was working during the last months of 1509 along with the lectures. Both of them still show how he "plowed through" the books that he studied, for they still bear the marks of his assiduous hand in countless markings, *nota benes*, and marginal glosses. In the volume of the *Sentences* these notes are sometimes so numerous that one gets the impression of having parts of lecture notes. Sometimes they are written as though spoken directly to the student: "Please underscore! Please note!"

A well-bred modern user of a library is somewhat surprised that Luther treated books that were not his own so very disrespectfully. But men of that time had not been well trained. They treated books as carelessly as they did the manuscripts they used in study. In the latter such additions are even more numerous. But since only the best rag paper was used for printing, it did not injure the appearance of the books nearly so much as it would today, especially if the learned biblioclast wrote in so small and yet so exceeding clear, neat, and regular a hand as did young Luther. How mistaken one would be if one were to draw conclusions as to the character of the writer from this almost feminine handwriting! The contents of these same marginal notes are anything but the effusions of a tender heart. On the contrary, they already reveal, step by step, the vigorous, indeed the passionate, temperament of the later Reformer. Even the critical vein, which is so strikingly characteristic of the older Reformer, begins to make itself strongly felt in the twenty-six-year-old *Sententiarius*. Already he is rigorously criticizing the style and contents of the books he reads and even at this time is able, with a happy penetration, to establish the spuriousness of two writings which in the Middle Ages were included among the works of Augustine.

The views and doctrines which Luther was expounding, however, still breathed the old Erfurt spirit. The fact that he no longer spoke of two, but of only one chief cause of redemption, and the fact that he no longer admitted the validity of free will but only of grace would indicate, as his deductions elsewhere show, a departure from the Occamist tradition in form but not in substance. Also his attacks upon the famous humanist, Jacob Wimpfeling, who had dared to dispute St. Augustine's authorship of the Augustinian Rule, prove that he was still completely absorbed in the views in which he had been educated in the Erfurt monastery. But in one respect he differed from Nathin and his colleagues. He was already studying Hebrew. To be sure, little came of it as yet. The textbook available to him, Reuchlin's *Rudimenta,* was quite deficient for that. However, an interest in the original languages of the Scriptures was kindled in him at this early date. For the present, of course, this interest extended only to the languages as such; that the Bible should be studied only in the original text was an idea that was still foreign to him. In 1514 he still gave unqualified preference to the church's Latin translation rather than to the original texts. It was not until 1515 that he began to doubt the authority of the Vulgate.

While he was thus quietly learning and studying in his cell in the Black Cloister—it was probably the cell over the east wing of the transept, which was destroyed by a fire in 1872 and afterward restored for the benefit of a curious posterity —Erfurt experienced its wild "mad year." In January, 1510, the old city council was overthrown by an uprising of lower-class craftsmen and apprentices who were rebelling against the intolerable tax burdens and the maladministration of those in the leading circles. On June 24 the unfortunate head of the Council of Four, Henry Kelner, was executed upon the insistence of those who achieved power. And on August 4 the chief building of the university, the great hall with the fine library in which Luther, when he was a bachelor of arts, first came in contact with a complete Bible, was demolished and ruined by the enraged mobs. During these disturbances every inhabitant of Erfurt had to espouse one party or another, if not openly, at least in his sympathies. Luther did this too, and even at that time he had decided unequivocally against the rioters. He never forgave the Erfurters for the violent outrages of this mad year. He later dated the decline of the city from the execution of Kelner, and on this occasion applied to Erfurt the proverb: "Proud spirit, secret jealousy, childish counsel: these three destroyed Rome and Troy."

Meanwhile he had finished his lectures on the first two books of the *Sentences.* Not very long after the assault on the great hall, therefore, he received the degree of *baccalaureus formatus* from the theological faculty. It is very doubtful, however, whether he finished expounding the whole of the third book. In all probability he had to break off suddenly in the midst of it.

CHAPTER VIII

TO ROME AND BACK AGAIN (1510-11)

The state of the Catholic Church at the beginning of the sixteenth century was in many respects similar to the condition of Prussia prior to the catastrophe of Jena. Sentiment for a thoroughgoing reform was present everywhere. Nor were proposals of reform and attempts at reform wanting. Except in Spain, however, all of these were frustrated at the very start. The opposition was too great. It was chiefly the ruling authority of the church, the curia, which resisted reform. It was not at all uncommon for the popes to violate and nullify resolutions of reform which they had just approved. They were more interested in high and low politics, in war, art, music, hunting, the comedy, and the carnival than they were in any of the reforms. They no longer had any understanding—or at least any adequate understanding—of the spiritual duties of their office.

We also find such efforts at reform in the Order of the Augustinian Hermits, and the generals of the Order were not the least zealous advocates of a revival of the old discipline. General Mariano da Genazzano, whom we remember as the bitter opponent of Savonarola, had actively championed this cause. But he was far surpassed by a younger brother of the Order who had been especially intimate with him and who, after numerous very brief terms as general, entered in June, 1506, upon a twelve-year period as head of the Order. This was Egidio Canisio of Viterbo. But Egidio had practically the same experience as his predecessors. The Conventuals, or representatives of the laxer discipline, usually did not have the slightest desire to be reformed. And the Reformed Congregations, of which there were but nine in 1507, made all sorts of difficulties for him because they were afraid that they might lose their privileges and believed that their local customs might be threatened. In this way they nullified his best and most promising plans. A characteristic example of this may be seen in the internal conflicts in the Saxon Congregation between 1507 and 1512.

In order to give the reform movement in Germany a wider scope, Egidio planned, at the end of 1506 or the beginning of 1507, that the vicar-general of the Congregation, John von Staupitz, should undertake the leadership of the Saxon Order in conjunction with his office as vicar and then, as provincial, gradually reform the deteriorating Augustinian monasteries of the Province. On December 15, 1507, Staupitz succeeded in getting a Bull from the German legate, Cardinal Carvajal, which empowered him to unite more than twenty monasteries of the province of Saxony, which had not been reformed, with the Saxon Congregation. At the same time this Bull instructed the archbishop of Magdeburg and the bishops of Bamberg and Freising to suppress all resistance to this measure, with force if necessary, and to deny any opponent the right of appeal to the pope. The attempt to win the Congregation for this plan was at first abortive. On this account Staupitz preferred not to publish the Bull immediately. It was only after the general had appointed him provincial of Saxony on June 26, 1510, and after he had pledged the members of both the Congregation and the Province, under threat of very severe punishment, to obey him implicitly, that he ventured to publish the Bull three months later, on September 30, 1510. Twenty-two of the twenty-nine monasteries of the Congregation then approved the union. The other seven persisted in their opposition, and prominent among these were the two largest and most influential, the monasteries at Nuremberg and Erfurt.

The Erfurters sent Dr. Nathin and Father Luther to Halle to get a *Vorschrift*, or permission to appeal, from the archbishop of Magdeburg through the intervention of the dean of the cathedral, Adolf, prince of Anhalt. But the archbishop undoubtedly refused. Thereupon Nathin and Luther, under orders from their monastery, appear to have set out at once for the conference to which the Franconian district-vicar, Simon Kayser, had invited the dissenting monasteries. This conference was probably held at the Augustinian monastery at Nuremberg. Despite the express prohibition of the Bull, and without obtaining the consent of Vicar-general Staupitz as required by the statutes of the Congregation, the conference decided to appeal to the pope and to send two of the brothers to Italy for this purpose. One of these was probably an older *pater* of the great Nuremberg monastery who was familiar with the way in which business was transacted at the Vatican and who had some mastery of the Italian language. The other was Martin Luther. We may properly conclude from this that Brother Martin was one of the most zealous spokesmen of the opposition. But inasmuch as he was only twenty-seven years old and had no knowledge of Rome, he was certainly not chosen by the conference (as Cochlaeus maintains) to be the *litis procurator,* or agent of the seven monasteries. He was merely selected to accompany the *litis procurator* as the so-called *socious itinerarius,* or traveling companion, required by the Rule.

It was in all probability before the middle of November, 1510, that the two *patres* set out from Nuremberg and journeyed to Ulm at a fairly leisurely pace. From Ulm they probably passed through Upper Swabia and the western part of Switzerland along the road which was frequently taken by the Nuremberg merchants, and thence through the Septimer Pass toward Milan. It can hardly be determined how they proceeded from this point across the Apennines. We can say with certainty only that they started out from Florence along the old imperial road which led them through Siena and Roncaglia on the way to Rome. The winter of 1510-11 was an unusually hard one in northern and central Italy. It rained in Rome almost continually from the end of October to the beginning of February. In Bologna there was a deep snow on the ground on January 2, on the sixth there was a severe blizzard, and on the thirteenth there was a heavy snowstorm accompanied by almost unbearable cold. Nor was it particularly pleasant to be traveling in South Germany or in the Alps during these months.

However, the two travelers were spared an inconvenience which can become very annoying to a traveler today. They never had to search very long for suitable lodgings for the night. Inasmuch as they were certainly provided with *litterae testimoniales* (letters of introduction) from their superiors, they could stop over anywhere along the way at the monasteries of the Augustinian Hermits. While they were in Italy, it appears that they generally stopped at the monasteries of the Lombard Congregation, which had made some sort of agreement with the German Observants in 1505. This Congregation had two monasteries in Milan, Santa Maria dell'Incoronata and Santa Maria de Castro. In Florence it had the magnificent monastery of St. Gall, erected by Lorenzo the Magnificent not far from the Porta San Gallo, and in Rome Santa Maria del Popolo. Luther himself does not name any of these monasteries. In fact, he mentions only one of the many places where he lodged on his journey to and from Rome. This was the wealthy Benedictine abbey on the Po River which had an annual income of 36,000 ducats, a full third of which was "used for the entertainment of guests." He was probably referring to the Abbey San Benedetto Po, in Mantua, of whose hospitality travelers to Rome were accustomed to take advantage in those days.

The year 1510 must have been drawing to a close when the two pilgrims finally reached the much celebrated spot on the ancient Via Cassia from which one catches the first glimpse of the Eternal City. "At this sight," Luther related later, "I threw myself to the ground and said, 'Blessed be thou, holy Rome!'" Not long after this the two brothers passed through the Porta del Popolo and, turning to the left, came to the entrance of the Augustinian monastery, Santa Maria del Popolo. They made this monastery their home during their stay in Rome.

They probably went to San Agostino the very next day in order to announce their arrival to the procurator of the Order, as they were required to do, and to solicit his support in the appeal of the seven monasteries. Legally the case was so clear that the procurator could have refused and sent the brothers back home at once. However, since the general was personally interested in the matter, the procurator in all likelihood deemed it necessary to confer with the general. Of course, Egidio had no intention of approving the appeal. On the other hand, he did not want to offend the appellants, for he was anxious to put an end to the controversy in the Congregation. Hence it appears likely that he did not deny the brothers' petition until he had decided to dispatch the German brother, John, to Germany as peacemaker. From all appearances, therefore, almost four weeks passed before the brothers received an answer to their request and could begin their return journey.

This delay gave Brother Martin time to look at the Eternal City with the help of the *Mirabilia urbis Romae*, the Bädeker of that time. He found time to do this despite the fact that the statutes of the Order required him to take part in all the daily services in Santa Maria del Popolo as long as he was a guest there. But he was more concerned about his soul's welfare than about sightseeing. So he probably inquired at once where he might make a general confession, for it had been a particular comfort to him all along to think that at Rome he would be able to unburden himself of all that weighed on his conscience. But in doing so he came upon "thoroughly unlearned people"—priests who did not know how to hear confession. It was an experience which the Catholic reformers themselves were later to have in many parts of Italy. This was the first and (remembering what his feelings were at that time) perhaps the deepest disappointment which the Holy City had in store for him.

After this he set out at once, after the fashion of the time, on the great pilgrimage to the seven principal churches of the city, which were open all day even in Luther's time. This was a very fatiguing trip, not only because it was customary to visit all seven in one day, but also because the roads were in an unbelievably poor condition. It was especially strenuous, moreover, when the pilgrims fasted the whole day, as they did, in order that they might receive Communion at the end of the pilgrimage. They usually began early in the morning with San Paolo fuori le Mura, at the southwestern extremity of the city, beyond Aurelian's Wall. From San Paolo they would walk along the ancient road della sette Chiese to San Sebastiano, which was on the Appian Way; the catacombs which are located near by were usually visited at the same time. From there they would go to San Lorenzo fuori le Mura, San Giovanni in Laterano, Santa Croce in Gerusalemme, Santa Maria Maggiore, and finally, cutting straight across the city, to San Pietro in Vaticano. Here the pilgrims were wont to have the sacrament administered to them, and they would drink from the flowing fountain whose water "is led into the pope's garden because it traverses the whole earth in the bones of saints." Brother Martin, like all other pilgrims, naturally did not fail to crawl up the twenty-eight steps of the so-called Scala Sancta (located at that time on the north side of the Lateran Palace) and to pray a Pater Noster for his grandfather Heine Luder, of Möhra, on each step after having kissed it piously. For it was said that one could "free a soul from purgatory by going up on one's knees." But he had hardly reached the top when a doubt, which he had probably just heard, occurred to him: "Who knows whether it is true?"

Luther also read mass a number of times, particularly masses for the dead. For there were a great many altars at the various sacred spots, and it was believed that the reading of a mass at one of these would immediately release a poor soul from the flames of purgatory. He was not always so fortunate as to find an opening at these sites, which were especially marked out in his guidebook. For instance, he tried to get such an opportunity in San Giovanni in Laterano, not far from the great archway in which the two bells, alleged to be the oldest in the world, were hanging. But Saturday after Saturday his efforts seem to have been in vain, so great was the press of priests on this weekday in front of the railing of the Sancta Sanctorum Chapel! It appears that he had better luck at the altar of Sebastian at San Sebastiano. Here and there—as at San Giovanni and San Sebastiano, for example—he could gain the same end without saying a mass. As a matter of fact, Luther found so much opportunity to do something for the poor souls of the dead that "he was downright sorry" that his father and mother were still living. He would gladly have rescued them, too, from the flames of purgatory "by means of his masses and other excellent works and prayers."

Besides visiting the seven principal churches, Luther also ran like "a mad saint through all the churches and crypts"— by the latter meaning all the catacombs which were accessible at that time. In all likelihood, therefore, he not only visited the cemetery at San Sebastiano, with its forty-six popes and eighty thousand martyrs who "lie crosswise" in the narrow aisles, but also the burial places at San Lorenzo and Santa Agnese fuori le Mura. At all events, Luther often mentions Santa Agnese afterward, although only to show how much this famous sanctuary had fallen into decay due to the greed of the popes. It is only incidentally, in fact, that any of these places are mentioned in his discourses, sermons, and writings. Most frequently he mentions the Pantheon, which was even then one of the greatest sights of the Eternal City. He refers twice to the "German church in the Spital," [1] and once to Santa Maria in Araceli and to San Pancrazio on Monte Gianicolo, where "the saint is exhibited in the

[1] See below, p. 66.

body, and countless martyrs in addition." But these are
certainly not the only holy places, apart from the seven
principal churches, which he sought out during those four
weeks in Rome.

What was it, then, that made him so "mad" as to run
through all the churches and crypts and to believe everything "that was invented there with stinking lies"? Primarily,
as he himself says, it was the pious desire to earn all the vast
indulgences which were available. And yet what could even
San Giovanni in Laterano offer in this respect when compared with the chapter house of All Saints in Wittenberg?
Accordingly other motives must have played a part too. The
wish to do something for the poor souls of his deceased relatives in purgatory must always have been present. At the
same time he was eager to see with his own eyes all the
magnificent and world-famous shrines which Rome called
its own. Unfortunately the most famous of these were not
accessible at the time. Special written permission from the
pope was required, for instance, to enable anyone to inspect
Santo Volto in St. Peter's (the handkerchief of Veronica)
and the other relics of the Passion which were there. But
the pope was in Mirandola and environs at this time and
could not be reached by Luther. As a result he could not
possibly have seen these shrines. The same was true with
respect to the heads of Peter and Paul which, to the delight
of all Rome, Pope Urban V had discovered in the palace
chapel of the Lateran, Sancta Sanctorum, on March 1, 1368.
They were enclosed in two costly golden busts, and in the
ornate ciborium prepared by Giovanni di Stefano they were
entombed above the principal altar of the Lateran church.
It is true that Luther frequently mentions these remarkable
relics, but he always described them quite erroneously as
"wooden heads." He never saw them with his own eyes, as
he himself once said expressly, but spoke of them only from
hearsay. Luther's pious curiosity was nevertheless fully satisfied by the sight of the less precious relics. However, he

refers specifically to only a few of these. Thus he mentions
the twelve feet of frightfully thick rope with which Judas
Iscariot is supposed to have hanged himself. (This rope, suspended from a column in St. Peter's near the altars of St.
Simon and St. Jude, was taken as booty by Schärtlin von Bur-
tenbach during the sack of Rome in May, 1527, and then solemnly hung up again in Schorndorf, Schärtlin's home town in
Swabia.) Luther also mentions having seen a number of
paintings alleged to have been the work of the Evangelist
Luke. He was probably thinking of the famous Madonnas
of Santa Maria del Popolo, of San Agostino, and of Santa
Maria in Araceli.

We have a more exact knowledge of the state of Luther's
mind as he wandered from church to church than we have
of the number and nature of the shrines which he saw. He
was still such a "mad and arrogant saint" that "he believed
everything that was invented there with stinking lies." He
never had the slightest doubt that the hundreds of *mirabilia*
(often so very curious) which he had been shown were
genuine, or that the "unsifted lies" which he had been told
about them were true. It was only afterward that he learned
to think differently about them. But he always remembered
one of the many churches in the Eternal City with gratitude. This was the German national church, Santa Maria
dell'Anima, behind the Piazza Navona, which he called the
"German church in the Spital." "It is the best church, and
has a German parson." He probably meant by this that he
got a better impression here because the service was conducted, as it still is today, in the German fashion, and because
the worshipers appeared to be more devout than those in
the Italian churches. For just as Italian visitors were astonished at the devoutness of the people and the dignity of
divine services in Germany, so the celebrants' haste and lack
of dignity and the irreverence of the worshipers in the Italian
churches struck the Germans as strange. Even at this time
it probably disgusted Brother Martin to observe, as he put

it later, that "the priests could say mass in such a cocksure
and slapdash fashion, as if they were doing a juggling act,
for before I had come to the Gospel, the celebrant beside me
had already finished his mass and was calling to me, '*Passa,
passa,* hurry up, have done with it!' " In the course of a single
hour he once saw as many as seven masses celebrated at one
altar in San Sabastiano! The German church, to which he
liked to refer, had suffered a decline at that time, and we
do not hear particularly fine things about the chaplains in
the college of priests. It is clear, however, that there was a
German parson (more accurately, a sacristan) at Santa Maria
dell'Anima by the name of Henry Bode, and there were
about a half-dozen additional German chaplains there. It
may well be, therefore, that Luther was animated by a somewhat provincial spirit when he expressed his opinions of
Anima. He was apparently delighted to find a place in the
Eternal City where he might meet Germans. And he must
have become acquainted with Germans here, among them
the so-called courtesans, or members of the papal court.

Such running about from church to church by pilgrims to
the Eternal City was nothing out of the ordinary at that time.
All Christians who visited Rome did practically the same
thing. During these four weeks, therefore, Brother Martin
did not do anything at all unusual but simply did what, with
the help of the customary guidebook, was expected of a pilgrim. He was unfortunate, however, in having very poor
weather, for rain fell in torrents almost all the time he was
there. Nor did he have the good fortune to see everything
which his guidebook had listed for the benefit and profit of
salvation-seeking northerners, for the most famous of the
shrines were not accessible at the time. Besides, he did not
participate in many church festivals in Rome—at all events,
not in a single one of the *great* festivals. Probably the most
important event during his stay was the pilgrimage to San
Sebastiano on the Appian Way, which took place on January
20 and in which all Rome was still accustomed to take part.

There was very little activity in church life, even in other respects, during his sojourn there. The Advent season was already past when he arrived. Hence he heard no sermons at all in the churches of Rome, and hardly had the opportunity to hear any while traveling through Italy. He never expressly mentioned that he did. Apparently he was speaking from hearsay when he described the character and defects of Italian pulpit oratory.

On the other hand, many a curious thing came to his attention which did not fit in very well with his conception of Holy Rome. He was particularly horrified by the stories about Pope Alexander VI and his bastard children—stories which were later demonstrated to be partly fictions but which were believed at that time by everyone in Rome, above all by Alexander's successor, Pope Julius II. Strange things were told him about this pope too. He was far more impressed, however, by what he learned from the German "courtesans" concerning the frivolous unbelief of Roman priests, the conduct of cardinals (which was often quite scandalous), and the predictions that calamity would fall upon Rome which were current in all Italy since the time of Savonarola. The impression of the leaders of Roman society which he formed in this way was not particularly encouraging. But he did not hear much to the credit of the common people either. There was more talk about "dissolute life, irregularities, and murders" than he was likely to have expected in such a holy city, and he must have been surprised to hear of the "exceedingly strict order" which the whoremaster Sier Nicolo Fieschi maintained in the narrow alleys of the inhabited part of the city. Less often, conversation drifted to the livelier events in the history of the previous decades, as, for example, the amusing account of the wicked Count Deifobo of Anguillara. On the whole he found little edification and pleasure in what he learned in the Eternal City—especially what he learned from his own countrymen in regard to the curia, the Romans, and even the German and Dutch "courtesans." We might imagine that this was a purely personal misfortune. But all the pilgrims to Rome of whom we know anything had practically the same experience. All of them were disillusioned, horrified, distressed, or at least astonished by what they had experienced or heard there.

Is this all that Brother Martin heard or saw in Rome? It is certain that he did not get to see the pope, who since August, 1510, had been sojourning in northern Romagna together with the larger part of his court, his Swiss Guard, his chancellery, and the foreign legates. All but two of the cardinals had left Rome too, and one of these was lying on his deathbed while the other was languishing in close confinement in the Castle of St. Angelo. Even the foreign petitioners and agents who were usually thronging the datary and the palaces of cardinals had followed the pope to his encampment. And so it was almost as quiet in Rome at this time as in a sleepy country town which has no economic life of its own. Speaking of economic activity, despite its population of about 40,000, Rome could not compare with Erfurt (with half as many inhabitants), not to mention Nuremberg or even Augsburg. As a matter of fact, if Brother Martin compared the city of the popes with these two highly developed industrial and commercial centers of South Germany, it must have given him the impression of a dead city, and at the same time of a city of the dead. For the extensive area enclosed by Aurelian's Wall included not only great tracts of uncultivated land, but also (and this astonished him) numerous stretches of ruins, alongside which the inhabited part of the city appeared small and insignificant. He tells us that he walked about among these ruins a great deal in spite of the danger threatening the traveler from the rabble which found shelter there.

What was it that interested him most in these dead quarters and in the narrow streets of the Eternal City? Without a doubt, the catacombs near San Sebastiano. He was interested in these because eighty thousand martyrs and forty-six holy popes were supposed to have been entombed there. Next to these, the Pantheon, the vast ruins of the Colosseum, and the Diocletian baths struck his fancy most. Among ancient sculptures he names only the statue, with its curious marble settle, which was allegedly that of Popess Johanna. To be sure, the number of works of art to be seen in Rome was then limited. Of those which had been excavated the better pieces were in the possession of private citizens. Such other fragments of ancient glory as a traveler might come upon in the streets and market places belonged in the category of archeological curiosities rather than of fine art. The fact that Brother Martin mentions only this one statue—and his attention was very likely attracted to it only because of the incident which it was presumed to picture—certainly shows that he had no interest in such things at the time. Nor does he betray the slightest interest in the new art, which must have been noticeable here and there, in contrast to the pure medievalism of the city as a whole. "The palaces of the right reverend cardinals" which, he commented, excel all the palaces of kings—he was probably thinking particularly of the Cancelleria, the Palazzo di San Marco, the Palazzo Condolmier-Orsini on the Campo di Fiore, and the palaces on Piazza Scossa Cavalli in Borgo—certainly caught his eye. They attracted him, however, not because of their beauty, but rather on account of their "luxuriousness," which was very offensive to his monkish sensibilities. It is not surprising, on the other hand, that he did not say a word about the building of St. Peter's because there was very little of it to be seen at the time. Only the four colossal pillars of the dome had been completed. The nave and the rostrum of the old basilica were still standing and were still being used for services. But there was another church in Rome which very worthily embodied the new style of architecture. Yet Luther was just as silent concerning this church—the Basilica di Santa Maria del Popolo—although he prayed and sang in it every day.

Luther appears to have had no more interest in the paintings of the new school than in the buildings. He must surely have had the Madonna of Santa Maria, ascribed to St. Luke, pointed out to him, but he seems to have been unmoved by the magnificent frescoes of Pinturicchio in the Chapel della Rovere and on the ceiling of the choir. Of course, one cannot conclude from this that he was by nature wanting in taste for the plastic arts. It simply means that he was wandering through the Eternal City with the eyes of a pilgrim. If he wished to see and to venerate only the most important of the accessible shrines listed in his guidebook, and if he wished to secure only the largest of the indulgences offered in these shrines, he had to husband his time and even regiment his thoughts so as to pass by many of the marvels of Rome which had no significance for his soul's welfare.

Consequently he saw nothing unusual, heard nothing unusual, and experienced and did nothing unusual in Rome. On the contrary, his experiences and impressions deviate hardly a hair's-breadth from the experiences and impressions of contemporary travelers to Rome. Even the disillusionments which he suffered correspond with the experiences of other pilgrims to Rome. But like them, too, Luther was not at the time shaken in his Catholic faith by these disillusionments. For he found not only the Unholy Rome, of whose existence he had previously known nothing, but also the Holy Rome, which had been dear to him from his youth. And he found the Holy Rome especially in the narrow passages of the catacombs, which moved his soul so deeply in those four weeks that the perplexing and repulsive impressions of the Unholy Rome could not at first prevail. It was only when he felt constrained to declare war against the Unholy Rome that these bad impressions became meaningful to him. At the same time they became weighty proof that he was not doing an injustice to the papacy when he undertook the "abominable, hateful business" of attacking it in speech and writing. But even in later times these bad impressions were never the sole basis for his opinion of Rome. What he learned after 1517 from contemporaneous literature, and from the accounts of German visitors to Rome and Italy who had observed the Eternal City for years rather than for only four weeks, influenced him quite as much, and perhaps more.

About the end of January or the beginning of February, 1511, the two brothers left the Eternal City. It may be assumed that they started out on the same road by which they had come. From Florence they apparently went to Bologna by way of Scarperia, Fiorenzuola, and Imola; and from Bologna by way of San Benedetto Po and Verona, to the Brenner Pass. When they had pushed their way through this pass, which in February is usually covered with snow, they turned westward from Innsbruck to the Schanitz Pass and, going by way of the much traveled road through Partenkirchen and Schongau, they reached Augsburg about the beginning of March.

It was only very occasionally that Brother Martin mentioned the experiences and impressions that he had on the long journey to and from Rome, just as he seldom spoke of his sojourn in Rome. Nor can the geographer and the historian of culture learn very much from these utterances. Nevertheless, all of them have some significance for an understanding of his mental and spiritual make-up. For this reason a biographer cannot lightly pass them by. In Nuremberg Luther was especially impressed by a clock which struck the hours; in Ulm, by the enormous size of the cathedral; in Swabia and Bavaria, by the great friendliness and efficiency of the innkeepers. In Bavaria he found the soil very unproductive. And yet, he says, there were very well-built houses and strongly fortified towns there. The people are not very intelligent, he thought, but on this very account they are upright, honest, and industrious. In Switzerland there is nothing but mountains and valleys, and the soil is very barren. Agriculture does not thrive there—only meadows and pastures. Yet the streets are very safe and pleasant, and the houses just as fine as those in Bavaria. The people are strong, upright, and brave. Since they cannot find enough sustenance at home, the men have to seek their livelihood elsewhere as mercenary soldiers. If there happens to be no war, they milk the cows and make the cheese, which is done else-where only by the women. Of neighboring Tyrol Luther says almost nothing; quite incidentally he remarks that Inns-bruck is a small town, but so uniformly built that it looks like a single, small house.

Nor does he say much of Augsburg, the first larger German town which he touched on the return journey. Here he seems to have been most interested in the famous miracle-maid, Anna Lammenit, who was also highly honored by Emperor Maximilian; it was alleged that she had lived for the previous ten years on the Host which she received every Sunday. Luther had a chaplain take him into the "virgin's" house, near the Church of the Holy Cross. But he was somewhat dismayed when the celebrated saint, who in 1512 was ex-posed as a shrewd impostor, bluntly answered his question whether she would not gladly die: "My word, no! I do not know how things are there; I know what they are here."

Luther's remarks concerning Italy and its people are equally scanty. He praises the country highly. It is a "most delightful region." Richly bearing olive trees spring up even out of the rockiest ground; there one learns to understand the words of the Psalm (81:16), "With honey out of the rock would I satisfy thee." He is particularly impressed by the fertility of the plains of Lombardy and the mighty waters of the Po. It also appears remarkable to him that the citron tree always has ripe as well as unripe fruit on it. He finds the climate to be very subtile, that is, dangerous. On this account one cannot sleep near an open window there. He and his companion tried it once, but suffered an attack of malaria as a consequence; they were cured simply by eating several pomegranates. The inhabitants please him much less than the country. True enough, they are more polite, refined, vivacious, and active, and also more sly and crafty than the "barbarous" North Germans. They do not drink nearly so much, and they dress better. For whereas the tailors in Germany put everything together higgledy-piggledy, there are special tailors in Italy who make nothing but breeches or jackets or coats, and this naturally results in better clothes.

But this is the best Luther can say in praise of the Italians. Their lively gestures struck him as ludicrous. Their roundelays and dances appeared to him to be highly lascivious, even though the men joined hands with the women with a cloth between them. He was amazed at the jealousy with which the men guarded their wives, so that they always had to go about veiled and were never allowed to be addressed in public. In fact, they were practically kept imprisoned. He was even more astonished at the ingenuousness with which the people openly performed their natural functions on the street corners. He deemed them no better "than dogs" in this respect. If a man wanted to protect his house against such indecencies, he had to post a picture of St. Anthony with the fiery spear. In spite of all this, they considered themselves better than all other people, especially the drunken, besotted Germans, and they took every opportunity to poke fun at the piety of the Northerners. They themselves had absolutely no reverence for that which is sacred. They blasphemed and joked about God and the saints in horrible fashion, and their characteristic name for a fool was a *bon Christian,* a good Christian. Among the Germans, the only ones who could compete with them in craftiness were the Lower Saxons and the Dutch; indeed, whenever such people settled in Italy, they became worse than the worst Italians, as the proverb says: "An Italianized German is a devil incarnate." Thus the Italians themselves would have nothing to do with the *Alemanni bassi* (Low Germans), but they highly esteemed and loved the *Alemanni alti* (High Germans).

Luther was not always unaware of the fact that these were

very biased judgments. "I do not understand the Italians and they do not understand me," he said once, "and this is in some measure a natural source of anger and hatred." He was thinking primarily of the difference in language. Although he had picked up a few scraps of Italian on the way, he had neither time nor opportunity to learn it properly. Nevertheless he had the quite correct impression that there were a great many dialects and that on this account the Italians often understood literary Italian very imperfectly.

Luther had little to say about the famous Italian towns through which he passed on his journey to and from Rome. He mentions Milan several times, but only to recall the fact that he had not been permitted to say mass there inasmuch as the Ambrosian Liturgy was still used in the diocese. Florence also is occasionally mentioned. But the buildings and the works of art, which today are esteemed as the landmarks of the city, did not make a great impression on him. He was impressed, rather, by the excellently managed hospitals and the famous foundling asylum, close by the Porta San Gallo where he lodged with the Lombard Augustinians. "When a patient is brought into the hospital," he relates, "all his clothes are taken off and are given to a notary for safe-keeping. Then a white nightgown is put on him and he is placed in a beautifully painted bed with clean sheets. Thereupon two physicians come to examine the patient. The attendants bring food and drink in clean glass vessels and do not touch the food, even with a fingertip, but offer it to the patient on a tray. The most noble matrons of the city, heavily veiled so as to conceal their identity, take turns nursing the sick for a few days at a time. In the foundling asylum the children are also sheltered in the best possible way and are very well nourished and taught. They all wear neat uniforms of the same color and are most paternally provided for." Concerning Siena he says, incidentally, that it was there that he heard an Italian (very probably a monk of the famous Augustinian monastery in Siena) say, "We have learned a great many epigrams from your emperor, Frederick [III?], this one in particular: 'He cannot rule who cannot dissimulate' (*Qui nescit dissimulare, nescit regnare*)."

It becomes quite evident that, as in Rome itself, Luther experienced nothing unusual on the journey to and from Rome, and that he always observed everything that was new to him from a very one-sided point of view. He had no eye for the charms of the landscapes in the regions through which he traveled. Like a peasant, he asked only whether they are productive and whether they are suitable for agriculture or only for stock farming. As to the towns, he simply notices whether they are large or small, well or badly fortified, and whether or not they are uniformly planned. He is interested merely in the size and outward magnificence of the many houses, palaces, and churches which he passes, and occasionally he notes the acoustics of the churches. He never mentions works of art, although he does notice mechanical curiosities like the Nuremberg clock. Yet he declares later, "The Italian painters can imitate and copy nature so skillfully and faithfully that their pictures not only have the genuine, natural colors and shape of all the parts, but also the expressions, and so they seem to live and move." Since, in later years, he never had opportunity to study the pictures of Italian painters, this appreciation probably reflects impressions received on the journey to Rome. The same may be true of his opinions concerning the frescoes of Pinturicchio in the Santa Maria del Popolo.

A like discernment is disclosed in Luther's remarks concerning the inhabitants and the accommodations in the countries through which he went. His comments permit us to draw some conclusion as to the character of the inhabitants. The things that every traveler notices at once—the condition of the roads and inns, the conduct of the innkeepers, the dress, customs, methods of trade, and language of the foreign people—naturally always struck him too. In addition, he shows an interest only in the religious usages, the religious behavior of the clergy and laity, the condition of the monasteries, and the life of the regular and secular clergy, all of which is quite natural for a priest and monk. As a rule he apparently saw only the superficial aspects of things. But there are also occasional observations which suggest that we are not here confronted by an observer of the common run. Characteristic examples of this are his remarks concerning the hospitals in Florence and his appreciations of the Italian painters and tailors.

At first thought it may seem somewhat bold to attribute to Luther, the monk, an interest in such altogether profane things as breeches. But the apparent incongruity disappears when one remembers how important the problem of dress was, and still is, in monasteries, and when we recall that even as an older man Luther had to mend his own breeches. He says, "Trousers seldom fit me well, so I have to make these [which he happened to have in his hands] last long. Even Electors Frederick and John mended their own breeches. In Italy the tailors are first-rate; there the pants-makers have a separate guild. But in Germany the tailors are careless; they take a lot of material, use no models, and cut everything— breeches, jerkin, and coat—from the same pattern." Additional citations are not lacking to show that he had an eye for such things and appreciated the aesthetic side of dress. "It makes my eyes smart," he said once, "to see a man go about in breeches looking like a ruffled pigeon." Contemporaneous styles in men's clothing could hardly be characterized more perfectly. However, such impressions were stronger in his earlier than in his later years.

About the middle of March, 1511, the two brothers went from Augsburg to Nuremberg. Here (in all probability shortly after their arrival) another conference of the seven dissenting monasteries was held in the Augustinian monastery and the travelers reported the result of their mission. It is nowhere stated that Luther took part in such a conference, but we may safely conclude from the position he had held in the opposition since October, 1510, that he was present. It appears that the conference received the impression, from the reports of the two paters, that the general would ultimately yield. It was accordingly decided, about the end of March, to send a new commission to Rome at once with the petition that, in case the general was not in a position to approve the requests of the dissenting monasteries, he at least allow recourse to law, that is, permit them to present their appeal to the pope. It was probably not until the new envoys were on their way to Rome, about April 2, that Luther started north on the road to Erfurt. Thus, in all probability, the controversy kept him from his monastery and his teaching for about five months. Presumably another brother had continued the lectures on the *Sentences* so that Luther could begin right where his substitute had left off. In those days this procedure was quite customary, and in view of the impersonal method of the whole system of higher education in the schools, it entailed no disadvantage to the student. But in the course of the summer an event occurred which made it necessary for Luther to leave Erfurt forever.

In April, 1511, the general of the Order was still firmly determined to consummate a union of the Congregation with the Saxon Province. But Staupitz, the man on whose co-operation he had especially counted, began to waver during the summer. To be sure, at a conference in Jena, in the middle of July, he told the deputies of the seven monasteries that he could not resign the provincialship of Saxony, but in other respects he made such concessions that they promised to lay his proposals of peace before their monasteries and to act upon them within two months. During the same month of July the discussion of this so-called Recess of Jena must have led to a violent disagreement in the Erfurt monastery. The majority of the *patres* rejected the Recess. But two of them, Luther and Brother John Lang, who was his close friend even at that time, voted to make peace with Staupitz. They apparently argued that a continuation of the opposition was incompatible with the vow of obedience to their superior, the vicar-general, and that it was harmful to the church.

Concerning the events immediately following we have only very meager information. We know only that Lang was sent into "exile," expelled from the monastery, and that he went to Wittenberg, where he was matriculated before August 17. We also find Luther in Wittenberg by late summer of 1511, and according to the letters which he wrote to Erfurt in 1514, his departure from Erfurt must have been marked by strife. It follows, therefore, that he was also sent into "exile." The admission of the two exiled brothers into the Wittenberg monastery obviously could not have taken place without the knowledge and consent of Vicar-general Staupitz, who, it appears, was in Wittenberg at the time. Indeed, we might go one step further and say that the two brothers turned to Staupitz after their banishment, and that it was Staupitz, as Luther once explicitly stated, who arranged for their transfer to Wittenberg.

Like the Erfurt monastery, the Nuremberg monastery also rejected the Recess of Jena, and it did this, as it appears, unanimously. Thereafter Staupitz considered the cause lost, and as early as late fall he decided to drop the union project entirely. He carried out this decision at the Chapter at Cologne in May, 1512. Peace was again restored to the Congregation. This peace was expressed outwardly in the re-election of Staupitz as vicar-general and in the temporary removal of his see to the Augustinian monastery in Nuremberg, the headquarters of those who had heretofore been his opponents. In Erfurt, meanwhile, a strong feeling of antipathy toward Luther and Lang persisted. At the Chapter of Cologne Luther had to have the mouth of an Erfurt slanderer stopped and, even as long afterward as 1514, he had to defend himself vigorously, in a sharp correspondence, against all sorts of unfounded accusations by Dr. Nathin, who once had been so well-disposed toward him. But it does not follow from this that the controversy between the seven

monasteries and the "Staupitzians" also continued after the
conclusion of peace at Cologne, which was really a victory
for the seven monasteries. Nor can such a conclusion be
drawn from the few critical remarks, concerning the attitude
of the Observants toward their superiors, found in Luther's
lecture notes of the years 1513 to 1516. It is probable that
no one heard these remarks at the time. For at that time the
Reformer used to let such allusions to current events, which
flowed from his pen while he was preparing his lectures, go
by the board when he delivered them. By the beginning of
1516 even the Erfurters were sufficiently reconciled to call
Lang back from "exile" and to raise no objection when
Luther, who then held the office of district vicar, set Lang
over them as prior.

But did these controversies also have significance for
Luther's inner development? As far as the journey to Rome
is concerned, the most that can be attributed to it is a negative significance, for it definitely destroyed his cherished
hope that he would find satisfaction for his inner needs in
Holy Rome. Even if the acquisition of the abundant indulgences in the Eternal City did give him some comfort at the
time, his old doubts and fears returned very soon. Now that
even this hope was shattered, his doubts and fears probably
caused him more anxiety than ever before. Accordingly if
he had been required to give an account of the effect which
this "mad pilgrimage" had on his inner life, he would probably have expressed it in the same words which he used a
quarter of a century later: "Like a fool, I carried onions to
Rome and brought back garlic."

But far more important, not only for his inner development but also for the progress and outcome of the Reformation, was the fact that the termination of the controversies
meant his transfer back to Wittenberg in the summer of 1511.
That he came into close contact with Staupitz, that Wittenberg became the forum and Electoral Saxony the cradle of
the Reformation movement, and the effect which this had

upon Luther, upon the shaping of German history, and upon the development of Protestantism in general and German Protestantism in particular—all this is directly or indirectly the result of this transfer. This is so in spite of the fact that it was never mentioned by his contemporaries or by himself and that it was undoubtedly painful to him at the time. For although we know little of the events which led up to it, we do know with certainty that he did not leave Erfurt voluntarily.

But why was he not permitted to stay? Because he felt himself impelled by his conscience to disagree with the majority of the brothers. As far as we know, this was the first time in his life that he dared to think and act differently from the "compact majority," and it was very likely not easy for him to do so. But "it was his salvation; it lifted him to new heights."

CHAPTER IX

DOCTOR AND PROFESSOR (1511-12)

"During the past summer we have used up, in building, about four hundred guldens of the sum which Your Princely Grace sent us, and yet we have not completed very much. We desire that Your Grace would favor us with some bricks from your own building [at the castle] so that we shall not be at a standstill."

The writer of these lines was John von Staupitz, the addressee was Frederick the Wise, and the building to which the lines refer was the new Augustinian cloister in Wittenberg. It is possible that Staupitz did receive some bricks from the Elector's builder after this appeal, but the Elector did little more than this for the rebuilding of the Black Cloister. When Frederick Mekum came to Wittenberg for the first time at the beginning of June, 1527, "no more than the dormitory for the monks had been built. The foundations of the new church, the cornerstone of which had been laid by the brother of the Elector, Archbishop Ernest of Magdeburg, before June, 1507, were begun, but they were only level with the ground. In the midst of these foundations the old monastery chapel was still standing, a very rickety frame building propped up on all sides, about thirty feet long and twenty feet wide." (To Luther's great sorrow it was not torn down until 1542.) "It had a small, old, rusty choir gallery in which at a pinch twenty persons could stand, and on the south wall a pulpit about five feet above the floor, made out of old, rough boards. In short, it had in all respects the appearance of those pictures which artists paint of the stable in Bethlehem where Christ was born."

Mekum's description, however, is not quite complete. He mentions neither the little garden behind the monastery near the town wall, nor the brewery of the old monastery in the southwest corner of the court, nor the building with its tower-like upper story connecting the dormitory and the brewery. Finally, he does not mention the famous pear tree which stood on the west side of the court, which was still open to the street.

It was in the shadow of this pear tree that the monks were accustomed, since there was no longer a cloister, to spend the prescribed time of recreation. Even Staupitz did this when he was staying in Wittenberg. One day when he was sitting under the pear tree—shortly before or shortly after the great ceremonies on September 16 and 17, 1511, when he conferred the doctor's cap on no less than four Augustinian Hermits in the presence of eleven doctors of the Order—he called Brother Martin to him and said, "Herr Magister, you must become a doctor and a preacher; then you will have something to do." How he had come to the opinion that Luther must have something to do will become evident later. On one of the following days, as he was again walking under the pear tree, he spoke of the matter to Luther again, and this time in earnest. But Luther immediately cited no less than fifteen reasons why he did not feel himself called to be a preacher and doctor. Staupitz, however, refused to admit any of these reasons. "Why, my dear fellow," he reproached him, "you don't want to set yourself up as wiser than the whole congregation and the Fathers!" Then Luther burst out with the words, "Herr Staupitz, you will bring me to my death. I will never endure it for three months." Staupitz replied jokingly, "Don't you know that our Lord God has many great matters to attend to? For these He needs clever people to advise Him. If you should die, you will be received into His council in heaven, for He, too, has need of some doctors." After this Luther had to acquiesce, willingly or not.

At this time every professor of theology was still required to preach and every preacher was required to have studied theology. Thus Staupitz in those memorable conversations

demanded of Luther both the assumption of the office
of preacher and the acquisition of the degree of doctor
of theology. The appointment of the preachers of the
Order was a prerogative of the vicar-general. So now Luther
had to begin at once to preach before the monks in the
refectory. Permission to receive the doctor's degree was
also conferred by the vicar-general. But more than a year
elapsed before Luther became a doctor. What was the
cause of this delay? From all appearances it was the distressing question of money. The fees for the doctor's degree
amounted to fifty guldens for ordinary candidates and seventeen guldens for mendicant monks. Staupitz, who was very
short of money at the time, was unable to raise this sum,
much as he wished to, apparently because he had exhausted
his funds in connection with the elaborate ceremonies held
on September 16 and 17. "The poor, newly founded monastery" at Wittenberg was hardly in a position to pay it either.
There was nothing Staupitz could do but appeal to the "dear
friend" whom he regarded as his "only refuge" next to God—
the Elector. But the Elector was willing to give only when
he had the assurance that it would contribute toward his
own salvation or help his new university. He therefore would
not provide the promotion fees until the vicar-general promised him that "for the rest of his life, Martinus would be
responsible for the lectureship on the Bible in the theological
faculty which formerly appertained to him" (Staupitz) but
which, in fact, Staupitz had not occupied for a long time.

In the meantime Luther was occupied only as a preacher
in the monastery. The time left over for his own study he
used, from all appearances, in learning Greek and reading
through Augustine's great works, *On the Trinity* and *The
City of God*. In the octave of Jubilate, 1512 (May 2-8), he
took part, presumably as a delegate of the Wittenberg monastery in the Chapter at Cologne, which put an end to the
controversy in the Congregation and which also concerned
itself in a number of ways with his own person. First, it

"stopped the mouths" of the Erfurt slanderers so that now he was (at least for a time) left in peace by the Erfurt brethren, and secondly, it appointed him as subprior of the Wittenberg monastery with the primary duty of directing the studies of the younger monks. Apart from this we know concerning this two-months' journey, which had to be made on foot according to the custom of the Order, only that when Luther was in Cologne he did not neglect to see and piously reverence the relics of the holy Three Kings.

About the beginning of June he assumed his new office in Wittenberg. On this occasion he was for the first time allotted a little room with heat for his own use. This room was in the tower-like upper story over the building connecting the dormitory and the brewery, in the southwest corner of the monastery. It had served as a dwelling for his predecessors in office. Even though it was small and was a remnant of the old monastery, he retained it as his work room for the rest of his life because he could not be so easily disturbed there. However, as early as 1532, he expressed the fear that "the great cannons, ramparts, and battlements of the new bastion in the southeastern part of the town would gobble up the poor little room from which he had stormed the papacy, wherefore it was worthy of eternal remembrance." After his death this very thing happened, for as he correctly foresaw, the Junkers (Scharrhansen) won the victory over him in this respect also.

In the fall of 1512 the negotiations with the Elector concerning his entrance into Staupitz' professorship had finally progressed so far that, on October 4, he could receive the "license," that is, permission from the theological faculty, to become a candidate for the doctor's degree. To receive this he had, among other things, to swear allegiance to the Roman Church. On October 9 he went to Leipzig to receive in person from the electoral chamberlains, who were there for the Michaelmas fair, the fifty guldens which the Elector had appropriated for the promotion fees.

Accordingly, on October 18 the preliminary celebration of the promotion, the so-called *vesperies*, took place in the castle church under the presidency of Professor Carlstadt; and on October 19, at seven o'clock in the morning, the promotion ceremony itself was observed in the same place, the *aula cathedralis*. On this occasion Luther was required to swear another oath, in which, among other things, he promised that he would not lecture on frivolous, strange doctrines which were condemned by the church and offensive to pious ears, and that he would inform the dean within eight days of anyone who should teach such doctrines. Thereupon Carlstadt, with sundry sententious remarks, handed to him first a closed and then an open Bible. Then the hat made of pure wool was placed on his head and the silver doctor's ring on his finger. After this there followed several hours of discourse and disputation in the style in which that oratory- and ceremony-loving age delighted. The formal ceremony was not over until ten o'clock. However, as a doctor he was still not a member of the theological faculty. It was not until three days later, on October 22, that he became a member by formal reception into the "*senate*," that is, the professorial staff of the faculty, which at that time consisted of only five persons. He began his teaching as the incumbent of the lectureship on the Bible the very next Monday, October 25, at seven o'clock in the morning in the auditorium of the Black Cloister. It appears that he started with a lecture on Genesis.

Luther later tells us that it caused a sensation that he had attained to such high honor and office at so young an age. But he himself was in no such mood. It is true, he was now "both master and doctor," but, as he said in a sermon on May 21, 1537, he "still did not know the light" for which he had been seeking so long. Indeed, it was in these first months of his professorship that he experienced especially severe suffering from the doubts and fears which had been tormenting him for more than seven years. What was the ultimate cause of this inner misery, and how was he freed from it?

CHAPTER X

DAWN OF THE REFORMATION CONSCIOUSNESS
(April-May, 1513)

Hundreds of men and women before Luther had entered the monastery to make satisfaction for their sins and to escape from the wrath to come. For not a few of these hundreds, the external occasion for their entrance was, like his, an emotional experience which suddenly put them face to face with the fear of death and divine judgment—a severe illness, an unexpected death, the murder of someone near them, or the like. Legend is full of tales of this kind. Even the "vocation" through a thunderstorm is not without precedent, as is shown by the story of St. Norbert of Xanten. Just as the motive and the external occasion which led Luther into the monastery were not extraordinary, neither were the experiences which he afterward had in the monastery out of the ordinary. Many monks had had similar doubts and scruples, but in the course of time they had found some sort of peace. The one thing, therefore, that distinguishes Luther from the great mass of ascetics is simply the fact that all the means of quieting such doubts provided for by the old monastic teachers not only failed but rather had a completely opposite effect; that is, they merely increased his inner distress and anxiety.

The most important of these means of pacification was confession. Luther had been taught that in the moment when the priest whispers the words, *"Deinde te absolvo,"* all sins are *sono sonato* driven out of the soul, except for a remainder, the so-called "tinder" of original sin, which, however, is not really a sin at all. But to his horror he was compelled to acknowledge repeatedly that confession did not have this effect upon *him;* that, on the contrary, he was just

the same after confession as before. However, he did not
at this time conclude from this that those doctrines were
therefore false, but only that he had not yet confessed in the
right way. He was not content therefore with one general
confession, as were other monks. He made such a complete
confession no less than three times—the first time at his
reception into the Black Cloister at Erfurt in September,
1505; the second time probably at his profession in September, 1506; and the third time at Rome in January, 1511. Besides this, for a time he confessed every day. Indeed, it
seemed that "as soon as he had confessed and turned to the
altar, he beckoned again for a priest" in order to ease his
conscience once more. But the result was always the same:
"Not for a single hour could he remain as he was [accord-
ing to the teaching of the Church] immediately after
confession."

As with confession so it was with the other means for
calming doubts and fears—private chastisement and exercises which had been used with success by the devout before
him. As previously mentioned, as long as he was under
the discipline of the master of novices he could not make
use of these means. But when he had made his profession
nothing prevented their use. The exercises to which he
subjected himself were the usual ones, such as fasting,
vigils, and prayer (that is, private devotional exercises).
But the end that he had in view was far beyond the customary. He not only desired to propitiate God with these extra
ascetic works but, as Loyola did later in Manresa, he wanted
actually to compel Him to take from his soul the burden of
his consciousness of guilt. But the desired result failed to
appear. His anxiety over his sins, instead of being diminished, was only heightened. And here again he blamed the
failure not upon the means employed but rather upon his
own carelessness in the use of these means. Thus these
failures only caused him to lay hold more harshly upon himself and to torture himself ever more severely by fasting,

vigils, and a multiplicity of devotional exercises. But, as he said, this only ruined his physical health. His anxiety over his sins remained. Indeed, the more earnestly he exerted himself to make God gracious by such extra works, the more dreadful did his thoughts of the Last Judgment become, the greater was his fear of Hell, and the more fervent his longing for the certainty of forgiveness. It is true that, especially in the beginning, moments were not wholly absent when he believed that he had done enough and was pleased to hear himself praised for his saintly life, but "when a little trial of death and sin appeared I immediately succumbed again."

Luther himself repeatedly designates as the chief cause of his inner distress the notion that man can do everything that he wills to do, and also that he is able to earn the reward of eternal blessedness by his own works. This notion had apparently been familiar to him from his childhood. It became, in a sense, an axiom for him in the Erfurt Occamists' doctrine of the unlimited power of the human will, and this axiom was confirmed again and again by what he was learning in the monastery. In the first place, as a student in the monastery ever since 1507 he had read and heard none but Occamists. In the second place—and this is more important —such matters as the absolute fulfillment of all the Commandments, even the command to love God with the whole heart and mind without the admixture of any selfish feelings whatsoever, which the Occamists set forth as merely *theoretically* possible, he accepted from the very beginning as a practical requirement. For, like all other monastic rules, the Augustinian Rule was of course based on the idea that every monk could fulfill its requirements. The old monastic teachers, Cassian, the author of the *Vitae Patrum*, Bernard of Clairvaux, Gerhard Zerbolt of Zutphen, John Momboir, and others who might be mentioned, some of whom Luther had read as a novice for edification, were entirely of the same opinion. Indeed, St. Bernard, whom he esteemed especially throughout his life, maintains in all seriousness in his little book *On the Love of God* that it is possible by means of constant cultivation of the soul and purely by one's own reason and strength, to rise from the lower affections of natural self-love to disinterested love of one's fellow-man and finally to the pure, sublime love of God.

But did Luther hear or read nothing at all of the grace of God when he was in the monastery? It is true that grace was constantly mentioned in the hymns, prayers, and lections of the Augustinian breviary from which he prayed daily. Grace was also discussed in the lectures which he heard. But his teachers in the monastery, as in the university, repeatedly emphasized that this grace was something that a man must first earn for himself. Only if he did all that he was capable of doing could he be entirely sure of grace. But it was just this which tormented him so—that he could never say to himself, "You have done what lies in your power," that is, "you have done what you should, and therefore what you could."

But was he not acquainted with the comforting doctrine which taught that so-called "gallows repentance," that is, the egoistic fear of punishment for sin, was sufficient for confession? Did he not know that this imperfect repentance *(attritio)* was changed into the perfect repentance *(contritio)*, which grows out of a pure love of God and a hatred of evil as evil, by the sacramental effects which accompany the act of confession? Did he not know that confession is therefore a means of attaining the pure love of God by a sort of magical process? Certainly, he knew this doctrine well, just as he also knew that "hangman's" doctrine of Biel that man can gradually acquire this pure love by his own power if he disposes himself, according to the prescribed method of St. Bernard, to ever higher and more difficult stages of love. But this teaching was just as comfortless as the other; more than this, it was a rack for his conscience. Why? Because it was in complete contradiction to his own experience. For he never had the feeling in his soul during the act of confession that this mysterious transformation of the fear of hell into the rapturous emotion of pure love of God was taking place. On the contrary, he always had the tormenting impression that his repentance was and remained imperfect.

But, since his reception into the Order had not Luther read the Bible daily, and with such zeal that in 1513 he knew the Latin version almost by heart? Would he not have realized from this that the doctrines and ideas which tormented him so had "no basis in Scripture"? If he had fully understood the Bible at this time it would, in truth, have been able to help him. But his eyes were still bound. Even in the Bible he saw only the demanding, angry God, not the gracious, merciful Father; he saw in Christ only the judge of the world "on the rainbow" who gives to each what he has earned while living in the body, not the Lamb of God who bears the sins of the world.

Then how is it to be explained that he did not turn away from the Bible? What drove him to immerse himself in it again and again, no matter how sorely it wounded his heart? We hardly go wrong if we reply that it was because he was under the overmastering impression that in the Bible the holy God, who would allow no bargaining with Him but demanded that absolute purity of will for which Luther's deepest feelings longed, was speaking to him in person. Like the seeker for truth who reaches out for the truth even when he knows that it will kill him, so Luther, just because he was yearning with all the fibers of his heart for the *certainty* of forgiveness, had to allow the voice of this God to work upon him again and again, even though in so doing he felt as if "it were shattering his bones." So from the very beginning his struggle for a gracious God was at the same time a struggle for a right understanding of the Bible. Indeed, his conscience, even at this time, was so completely "imprisoned in the Word of God" that, despite his most passionate longing for inner peace, he had absolutely rejected every solution of his doubts which he had not been able to harmonize with the Bible.

But was he so deeply immersed in the prevailing doctrine of works and merits that the obvious idea of trying some other way to salvation never occurred to him?

Luther says later that he too was once caught up into the first heaven and that he had felt as though he had sojourned with the choirs of angels. Accordingly he, too, once tried the mystical way of salvation, and strove, according to the precepts of St. Bonaventura and Pseudo-Dionysius the Areopagite, to "climb up into the Majesty" and "gaze at the naked Majesty," and thus experience union with the pure Godhead. He even succeeded on one occasion in attaining a sort of rapture, but never the experience of union, despite his striving for it so hard that he "became quite mad." Furthermore, by this time he had probably read some of the much used mystical devotional books which he mentions later, such as the writings of Gerhard Zerbolt of Zutphen and John Momboir, and St. Bernard's sermons on the Song of Songs. Thus he had also become familiar with the methods of the mystical *Jesusminne*. Perhaps he had even meditated upon the life and passion of Jesus with the technical correctness prescribed by these methods, as so many monastics did, for later he shows that he was very well acquainted with them. But he found no peace of soul on this much traveled road either. Nevertheless, he did not conclude from all this that the mystics were striving for the extraordinary. He simply concluded that he was not yet pure enough to be able even to desire anything so exceedingly high as immediate contact with the most high God. So these efforts also drove him back again to examine his impure soul and, if possible, to chastise and torture himself even more than before.

Everything that had apparently been of such great help to hundreds of others in a similar circumstance affected Luther like poison. Superficial observers have been quick to conclude from this that there must have been something wrong with him. They have believed that they could strengthen the force of this conclusion by the assertion that Luther repeatedly suffered these "attacks" (*Anfechtungen*) even in his later years, and that by his own testimony these later "attacks" gave him more trouble than the fits of fear he suffered while in the monastery. In point of fact, he did have repeated "attacks" in later years, and some of them afflicted him more severely than the grinding struggle for certainty of salvation in the early years. But what was the cause of these later "attacks"? Primarily worry over his work, grief over the frivolity and moral shortcomings of the evangelical princes and lords, and disillusionment over the ingratitude and sensuality of the masses. At times it was also the thought which he calls his greatest and severest trial: "You alone are the cause of this state of affairs. Now, if it is wrong, you are responsible for as many souls as go to hell." Moreover, these later "attacks," as he himself acknowledged, were also physically conditioned. They were evidently closely connected with the nervousness which had given him so much trouble ever since 1521, when it became necessary for him to use opiates. They seized him especially during the night, which prompted him to utter the well-known saying: "My night battles are worse than my day battles." He tried to prevent them by external means in that, when he felt them coming on, he intentionally ate and drank more copiously than usual even though he had no appetite. He wanted this to be considered not as gormandizing, but rather as fasting, since it was done without appetite. These later "attacks" must not be indiscriminately confused with the spiritual "temptations" with which we are here concerned.

Nevertheless, the fact remains that the means and methods of the monastic soul-cure, tried a thousand times, failed to help Luther. Hence the suspicion remains that this can in some way be connected with a psychic defect — for example, a disposition toward melancholy or epilepsy. If this diagnosis were correct, some clear, definite traces of mental disease would surely be established. One such sure indication, for example, would be inability to perform any mental work which requires a vigorous exertion of the power of will and thought. But this characteristic symptom is entirely absent in Luther. On the contrary, it is in these critical years that he showed an extraordinary capacity for work. He attended and delivered lectures on subjects which placed the heaviest demands upon the logical faculties of the hearer as well as the speaker. He studied books which can be worked through only with the most intense concentration. And, what is of more importance, he learned two new, difficult languages at the same time — Hebrew and Greek — without a teacher and with the most meager of aids.

However, even if it cannot be proved that Luther was mentally abnormal, still it cannot be denied that the failure of the tested remedies of the monastic cure of souls must somehow be connected with the peculiar constitution of his psyche. As a matter of fact, his psyche was somewhat differently constituted from that of the average normal European of that day. In the first place, he did not possess the enviable gift of deceiving himself. He could not persuade himself that confession liberated him as with a magic stroke from his faults and evil tendencies. No matter how hard it was for him, he had to bow to the truth and acknowledge that, no matter how much he might desire it, *he* was unable to experience the magical effect attributed to the sacrament. And as time went on he was no more successful in deceiving himself concerning the fact that he was absolutely incapable of performing what the Occamists and the Rules and Constitution of his Order represented as possible and obligatory. To his sorrow he had to declare that, no matter what might be true for others, *he* was not able to coax these desired emotions from his soul; in fact, that he was even incapable of wholly and completely willing what he had earnestly made up his mind to will. It is significant that he could not bring himself, as the ordinary person would, to reduce the requirements which he had placed upon himself. He simply was not satisfied with the minimum standard of external respectability and sanctity which even the average person may attain with a little application.

In the final analysis, the real cause of Luther's inner distress was, first, the conviction — the consequences of which he realized fully and which he held so firmly during all these years — that God requires absolute purity and total surrender; and, second, the inexorable rigor and honesty with which he always judged his own heart. The prevailing belief in works and merits, the Occamist doctrine of will and grace, and the scholastic doctrine of penance were not the cause, as Luther himself later says, but only the external occasion of the inner struggles which he had to endure. If he had not interpreted the words, "Thou shalt!" so strictly and definitely, and if he had not applied this interpretation to himself so scrupulously and literally, all these doctrines and dogmas would not have given him any more trouble than they gave all the honest, average persons who took the cowl when he did in order to make satisfaction for their sins, but who never experienced any of the severe trials which he endured. But in that case he would in all probability have become nothing more than an ordinary, average monk and professor, and every trace on earth of his life would long since have disappeared. But it was just this insight and this unrelenting conscientiousness in judging himself which were now causing him so much distress. Here was the living force that drove him onward and forced him further and further away from the beaten track of the old faith, for this compelled him ever and again to ask the question — in the opinion of all pious Catholics a highly impious question — "How can *I*, as an *individual*, be assured of the forgiveness of sins and thus of the favor of God?"

This analysis recognizes that the restraint which made it so difficult for Luther to escape from the maze in which he was entangled was just as important as the constraining power which drove him onward. This restraint was the pronounced conservative tendency of his mind which would not permit him to declare a dogma, or even a mere scholastic opinion, false simply because it contradicted his own experience. So in this very critical period he clung with the greatest tenacity even to the doctrines which caused him the greatest torment; indeed, he probably would have adhered to them firmly for the rest of his life, in spite of all doubts and scruples, if their validity had not been shaken for him, contrary to his expectation, by *the* authority, the voice which was for him the voice of God Himself — the Holy Scriptures.

It hardly needs to be said that in this inner struggle, as in every long struggle, periods of peace were not lacking. To use Staupitz' phrase, when Luther had something to do, — lecturing or debating, or learning Hebrew, or when, as during the journey to Rome, he was under the necessity of accomplishing some task which had been committed to him — then, of course, he had no time to be constantly giving heed to the complaining and accusing voices in his breast. As he himself says, during these eight years he also had occasional moments when he felt truly comforted and happy, as when he listened to the beautiful ancient and medieval hymns in the monastery church, or when he succeeded in "reading a mass well." Indeed, there were times when he felt that at last the time of his "spiritual temptation" was over, and he drank in with pleasure "the sweet praise and fine words" which his friends and superiors lavished upon his saintly conduct. But these were only "bright moments." A single word — for instance, the word in the Thirty-first Psalm: "Deliver me in thy *righteousness*"—was enough to cast him down again into the hell of a tormented conscience, so that for a long time he "was again completely prostrated."

But, like many young men, Luther, too, would gradually have become apathetic and weary of the fruitless striving for an ideal that was probably unattainable, if he had not been suddenly seized with tremendous power (apparently not until after the journey to Rome) by a new problem — the question whether he belonged to the elect or to the eternally damned. We may very well conclude from this that he was no longer satisfied, as he had been in 1509-10, with the easy way out offered by the Occamists who declared that God has, on the basis of His foreknowledge of the conduct of men, predestined some to salvation and others to hell. We may also conclude that he had meanwhile exchanged this view for Augustine's doctrine of predestination, probably under the overpowering influence of the reading of the great work, *The City of God.* Augustine's doctrine must have seemed very illuminating to him at that time, for it harmonizes much better with the Occamistic view of God than the extremely inconsistent construction of Master Gabriel Biel which made now the divine and then the human element the deciding factor in salvation.

But this doctrine unquestionably introduced a new kind of anxiety into his inner life and intensified his misery to the deepest despair. If there was anything that was certain for him from childhood, it was the belief that God is just, that He holds inviolate the laws and regulations which He has created of His own free will, and that "He guarantees His grace unfailingly to everyone who does what he can." Now the God who for him had been a supernatural personality bound by clearly discernible laws had suddenly become a Being of Force completely incomprehensible even in His activity. But this idea became a source of the most dreadful inner torture only when he realized that he was at the mercy of this Being of Force, who could be moved to grace or disfavor neither by human desire nor human acts, so that he himself had absolutely no power to change the fate to which he was destined from all eternity; indeed, that he was not even able to determine whether he belonged to the elect or to the reprobate. This feeling of being hopelessly bound, which always accompanies this conception, also awakened

in him strong defensive reactions. Wild hatred welled up
within him. Words of blasphemy crowded to nis lips; indeed,
there surged up in him the mad desire, if possible, to kill this
dreadful God.

Yet he was under no delusions. He knew that he had no
claim on grace, that God had a right to be angry with him,
that He *must* be angry with him, for even in this period he
never lost his belief in the holiness of God. The paroxysm
of hate resolved itself again into the paroxysm of despair, so
often described by him out of the depths of his own experience. It seemed to him that he was having a foretaste of
all the tortures of hell. "No tongue can tell, no pen can
write," he says in the most famous of these descriptions,
"what a man suffers in such moments. . . . If this suffering
were to last for only a half-hour, yea, only the tenth part of
an hour, he would be utterly destroyed and his bones would
turn to ashes. At such a time God in His wrath appears
dreadful beyond all imagination. And like God, so the whole
creation. No flight is possible. There is nothing that can
comfort. Everything accuses."

So he came to Wittenberg in the summer of 1511 in a
state of profound spiritual agitation. He was also in such
poor physical condition that he believed that he could no
longer undertake anything at all. But the change was good
for him, for it brought him to Staupitz.

John von Staupitz, as a disciple of the Cologne and
Leipzig *Antiqui*, had views on the questions that were tormenting Luther fundamentally different from those of the
philosophers and theologians with whom Luther had been
exclusively associated up to this time. He denied most vehemently that man can either know, will, or do good by his
own reason or strength. On the contrary, Staupitz believed
that such ability is granted to man only if he belongs to the
elect and receives the heavenly medicine of grace which is
poured in through the sacraments. There were, to be sure,
no infallible signs of election, but there are "infallible signs

which are appointed to make hope certain and to drive out
despair." These signs are the seven sacraments. That is to
say, one could overcome anxiety in regard to predestination
through the diligent use of the sacraments. That such
anxieties can be only temporarily suppressed in this way
but can never really be removed, Staupitz does not appear
to have realized even in 1517, though in the meantime he
had learned in his pastoral intercourse with Luther how
severely "this worst of all temptations" could torture a
devout man. It is evident that he was not the kind of person
who feels such problems as a thorn in the flesh, but that he
was simply content with the solutions offered by vulgar
Thomism.

But Staupitz, the Thomist, is not the whole Staupitz. Even
in his otherwise wholly Thomistic book, *On Predestination*
(1517), he declares in one place that the principal problem
of religion is not how man is enabled to do good works
which will make him worthy of the reward of eternal
blessedness, but rather how he can attain to the saving love
of God. In the little book, *On the Love of God*, which
appeared at the end of 1517, he further maintains that one
can no more learn this love from others than one can learn
from others to see, taste, hear, feel, or smell. Nor can one
acquire it by the processes of reason, or by reading the
Bible. "On the contrary, it is born only out of the revelation
of God's love toward us." Where is this revelation to be
found? In the life, sufferings, and death of Christ. But it
becomes a revelation to the individual only if he belongs to
the elect. Enabled by the Holy Spirit, the elect know Christ
inwardly, not only outwardly. Thus this revelation is never
a product of human effort and work, but always a "pure,
unalloyed grace." This is so not only for the beginner who
still loves other things besides God, but also for the one who
has advanced and learned to use all things to the praise and
love of God, and equally so for him who has attained perfection, who has wholly renounced all personal choice and

activity and waits in utter obedience and perfect resignation
to hear only what God would speak and do through him.
He who possesses this love can do no evil; for him even the
heaviest burden is light and all pain is sweet, for to love is
in itself always sweet. But the surest sign that such love
dwells in us is that we are independent of all creatures and,
without even thinking of our life or study or even of our
own soul's salvation, we seek nothing but the glory of God.

These statements show that Staupitz, like so many
Thomists, was a disciple of the so-called *devotio moderna*,
or the later mysticism of the Netherlands. Like Thomas
à Kempis, the best-known representative of this religious
tendency, he is no longer seriously concerned about the
ultimate goal of genuine mysticism, the union of the part of
God enclosed in the soul with the undivided God-substance.
On the contrary, he designates as the highest experience
and foretaste of blessedness the nuptial union of the soul
with Christ, in which there is only a blending of the will and
the feelings, but not a temporary suspension of the essential
distinction between God and man. However, there is no
contradiction between these mystical ideas and the vulgar-
Thomistic ideas which Staupitz otherwise advocated. They
rather complement each other and consequently do not exist
in his mind as unconnected ideas, as is shown by the assertion that only the elect can share in the "pure, unalloyed
grace" of saving love toward God.

Staupitz was, therefore, at once a Thomist and a mystic,
as Loyola and his first disciples were later. That indicates
that this combination is by no means un-Catholic. As a
matter of fact, it was just this combination which effected a
revival of Catholic piety in the sixteenth century and which
ultimately made it possible for the Catholic Church to maintain itself against Lutheranism. It is, therefore, not surprising that there is absolutely nothing un-Catholic in those
writings of Staupitz which are undoubtedly genuine (the
book, *On Faith*, which appeared posthumously does not

belong to this class). He relies not only upon the merit of Christ but upon the merits of Mary and the saints as well. Like Thomas Aquinas, and with his limitations, he adheres to the idea that salvation can be earned; and even in 1517 he denounces as a *satanic temptation* the opinion that man can be saved only by divine mercy and not by his own works. Thus, as far as the basic tendency of his piety is concerned, and despite the fact that later he once called himself a "forerunner of evangelicalism," he actually stood closer to Loyola than to Luther. Nevertheless, he was able to help Luther more than all the other medieval saints. Consequently, it is at this point in Luther's development, if anywhere, that it ought to be evident how much help he could still receive from Catholic piety, and how far he had already outgrown this piety, even in its noblest form.

Staupitz, like most Saxons, could not help "being kind and gracious" to everyone. It was therefore not hard to approach him. To be sure, whenever his kindness threatened to involve him in serious conflict, he immediately withdrew, for it was not his nature to pledge himself wholeheartedly to a person or cause. It was not his nature; as Luther says, he was "too cool and too dispassionate" to do that. It was therefore more an evidence of weakness than strength when for the sake of peace he relinquished his own long-cherished pet plans for the unification of the Saxon Congregation with the Saxon Province of the Order. He could never make up his mind to oppose open violations of the law and merely comforted himself by uttering the pious words, "God grant us patience!" or the proverb which he considered the quintessence of all the wisdom of life, "Things cannot be right in this world anyhow"; or even brushed aside everything disagreeable with a more or less coarse jest, for he had a pronounced humorous vein. But many people feel that it is convenient to have such people about who can reconcile themselves so easily, not only to the imperfection, but also to the injustice, of the world.

It is, therefore, not surprising that throughout his life
Staupitz enjoyed unusual popularity in all circles of society,
but especially in circles of authority and culture. He was, as
it appears, so close to Frederick the Wise from childhood—
his native town, Motterwitz, lies only a few hours from
Grimma where Frederick was reared—that he could without
reserve call him his dearest friend. He was always welcome
in the courts of Berlin and Munich and the petty courts of
the counts of central Germany, and he so captivated even
the suspicious patricians of Nuremberg, when they learned
to know him personally, that they even thought his preaching
was very fine, though Luther considered it very "irksome."
The fact that as a born nobleman he was well acquainted
with court society, and that as a true North German he always
remained friendly and courteous when another might have
become excited and angry, as was apt to happen with Luther,
certainly enhanced the pleasing impression of his personality.
But the feeling that he was not motivated by selfish ambitions, that after his own fashion he meant well toward everyone, contributed even more to that impression. It was for
this reason that he was frequently called in as an arbitrator
of purely secular affairs. But in such cases he achieved success only when the differences were not particularly deep.
Whenever the opinions and views of the disputants were in
sharp opposition as, for example, in the affair of the Erfurters
with Electoral Saxony, he failed because he was unable to
throw the weight of a superior will into the balance; and as
a true mystic, he really had no profound interest in the
dispute as such, and therefore did not possess the ambition
to effect a definite decision.

How, then, did Luther come into closer relations with this
man? He says himself that he often confessed to Staupitz—
not tales concerning women, however, for sensual desires
gave him very little trouble while he was in the monastery.
When women did come to confess to him Luther did not
even look up. In Erfurt, however, none came to him, and

in Wittenberg only three. What he confessed to Staupitz
were, rather, the "real, knotty difficulties," above all, the
doubt as to whether he was one of the elect. At first Staupitz,
like the other father confessors, dismissed him with the poor
comfort, "I do not understand you." "Then," said Luther,
"I thought that I was the only one who had ever experienced
these 'spiritual temptations' and I felt like a dead man.
Finally, one day as I sat at a table, sad and downcast, Staupitz asked me, 'Why are you so sad?' I replied, 'Oh, where
can I go?' Then he said, 'Oh, you do not know why it is
necessary [for you to be thus tempted]. Otherwise, nothing
good would come of you.' He thought, of course, that I was
a scholar, and that if I were not tempted I would become
proud." Thus Staupitz never understood Luther's affliction
because he himself had never experienced anything like it,
as he openly admitted, and so he underestimated the peril
in which the young man found himself.

It was not until Luther had confessed to him another time
that Staupitz began to suspect how deeply the poor brother
was suffering inwardly. "If anyone wishes to dispute about
predestination," he now said to Luther, "then begin to speak
of the wounds of Christ. Impress deeply upon yourself the
image of Christ, who was predestined by God to suffer for
sinners, and thus predestination will be solved." Did he
actually mean that predestination, the problem that was
tormenting Luther, would thus be completely solved? Certainly not, for if that were the case he would hardly have
neglected to repeat this advice in his book on this subject.
What, then, did he mean? The answer simply grows out of
the situation. He wished in this way to put an end to Brother
Martin's preoccupation with the problem which was disturb-
ing him so much. And he was completely successful in this
purpose. As the Reformer himself said later, sometimes even
a chance word, casually dropped in the hour of temptation,
which suddenly diverts the attention in another direction,
can bring immediate release. Staupitz' words had just this

effect upon him. The dreadful visions of the terrors of hell
which had so long tormented him were suddenly displaced
by the comforting image of the wounded Christ, and with
that disappeared, at least for a while, the horrible anxiety
under which he had just been suffering. Thus it is not a
mere imaginary statement when Luther later praises Staupitz
as the one who had saved him from hell. In actual fact,
Staupitz had by these words helped him to overcome the
severest temptation he had endured up to this time.

Luther also learned many another "comforting and salutary word" from Staupitz. For example, the saying, "True
repentance *begins* with the love of God." "These words,"
he writes in 1518, "struck me like a thunderbolt from heaven
and lodged in my soul like the arrow of a mighty man."
Why? Because they flatly contradicted the assertion of
Gabriel Biel that repentance normally begins with the love
of self and then, if the penitent understands the art of con-
trolling his feelings in the manner prescribed by Bernard of
Clairvaux, ends with the love of God. And his words, "I,
too, once confessed daily, and daily resolved to be devout
and remain devout. But every day I failed utterly. Then I
decided that I could deceive God no longer; I could not
have done it anyhow. I shall await an opportune hour that
God may come to me with His grace. Otherwise everything
is lost . . . . It is a great mountain, says the Law. I will
surmount it, say the flesh, hypocrisy, and self-confidence.
You cannot, says the knowledge of sin. Then I will leave it,
says despair." This confession likewise moved Luther very
deeply, for it, too, contradicted everything that he had
learned from the Erfurt Modernists. But it was just for this
reason that it impressed itself indelibly upon his memory.
However, the deepest impression was made upon him by
the admonition, "One must contemplate that man who is
called Christ," that is, believe that Christ has died upon the
Cross for the sins of men, for, like all Occamists, he had
heretofore been of the opinion that the death of Christ was

not sufficient to atone for the sins of men, but that it helped only those who were able to complete the merit of Christ with their own merit.

What made these words of Staupitz so memorable to Brother Martin was not, in the last analysis, their contradiction to the doctrines which, even though he had been reared in them, had caused Luther such great inner difficulties in these last years. It appears that Staupitz would never enter into a regular discussion of these doctrines with him, but was rather content to put him off with a curt suggestion of a difference of opinion. So at first he succeeded only in confusing Luther and driving him to "begin to compare his words with the words of Holy Scripture." But the fact that Luther did this proves at any rate that he had now finally awakened out of the dogmatic slumber in which "the disputatious theology" had held him so long, and that he now felt the necessity of formulating his own opinion with regard to the questions which were tormenting him upon the basis of Holy Scriptures without regard to theological tradition. In other words, he began to go his own way as a theologian.

But Luther was always conscious of having received from Staupitz definite suggestions of a positive kind. In the spring of 1531 he once declared at table, "I have received everything from Staupitz." Shortly before this he said, "Staupitz originated the evangelical doctrine," because it was he who taught that "one must contemplate the man who is called Christ." Can we accept this opinion? That Staupitz first made him familiar with the old message of Christ the Lamb of God that bears the sin of the world, and made him familiar with it in such a manner that it made an overwhelming impression upon his broken spirit, is a certainty. But it is also certain that Luther was still not in a position at this time to grasp this message in its entirety and adhere to it permanently. But why was he still incapable of holding it fast? Because no matter how much he tried, he could not bring it into accord with the view that God could pardon him only when he had "done what lay in his power"—the view which had been his since his youth and which had actually become an axiom for him in the school of the Erfurt Modernists.

Could Staupitz help him over this difficulty? No! For, even though, as a Thomist, he ascribed considerably greater importance to grace than did the Modernists, Staupitz still held fast to the idea that man could not be saved by divine mercy alone, but that the merit of Christ must somehow be completed by the merit of the individual. Like so many other words of the Bible, the Reformer could fully understand the word of the cross and make it inwardly his own only when he had come to realize, on the basis of Romans 1:17, that the view of God's nature and work which had been indigenous to the Catholic Church for more than a thousand years, was not in accord with the Gospel. But, if this is correct, how then is it to be explained that the word of the cross became for him the "first and chief article of faith," rather than the "word of enlightenment" (Romans 1:17), without which he -could not have understood the word of the cross? We can only reply: Because it was the fact to which the word of the cross points that gave him the initial certainty that he had rightly understood Romans 1:17, namely, that in His innermost being God really is, as the Apostle here assumes, "pure grace and mercy"; for without this fact, which is wholly independent of human delusions and desires, he would never have been able to hold to this understanding, so new was it to him and so completely contrary to all reason and common experience.

Nevertheless, it appears that from the very beginning Luther's thought concerning the cross was somewhat different from that of Staupitz. Luther did not see in the death of Christ a revelation of the love of God, as Staupitz did, but rather a manifestation of the "unalterable sternness of God with sin and sinners." God's gracious will Luther first found definitely expressed in the resurrection of Christ. Henceforth he would acknowledge only Christ as Redeemer and Saviour and would have nothing more to do with the merits of Mary and the saints. But even though he later held a somewhat different view of the cross than Staupitz, he never forgot that Staupitz had first emphatically pointed him to the Crucified, for he was grateful by temperament. He always remembered with pleasure the men "through whom God had helped him," and he was inclined rather to overestimate the help he had received from them than to underestimate it. And so he also occasionally overestimated the part that Staupitz had had in his "redemption from the hell" of despair. He had even given Staupitz himself the idea that he was "the forerunner of the Gospel." In truth, however, Staupitz was still very far from the Gospel. This is proved by the letter, the exact text of which has unfortunately not been preserved, which he addressed to the young brother after his departure from Wittenberg in October, 1511. He wrote somewhat as follows: "You desire to be without sin and yet you have no real sins. Christ is the forgiveness of real sins, such as parricide, public blasphemy, contempt of God, adultery, and so forth. These are the real sins. If Christ is to help you, you must have a register in which the real sins are recorded. You should not concern yourself with slips and imaginary sins and make a sin out of every breaking of wind."

Was Luther likely to commit such gross offenses as are here enumerated? No! Why, then, does Staupitz advise him henceforth to register only such "real sins"? Because he thought that in this way he would be able to drive out of Luther's head the idea that he was an especially grievous sinner. So little did he know the young brother, even after months of the most intimate fellowship, that he thought it possible to cure him of his obviously incomprehensible fear of sin with such altogether superficial and artificial expedients. He hardly observed that the real cause of Luther's inner distress was not so much fear of hell as the yearning for certainty of forgiveness. But even if he had divined it,

Staupitz probably would have counseled him, after the manner of St. Thomas, by saying that such a certainty is to be attained only through special divine revelations (such as dreams, visions, and heavenly voices), and that it is therefore granted to only a few especially favored saints. To demand such extra revelations, however, would be very impious. The truly humble man will rather reconcile himself, without murmuring, to the fact that it is God's will that he should never escape being tossed between fear and hope, and will be thankful if, after scrupulous searching of his conscience, he is able to conclude from his conduct that he *probably* stands within the grace of God.

Neither at this time nor later did Staupitz realize that Luther could not be satisfied with this kind of probability, or even with a certainty that was based on visions or similar "very dubious and delusive" ecstatic experiences such as the saints of the past were supposed to have had and which Loyola in Manresa believed he had, ten years later. He manifestly did not realize that Luther could be satisfied with nothing less than a revelation, entirely independent of his own personal sensation and experience and open to and attainable by every man, which proved to him that God is ready to forgive every sinner, not only now and then, whenever He happens to choose, but always and, as it were, on principle. Thus on this decisive point the Reformer had already outgrown medieval piety in its noblest and most promising form. But what it could give him, Staupitz gave him. It awakened him out of the dogmatic slumber into which the modern theology had put him, and it directed him to the crucified Christ. So when in his last letter to Luther on April 1, 1524, Staupitz speaks of himself as a "precursor of the Evangelical doctrine," he does so with a certain right, and he is equally right when, in the same letter, he says to Luther: "You have led us from the husks of swine back to the pastures of life." For it is beyond doubt that in later days Luther also exerted an influence upon Staupitz.

But like so many of the devout of mystical inclination, he had allowed himself to be carried away further by it than was really compatible with his religious principles and his nature, and therefore at the end of his life he renounced his once beloved and respected friend and broke away from his Order.

Unfortunately we no longer possess any of the numerous letters which, according to his own statement, Luther addressed to Staupitz during his years in the monastery. We know only that one of these letters, which must have been written between November, 1511, and April, 1513, contained the mournful words: "Oh, my sins, sins, sins!" Thus his anxiety over his sins gave him as much trouble after the critical meeting with Staupitz as before. The inner struggle in his soul continued with scarcely diminished vehemence. It was not until April or May, 1513, that an almost sudden change took place.

It was at this time that Luther was busy composing so-called *argumenta*, or brief content summaries, for the text edition of the Latin Psalter. He intended to use these as a basis for his lectures after the summer vacation (July 12 to August 15). Since he had long known the Psalms by heart and had at hand the latest commentary on the Psalms, the *Psalterium Quincuplex* of the French humanist, James Lefèvre d'Étaples, he probably proceeded with this task with little difficulty to Psalm 30, according to the numbering of the Vulgate. But after he had summarized the contents of this Psalm, freely following Lefèvre, and had written his notes in the margin, he suddenly had to lay his pen aside. He was profoundly disturbed. His eyes had fallen upon a long familiar passage which again struck his lacerated soul like a blow of the fist. *In justitia tua libera me* (In *thy righteousness* deliver me). In connection with this turn of expression, which appears so frequently in the Psalms and the Pauline Epistles, Luther was accustomed to think of the judicial righteousness of God which, in the feeling of his own unworthiness, he feared so greatly. It was for this reason that he actually hated the word "righteousness." He fairly fled from it. In fact, up to this time he could never bring himself to study Paul's Epistle to the Romans carefully because the idea of the righteousness of God plays such a large role in it. Nevertheless, he had a vague feeling that perhaps this idea could have a different sense in the language of the Bible than it had in the language of the philosophers, and he felt a strange urge finally to make up his mind about it.

He therefore turned to the famous passage in Romans 1:16-17, in which the Gospel is characterized as the saving power of God for all who believe, because in it the righteousness of God is revealed from faith to faith. But at first the study of this passage only made his heart grow heavier and the darkness deeper. "Thus the Gospel, too," he said to himself, "is only a revelation of the punitive righteousness of God, only a means of further torturing and tormenting men who are already fearfully burdened with original sin and the Ten Commandments." And just as so often before, as he pondered this, there now rose up in him again a feeling of passionate hatred for this cruel God who always requires love, love, and yet actually makes it impossible for His creatures to love Him. "So he raged" in his little room in the tower of the Black Cloister "with a wounded and confused spirit, and beat importunately on that passage in St. Paul, thirsting with a most ardent desire to know what the Apostle really meant, until finally, after days and nights of thinking, he hit upon the idea of examining the context more carefully." The righteousness of God is revealed in the Gospel. "The just shall live by faith." Therefore, he concluded, what is meant here is not the punitive righteousness of God, but rather the forgiving righteousness of God by which in His mercy He makes us just, as it is written, *justus ex fide vivit*. "Then it seemed to me as if I were born anew and that I had entered into the open gates of Paradise. The whole Bible suddenly took on a new aspect for me. I ran through it, as much as I had it in my memory, and gathered together a great number of similar expressions, as 'work of God,' that is, that which God works in us; 'power of God,' that is, the power through which He makes us powerful; 'wisdom of God,' that is, the wisdom through which He makes us wise .... As much as I had heretofore hated the word 'righteousness of God,' so much the more dear and sweet it was to me now. And so that passage of St. Paul became for me in very truth the gate to Paradise."

If we ask what that decisive hour produced, Luther himself gives us the answer: a new insight and a new sense of life. The new insight is reflected in the argument to Psalm 31, probably written on the same day: "Concerning the means of true repentance, that sins are remitted, not by any works, but alone by the mercy of God without any merit." But this sentence still does not clearly express what is, in the last analysis, treated of here; namely, not merely the conditions of the forgiveness of sin, but rather the nature of God and His gracious will toward us. However, he was always of the opinion that in this he had uttered nothing new, but had "only restored the Holy Gospel again." In reality, in this, the head and heart of his message, he is not an innovator but a renovator. Therefore, of all the names that his or later generations have invented to characterize his unique position in the history of the Christian religion and religion in general, none fits him so well as the name *Reformer*, which was coined especially for him.

In the first place, this term clearly expresses that he was not the founder of a new religion, nor even that he was one of those many well-meaning, alleged renovators of "true" Christianity who think that they can restore original Christianity by an external, mechanical imitation of primitive Christian ordinances for congregational life, or by a literal, verbal application of primitive Christian doctrines. He was rather the rediscoverer and reviver of what was essential and specifically Christian in primitive Christianity. This is evangelical faith in God, or, to put it in another way, the Gospel of the grace of God in Christ.

In the second place, this name is also very fortunate in that it fixes and symbolizes in the simplest manner the significant distinction which exists between Luther's religious self-consciousness and the self-consciousness of most other great personalities in the history of religion, Christian and non-Christian. If there is anything that is characteristic of the latter, it is the consciousness of being a bearer and instrument of a special revelation which is believed to have been received in visions, dreams, and other ecstatic experiences and confirmed by miracles and signs. Luther never had such ecstatic experiences. Nevertheless, he never doubted that the "insight" which had made him a reformer had been "given to him by the Holy Ghost," or "revealed" to him. The suddenness with which this "insight" emerged, after days of agonizing thought and search, and the profound emotion and the feeling of being liberated which accompanied it certainly contributed toward strengthening him in this conviction. But it is unquestionable that his conviction was confirmed by the impression that God had been especially near to him in that moment; and it was corroborated by the certainty that "his teaching was not his but rather the true, pure Word of God," and that he had received it not in visions and dreams, but in a completely normal state of mind. For in his opinion visions and dreams are always very dubious and delusive, dependent upon the temperament and disposition of the individual who has them, often caused by evil spirits, never equal in value to the Gospel even when they are genuine, and, for that matter, no longer necessary to Christianity now that it possesses the Gospel.

Furthermore, like most prophets and founders of religion, after 1520 Luther was accustomed to express the conviction "that God was pleased to work through him," or that he was an "unworthy instrument" of God, and that "since he had received the Gospel, not from men, but from heaven through our Lord Christ, he, too, could well boast and call himself a servant and Evangelist" (March 5, 1522). Indeed, "in order to spite the Devil and his enemies," he even allowed himself for a time to be called by the "pompous" title bestowed upon him by his admirers, "the prophet of the Germans, the apostle and evangelist in German lands." Nevertheless, he was always conscious that he was "not sent directly from heaven" and that he had not "received his call through a vision of God," and accordingly he never felt the need, as did George Fox a hundred years later, of verifying his mission through miracles and signs. His opinion of these petty miracles, which can in no wise be compared with the great everyday miracles of God, is fundamentally the same as that of visions and dreams. He is convinced that they also are highly delusive, often caused by evil spirits, not equal in value to the Gospel, and no longer necessary to Christianity. However, the passages in which he exhibits such an unusual degree of self-consciousness can be counted upon the fingers. As a rule he bases his work as a reformer simply upon the common duty of every Christian to stand up with all his might for divine truth and his own confused and weak conscience.

Moreover, Luther emphasizes repeatedly that he was drawn into this affair against his will "because of his office"— that is, through the conscientious performance of the duties of his preaching office, an office which had been pressed and forced upon him. The obvious objection that this office gave him authority only in his "assigned parish," that is, "in Wittenberg, but not to teach publicly in the whole world," did not occur to him at the beginning. It was not until, against the unordained Anabaptist preachers, it seemed necessary for him to give explicit enunciation to this principle, which had already been familiar to him since 1520, that it began to weigh upon his conscience. Then it became a matter of great satisfaction to him that he had been forced to become a doctor "against his will." For it was his opinion that as a doctor he had been "forced and driven to expound the Scriptures to the whole world and teach everybody" (1530). So now he laid the greatest weight upon his doctorate which, for a time (1522-23), he had looked upon only as a worthless papistical masquerade. Indeed, he declares, "I would not take all the world's goods for my doctorate, for if I did not have this great, heavy responsibility which rests upon me, I would surely be driven to despair and to doubt whether I had not begun this cause without call or command, like a sneak-preacher. But now God and all the world must bear witness that I began it publicly, in possession of my doctorate and my preaching office, and that I was led to it by God's grace and help" (1532).

Much as Luther's self-consciousness may at times resemble the self-consciousness of the ancient prophets, it was, nevertheless, of an entirely different kind and origin. Above all, it did not rest upon any kind of ecstatic experience, but rather upon an "insight" that came about entirely unattended by such abnormal spiritual phenomena. But he never drew the conclusion that this "insight" was true because of the effect which it had upon his spirit or the feelings which it aroused in him, but rather that it was true because it was in agreement with the clear Word of God. Furthermore, he did not feel inwardly exalted on account of the prominent position which he occupied among his contemporaries; on the contrary, he felt distressed and disquieted. It was for this reason that he had to reassure himself again and again that he had not undertaken such great things out of meddlesomeness and presumption, but because of the offices which had been thrust upon him, that he had been "driven and forced" to do it. He had to reassure himself that he was not doing anything strange and extraordinary, but that he was rather simply fulfilling a common Christian duty when he was fighting in word and deed for divine truth and helping his fellowmen to gain the true "insight" and the blessed liberty of the children of God. Just as he had not become certain of the grace of God without "spiritual temptations," so he had to struggle again and again for the certainty that he had done right in raising his voice against what was anti-Christian in the church of God. But he mastered *these* "spiritual temptations," which were strongly conditioned by his chronic ill health, especially his nervous insomnia (cf. p. 93), when he considered that his teaching was not his own but the teaching of the Scriptures and the pure Word of God. For then he always arrived at the clear and indubitable conviction that he never *could* and never *should* have acted otherwise. The certainty that he had the Scriptures on his side, that he was not standing upon what was merely his own—his own experiences, sensations, and visions—this was the root and unshakable foundation of his consciousness of being called to be a reformer. But in his development, this consciousness of being called was not, as with most other religious leaders of mankind, conditioned by a consciousness of being the bearer and chosen vessel of a charism—a higher, supernatural gift— and by a furious zeal, regardless of all considerations and cautions, to exemplify this charism, but rather by a consciousness of obligation to known truth. For him, an act never became a *must* until it had first become an *ought*, that is, until it had been recognized as a duty and, therefore, as a command of God.

But the above-mentioned facts have decisive significance not only for the understanding of his religious self-consciousness and his consciousness of being called to be a reformer, but also for the understanding of the historical consequences of his message. As is shown in a classical manner by the ecstatic experiences of Loyola, visions, auditions, and inspirations—no matter whether they are the result of conscious, hyperconscious, or dream states—almost never have a single meaning, and like all visionary complexes are not very easily retained in their original form. "Insights," however, always have a single meaning and are not easily altered. Thus they can later be recognized as false but are never again entirely forgotten. This in itself explains why they naturally have a more permanent effect upon the consciousness than such "parapsychological" states. Whereas the typical ecstatic can hardly ever think and act consistently, unless he happens, like Loyola, to be by nature a man of outstanding power of will and intellect who never allows his visions and illuminations to have any influence upon his actions, the man of "insight" always moves more or less in the direction toward which his "insight" points him, even when he is following an impulse of the moment. While the former usually betrays a strong inclination toward extravagant peculiarities in speech, gesture, and mode of life, the latter, as a rule, behaves quite like other people and is therefore in a position to influence much broader circles. This contrast may be illustrated with a drastic example simply by comparing Luther's development with that of Fox. Furthermore, while it is true that ecstatic experiences are transferable from person to person, they are hardly ever communicable without certain modifications in conceptual content. "Insights," on the contrary, may be detached completely from the person of the originator and transmitted to others in very much their original condition, without any difficult process of translation and interpretation. Naturally, this frequently results in the "insights" being handed down as a mere formula, appropriated merely by rote and not inwardly assimilated. On the other hand, it also means that they reach much wider circles, that they may be readily translated into action, indeed, that they can actually change the face of the whole world without their originator having moved a finger. Of course, "insights" have such a strong intensive and extensive effect only when they are looked upon as irrefutably true and absolutely binding, so that every man feels compelled in his conscience to submit himself to them. Luther's message had such power over souls because it had been drawn from the book which everyone at that time respected as God's Word; that is, as an absolutely binding authority. Thus, in the last analysis, the historical result of his message is also to be explained by the fact "that his teaching was not his own imagined dreams, but rather the Scriptures and the clear Word of God."

But in April and May, 1513, Luther himself had no conception of these far-reaching consequences of his new "insight." He perceived at first only the liberating and reviving effect it had upon him. The oppression which had weighed so long upon his soul had suddenly vanished. The brazen wall against which his thought had beaten in vain was finally broken down. Now the stream of his ideas could pour forth unhindered and flow onward in a constantly rising flood. But he was still permitted to mature for four full years, without suspecting what his real destiny would be. What he then proclaimed to the world was almost entirely the acquisition or, at least, the fruit of those four quiet years in which, still pursuing his own needs, he was able to deepen and extend his new "insight."

CHAPTER XI

YEARS OF SILENCE (1513-17)

In Wittenberg, as elsewhere, instructors in the so-called higher faculties were not particularly burdened with official duties. They were not obliged to announce more than one course, nor did they have to lecture more than two or three hours a week. And as far as we know, Luther offered only one course a year from 1512 to 1521, and it appears that he never lectured more than two hours a week. It was only in the years 1524 to 1531 (following the period from Easter, 1521, until the spring of 1524 when he did not lecture at all) that he lectured three hours. As professor of theology, moreover, he was not required to adhere to a prescribed rotation of courses or to observe the divisions of the academic year. Hence he was always free to select the topics of his lectures, and he could continue his discussion of the same subject year after year. In fact, he did this without hesitation. His first lectures on the Psalms extended over two years (August 16, 1513, to July 13, 1515) and his second three years (April, 1518, to March 21, 1521), but his last lectures on Genesis covered almost ten and one-half years (June 3, 1535, to November 17, 1545). Even at that, Luther did not consume nearly so much time as his colleagues in the late Middle Ages, for the latter often spent two or three years in the exposition of as little as a single chapter of the Bible. It is not surprising, therefore, that Luther gave only sixteen courses of lectures, and that in these sixteen he treated only thirteen books.[1]

But one must not forget that, as professor, Luther had not only lectures to deliver but also disputations to participate in,

[1] Genesis, 1512-13 (?), 1535-45. Psalms, 1513-15, 1518-21, 1532-35. Isaiah 1528-30. Minor Prophets, 1524-26. Song of Solomon, 1530-31. Ecclesiastes, July to November, 1526. Romans, 1515-16. Galatians, 1516-17, July 3 to December 12, 1531. I John, August 19 to November 27, 1527. I Timothy, January 13 to March 13, 1528. Titus and Philemon, November 1 to December 18, 1527. Hebrews, 1517-18.

and that he was not merely a professor but always filled several other offices in addition. Since the fall of 1511 he had been preacher in the monastery and, beginning not later than the end of 1514, he also occupied the pulpit of the parish church in Wittenberg. So he was already preaching at least twice a week at this time—all together 170 times a year. Besides, since May, 1512, he had been subprior and regent of the school connected with the Black Cloister. In this capacity he probably had to tutor the student-monks at least an hour a day, deliver a private lecture on occasion, and constantly superintend their studies and counsel them. Then in May, 1515, he was made district vicar—overseer of ten, and later eleven, monasteries of the Saxon Congregation in Meissen and Thuringia. At the same time he was still *lector mensae* and as such had to read the prescribed lections at the common meals in the refectory. All these duties gave him so much to do after 1515 that he "seldom had enough time to discharge the canonical hours and celebrate [mass]." And then when he began (1518) to write more extensively, it often happened that he did not get to read his breviary at all during the first days of the week. In order to make up for what he had missed in this way, he would lock himself in his room on Saturdays and often devote the whole day, without eating or drinking, to prayer. He traced his nervous insomnia, from which he suffered constantly after 1520, to this practice. The roots of the malady probably lay deeper. But there is no question that such a peculiar practice of prayer also contributed to it.

In what measure was he able to do justice to the varied duties of these four offices? We do not hear much about his activity as superior of his Order. The letters which he wrote as district vicar, especially those written during a visitation which lasted several weeks in the spring of 1516, nevertheless reveal that he allowed no departure from the Rule and Constitutions to go uncensored and that he did not shrink from applying vigorous measures for the restoration of discipline and order. Yet he never failed to exercise a strong pastoral influence on those committed to his care. There is no trace of "liberal opinion or laxity of practice" in his decisions. On the contrary, he was obviously stricter in the observance of the Rule than his immediate predecessors in the office.

We are far better informed about Luther's activity in the pulpit and in the professor's chair. We have somewhat more than a half-hundred sermons and fragments of sermons dating from this period. From them we gather that he still employed a thoroughly traditional method in the pulpit. Like all conscientious preachers of the day, he worked out every sermon in Latin beforehand. As far as we know, it was only in most exceptional instances that he extemporized, then or later. Even as an old man he would sometimes wake up at night, bathed in perspiration, because he dreamed that he had to preach without having prepared a sermon manuscript. Nor was he departing from tradition when he preached an occasional series of sermons on single parts of the catechism. So, for example, he preached a series on the Ten Commandments in the parish church from June 21, 1516, to February 24, 1517, and on the Lord's Prayer during the next six weeks.

But was Luther's preaching conventional in other respects, too? One of these sermons is still extant in his own handwriting. It is probably the oldest we have, for it must have been delivered a long time before Christmas, 1514. The text on which it is based is rather curious: "Moab is the cook-pot of my hope" (Psalm 60:8). But the exegesis is even more curious. The cook-pot is the world. The three legs of the pot are the three evil lusts mentioned in I John 2:16—lust of the flesh, lust of the eyes, and vainglory of life. The cook is Christ. The meat which is being cooked in the pot signifies men, particularly martyrs, who are in this manner being prepared as a savory dish for Christ and the angels. Christ is constantly stirring up the fire. Meanwhile

He allows the ungodly to prosper and permits them to torment the saints in every way. If the water does not come to a boil, He puts a lid on the pot; that is, He allows temptation to increase. Thus the saints not only get to boil, but also to steam; that is to say, they send up the incense of their prayer to God.

One cannot help asking, as one reads this oldest of Luther's sermons, Is this really Luther's? Is it not rather a sermon of Geiler von Kaisersberg, whom Luther may already have known at this time? If one examines it more closely, however, one will soon notice that there is a great difference between this and Geiler's work. The renowned Strassburg preacher aimed to amuse his hearers. Luther remained as grave as a tomb even when he drew comparisons which must strike the modern reader as comical. It is obvious that it did not occur to him that they could provoke laughter. He used such comparisons only because he interpreted the text—which was probably not chosen by himself, for he was accustomed to preach on prescribed texts all his life—allegorically as well as literally, as it was commonly done. He continued to do this frequently in his later *Church Postils*. But as far as this early sermon is concerned, which at first glance reminds one so strikingly of Geiler's method, it simply demonstrates that Luther was still treating a prescribed text strictly in accordance with the customary fashion. It certainly does not reveal any tendency in the direction of establishing a new type of preaching.

Considerable portions of his earliest lectures as well as of his sermons have come down to us. Of his first course of lectures on the Psalms (about August 16, 1513, to October 21, 1515) we have all except two leaves of his manuscript for the *glossae* and about two-thirds of his manuscript for the *scholia*, and in addition a part of his preliminary work in the marginal notes of his copy of the Lefèvre Commentary. The complete manuscript of his lectures on Romans (November 3, 1515, to September 7, 1516) is still extant, besides several fragments of students' lecture notes. On the other hand, we have only students' copies of the lectures on Galatians (October 27, 1516, to March 13, 1517) and on Hebrews (March, 1517, to April, 1518).[1]

When we compare these old manuscripts and copybooks with the lecture notes of other contemporary professors, we notice at once that Luther's lectures, like his sermons, follow an entirely conventional pattern. He always began with a brief explanation of the words, the so-called *glossae,* which the students were supposed to copy at once into a specially prepared copybook with ample space for writing between the lines of the text. Then he dictated *scholia* to them, sometimes long and sometimes short. These were biblical-theological or dogmatic comments on particular passages which seemed important to him. He also followed the customary procedure in the exegesis of the text. He based it not on the original text, but on the Vulgate. In fact, at first he gave the latter preference. He abandoned this practice as he proceeded with his lectures on the Psalms, but inasmuch as only the Vulgate was available to and understood by the students, he had to continue making this text his point of departure. But now it became a principle for him always to adduce the original text, provided he had access to it himself. Thus in the lectures on Romans he always took the original text into consideration after the Greek New Testament of Erasmus had come into his hands.

Like all his contemporaries, Luther proceeded, in his interpretation of details, on the principle that every verse of the Bible has not only a literal, but also an allegorical, a tropological or moralistic, and an anagogical meaning. The first, that is the literal or grammatico-historical sense, is actually not applied at all in his lectures on the Psalms, for to him the Psalms comprised a prophetical book and hence every Psalm referred directly to Christ. Considered purely as a work in exegesis, therefore, these lectures are not supe-

[1] Erich Vogelsang suggests April 21, 1517, to March 26, 1518, for Hebrews.

rior, but inferior, to the works of the great medieval exegetes, Nicholas of Lyra and Paul of Burgos. Of course Luther was very well acquainted with these works, but he was in constant conflict with them because they depended too much on their "Rabim," or Jewish interpreters. Nor did he learn as much as one would expect from the two humanists, Lefèvre and John Reuchlin, whose works he also used. There was at the same time a great unevenness in Luther's exposition. Here he writes a long essay on a single verse, and there he passes over the most difficult and interesting passages without batting an eyelash, as if he wore blinders. Hence the word "deficient" seems to be almost too mild a censure to apply to these lectures, for the general impression they make upon the modern reader, despite many excellent isolated remarks, is very unsatisfactory when compared with the *Glossae* of Lyra and Paul of Burgos or with the *Commentary* of Lefèvre, which certainly cannot be called masterpieces either.

Before one can make such a comparison, however, one must in justice inquire whether Luther's lecture notes may properly be compared with these works at all. It is clear that they cannot. For Luther's lecture notes do not comprise a regularly worked-out commentary intended for publication, but simply a collection of materials intended exclusively for the personal use of the author. The freedom with which he was accustomed, in his lectures during the first months, to deal with these materials—it appears that he often assembled them hurriedly at the last moment—is revealed by a comparison of his own manuscripts on the Epistle to the Romans with the extant fragments of students' notes on the same epistle. Luther's own notes are hardly recognizable in the latter, so much did he reduce them and recast them in both form and content (one sometimes wonders why) in his oral delivery. Where only Luther's own notes are extant, as in the case of his lectures on the Psalms, we can no longer determine what he may have said in the lecture hall. On the other hand, where we have only students' notes, as in the case of the lectures on Galatians and Hebrews, try as we may, we can no longer divine what his own notes may have contained.

In studying these materials, however, one should not overlook the fact that, as early as his first lecture on the Psalms, which probably took place August 16, 1513, at seven o'clock in the morning, Luther set up new principles for exegesis which are deserving of the most careful consideration. Of course he was able to express them much better later on. Perhaps he summarized them best on that famous scrap of paper (February 16, 1546) on which he set down the very last thing which he wrote: "No one can understand Virgil in his *Bucolics* and *Georgics* unless he has been a shepherd or farmer for five years. No one can understand Cicero in his *Letters* unless he has busied himself with the affairs of a large state for twenty years. Let no one think that he has studied Holy Scriptures sufficiently unless he has governed congregations with the prophets for a hundred years. . . . We are beggars, it is true!" What did Luther mean? To understand an author requires an inner relation to the matter which the author is treating. So a certain measure of religious experience is essential to an understanding of the Bible. Such experience always presupposes a certain "conformity of disposition" between the exegete and the sacred writers, "for a man judges as he is. Anyone whose attitude toward the mysteries of Holy Scriptures is like that of a horse or mule will never understand the Scriptures." The intelligence and education of the reader do not play a part in this kind of understanding. Hence the learned are often less fit for this than the unlearned, and shrewd, rational persons are generally inferior to plain, simple people who are not merely guided by their reason, but also have an eye for that "which no intellect of intelligent men sees." And it is just this which is the chief thing in the Bible.

Of course Luther did not mean by this that grammatical

and historical exegesis is superfluous, but simply that it is insufficient, and that true understanding only begins when the text is thoroughly explained from the linguistic and historical angle. As a matter of fact, when he prepared his lectures on the Psalms, Luther himself had scarcely succeeded in gaining this understanding. But he had at least recognized clearly, even then, how necessary it is. In the history of scientific exegesis, therefore, deficient as this course of lectures may appear from the standpoint of grammatico-historical exegesis, it nevertheless represents an advance. And this can certainly not be said of Lefèvre's *Commentary,* nor can it be said in the same measure of Lyra's *Glossae.*

In the succeeding course of lectures on the Epistle to the Romans, Luther furnished an example of this art of understanding for the first time. Here he had material which was particularly suited to him. Here he could draw on the depth of his personal experience—a thing which neither the scholars of the ancient or medieval church nor even the humanists had ever succeeded in doing. It was a matter of comprehending from within and of making intelligible what Paul felt, thought, and taught. In a sense, Luther enabled mankind to rediscover the great apostle who had been an object of fruitless research for so long a time. But even if we regard it simply as a scholarly performance, this course of lectures demonstrates how rapidly Luther was now developing. In the external arrangement of the lectures he still followed medieval usage. The explanation of words (*glossae*) was separated from the interpretation of the contents (*scholia*). He continued to use part of the exegetical apparatus of the Middle Ages, but he had freed himself almost wholly from medieval exegetical method. Now he interpreted the text only grammatico-historically and "pneumatically." From this time on he ceased to use allegory in the treatment of New Testament texts, except in the pulpit. Now that he was in a position to do so, as remarked before, he made it a principle always to go back to the original text, and with ever

increasing assurance he reached independent conclusions in
the discussion of linguistic and historical questions. For
example, he was already questioning the tradition of St.
Paul's journey to Spain, and he asserted that the passage to
which Lefèvre appealed in its defense is "apocryphal." Moreover, he called attention for the first time to the difficulties
which the long list of greetings in the sixteenth chapter of the
Epistle offers to exegetes.

In short, he had already learned to see with his own eyes.
He took an independent stand over against the opinions
of learned authorities of his own time—Erasmus, Lefèvre,
Reuchlin—as well as over against the ecclesiastical tradition,
and he did not hesitate to give public expression to his
divergent view whenever this seemed necessary to him. So,
for example, he declared (probably in a disputation in September, 1516), that the chief authority of the Middle Ages
on the doctrine of penance—the work on true and false
repentance ascribed to Augustine—was, on internal evidence,
not genuine. This was a great shock to his colleagues, especially to Dr. Carlstadt, for the book had found abundant use,
as a genuine work of Augustine, not only in the *Sentences*
of Peter Lombard but also in canon law.

At this time Luther was commissioned, probably by Elector Frederick at the suggestion of Spalatin, to revise for
publication his lectures on the Psalms. He complied very
unwillingly with this request. He worked over just a few
of the Psalms in the fall of 1516 and then abandoned the
task. But the few fragments of this revision which have come
down to us are very interesting because they show what
progress he had been making in the treatment of Old Testament as well as New Testament texts. In the case of Old
Testament passages, too, he now went back to the original,
on the basis of which he corrected the Latin translation. He
no longer regarded the Vulgate as a canonical authority, but
simply as an aid. Moreover, he was more successful in his
exegesis, although he still adhered to the prophetical inter-

pretation of the Psalter. More striking is the difference in
plan and presentation. The separation of *glossae* from *scholia*
had disappeared, the scholarly apparatus had been reduced
to the most essential matters, and the presentation of the
religious content had become the chief thing.

Unfortunately only students' notes of the lectures on Galatians (October 27, 1516, to March, 1517) and on Hebrews
(March 27, 1517, to April, 1518) have come down to us.
Those on Galatians were obviously written by a student who
was not particularly gifted, for they teem with errors of
hearing and writing and with the worst kind of trumpery.
Little can be done with such insufficient materials. They
do show, nevertheless, that Luther continued to grow in
wisdom and knowledge between the years 1516 and 1518.
He did not explicitly reject the fourfold sense of the Scriptures, but he held that St. Paul and the ancient teachers
recognized only a literal and a spiritual sense, and that the
anagogical sense was quite a recent invention. He himself,
therefore, expounded the text in the grammatico-historical
and spiritual senses. He knew, better now than he did in the
lectures on Romans, how to grasp the religious content of
the text and present it clearly and precisely. In fact, he was
already successfully attempting to sum up the religious
values in short formulas.

As early as the spring of 1515 Luther himself referred
with gratitude and joy to his "progress in reading and writing." But much as he was convinced of the significance of
"languages" for the exposition of the Bible, he was not thinking here of the progress which is at first most apparent to
the observer who studies these old, long-lost lecture manuscripts. He was thinking, rather, of his progress in the religious understanding of the Bible, "in the knowledge of God
and of Jesus Christ." If we pay attention only to the concepts
which he employed, we shall perhaps notice only a little of
this progress at first because he was constantly putting the

new wine into old bottles. He retained the old scholastic terms—original sin, infused grace, faith, good works, justification, and so on—but he gave them an entirely different content. For instance, when he defined original sin, he simply repeated the scholastic formula used since the thirteenth century. But what the scholastics considered an effect of original sin—evil desires or concupiscence—he designated as its nature; and what they looked upon as the characteristic expression of concupiscence—sensual lust—appeared to him simply as an accessory symptom. The real nature of concupiscence, and of sin generally, was for him the *proprius sensus*, selfishness. Selfishness dominates the whole instinctive and volitional life of natural man. It does not destroy freedom of choice, which is essential to the human will, but it destroys the capacity to will freely, cheerfully, and fully what is good, for to will the good means to will it freely, cheerfully, and fully. If a man acts under constraint, indifferently, or half-heartedly, he does not really do good at all even if outwardly his conduct appears to be without reproach. As one ponders this, one will speak, after Augustine, of a *servum* rather than of a *liberum arbitrium*, and if one wishes to determine the relation of man to the good, one will speak of a *noluntas* rather than of a *voluntas*. In the final analysis, selfishness is idolatry, for it always reduces itself to this, that man regards his self as an idol and hence does not trouble himself either about God or about his neighbor. Yet it is not only that he does not trouble himself about God; in his pride he also resists the merest suggestion of allowing God to help him and prefers at all costs to try to become good or righteous by his own reason or strength. Such conduct is unbelief. And so unbelief can be designated as the fundamental and chief sin.

In his lectures on Romans Luther still answered the question, How can man get rid of his sin? exactly as the scholastics did: Through "the grace which is infused" into him. But what did he mean by grace? It is not a supernatural medicine which is poured into man through the sacraments, but something altogether spiritual and personal, the "living, moving, and active Spirit of God" by which God engenders new life in the soul. Since this action of God upon the soul is an outpouring of His forgiving love and favor, grace can also be defined as the favor of God. But it is more than a favorable *attitude*. It is the will of God manifest in redeeming *acts*, and in these acts God is always personally present.

What, then, is the effect of grace upon man? Again Luther answered precisely as the scholastics did: Justification. But to him justification was not an instantaneous physical miracle by which sin is suddenly destroyed by the supernatural quality of the grace infused into man's soul, but it is a spiritual and psychological miracle which is accomplished in the soul of man without any material means whatsover, and it always produces three effects in man. First and foremost, it produces a new disposition. This is faith, or an unreserved trust in the forgiving favor of God. Second, as a natural consequence, a "connection" or personal communion is established between the soul and God. And finally, a start is made in the direction of moral renewal. This occupies the whole subsequent life of man, for selfishness is unconquerable. Certain "remnants of the flesh" still cling to even the most saintly of men. Such men, too, are constantly in need of forgiveness until their last breath is drawn. Accordingly when they consider the sorry results of their moral endeavor, even they would despair if it were not for the certainty that Christ has made satisfaction for them, too, and that God reckons Christ's righteousness to their account. So everything depends on this, that man attains to certainty or comes to faith. It follows that faith is in no sense a human achievement. It is a humble and obedient surrender to God, effected by Him through His Spirit, which enables the sinner in the first instance to trust the promise, "Thy sins are forgiven." At the same time this surrender awakens in man the certain confidence that all the other promises of God will afterward be realized too. Faith is consequently not only trust, but it is at the same time a continual hope and expectancy, connected always with a cheerful, childlike, confident assurance that God, who has put such trust and expectancy into man's heart, is "disposed to love and favor" him.

But how is this wonderful feeling produced in the soul of man? It comes into being, said Luther, through contact with the Word of God, the Gospel. For in, with, and under the Gospel, God works upon the soul through His Spirit. The soul, meanwhile, remains quite passive and receptive, like a woman in the act of conception. It begins to stir and to move only when it has become aware of the sweet sense of God's love which streams into it from the Gospel.

Thus the Word of God had already become more important for Luther than the sacraments. The preaching of the Word of God, rather than the administration of the sacraments, is the chief mission of the church, he asserted, for the Word is the means by which Christ founded the church and continues to preserve and govern it. In the preaching of the Word He Himself is always instrumental and is constantly creating new believers. Hence it follows that the church, in its most essential nature, is a spiritual or invisible communion and that by no means all who call themselves Christians belong to it. But, although not visible to the physical eye, it is always present. Moreover, it is always present as a fellowship, for its members are all united with one another —first, by subordination to the common Head, Christ; second, by the intercession which they make for one another; third, by the quiet influence which they exert upon one another; and fourth, by the love which they have for one another, even if they are not known by sight. By believers, mutually associated in this fashion, the church is propagated from generation to generation. One may consequently say (although Luther did not yet express this), that it depends upon the *successio fidelium* (the succession of believers) and not, as the Roman Church teaches, upon the *successio epis-coporum* (the succession of bishops).

Much as he was already emphasizing that the church is by nature spiritual and invisible, Luther nevertheless always emphasized, too, that the external, visible hierarchically constituted church, despite its grave crimes, possessed the Gospel. For this reason he looked upon it, if not exactly as the organization, at least as an organ or instrument, of the invisible church, and required everyone to give implicit obedience to the visible representatives of Christ—not, however, without impressing upon the latter that it was their primary task to proclaim the Gospel. Even at this early time Luther manifested no sympathy at all with the sectarians, who in their pride were making the vain attempt to found a holy community, or with the Enthusiasts, who were appealing to new and special revelations of God and believed that they could do without Christ, the Gospel, and other means of help and protection which God had offered to believers.

Luther was already being reproached at this time by the wise of this world (that is, probably by his colleagues at the university) with the charge that according to his teaching it is not necessary to do good works. He could properly dismiss this assertion as "foolish babbling," for he was already stressing again and again that faith is never idle, but is a living, busy thing. Faith is of itself constantly active, and it must be constantly active, for if we ask why God grants us justification (the forgiveness of sins), the answer is: To enable us to do good works. This suggests that man, just as a tree from which one expects good fruit, must *be* good before he can *do* good. The opposite opinion of Aristotle, that man can make himself good by the gradual process of consciously and methodically practicing the virtues, is obviously false because man is not good by nature. The will to be good must first be created in him by God through conversion. Only then, being mindful of the benefit received, is he able to do good freely and cheerfully—and this is the important thing. Only then is he free from the requirements of the Law, whether as a drive or as a guide, for the love of good is in itself sufficient to keep him on the right path. Of course, this impulse of love is not always present with uniform purity and strength. As long as he lives, the old Adam will continue to plague him and cause him to stumble. So he must ever be making a new start, and he must ever remain in motion. Like St. Arsenius of old, he will never get beyond the feeling that he is just beginning to live as a disciple of God. But this feeling does not have a paralyzing effect upon him. On the contrary, it strengthens him in the two principal and basic virtues of the Christian which embrace all the other virtues—humility and obedience to God. At the same time it guards him against the most wicked and incurable of all vices—self-righteousness or hypocrisy.

But what does it mean to do good? Luther answered this question very simply at first, and just as thousands had done before him: To love God with the whole heart and one's neighbor as oneself. But to Luther this old commandment now meant something quite different from what it had meant to the scholastics. The latter had maintained that only the negative prohibitions of God are always and absolutely binding; the positive commandments are binding only when a special reason for their observance is present in the given situation. Over against this view Luther declared, as early as 1513, and expressly with reference to the commandment of love toward God, that sins of omission of which we are not aware are also sins in the real sense of the word. From their distinction between prohibitions and commandments, the scholastics had drawn the further conclusion that the commandment of love toward God can and need be fully observed only in the life to come. In this life it is sufficient if one performs such an "act of love" once in a while and never desires anything which is directly in conflict with love toward God. Of course, the scholastics maintained, there is more merit in restricting one's preoccupation with mundane

things to the minimum and devoting oneself, as far as human
frailty permits, exclusively to the loving contemplation of
God. As far as love of one's neighbor is concerned, they
maintained that, inasmuch as Christ commanded that we
love our neighbor as ourselves, He expressly declared love
of self admissible; indeed, He took it for granted that man
always loves himself more than his neighbor. Consequently
the love of self stands first in the natural order of love; then
follow the members of one's immediate family, relatives,
friends, and so on; then remoter acquaintances and finally
unknown fellow-creatures and enemies. For even the concept of neighbor was subjected by the scholastics to casuis-
tical dismemberment which sharply modified the gravity of
the commandment. For example, in their opinion one need
help an unknown fellow-man only if he is in extreme distress
and if one is in the fortunate position of having more than
is needed to maintain oneself in one's accustomed station in
life. As for an enemy, however, one need entertain only a
disposition to do him good in case he should fall into need.
To pray for him, or even to suppress natural expressions of
ill will in one's relations with him—as, for example, not to
speak to him—goes beyond what one is obliged to do and is
only to be expected of super-Christians (that is, members of
religious orders) who strive for perfection.

This artificial construction placed on the words of Jesus
was cast into the discard as early as the spring of 1515 when
Luther asserted that the law of God is unchangeable. It is
always valid, and its validity is always absolute. It always
requires that we love God with our whole heart and do good
to every man, whether friend or foe, good or evil, worthy
or unworthy. That classification of love, devised by the
learned, in which the self leads the procession of the objects
of love, is altogether alien to the law of God. On the contrary, God's law condemns self-love and puts hatred of self
at the beginning of the procession. Moreover, it always
demands the correct attitude as well as the correct act. Thus

neither a mere outward conformity without the proper inner disposition, nor a mere good intention toward one's neighbor which fails to eventuate in deeds, especially if this good intention is coaxed artificially from the soul, is valid as a fulfillment of the evangelical requirement.

In this way Luther restored the evangelical requirement in all its absoluteness, although he was well aware that it exacts something heroic, whether actively or passively, from frail man. For this reason he was at a loss to know what to do with the old Catholic distinction between commandments which are binding and evangelical counsels which are not binding, and with the equally old distinction between mortal and venial sins. For Luther, good and evil were not merely quantitative distinctions but were absolute opposites. There are no such things as morally indifferent actions, he said. Man always does either good or evil. Neutrality is just as incapable of application in the field of morality as it is in the sphere of religion. Of course, Luther did not conclude from this absoluteness of the evangelical requirement that all persons must always do the same thing. Everyone should give practical proof of the obedience which he owes God in that estate and vocation to which he has been called. "I, for instance, fulfill the commandment when I teach and pray, the farmer when he listens and does his agricultural work faithfully. . . . Elector Frederick and his officials do not fulfill it, however, if they do not allow themselves to be found when they are needed, but say, 'I must pray and serve God,' and thus, in their failure to understand God's will, refuse to serve God [aright]." The character of the calling does not matter at all. God does not look upon the work, but upon the disposition in which it is performed. The humbler and more despised a task is, the more exalted in God's eyes is the man who undertakes and performs it in obedience to Him.

The idea of a calling, therefore, was already present in Luther's thought at this time. In fact, it was present in a form developed far beyond Tauler, Gerson, Antoninus of Florence, and the German Dominicans Nider, Herolt, and Markus of Weida. For, ready as these men were to admit that a layman can secure salvation in his worldly calling and that a God-fearing layman has a better prospect of heavenly reward than an unfaithful monk, all of them regarded the religious estate as the surest way to salvation and hence ascribed to it a marked superiority over all other callings. As for Luther, by 1516 he no longer ascribed such religious superiority to monasticism. It is true that he still gave a brisk affirmative reply to the question, Is it a good thing to become a monk at the present time? But why? His reason for the reply was that no estate was so despised as the monastic estate. There is no estate, he wrote, in which one must suffer so much shame and in which one must bear such a cross, imposed even by bishops and priests. And since there is nothing so valuable for the cultivation of Christian character as unmer-ited suffering, it was better to become a monk at that time than it had been at any time in the previous two hundred years. One should assume the cowl not in order to escape from the pressure of the wicked world, but on the con-trary in order to experience this pressure in the strongest conceivable form. Indeed a curious recommendation of monasticism!

Quite in keeping with this, Luther derived from the com-mandment to love one's neighbor the obligation of associating with men—all men—including the unbelieving, the irascible, and the unlearned. Whoever, like the Bohemian Brethren, evades this obligation under the pretext that he cannot be and remain good among wicked people will not become better but worse and "flees from salvation for the sake of salvation." The true Christian will never make so bold as to declare that a wicked man is absolutely incorrigible and eternally lost. He knows well that tomorrow God can save the man who today seems to be eternally lost. Nor will the true Christian ever forget that God wishes to win others

through him, exactly as He has won him through others. To
associate with others, therefore, always means to serve them,
and primarily to serve their souls. But for the Christian this
service to one's neighbor is not simply a duty growing out
of the commandment of neighborliness; it is also a necessity
which presses itself upon him instinctively. He feels a natural
impulse to repay God for the benefit received. But he can
express this impulse only by turning to his neighbor, for
there is only one way in which he can show his gratitude
directly to God himself, and that is by thanking Him for
the benefit. Hence love of one's neighbor ultimately springs
from love of God or, more correctly, from the sense of happiness which takes possession of the soul when it becomes
aware of the love and favor of God. In Luther, therefore,
ethical requirement was already intimately bound up with
the new religious understanding of the Gospel. Besides, the
summarization of his new ideas in terms of "Christian liberty," which was later to become so popular, was already
emerging. The Christian is a free lord of all things on
account of his faith and a servant of all his fellow-creatures
on account of his love. But this servitude is the highest
liberty, for it has need of no one, it receives nothing, it
always gives, and gives always in freedom. This is so because
the Christian has made himself servant of all, not under
compulsion but voluntarily.

Almost all the themes of Luther's later teaching had therefore been touched upon in his early lecture notes on the
Psalms and on the Epistle to the Romans. The new religious
and ethical principles which he was destined to herald were
already complete in their major outlines when he wrote the
last words of his lectures on Romans. To be sure, they still
needed to be supplemented on many important points. On
marriage and celibacy, for instance, he still subscribed wholly
to the traditional notions. Nor was he entirely in the clear
concerning the value of civil government. He held that it

was by all means necessary and lawful for the secular authority to punish thieves and murderers severely. And yet a
Christian would be acting in ungodly fashion, said he, if he
would claim the protection of the law in his own interests.
He dare not resist evil in any way. He must allow himself
to be trodden under foot, and even killed, without murmuring and without considering the serious consequences to the
stability of the legal system which might result therefrom.
Of course, a Christian may not engage in war. When a pope,
like Julius II, takes the liberty, he simply commits a sin, even
if he does so only to recover stolen church property. Even
a secular prince can wage war only as a prince, not as a
Christian. Nevertheless, the slogan, "Resist not evil," did not
have unlimited validity in Luther's eyes at this time. The
Christian, too, must as a matter of course fight for the truth
at all times—with words and not with the fist—and he dare
not, like a dumb dog, tolerate injustice and manifold abuses
in the spiritual and secular government. As on this point, so
on others, his new principles were still incomplete, unclear,
or at least inadequately formulated. Contradictions, therefore, are not seldom found in these old pages, especially in
the notes on the Psalms. It is only in the course of his lectures on the Epistle to the Romans that he gradually overcame the Occamistic notion, for example, that man can and
must prepare himself somehow for the reception of grace.
Here one can see what effort it sometimes cost him to shake
off the views on which he had been brought up. But he did
not shrink back from this effort. He thought through his
new ideas again and again, and he constantly tried to formulate them in a new way until he had finally found a mode of
expression which satisfied him.

The lecture notes on the Psalms and on Romans reveal
this with particular clarity because his flying pen committed
to paper everything "that happened to come into his mind"—
even flashes of thought which had no direct bearing on the
text which he was treating at the time, and remarks which

he could hardly have used in the lecture room. So they are as revealing as a diary. Not only do they allow us to listen in on the young professor while he is at his work, but they also permit us to catch a glimpse of his inner life from time to time. It is as if we can sometimes actually feel the powerful breath of his spirit. Consequently these notes enable us to determine very precisely the progress which he was making in his reading and writing. He was himself right when he spoke only of advances, and not of wholly new discoveries, for closer scrutiny reveals that his whole spiritual growth in this period was actually only an unfolding of that fundamental "insight" which had been imparted to him in April or May, 1513. Throughout the rest of his life he held to the opinion that, like himself, others could arrive at this "insight" only through a miracle, that is, through the influence of the Holy Spirit on their souls. But he clung just as tenaciously to the conviction that the Spirit does not do this without means but, just as once in his own case, does this with, in, and under the Word of God, that is, by means of the Word as this is heard from or read in the Scriptures. If we would understand Luther's teaching, therefore, we must ever and again recall what it was that he had come to know and experience in that critical hour.

But is this adequate for an understanding of the progress which we have just tried to describe? Luther himself tells us that he read Augustine's work, *On the Spirit and the Letter*, after that critical hour and that, contrary to his expectation, he found an exposition there of the concept of God's righteousness which was similar to that to which he had himself come. He added that "this pleased" him. We can no longer determine when he became acquainted with this work of Augustine, but we can establish what influence this discovery had on him. It led him, in the first place, to read "almost all of Augustine" that he had not known before, especially the writings against Pelagius and the Pelagians (these interested him particularly) in which Augustine set forth, in all its consequences, his teaching on sin, grace, and predestination. This naturally helped to clarify his own views on these questions. But more important was the impression he gained that in his convictions he was not standing alone, that the greatest teacher of the church was on his side. To be sure, this was not entirely correct, but it strengthened him not a little in the belief that he was not an innovator but an adherent of the old, genuine, and pure Catholic doctrine. Yet Augustine's influence on him was not only stimulating and encouraging, but also restraining. Augustine's authority persuaded him, for instance, to retain the notion of "making just," although it was not entirely suitable for the presentation of his new religious views. He also held on to many other notions and ideas which, even at that time, no longer harmonized with his convictions.

Later he prized the greatest religious genius of the Middle Ages, Bernard of Clairvaux, almost as highly as Augustine. But Luther nowhere suggested that Bernard gave him any help, nor is it evident in his writings. What made him love and esteem the great monk, it would appear, was simply the impression that "despite many errors, in his faith he was a real, earnest Christian, and that of all authors he had in his writings preached Christ most sweetly." Later on Luther sometimes mentioned the great French publicist, Gerson, as the only teacher of the church who had written about spiritual temptation, but in this case, too, without adding that he was in any way indebted to him. In his *Table Talk* he also mentioned with praise many another theologian of the ancient and medieval church. Yet he never ascribed positive influence on his development to anyone except Augustine.

Meanwhile we must also count on the possibility that Luther may have at times unconsciously taken up ideas from his environment which, if not directly, at least indirectly contributed to his development. Such an influence, of which he himself was not quite conscious, is supposed to have been exerted, for instance, by Gregory of Rimini (died 1358). In philosophy Gregory was a follower of Occam. But he would have nothing to do with the theology of the Modernists. In theology, especially in the doctrines of sin, grace, and predestination, Gregory reverted most decidedly to Augustine. Even if Luther had never mentioned him later, one might perhaps have jumped to the conclusion that he had been led by the citations from Gregory's works in Biel's commentary on the *Sentences* to study this Augustinian of the fourteenth century and that Luther had been unconsciously influenced by him in his views. However, although he often mentioned Gregory, he did so only after 1519. In all likelihood, therefore, he read him for the first time in 1519, and hence first made his acquaintance at a time when he could no longer learn anything from him.

More frequently than Gregory, Occam, and the Occamists, the theologians whom he opposed with such vehemence after 1515 have been designated as Luther's real teachers and masters. In fact, it has even been asserted that Luther was in the last analysis nothing but an "ossified Occamist." This opinion, like almost all opinions, is based on a correct observation. Like most other men, Luther never entirely outgrew the influence of the method of thinking and teaching in which he had been trained. For instance, his later statements concerning the omnipresence of the glorified Body of Christ in his writings on the Lord's Supper, and the concepts, proofs, and analogies which he adduced to support this doctrine, he got wholly from Occam, d'Ailly, and Biel. Similarly, his teaching on the inviolability of the seal of confession and the admissibility of "white lies" (later to have such practical significance in the bigamy case of Philip of Hesse), his teaching on natural right and natural law and on the position of the secular government toward natural law and statute law, and, above all, the conviction, to which he clung with the greatest vigor until he drew his last breath, that reason is utterly incapable of apprehending the mysteries of faith—all this and much more goes back ultimately to Occam. Accordingly Luther's theology cannot really be understood, nor his whole *Weltanschauung*, unless the fact that he was schooled under the "Modernists" is constantly borne in mind.

But may we on this account label him an "ossified Occamist"? Such an offhand conclusion would do violence to the truth. For if we consider the *religious* ideas which are basic to his teaching—his conceptions of evil and of sin, of the forgiveness of sin and of grace, of Law and Gospel, of piety as a religious and piety as a moral attitude—we shall have no difficulty in recognizing that these basic ideas were reached in a struggle *against* the "modern" theology. His *Christianity*, therefore, is anything but an "ossified" or modified Occamism. In all its essential features it is rather the greatest conceivable antithesis of Occamism. Yet this is not to deny that although Occam may not exactly be said to have helped him, he nevertheless made it easier for Luther to overcome the medieval religion. The late medieval thinkers were not yet in a position to grasp that the spiritual is something purely spiritual. Just as they always thought of God in terms of substance, so they considered sin, while not exactly a substance, at least as an absence of substance. Grace, meanwhile, was defined as heavenly matter which makes up for the absence of substance in sin, and justification as the transaction by means of which this absence is compensated for and man is converted in a trice from a sinner into a righteous creature. Duns Scotus was the first to attack these materialistic conceptions, and he was soon followed, with even greater force, by Occam. As he thought of God strictly in terms of will, so Occam thought of sin simply as an act of the will, and grace was for him actually no more than a "spiritual ornament" or a sort of stamp by which God acknowledges that the attainments of man are acceptable. In keeping with this, forgiveness of sin no longer meant to him the infusion of the substance of righteousness, but merely the nonimputation of sin. He retained "justification" in Augustine's sense as an independent transaction following the nonimputation of sin, but in reality he did not know just what to do with this dogma. Hence Luther needed only to cast overboard those thoroughly meaningless and empty notions which the "Invincible Doctor" had retained and, in the light of his own religious outlook, to put new content into the hollow concept of the "nonimputation of sin." And here Luther was through with the Catholic system.

Of course, this did not come about so easily and quickly as it may sound today. It cost him bitter struggles and hard work. There is no doubt that Occam had made this work easier and had provided a formula, in the notion of the "nonimputation of sin," which could conveniently be adapted to the presentation of Luther's own views. But did not Occam and the Occamists also help him directly, by means of positive suggestions and cues, to extricate himself from the labyrinth of doubt and the pangs of conscience into which they had previously thrust him? When one reads what the "Invincible Doctor" himself had written, for example, in his famous dialogue on the Holy Scriptures, it appears that, although he did not show the young monk the way out of his inner perplexity, he at least referred him unmistakably to the only place where he could find the help he needed. This work emphatically states that the Holy Scriptures are infallible. Hence, wrote Occam, the Christian is bound to believe only what is written in the Bible or what follows as a logical consequence from the words of the Bible. Yet this hint could have profited Luther only if Occam had at the same time furnished the key to an understanding of the Bible. But the "Invincible Doctor" was utterly incapable of doing this, for, highly as he thought of the Bible in theory, he actually saw nothing more in it than a fortuitously assembled *omnium gatherum* of divine oracles which are contrary to reason and the meaning of which can only be ascertained with the help of Catholic dogma. As a matter of fact, therefore, the dogmas

of the church were the highest authority for him too. If
Luther had simply followed in Occam's footsteps, the Bible
would have remained for him a book with seven seals and
it would never have occurred to him, even remotely, to try
impartially to find out what the Book actually contains.
Nevertheless, it was not entirely without significance for his
development that he came out of a theological school which
in theory attached such supreme importance to the Bible.
But this principle became fruitful for him only because he
felt constrained to take it very seriously in practice as well
as in theory.

Meanwhile, those who feel that it is necessary to trace
Luther's religious views back to some earlier influence are
now accustomed to have a decided predilection for the so-
called German mysticism. When did he come into contact
with this movement, and what significance did it have for
his development?

It was probably during the visitation which he conducted
as district vicar in Meissen and Thuringia during May, 1516,
that Luther became acquainted, at the home of his friend
John Lang in Erfurt, with a German book of sermons which
so captivated him that he took it along to Wittenberg that
he might study it at his leisure. The author of these sermons
was the Dominican, John Tauler, of Strassburg (died 1361).
Some time later he came (we do not know where or how)
upon a little work of a similar nature which pleased him so
much that he had it printed in December with a short preface
to recommend it. In the spring of 1518 he came upon a
complete text of this work. Here a priest and curator of the
Teutonic Order in Sachsenhausen, near Frankfurt, was mentioned as the author of the "spiritually estimable little book."
This discovery caused Luther to put out a new edition of
the work and add to it the title, *Ein deutsch Theologia.* So
he became acquainted with Tauler as well as with the mystic
from Frankfurt only after his new religious views had, in

their essential features, attained maturity. It simply is not true, therefore, that it was his acquaintance with these two old men of God that transformed him "from a man of despair, struggling in a gloomy sea, into a Reformer."

How, then, can we explain the fact that in these very years he praised both so extravagantly and recommended them so warmly? A satisfactory answer to this question is found in the marks and marginal notes which Luther made in his own copy of Tauler's sermons, which we still possess, and in those passages of his works in which he expressly or tacitly cited Tauler or the mystic from Frankfurt. Here we observe that the passages in the writings of these mystics which made a particular impression on him were the ones which depict in strong words the anguish, the pressure, the tension, the inner distress—in short, the "travail"—which necessarily precede the "birth of God in the soul," or the union with the undivided Godhead of the particle of God enclosed in the soul. But to what did Luther apply this typical description of the typical mystical experience? He applied it to the great temptations which, in his own case, resulted from the anguish of a terrified conscience and the uncertainty of election.

Luther was also very much affected by the sermon in which Tauler asserts that man has not gained full mastery over himself until he feels inwardly ready—be it out of love toward God, be it out of affection for his brethren, or be it to make satisfaction for his sins—to go so far as to take upon himself the dreadful fate of eternal damnation. But not even this was appropriated by Luther without giving it an entirely new interpretation. "Readiness to go to hell" (*resignatio ad infernum*) was for him not a disposition which man can produce by his own strength, not an act of voluntary humility, but a condition of the soul into which he is put by God. For the influence of the Holy Spirit has reached its goal only when man finds that he is forced to submit unconditionally to the just judgment of the holy God and no longer wills anything but what God wills. On this account it is the elect whom God allows to experience such things. And this is so because religion is concerned, not to satisfy the creature's desire for life and blessedness, but rather to do justice to the unabridged will of God.

Moreover, the vigorous protest of the two old men of God against a vulgar, reward-seeking piety was very welcome to Luther. But why was the "reward-seeker" so odious to these mystics? Because such a man has too low an estimate of his own moral power and is unwilling to yield that measure of "self-deprivation" which is the prerequisite for merging the "self in the still, formless Godhead." Why, on the other hand, did Luther have no use for the "reward-seeker"? Because such a man has too high an estimate of his own power and, in addition, is so presumptuous as to expect God to reward his paltry works.

Finally, the constantly repeated exhortation of the two old seekers of God, "Suffer God, for everything depends on it," was also very precious to Luther. But what was he thinking of in connection with "suffering God"? Of justification. And what were the mystics thinking of? They were thinking of the travail of God's birth in the soul which must always be preceded by a very vigorous preparation on the part of man, by a rigorous self-discipline of the soul. Thus Luther always read his own thoughts into the two mystics. He reinterpreted the whole mystical terminology and gave it his own meaning, as can be seen especially in the second course of lectures on the Psalms (1518). It will suffice to demonstrate this by taking one idea which was of the greatest significance to him at that time, the idea of humility. What did humility mean to the mystics? Voluntary self-abasement. With such voluntary self-abasement Luther would have nothing to do. In his eyes it is only a sham, artificial humility, the lying mask for the most dangerous variety of pride: spiritual pride. True humility is something quite different, something which man can never secure for himself. It is an unconditional self-condemnation to which man comes, against his own wish or will, when the judgment of God (the standards which he finally acknowledges in his conscience as just, much as he may kick against the pricks) overtakes him in the hour of moral collapse. Thus Luther had exactly the same experience with these two old men of God that he later had with Huss, Wessel Gansfort, Goch, and Savonarola. He unwittingly transformed them, though they were headed in quite a different direction, into confederates and colleagues because, in everything that he read, he was always seeking answers to the very personal questions and problems which were raised by his own reflection and experience. He misunderstood them. And in the last analysis it was only because he misunderstood them that he could use them, in modest measure, as aids in his struggle for an ever clearer grasp of his own religious insight.

But this is not all that need be said concerning Luther's relations with mysticism. It was undoubtedly of the greatest importance for his inner development that while in the monastery he became thoroughly acquainted with mysticism in all its characteristic manifestations, from Dionysius the Areopagite to the representatives of the "modern devotion." For it was in mysticism that he encountered most powerfully the impulse toward religion, even if under a strange cloak. Here he came upon the fervent longing to experience God, to experience Him personally, to experience Him now, and in connection with this he learned that such an experience is impossible without absolute purity of heart. That this longing of the mystics found an echo in his soul is just as certain as the fact that God meant something quite different to him and that consequently he could never have come to God in the way they recommended. Similarly, there can be no doubt that the mystics encouraged him again and again in his striving after absolute purity of heart and in his inclination to rigorous self-examination. But he was more in earnest about this than even John Tauler and the mystic of Frankfurt, and for this reason he reached an entirely different conclusion—the conclusion that man, while he can will the good now and then, will never succeed here on earth in willing *only* good.

Just as mysticism furnished his seeking and longing with wings, so it also helped to lead Luther directly to a primitive Christian idea which, in his eyes, was always a part of the Gospel. This was the conviction that unmerited suffering, or the cross, is not an intolerable fate, but grace. But this conviction, too, was different for Luther than for the mystics. The mystics had changed the message, "Blessed are they that mourn," into a flat imperative, "Blessed are they that seek occasions of mourning." And for this reason they devised the most monstrous and absurd self-torments and literally reveled, after the manner of Indian penitents, in such sufferings of their own invention. There was no longer any trace in Luther of such pathological eccentricities. "Not the suffering which you devise for yourself," he warns by the beginning of 1517, "but the sorrow which comes upon you against your choosing, thinking, or desiring—this is the way of the cross. Follow this, let this be your discipleship, this is the hour in which your Master comes to you." So highly did he think of this true, genuine, "holy cross," from the patient endurance of which the Christian can alone learn whether he is in earnest about the Gospel and about following Christ, that to give it adequate expression he now preferred to call his whole teaching the Theology of the Cross. For the cross, he wrote, is the symbol of the gift of God (*donum*), through which man becomes the child of God, as much as it is the symbol of the highest task which is set before him, the imitation of Christ (*exemplum*); it is also the mark (*signum*) by which the children of God are distinguished from the children of the world and the "certain sign" (*indicium*) by which they themselves can recognize that they "are in God's kingdom and possess eternal life." Indeed, so thoroughly convinced was he of the necessity and blessing of the cross in the last sense that he wrote: The worst temptation is not to

experience any temptation at all, for anyone who takes the
Gospel seriously must provoke the world to hate him, and
this inevitably results in all kinds of inner temptations.

The rejection of the mystics' high regard for self-imposed
suffering was necessarily accompanied by a rejection of the
cathartic asceticism which the mystics recommended and
assiduously practiced as a means by which man's sensuous
impulses were to be completely eradicated. But it was some
time before Luther realized this. In his *Treatise on Christian
Liberty* (November, 1520) he still considered cathartic
asceticism in some measure necessary to guard the inner life
against the exceedingly strong influence of the sensual appetite. But even at this time he was through with an actual
mortification of the natural impulses. And later he countenanced only those two forms of asceticism which are compatible with the Gospel—caritative asceticism, which voluntarily renounces permissible pleasures for the sake of the
brethren, and gymnastic asceticism, which seeks to strengthen
the moral will by means of freely chosen exercises of activity
and renunciation. He did not fail to point out, however, that
such gymnastics can easily produce the opposite effect—a
stronger excitement of the natural impulses—if it is not
accompanied and supplemented by prayer and devotion.
On this point the influence of mysticism on his thought and
feeling was still apparent up to the time of the Diet of
Worms. For the mystics' basic religious ideas, however, he
no longer had any use even at the time when he became
acquainted with Tauler, although it was not until 1518, in
his second course of lectures on the Psalms, that he formally
repudiated them. As a matter of fact, he had never known
what to do with them.

So Luther's attitude toward mysticism, just as his whole
development, confirms the fact that man, like a plant, takes
from his environment only what agrees with his nature. He
became acquainted with all the varieties and practically all
the prominent representatives of this movement, from

Dionysius the Areopagite to John Momboir, the last influential author of the Modern Devotion, and in his first years in the monastery he often made an honest effort to mold his spirit according to their directions. But he never succeeded in understanding their peculiar conception of God and the soul because their dominantly pantheistic mood and outlook were always entirely foreign to him and beyond him. On this account he was also unable to understand those teachings of Augustine which originated in such an outlook. In Luther's eyes evil is never simply an "absence of being." Nor in so far as it exists, was it for him, like everything that is or participates in being, good. But evil is always the absolute opposite of good, and consequently never simply a *longe a Deo esse* but always a *contra Deum esse*. This explains why it was never possible for Luther to agree with Augustine that there is something in evil or in sin which does not destroy the order and beauty of the world but, rather, like the dark shadows in a painting, belongs to its inherent order and beauty and, in fact, sets them off effectively. Luther always saw in sin something which should not be, something which must by all means be removed.

The natural and necessary consequence of this is that, from the beginning, Luther's attitude and disposition toward the conditions which he found in the church were altogether different from what we observe in Augustine and the mystics. While the latter were not sensitive to the phenomena in the church of their time which were at variance with their ideals and—in so far as they did become conscious of them—did not allow them to disturb their peace of mind, such impressions and experiences always roused Luther to such an extent that he had to give vent to his discontent. As soon as he was sure of his new understanding of Christianity, therefore, he began at once to apply it as a standard to the teaching of the church and to oppose abuses in ecclesiastical administration and the practice of religion.

Already, in the lectures on the Psalms, Luther once com-

plained that "the state of the church has never been so
unhappy as it is in these days." Outwardly, to be sure, peace,
well-being, and security prevail, he said. Nor is there any
want of divine services. But deeper examination reveals
everywhere the characteristic signs of the Last Day: apostasy
and decay. The pulpits echo with fables, scholastic and juristic hair-splittings, and exceedingly coarse jests. The Gospel
has been entirely, or all but entirely, silenced. Aristotle is
the idol of not a few preachers. The average Christian consequently no longer knows what the life and passion of
Christ mean. Like the pulpit, the altar is no longer what it
once was. The sacraments are administered in the most
frivolous and profane fashion, and prayer has become luke-
warm, dry, and spiritless. Lukewarmness is prevalent everywhere, as a matter of fact, and connected with it is the
attempt "to make the way to heaven as easy as possible for
the people by means of indulgences and false teachings."
Moreover, the administration of the judicial and executive
power in the church is very poorly managed. "And who can
count up the abuses which take place in the bestowal of
benefices?" Bishops, clerics, and monks seek only power and
money. They defend the worldly possessions of the church
as zealously as if its eternal foundation were at stake, and as
if the church did not have to be as willing to suffer loss and
injustice as the individual Christian. There is no reluctance
to use force of arms to defend these possessions. Not even
the popes shrink from waging the most inhuman wars for
their patrimonies. Among the bishops there are some who,
in their quest for worldly power, have succeeded in gaining
control of a considerable territory, and they rule over it like
princes and kings. Even the monks are so secularized now
that they submit their quarrels to secular princes and think
only of how they might make money out of their brother-
hoods and indulgences. But much greater is the abuse in
which the popes and bishops engage with their indulgences.
They are not concerned about increasing the treasure of the

church, but only about reducing it. But that there really is such a treasure from which the church can draw to bestow indulgences, and that this treasure is ultimately inexhaustible —about these things Luther did not entertain any doubt at this time.

Luther expressed himself much more sharply when he discussed similar abuses in his lectures on the Epistle to the Romans. "The Roman Curia," he asserted here, about the middle of the year 1516, "is thoroughly corrupted and infected, a colossal chaos of all conceivable debaucheries, gluttonies, knaveries, ambitions, and sacrilegious outrages. Today Rome is carousing as much as in the time of the Caesars—if not more. Hence it has even more need of the apostles today than it did before." The popes are entirely preoccupied with the interests of their secular power. "Even if you were to have all the vices which the apostle enumerates in II Timothy 3, as long as you defend the rights and liberties of the church, you are the most pious of Christians. However, if you do not do this, then you are not a faithful son and friend of the church." The popes and bishops are very liberal in bestowing indulgences for these secular interests. But to grant indulgences to poor souls for nothing—this does not occur to them. They no longer have any conception at all of what spiritual rule means. And this spirit of secularization is now spreading through the whole church. For the building of churches, for gold and silver sacred vessels, and for organs and other outward pomp, enormous sums are expended. But the commandment to love one's neighbor is forgotten. The most ignorant and insipid babblers, who encourage the little man to perform such external works but do not show him what everyone must do in his calling, are promoted to the position of preachers, especially indulgence-preachers. And liturgical prayer is read, by both priests and monks, so irreverently and thoughtlessly that they actually fall asleep and snore while engaging in it. Quite in keeping with this, Luther continued, is the practice of the bishops, who immediately place a whole city under the ban and interdict when some damage has been done to a church building, but who quietly put up with, and even look with favor on, the worldly, sensual, self-seeking behavior of the ignorant, useless carriers of moral pestilence whom they admit to holy orders. Since so much fuss is being made about the hatred and hostility of the laity toward the clergy, one really ought to inquire why the clerics are so unpopular and why the apostles and saints never experienced such hostility.

Not only were the complaints of Luther now becoming sharper and more concrete, but after 1516 they were also directed with growing frequency against the institutions of the church and were connected with definite proposals for reform. Fasting still had value for him as a wholesome exercise, but obligatory fasting was, in his opinion, a mischievous thing and should therefore be given up. The number of holidays must be reduced, church worship must be cleansed of unnecessary ceremonies and all superfluous pomp, ecclesiastical law must be reformed, and the Jewish superstition connected with all of these must be rooted out. But, said he, just as it is false to declare that such usages are necessary for salvation, the opposite opinion of the Bohemian Brethren, that they must be radically abolished, is just as false. Out of consideration for the weak who are attached to these things, and particularly also in the exercise of voluntary obedience, one must observe what the consensus of the church has established in ancient times.

New, too, was the fact that Luther now began to censure and criticize particular individuals. For the most part, to be sure, he expressed only casual reproof of those who had provoked his displeasure; for example, Pope Julius II, Duke George of Saxony, and Archbishop Albrecht of Mainz. He dealt at greater length only with his own ruler, Frederick the Wise. What particular fault did he have to find with him? In the first place, said Luther, the fact that he is so "foolish" as to increase the services in the Wittenberg castle church; in the second place, he has the ambition to gather more relics in this church than Archbishop Albrecht of Mainz has in his new chapter house in Halle on the Saale; in the third place, he is building too much ("I fear that the monastery [the alterations in the Black Cloister] will bring a great deal of misery to its wretched founder, even as the new castle church will"); in the fourth place, he cannot be found "when he is needed" and he neglects his duties in the affairs of government on account of his preoccupation with churchly devotional exercises. Only with Frederick's love of peace was he entirely in agreement, for he still held that every war, even the purely defensive war, is wrong. Yet he could not suppress the suspicion that Frederick's love of peace was not based on noble motives alone, but also on the fear of injury. Thus Luther already understood Frederick quite well and formed a more exact estimate of him than any of his contemporaries.

This example shows that Luther was already quite aware of abuses in the secular government. In general, he said, the secular government is doing its duty more than the spiritual government. It would therefore be of economic advantage to the lower clergy if ordinary benefices were placed under secular control. Yet he observed that the administration of civil justice is thwarted by the jurists' interpretation of the law; the princes pay too much attention to the jurists anyway. So he already bore something of a grudge against this profession. Especially the canonists, the ecclesiastical jurists, were abhorrent to him because they were the mainstays of that confusion of religion and law in the preaching and administration of the church which he found so intolerable. But neither was he very fond of the secular jurists. It may be said that the whole attitude toward the world and life on which jurisprudence rested—placing law above love and emphasizing form as over against norm— was very repugnant to him. Besides, he had the impression

that no profession accepted so many "tips"—that is, was so
easily bribed—as the jurists.

But Luther was dissatisfied with the other professions, too.
The artisans work, he said, as if they were asleep. The merchants are daily devising new tricks to outwit and overcharge
their customers. Even the farmers have come to master the
art of deception. Luther also expressed sharp displeasure
with the gluttony and drunkenness which were spreading
through all classes, with the more than heathenish jealousy
and malice which characterized the relationship of nations,
and with the activity of the astrologers. But his sharpest
attack was always reserved for the "swinish theologians" (the
Occamists) and the "no-account preachers" who, by pointing
to indulgences and other pledges of "present grace," rocked
the people in a cradle of deluded security.

"I pray earnestly that no one will imitate me," Luther
wrote on one occasion, "when I say such things in obedience
to my duty and the burden resting upon me. Practical application to the present makes the understanding of the text
easier. Moreover, by virtue of papal authority I hold a
public teaching office. Accordingly it is one of my official
duties to strike out against all the wrong of which I become
aware, even if the wrong is done by persons in high position." So Luther already considered himself bound, as a
doctor of theology, to criticize conditions in the church. But
does it follow that Luther included in his academic lectures
all the remarks and allusions of this kind which we find in
his notes? Not at all. If this were so, such passages would
also be found in the students' copybooks which contain the
notes they took during Luther's lectures on Romans and
Galatians. But this is not the case. Hence in his lectures
Luther generally, if not always, let these "rantings" go by
the board. In all probability he dealt just as freely with his
sermon manuscripts. The discovery of critical utterances—
rare, incidentally, in these sermon notes—does not permit
the hasty conclusion that Luther was then preaching such

things from the pulpit. Only on the subject of indulgences and certain excesses in the worship of saints is there clear evidence that he spoke his mind frankly from the pulpit at this time.

This means that the scope of Luther's criticism must not be overestimated. For the most part it remained on paper. Only in exceptional cases did any of it reach the ears of students and burghers. Moreover, it must not be forgotten that Luther was still thinking and teaching in irreproachable Catholic fashion with regard to the articles of faith which had been the chief objects of attack by medieval heretics and which were consequently considered the actual touchstones of Catholicism—the papacy, purgatory, the sacrifice of the mass, the sacraments, and the veneration of images, saints, and Mary. In a sermon on the festival of the Assumption of Mary, August 15, 1516, he celebrated Mary with the customary extravagance, and he always referred to the saints in warm and reverent terms. There is evidence only that at this time he was speaking sharply from the pulpit against the abuse of ascribing definite functions to the saints, as, for example, calling upon St. Anthony as a remedy for erysipelas, St. Sebastian for the pestilence, St. Valentine for epilepsy, St. Apollonia for toothache, St. Laurentius for danger by fire, or St. Louis to keep beer from becoming sour. Similarly he was now attacking the cult of St. Christopher and the use of Christopher medals, which were very popular in Wittenberg. And he probably did not keep from the Wittenbergers his opinion of the absurd fables in the legend of St. Bartholomew. But even if some of his hearers took exception to this criticism, it was not un-Catholic. Indeed, he could well believe that he had done the "dear saints" a service by pointing out that, in addition to calling upon them for special cures, people can and should have recourse to the intercession of the saints in every kind of physical and spiritual need.

Now, when and how did those who were near Luther come to the realization that there was something more in him than an ordinary friar or professor?

In the summer of 1514 the Benedictine Paul Lange, of Posa, near Zeitz, visited the universities of eastern Germany to gather material for a new edition of Trittenheim's dictionary of authors. In Wittenberg, too, he unearthed and sought out quite a few celebrities on this journey. But he overlooked Luther. And he did so in spite of the fact that his definition of the term celebrity was by no means narrow. On the contrary, he was inclined to give some space in his notebook to even the most insignificant professor who might in time become a *vir inluster* (celebrated man) and to list the works which such a man was only planning to write. If Dr. Martinus had been reckoned among the lights of the university, the conscientious and diligent Benedictine's attention would surely have been called to him. The fact that this was not done demonstrates that, even in Wittenberg, Luther was still quite an unknown quantity. Outside Wittenberg he was known to some extent, but only in his Order. Here, as a matter of fact, he amounted to something, especially in the eyes of the head of the Saxon Congregation, John Staupitz. For this reason Staupitz did not fail to push him forward wherever and whenever he could. Thus, for example, he commissioned Luther to preach the festival sermon before the superiors of the Congregation at the chapter meeting at Gotha on May 1, 1515, and had him elected district vicar shortly afterward. Nor did Brother Martinus disappoint his expectations. His sermon on the vice of fondness for gossip made such an impression on his hearers that even the humanist and canonist of Gotha, Conrad Mut (called Mutianus), who thought so little of the barbarous monks, desired to make Luther's acquaintance, and Luther's fellow-monks and friends were pestering him for copies of his sermon manuscript a year later.

Meanwhile, Luther's position was undergoing a change

in Wittenberg too. By the time John Oldecop, of Hilde-
sheim, was matriculated at the university on April 16, 1515,
"he already had many auditors." Oldecop enjoyed attending
Luther's lectures, especially because he "put every Latin
word into such stout German"—that is, because he often
used German in his lectures to help his auditors to understand. In fact, some men were already coming to Wittenberg expressly to hear him. The first man reported to have
come for this reason was the former mayor of Brück, Gregory
Heyns, father of the Wittenberg pastor, Simon Heyns, and
of Gregory Brück, later chancellor of the Elector. Despite
his age and his frail health, as Melanchthon tells us, Gregory
Heyns was not discouraged by the long distance between his
home and the Black Cloister from coming again and again
to "hear the comforting teaching of the Son of God" from
Luther's lips. So it was the religious content of Luther's lectures which especially attracted him. More even than in
his lectures, this side of Luther's nature came to the fore in
his sermons. John Oldecop later confessed that he did not
miss a single one of these sermons although, even then, he
did not agree with Luther's criticism of the popular worship
of the saints. But he went to hear Luther, as he added,
because "he was vigorous in the pulpit and condemned sin,
as is right, without any distinction or fear." For instance,
Luther preached against the participation of young girls in
the festive carousals of students and spoke "so severely and
sharply that thereafter parents kept their marriageable
daughters at home. This gave him a following, fame, honor,
and praise among the most prominent citizens."

More important than all this was the fact that Luther's
influence on his colleagues in the university was gradually
increasing and that he found a patron at the Elector's court
who shared his views and hopes. This man was the Elector's
librarian, secretary, and court preacher, George Burkhardt,
of Spalt, near Nuremberg, who was called Spalatin. As
early as the end of 1513 Spalatin called Dr. Martinus "an

excellent man and scholar, whose judgment I value very highly." By March, 1514, Spalatin was expressing the wish "to become wholly his," and in May, 1515, he had become "his" so completely that he revered and consulted Luther like an oracle. When he himself was consulted by his lord, Spalatin seldom failed to ask for Luther's opinion beforehand, either orally or in writing. Elector Frederick's dealings with Luther also passed through Spalatin's hands from the beginning, for it went against Frederick's nature to deal with Luther directly. Never in his life did Frederick exchange so much as a word with the Reformer. Hence it was of the greatest importance for Luther to have a friend and ally at the electoral court who always interceded for his cause, as Spalatin did, with the purest zeal and who always knew how to meet the Elector's objections in such a way that Luther's wishes were usually taken into account, at least to some extent. Frederick never succeeded in coming to a real understanding of the teachings of the Reformation and never had any interest, beyond the customary measure of princely benevolence, in the personality of the Reformer (which always made him exceedingly uncomfortable and, to say the least, somewhat uneasy) despite the fact that he was pleased with the glory which the bold monk had brought to his obscure university. If Spalatin had not continued to encourage him and if his other advisers—Hirschfeld, Dolzig, Einsiedel, Feilitzsch, Planitz, and Thun—had not been "good Lutherers," Elector Frederick would probably have dropped the "Herr Doctor," who was so difficult to manage, at the first opportunity which presented itself. For it was not at all like him to burden himself with such "dangerous and troublesome matters." Accordingly his whole attitude toward the Lutheran question was really determined by that modest man who never had the ambition to cut a figure himself, but who said that it was his life's task to serve one who was greater. Meanwhile Spalatin had the rare gift which enabled him to guide his lord's intentions, with utmost submission and gentleness and without the latter's awareness, into the channels he himself wished.

It appears that Spalatin at first used Luther chiefly as a literary adviser. But inasmuch as he was the Elector's right hand in the affairs of the university, Spalatin naturally began to consult Luther on all university questions too. Without seeking it, therefore, Luther gained an opportunity to create sentiment at the electoral court for a reform of the university according to his own notion. The goals he had in mind—doing away with the dominance of Aristotle, or Scholasticism, in the arts and theological faculties and the founding of regular chairs for the Greek and Hebrew languages—coincided approximately with the humanists' program of reform with which Spalatin had long since come into hearty accord.

This naturally brought Luther into closer connection with the humanistic circles. But he remained completely independent of humanism. When, for example, in the controversy between the Cologne Dominicans and Reuchlin, he supported Reuchlin unreservedly both in his correspondence and in the lecture hall, he did not do so because he shared Reuchlin's opinion that the Talmud is indispensable for an understanding of the Bible and that the Cabala is important for an understanding of the world. He did so, rather, because he judged the behavior of the Dominicans toward the great scholar to be impious and because, in his opinion, the classical testimony for the fulfillment of the biblical prophecy that the Jews would become blasphemers of their God and Messiah could be found in the Talmud. Moreover, he had as little patience with the "impudent" polemic of the Reuchlinists, especially with the buffoonery of his former friend Crotus Rubeanus in the famous *Letters of Obscure Men*, as he had with the "stupidities" and "wolfish" manners of the anti-Reuchlin poetaster, Ortwin Gratius. When he now began to exchange letters with humanists abroad, the initiative was never taken by Luther, but always by the humanists. Yet they were already getting on his nerves with their annoying habit of attaching themselves, with their brazen adulations, to every imaginable person of prominence, whether they knew him or not, in the hope of wheedling out of him a responsive hymn of flattery out of which they might make literary coin.

Even less acceptable were the humanists' plans for religious reform. Luther still dealt gently with Lefèvre. But by 1516 he was so opposed to the views of Erasmus that in October of that year he tried earnestly to convert the great critic through Spalatin. Then in March, 1517, he wrote: "My opinion of Erasmus decreases from day to day. I must confess that his sharp and undiminished attack upon the ignorance of the priests and monks pleases me. But I fear that he does not promote the cause of Christ and God's grace sufficiently. For him human considerations have an absolute preponderance over divine. . . . No one is truly wise in the Christian sense simply because he knows Greek and Hebrew. Despite his five languages, Jerome was not the equal of St. Augustine, who knew but one. Erasmus has quite a different opinion of this. But the opinion of him who attributes significance [in salvation] to man's will [Erasmus] is far different from the opinion of him who knows nothing but grace [Luther]." Nevertheless, Luther had not given up the hope that Erasmus might change his mind. Consequently he did not deem it expedient to come out openly with his opinion just then because, as he put it, the phalanx of the numerous opponents of "the new Aristarchus might be strengthened" thereby. Despite all inner differences, therefore, Luther was still conscious of the community of interest which existed between him and the great humanist. As a matter of fact, they were both attacking the same opponents —Scholasticism and the "inveterate ignorance of clerics and monks." Both looked for a reformation of the church in a return to the oldest sources of the Christian religion and both enthusiastically championed the study of Hebrew and

Greek. But, now as before, Luther did not become a humanist. Only in little externals did he adapt himself to the
humanistic manner at this time. Since October, 1517, he no
longer signed himself Luder, but Luther or Eleutherius
(Elutherius). The last form of his name he used only until
the beginning of 1519, however, and then only in intimate
letters to his three humanistic friends, Spalatin, Lang, and
Melanchthon. In these letters, after the humanistic fashion,
he allowed an occasional Greek word to slip in. But this
playfulness also ceased by 1519.

Important as these formative relations to humanism were
for the future of Luther's cause, more important for him at
the time was the fact that his teaching had, by the beginning
of the year 1517, gained the upper hand in the theological
faculty at Wittenberg. The occasion for this triumph was a
disputation in September, 1516, in which his pupil, Bartholomew Bernhardi, of Feldkirch in Swabia, sharply
attacked the Occamistic teaching that man can fulfill the
commandments of God by his own reason and strength.
Professors Carlstadt and Lupinus vigorously contested the
theses which the enterprising young Swabian had drawn up
with the help and approval of Luther. Even Professor
Nicholas von Amsdorf was not a little astonished at them.
But he soon came to terms with them. Lupinus also submitted when Luther set him right with the help of Augustine's writings. But Carlstadt set out for Leipzig on January
13, 1517, in order to buy an edition of Augustine's works
that he might, on the basis of these, thoroughly refute
Luther. But when he studied these folio volumes he soon
came to see that Luther was right, and in 151 theses he at
once (on April 26) took a public stand for the new teaching.
That decided Luther's victory in the theological faculty.
"Our theology and St. Augustine," he wrote to John Lang
on May 18, "now prosper and reign in our university. By
degrees Aristotle is falling into decline. The lectures on the
Sentences have fallen into discredit in an amazing fashion.

No one can count on having auditors unless he lectures on the Bible, or Augustine, or some other recognized teacher of the church."

Simultaneous with Carlstadt's posting of his 151 bristling theses on the door of the castle church, Luther also published a work, *The Seven Penitential Psalms with an Exposition in German,* which presents his views very positively and without any polemical barbs. But Luther did not regard this work as an announcement of a program of reform. All he intended was to supply the printer, Grünenberg, with a manuscript to substitute for the revision of his lectures on the Psalms which Luther had promised to furnish for the press but had not completed.

Nevertheless, Luther now felt that it was necessary to make a public declaration of his position. This purpose was served by the ninety-seven theses against scholastic theology on the basis of which his student, Francis Günther, of Nordhausen, engaged in a disputation on September 4, 1517. Luther had these theses printed. He sent them to Erfurt and Nuremberg. He asked his new friend, the Nuremberg patrician Christopher Scheurl, to show them to the very learned and wise Dr. Eck of Ingolstadt. And then Luther waited with suspense and inner agitation for an echo from the learned world. But in this he was disappointed. It is true that the old Erfurt Occamists angrily shook their venerable heads at his paradoxes and cacodoxies, and in Nuremberg there were even a couple of persons who read the little work with approval. But neither these nor the others considered it necessary to engage in a further discussion of the questions which he had raised. These ninety-seven theses which contained an almost complete outline of his new theology—in a negative and intentionally sharp form, to be sure—passed by the world of scholars, to his amazement, without as much as grazing their skins. Not these theses but, contrary to his expectations, another set of theses which, similarly clothed in the heavy garb of learned language, he now directed against an abuse in the church's practice of piety about which "all the world complained," suddenly started the ball rolling. In such wondrous ways was the dictum fulfilled in Luther's case too: "Good work is done when one neither intends nor knows it."

PART TWO

BEGINNING OF THE GREAT STRUGGLE

CHAPTER XII

THE NINETY-FIVE THESES

A study of the literature of legends and visions of the early Middle Ages gives the impression that the people of that time feared purgatory almost more than hell. The cause for this is not hard to find. It was believed that one could escape the eternal punishment of hell merely by contrite repentance, but that the temporal punishments of purgatory could be escaped only if one had conscientiously accomplished the satisfactions and penances imposed upon the sinner by the church. But these penances were very severe: three, five, seven and more years of fasting on bread and water, exile for years, long pilgrimages, loss of the right to bear arms and buy and sell. Everybody was therefore endeavoring in every way possible to lighten the weight of these severe works of penance.

Even the church was doing this. From the sixth century onward the church permitted penitents, first in Ireland and then elsewhere, to exchange (commute) difficult works for easier ones. In the Germanic lands, however, the church was influenced very early on this point by the Germanic legal idea that all corporal and capital punishments are commutable to money penalties, and in accordance with this idea a sinner might, for example, be permitted to pay a money penalty instead of fulfilling an imposed penance of fasting. The church also followed the Germanic idea of representation in that it occasionally permitted a penitent to have a relative or vassal, or some person specially designated for this purpose, wholly or partially discharge the penalty which had been imposed upon him. At first, however, such easements were permitted only in individual cases, each case being decided upon its own merits.

It was not until the year 1030 that several bishops in the province of Limousin, in southern France, conceived the idea of promising to all penitents a *partial* remission of penance as a reward for any kind of pious work. The innovation was very popular. Nevertheless, it would hardly have succeeded without a conflict if the popes had not sanctioned it and themselves proclaimed, from 1063 on, such *general* remissions of penalty—even to a greater extent than the bishops in that they promised *total* remission of penances to penitents, especially for one particularly pious work, that of participating in the religious war against Islam. The great success that Urban II had with this new method of recruiting troops for the First Crusade in 1095 induced the church not only to retain this custom but actually to remodel it into a new means of grace which was usually called an indulgence.

Thus, in its original form, the indulgence was nothing more than a general remission of all (plenary indulgence) or part (partial indulgence) of the canonical satisfactions or penances. But since these penances were accounted as substitute penalties for the temporal punishments of purgatory, the indulgences also signified a partial or complete remission of purgatorial punishment. Thus the fear of purgatory is the religious motive out of which the indulgence arose and which governed its further development. Where purgatory was not recognized, as, for example, in the Eastern Catholic Church, indulgences never found favor despite the lively communication that existed between the East and the West in the Middle Ages.

There were two prime factors, therefore, which were of decisive significance for the further development of indulgences: first, the growing financial needs of the popes; and second, the Germanic legal ideas mentioned above. As early as 1166 the English bishops, with the approval of Pope Alexander III, granted a partial remission of penance even to persons who could do no more than contribute a money offering to the crusade proposed at that time. Then in 1187 Pope Gregory VIII granted full absolution, not only to such alms-givers, but also to anyone who would pay the cost of a substitute for the crusade; and under Innocent III this privilege had already become a permanent arrangement. Henceforth it was no longer necessary to go to war in order to receive an indulgence. One could be content with furnishing a substitute or giving a money contribution. In the latter case, to be sure, one received, under Innocent, only a partial indulgence, according to the amount contributed. The indulgence thus became a money-making scheme that was capable of being used in many different ways.

But it was possible to gain larger profits by this means only as long as the demand for indulgences was kept alive among the masses by ever new forms of publishing indulgences, and, at the same time, by making it ever easier to procure the pardons. As long as the crusades were popular, the indulgence of the cross was quite sufficient for the former purpose. But when the great campaigns to the Holy Land ceased, it was necessary, in order to satisfy the demand for indulgences among the masses, as well as the Curia's need for money, to devise some new form of indulgence which would promise as large a sale as the "crusade indulgence." It was for this reason that Pope Boniface VIII came to establish the so-called jubilee indulgence in the year 1300.

The jubilee indulgence, or *jubilaeum*, promised a full remission of penance to all who visited the graves of the apostles in Rome once a day for at least fifteen successive days during the jubilee year. Boniface decreed that such a jubilee should take place only once every hundred years. However, in 1343, Clement VI was moved to reduce this interval to fifty years. Then, in 1389, Urban VI set it at thirty-three, in remembrance of the thirty-three years of the earthly life of Jesus, and finally, in 1470, Paul II reduced it to twenty-five years in view of the brevity of human life.

In other respects the development of the jubilee indul-

gence was quite like the development of the crusade indulgence. From 1390 the church also granted this indulgence
to persons who were unable to make the pilgrimage to
Rome in the jubilee year. Instead of this personal act, a
material consideration, a contribution of money, was then
required. At the same time the popes began to grant such
plenary absolutions even outside the jubilee year and for all
other possible purposes. Thus they turned this most important and most lucrative indulgence into a veritable commodity (*merx sancta*), and from the fifteenth century
onward allowed indulgences to be offered for sale in the
most varied forms, just like merchandise by traveling sales-
men, first in this church province and then in that, and then
throughout the whole West. Thus the sale of indulgences
came to be referred to, even officially and entirely without
any ironical implications, as a holy trade (*sacrum negotium*).

But frequently as they were now offered for sale, these
"holy commodities" were still not available at all times. If
one wanted to be quite secure from the torments of purgatory, one would need to have them, as it were, in reserve,
so as to have them on hand when the need was greatest. The
popes took account even of this need, and from 1294 on they
granted to certain persons of high position so-called confessional letters, which empowered them to receive complete absolution from any priest whom they chose, once
during life and once "in the article of death." This was the
rule at least from the end of the fourteenth century. But
the demand for the new means of grace was so lively that,
from 1350 onward, such letters were granted to anyone who
was able to pay the required tax. Thus the confessional letter
also became a means of raising money.

Then the Curia naturally had to invent new privileges for
noble sinners, both male and female, whom it desired to put
under obligation to itself. From 1370 onward the Curia
granted to certain nobles a full absolution, at first *toties
quoties*—that is, as often as they were in danger of death—

and, in addition, twice during life; then, later, once every year, sometimes even four times a year; and finally, after Sixtus IV (1471-84), at every confession. In addition, the Curia presented them with dozens of confessional letters to use as they pleased, so that they were in a position to parcel them out as favors to all sorts of people. This new means of grace was thus quite unashamedly employed for the advancement of the Curia's most worldly interests.

However, the demand for absolutions was still not satisfied by the creation of the confessional letters. As soon as the idea of indulgences arose, there also arose among the laity the desire to procure this grace also for poor souls in purgatory. From the thirteenth century onward, the crusade preachers strengthened the people in this opinion and the theologians after Thomas Aquinas generally seconded them. The canonists, with few exceptions, would have nothing to do with an indulgence for the dead until well into the fifteenth century; nor did the popes think it advisable to yield to the desire of the people on this question, for since most of them were themselves jurists, they heeded the jurists rather more than the theologians. Pope Calixtus III was the first to abandon this cautious policy (1457). However, he sanctioned such indulgences only for his native Spain. Thus, at first, outside of Spain, scarcely any notice was taken of the Bull sanctioning them.

The indulgence for the dead was first actually established by Pope Sixtus IV in 1476. The innovation stirred up a great sensation, but it was so popular that it met with immediate success everywhere and gave a fresh impetus to the indulgence traffic, for there were pious people who desired such indulgences for all the dead who were dear to them, and bought them by the dozen. Nevertheless, Rome felt it necessary to increase the sales of the holy merchandise by offering all sorts of extra inducements. Now the purchaser of an indulgence was usually granted, first, a confessional letter; second, a butter letter (that is, a license to eat butter, eggs, cheese, and milk, though not meat, on the prescribed fast and abstinence days); third, permission to substitute other good works for vows, even those sworn upon oath, excepting vows of chastity and monastic vows; fourth, a share in the spiritual treasure of the church (that is, in the power of grace resident in the good works of the saints); and finally, fifth, for a slight extra charge, even the right to retain and use with a good conscience illegally acquired goods, in case the legitimate owner could no longer be found. These extra inducements were eminently well calculated to make the holy merchandise increasingly attractive and also to make it desirable to very worldly-minded people.

Even the the late Middle Ages people were not lacking who absolutely condemned indulgences. The Cathari and the Waldensians, for example, would have nothing to do with them because they did not believe in purgatory. But among the ecclesiastical theologians of that time there was only one—Abelard—who sharply rejected them. All the rest defended them. Then the great scholastics of the thirteenth century sought in their thoroughgoing manner to justify dogmatically this contrivance of the church. But an even greater service was rendered in the promotion of the new means of grace by the French Dominican, Hugo of St. Cher; it was he who in 1230 first discovered and described the heavenly capital from which the church militant might dispense indulgences: the treasury of the surplus good works of Christ and the saints. It was formerly the opinion that this idea was copied directly from the late-Jewish dogma of the treasure of the patriarchs (sechus owaus). But this is out of the question. On the contrary, as so often happens in the history of religion, we have here two views which are analogous, or more correctly homogeneous, but not dependent upon each other. Since the scholars were in disagreement only upon the question of the admissibility of indulgences for the dead, in which the popes were not yet interested, the

Curia had no occasion at this time to give explicit definition of a dogma of indulgences.

It was not until the end of the fourteenth century that the number of determined opponents of indulgences began again to increase. Wyclif and his disciples, of course, would not approve of this contrivance of the church. But their opposition made so little impression in orthodox circles that Martin V could be content with condemning as heretical Wyclif's statement that "it is foolish to trust in the indulgences of bishops and popes." At the end of the fifteenth century several new critical voices were raised. But of these the two critics who might have become dangerous to the Curia because of their official position—the Basel professor, John Ruchrath of Wesel, and Peter Martinez, professor in Salamanca—acquitted themselves in 1479 by a "laudable recantation of their errors." Wessel Harmenss Gansfort, of Gröningen, who was intellectually most significant, excited a passing sensation only in his native country. One can scarcely say even this of the Parisian cleric, John Laillier (1484), and of the Franciscan, John Vitrier, of Tournay. Only the cases of Martinez and Laillier came to the ears of the Curia. However, neither case seemed important enough to justify any further action on the indulgence question. Hence, at this time there was no formal definition of the dogma of indulgences. But if in 1517 there was still no formal decision (*solemne judicium*) of the church on indulgences, it was nevertheless sufficiently established by a long series of papal pronouncements that it was heretical to doubt the saving power of indulgences and the right of the popes to administer the treasure of the church.

In recent times the selling of indulgences has often been compared to preaching missions. This comparison, however, is unsound. The missioner is concerned only with the salvation of the souls of his hearers; the indulgence preacher has designs, if not exclusively, at any rate chiefly, upon the believer's money. Moreover, at the end of the Middle Ages, the selling of indulgences was for the Curia purely a business. One cannot seriously ascribe pastoral motives to the Renaissance popes, and least of all in the administration of the indulgence institution. They saw no harm, therefore, in engaging the assistance of the great banks in the administration of this institution. As early as the middle of the fifteenth century the Medici had already performed excellent services for them in this connection, in return for a large commission. But the great house of Fugger, in Augsburg, had had so much to do with indulgences since the days of Alexander VI that in 1514 it turned its branch office in Rome into a regular indulgence agency. However, we must not conclude from the use of these capitalistic methods in the administration of the indulgence institution that the Apostolic Exchequer was the only one profiting by the indulgences.

In the first place, there were a great number of spiritual societies and so-called station and pilgrimage churches which claimed the right, mostly on the grounds of forged documents, to offer indulgences to believers everywhere through their pardoners (*quaestores*) and "stationaries." The Curia received none of the profit from these indulgences. There was also a large number of churches which, by papal sanction, had the right to grant a partial or plenary indulgence one or two days in the year to all believers present at the exhibition of their relics. The castle church at Wittenberg was so empowered. The Curia, of course, was always well paid for granting this right, but it received none of the profit from the indulgences themselves. However, it always shared the profit from the plenary indulgences which were granted upon application to individual spiritual or secular lords for the purpose of assisting some so-called good work — for example, the building or restoration of a church, the erection of an academic building for student monks, the building of bridges, roads, fortifications, dams, or dikes, or even merely for the payment of the debts of some financially embarrassed prelate who owed the Curia a considerable sum and appeared

unable to pay it in any other way. In these cases, from the
end of the fifteenth century onward, the petitioner, besides
paying the very high fees for the drawing up of the necessary
documents, also had to make either a so-called "composition"
(lump payment) or a promise to pay a third, or a half, or
even two-thirds of the profit to the Apostolic Exchequer—
after Leo X (1513-21) it was always half.

Finally, the Curia could not, at least legally, use in any
way it pleased the profits of the many great indulgences
which were published entirely upon its own responsibility
and risk, such as that for the war against the Turks and the
building of St. Peter's in Rome. In these cases, the Curia
was morally and, if the appointed indulgence commissioners
did their duty, factually bound to apply the incoming monies
to the stated purpose. However, most of the commissioners
were not so conscientious, and most of them were themselves
unable to resist the temptation, especially in times of financial pressure, to appropriate such monies for other purposes.
For example, Leo X often assigned indulgence money from
St. Peter's to his own private treasury, for he needed enormous sums for his private pleasures, especially his passion
for cards, which he played every day. Thus there was only
one source of income of this kind which the popes could
rightfully dispose of in any way they pleased—the jubilee
indulgence which was offered every twenty-five years, and
which at that time still brought in very large sums of money.
But, then, neither did they exercise the least restraint in the
expenditure of these sums even when they had pledged
themselves, as Alexander VI had in 1500, to use them for
the war against the Turks. For example, the greatest part
of the jubilee indulgence went to His Holiness' illegitimate
son, Cesare Borgia.

Besides the popes, however, a great number of other
persons always shared in the profits of the jubilee indulgence
and all the other indulgences published at shorter intervals.
Considerable sums were always swallowed up particularly

by the bankers, to whom, from the beginning of the sixteenth century, almost the whole of the organization of the indulgence business had been entrusted. As a rule, the princes and town councils of the territories in which the sacred wares were to be offered for sale also received their share of the profits, for they usually would not permit the commissioners and quaestors to enter until they had been guaranteed a "composition" of from one-sixth to one-half of the proceeds. Occasionally they would even refuse to permit the sale unless the indulgence appeared to serve their own interests or the interests of the territory. Thus they looked upon the indulgences as primarily a financial operation, not a religious institution. Otherwise, in permitting the holy trade, they could not have emphasized the financial side so unabashedly.

But secular rulers were not the only ones who had this conception of indulgences. The "whole world" was of the same opinion, including Luther. But as early as 1515 Luther was troubled more by the evil effects of indulgence preaching and the indulgence traffic upon the religious and moral life of the indulgence purchaser than by the base motives for granting indulgences. He accordingly felt it his duty occasionally to deal with the indulgence question quite plainly from the pulpit. We still possess two of these sermons. The first was delivered on a day that was especially appropriate for such instruction, namely, on the eve of the great indulgence festival in the castle church on October 31, 1516. The indulgence, he already argued here, is nothing more than the remission of the canonical penalties imposed upon the penitent by the priest at confession. However, it is to be feared that it often militates directly against *true* repentance, that is, the inner penitence of the heart which should pervade the whole life of the believer; for one who feels real remorse for his sins does not try to evade punishment, but rather actually longs for punishment. "Nevertheless, I affirm emphatically that the purpose which the pope has in view is good—at least as far as it can be ascertained from the wording of the indulgence Bulls."

Luther expressed himself much more sharply on the same question in the conclusion of his sermon on St. Matthew's Day (February 24), 1517. Here he charged that the wholesale distribution of indulgences results only in causing the people to fight shy of punishment. All too little of the blessings of indulgences is to be observed; rather there is a sense of security from punishment and a tendency to take sin lightly. Hence, he said, indulgences are well named, for they indulge the sinner. At best, such absolution is suitable for people who are weak in faith and who are easily frightened by punishment into doing penance. With the rest it has only the effect of preventing them from ever receiving the true absolution—divine forgiveness of sins—and hence they never truly come to Christ. "O how great are the perils of our times! How fast asleep are the priests! O what worse than Egyptian darkness we are in! How safely and securely we go on living in the midst of the most grievous sins!"

One can understand why Luther "received scant thanks" from Elector Frederick for such sermons, for indulgences, which also played a very great part in the budget of the electoral castle church, could scarcely have been more poorly recommended. But more important for us is the fact that Luther had positively rejected indulgences as early as October 31, 1516. Why was it that even at this date he would have nothing more to do with this means of grace? Because it had the effect of militating directly against true penitence and lulled the believer into a false security. His criticism therefore was not directed against the accompanying external evils, and this distinguished him from all the other opponents of indulgences of his time. On the contrary, his criticism was directed against the dangerous effect of indulgences upon the soul, and hence against the religious motives from which the whole indulgence institution sprang— the fear of purgatorial punishment and the craving for the most tangible and absolutely sure guarantees of salvation possible.

But this craving was after all one of the leit-motifs of Catholic piety. It had led the church at a very early time to declare that the efficacy of its means of salvation was entirely independent of the personal worthiness of the one administering the sacrament as well as the religious state of the recipient (*opus operatum*). This same craving had also induced the church to increase from century to century the number of those means of grace which had a material, objective effect. And this was done to such a degree that finally, at the end of the Middle Ages, it had actually become in the minds of the people a sort of insurance company for salvation. Nowhere, however, does this craving manifest itself so crudely and directly as in the popular belief in indulgences, and by no ecclesiastical institution was it so fully satisfied as by the purely commercial trade in indulgence certificates.

What was the indulgence certificate? It was a spiritual check, always made out in favor of a definite person, irrespective of whether he was among the dead or the living. In case he was dead, it immediately promoted the designated person from purgatory to heaven. In case he was still among the living and had made proper confession to the indulgence priest, it guaranteed him absolution from all temporal penalties for sin previously incurred, and hence also from the corresponding purgatorial punishments. Thereafter, whenever the bearer was troubled by the remembrance of sins committed, he had only to produce this certificate to quiet his conscience. But this certificate always included a letter of confession. It therefore also empowered him from that time forth to be absolved, as frequently as he desired and by any confessor he chose, from all ordinary offenses once in life and once in the article of death, and in addition from the special offenses and penalties legally reserved to the absolution of bishops or the pope.

The certificate therefore represented a title deed to salvation, visible to the eye and absolutely sure if correctly used. Consequently it gave the possessor an exceedingly comfortable sense of security which permitted him henceforth to do what he pleased without any pangs of conscience and actually made the Gospel call to repentance appear ridiculous. As early as 1515, Luther had been most vigorously combating this sense of security (*securitas de salute futura*) because he found it utterly impossible to reconcile it with either his view of God or his conception of salvation. For what did salvation mean to him? It meant to will what God wills. But man can only will what God wills when he has become wholly certain of God's favor (*certitudo salutis*); and again, he can only keep this certainty if he continually seeks God—that is, continually strives to do good. Nowhere did this sense of security, nurtured and encouraged in every way by the church, appear to him in such a gross and crude form as in the conduct of the purchasers of indulgences and the "market traffic" of the indulgence sellers. It is, therefore, no mere accident that it was the indulgence that first made him conscious of that inner opposition to the accepted piety of the church into which he was gradually slipping, and that his formal and at first so moderate criticism of the effects of indulgences provoked such immediate opposition on the part of the staunch representatives of the ancient faith. They immediately perceived that he had touched the vital nerve, not only of the hierarchical system, but also of the whole traditional practice of religion; and so, by their opposition, they forced him to carry his criticism further and further until, at last, before the pope had yet spoken his last word, he realized one day, to his own astonishment, that inwardly he had completely broken with "popery" (letter of February 24, 1520, to Spalatin).

But what caused Luther to reach for the war hatchet at this particular time? In April, 1517, the news spread abroad in Wittenberg that in the district of Magdeburg the Holy

Father Leo was publishing a new indulgence with very extraordinary benefits, for the rebuilding of St. Peter's in Rome. The townsmen and students who could scrape up a few groschen "ran like mad straight for Jüterbog" or Zerbst to procure the new indulgence. Some of Dr. Luther's penitents, who had often had to listen to hard words from him on account of their loose living, also took advantage of this opportunity to buy an indulgence certificate and a confessional letter, since the holy wares could not be offered for sale in Wittenberg because, unfortunately, the Elector Frederick had closed the borders to them. When they returned they told astonishing tales of what they had seen and heard across the border.

Whether John Tetzel, of Pirna—for it was he who, as sub-commissioner general, was the chief manager and spokesman for the new indulgence in the Magdeburg territory—actually uttered all the monstrous statements which the people attributed to him, we must leave undecided, for no one wrote down the sermons which he preached in Jüterbog and Zerbst. The model sermons which he wrote for his subordinates about the same time, and which we still possess, are, however, considerably milder in form, although they do prove that he did not shrink from using the strongest words and expressions in order to attract buyers for the wares entrusted to him. However, as far as their content is concerned, they follow quite the traditional ideas of the indulgence specialists of the time. Even the much-discussed sentences concerning the automatic effect of the indulgence for the dead—which were later compressed into the famous rhyme, "So soon as coin in coffer rings, the soul from purgatory springs"—were not in substance new, but merely an apt practical application of the commonly accepted doctrine, as it had been publicly set forth, for example, only a few years before by Luther's fellow-Augustinian, John Jenser of Paltz, in his *Coelifodina*. Tetzel differed from Jenser only in the boldness with which he drew the consequences for the practical administration of the indulgence from the commonly recognized doctrine, and the undeniable skill with which he translated the heavy formulas of scholastic dogmatics into the drastic language of the people.

In other respects also, Tetzel must have possessed all the characteristics which help to influence the masses. "Physically, he was a large, strong man, eloquent and very bold of speech, sufficiently educated, and his mode of life so-so," that is, neither too strict nor too lax. When he had finished his sermon, he would himself usually go to the indulgence chest and buy a certificate for his father or some other dead person, and when the money tinkled in the chest, he would cry out, "Now I am sure of his salvation; now I need pray for him no longer." In this way he stirred up the people, "especially the sentimental matrons," so that they too came to the chest and bought certificates. In fact, such power did he wield over the masses that on one occasion in Annaberg, Saxony, he prevailed upon the miners who had treated with disrespect the relics of the wandering monks of St. Anthony to follow the Anthonins in a crowd a distance of three miles to do penance for their offense. This he accomplished by threatening that all the mines would cease operations. He was always quick to utter threats. Whoever challenged his authority was immediately discomfited and reminded that he was also an inquisitor. Thus he always knew how to silence all critics, including the clerics who had been injured by the indulgence.

Apparently the unusual talent of this member of the Dominican Monastery of St. Paul in Leipzig for the business of selling indulgences was not discovered until quite late by his superiors. It was not until 1504 that he entered upon this career. After this time he was almost constantly active as an indulgence preacher. In the course of years on his journeys throughout Germany he also acquired a wide commercial experience, which later proved exceedingly useful to his employers. For example, when he could not get rid of his wares at the price demanded, he would immediately have the indulgence cross taken down again. Then after a time he would return and sell the indulgences at a substantially lower price. But he was also quite conscious of his own worth. "I am well known in Italy, in many other kingdoms, and in all Germany," he wrote on January 24, 1517, to a critic who had presumed to remark that he was not a doctor but only an ordinary begging monk. "I have showered my knowledge of theology and canon law upon many German universities and no one has ever treated me with contempt. On the contrary, every one of them, as long as ten years ago, begged me most urgently to take my degree of doctor of theology with them. If I had wanted to, I could have been a doctor before you had ever seen even the outside of a *Corpus Juris Civilis and Canonici.*"

Just because Tetzel thought so highly of himself, he was by no means inclined to sell himself too cheaply. For instance, for his co-operation in the Mainz indulgence enterprise he demanded eighty guldens monthly in cash, besides free transportation and free maintenance for himself and his companions and ten guldens extra for his servant, Veit. Thus this servant received in cash twenty guldens more a year than the highest official of the wealthy town of Leipzig! And for handling the external details of the holy trade he also demanded large sums of the Fuggers, who had financed the venture and allowed the retail sale of the holy wares to be taken care of by their agents. It is very doubtful whether he was always wholly conscientious in handling the large sums of money that passed through his hands. And the assertion that he had had two illegitimate children can scarcely have been fabricated. The restless, wandering life that he led and the great independence that he enjoyed were at all events a very great temptation for him to let himself go rather beyond what was fitting for a monk.

At this time, however, Luther had not yet heard these rumors which were so ruinous to Tetzel's calling. So far, he had heard only various reports concerning his bombastic assertions and fulminations. But these reports were enough to cause Luther the greatest concern because they struck him as being nothing less than blasphemy. His agitation increased when he was assailed with verbal and written inquiries from acquaintances and strangers concerning this blasphemous talk, and when he learned at the same time that the avarice of the priests was now the daily topic of conversation in the taverns and that the pope's power of the keys was the butt of the most vulgar wit. So by letter he implored several "magnates of the church" (that is, bishops) to put a stop to the scandalous conduct of the new indulgence preacher. Some of these great lords received his complaint kindly. Others found it ridiculous. None of them, however, dared to do anything whatsoever about it for fear of the pope and the censures threatened in the Mainz indulgence Bull. He also laid the matter before his juristic colleagues. But they certainly did not encourage him to pick a quarrel with the dangerous preacher-friar. So he worried over this matter during the whole summer without coming to any definite conclusion.

Then, probably in October, long after Tetzel had departed from the Magdeburg territory, there fell into his hands a little book, handsomely adorned with the arms of the archbishop of Mainz, "containing several such articles as Tetzel had set forth and which the quaestors (indulgence sellers) were ordered to preach." Now he found the indulgence actually recommended as a reconciliation of man with God, even in this booklet which was the archbishop's *Instructio Summaria* for indulgence sellers, and read that one could also buy indulgences for the dead without having repented and confessed one's own sins. So he said to himself: Now, as a publicly appointed teacher and doctor, you may not keep silent any longer. Now you *must* seek to prevail upon the archbishop, who doubtless gave his name to this bungling piece of work merely from misunderstanding and youthful inexperience, to suppress this book completely and recommend a different form of preaching to the indulgence sellers. Apparently he thought at first that he would be able to achieve this end by means of a scholarly treatment of the subject of indulgences, and he immediately prepared such a paper. However, he soon realized that the only way that he would be able to change the archbishop's mind would be to exert mild pressure upon him by means of a public announcement.

Since it was just at this time that the great indulgence festival of the castle church (November 1) was approaching, he decided to summarize his scruples, doubts, and critical considerations concerning the indulgence question in the more concise form of a number of theses, to have these theses printed on a placard, and then by means of this placard invite the members of the university to a public disputation on the saving power of indulgences. He proceeded in the manner customary at the time—by posting the theses on a church door. It is probable, however, that he had the premonition that in doing so he was undertaking something which might entangle him in all sorts of serious complications. Therefore, before he set to work, he first went down on his knees to submit the matter to God. Then he wrote the placard and had it printed by John Grünenberg across the street. But he said nothing of his project to any of his friends and colleagues; nor did he show anyone the placard containing the *Ninety-five Theses* on the power and efficacy of indulgences. Thus no one in Wittenberg suspected what he had in mind until, on the eve of All Saints (October 31), 1517, shortly before twelve o'clock noon, accompanied only by his famulus, John Schneider of Eisleben, called Agricola, he walked from the Black Cloister to the castle church, about fifteen minutes away, and there on the door of the north entrance, which had often been used as a bulletin board before the great festivals, he nailed the placard with the *Ninety-five Theses*.

But this was for Luther only a formality which frequently occurred in the university life of the time. He was far more concerned with the fate of the packet which he had sent, probably the same day, to the Magdeburg councilors in Kalbe on the Saale to be delivered to His Electoral Highness, the archbishop of Mainz and Magdeburg. This packet contained, first, a copy of the theses placard; second, a fair copy of the previously completed brief treatise on indulgences; and third, a letter to the archbishop, which is still extant in the original at Stockholm. In this letter, after briefly calling attention to the objectionable passages, he begged the prince for his own good immediately to suppress the *Instructio Summaria* and set Tetzel and his associates right, lest it come to pass that someone should write a polemic against the *Instructio* and the indulgence sellers, which would be highly injurious to His Electoral Highness' prestige. Luther sent a similar petition under the same date to his diocesan, Bishop Jerome Schulze of Brandenburg. The remaining, apparently not very numerous, copies of the placard he retained in his possession. Even Spalatin had not yet received a copy by the ninth of November, for Luther wrote to him, "I do not wish the Elector and his councilors to see my *Theses* before they are seen by the persons for whom they were meant, lest perchance it be thought that I wrote them at the instigation of the Elector, as I hear many have already asserted. It is a good thing that I can even swear an oath that they were published without the knowledge of the Elector." He was alluding to the ill humor that was still prevailing in the electoral court over the severe political defeat which the house of Wettin had suffered through the elevation of the youthful Hohenzollern in the great ecclesiastical domains of Magdeburg, Halberstadt, and Mainz, which surrounded and cut through the Wettin lands. It was quite natural for people who knew neither Luther nor the Elector intimately to jump to the conclusion that the Elector had made use of him to deal a blow at the Hohenzollern prince of fortune. It was very gratifying to Luther, therefore, to be able to repulse such gossip with a clear conscience.

The Ninety-five Theses, from the first to the last letter, confirm this completely unpolitical purpose of Luther's first reformation act. They are a proclamation, moving quite in the conventional forms of the academic style of the time, inspired solely by religious and spiritual views, and following exclusively religious and spiritual tendencies. But just because they were intended to serve a definite, purely practical and pastoral purpose, Luther here set forth his new religious views only so far as this seemed to him necessary to accomplish his immediate purpose. His purpose was a criticism of the Mainz *Instruction* and the Mainz indulgence preacher.

In Theses 1-4 Luther began by setting forth what it means to do penance. "Our Lord and Master Jesus Christ, when He said *Poenitentiam agite*, willed that the whole life of believers should be repentance." (1) Hence true repentance is not an occasional transaction speedily dispatched with the help of a regularly ordained priest, but rather an inner process that continues throughout the whole life of the Christian. *Poenitentia* is connected with *poena*, penalty. It follows that penance and impunity, penance and evasion of punishment, are antithetical, nay, mutually exclusive. He who does penance in the proper way will never cease to punish his old Adam—that is, mortify him with all manner of ascetic discipline.

Theses 5-7 lay down the general principles by which the saving power of papal indulgences is to be judged. It stands to reason that the pope can remit only such penalties as he is also able to impose. However, he cannot remit guilt at all; this God alone can do. But God never remits guilt without at the same time bringing the penitent into subjection to His vicar, the priest. In Theses 8-29 Luther deals particularly with the indulgence for the dead and the assumption on which it is based, the alleged power of the pope over purgatory; while Theses 30-40 deal with indulgences for the living.

With respect to indulgences for the dead, Luther stated that it should first be noted that all penalties, including canonical penalties, are effaced with the death of the penitent, and consequently the pope cannot bestow a remission of punishment upon the poor souls in purgatory. He can help them only by his intercession. But whether, and to what degree, this intercession will be favorably received by God no one knows. Concerning indulgences for the living, Luther again declared that he who truly repents of his sin does not flee from punishment but rather yearns for punishment (40). He who feels such remorse already has forgiveness of his guilt without indulgences (36-37). Those who believe that they can be sure of their salvation because they have purchased an indulgence will fall into eternal damnation together with their teachers (32).

In Theses 41-51 the indulgence and the contributions for the rebuilding of St. Peter's collected by means of the indulgence were then compared with other *good works* of mercy. He who fails to help a poor man in order to buy a letter of pardon does not gain God's favor but only incurs the wrath of God. He who has only enough to live by should not in any case buy an indulgence. Indulgences are useful only if one does not put his trust in them (49). Such trust would be vain even if the pope himself were to stake his own soul upon the salvation of the indulgence purchaser (52).

In Theses 53-80 the preaching of indulgences was then compared with the preaching of the Gospel, or the Word of God. They are enemies of Christ and of the pope who bid the preaching of the Gospel to cease entirely as long as the indulgence is being preached (53-55)—as was actually the case at every indulgence proclamation. In Theses 56-68, over against the doctrine of the treasury of the church is placed the statement that the true treasure of the church is the Holy Gospel of the glory and grace of God (62). Theses 69-80 embody a criticism of the "dreams" of the indulgence preachers. These were the scandalous utterances ascribed to Tetzel.

Finally, in Theses 81-91, Luther marshaled the "shrewd arguments" which the laity presented against the indulgences. Why does not the pope, out of Christian love and mercy, empty purgatory all at once (82)? If those poor souls who have been released by indulgences no longer need our intercessions, and since it is supposed to be wrong to continue to pray for such souls, why is it that the mortuary and anniversary masses endowed for this purpose are permitted to continue, and why are not the countless benefices established for this express purpose suppressed (83)? For money the pope permits the most impious man to release a soul from purgatory; but to do this gratis he refuses (84). Why does the pope, in spite of his enormous wealth, build the church of St. Peter with the money of poor believers and not at his own cost (86)? What is it that the pope bestows upon those who, by perfect contrition, already have a right to full remission (87)? Why does the pope, since by his pardons he is supposed to be seeking only the salvation of souls, suspend all other indulgences, even though these are supposed to have equal efficacy (89)? To repress these doubts of the laity without giving reasons, by force alone, would be to expose the pope and the church to the ridicule of their enemies (90). But these doubts would all be readily resolved, nay, they would not have arisen at all, if the indulgence were preached "rightly," or, as Luther put it, "according to the true intention of the pope."

At this point, Luther was in reality finished with his argument, but he felt the necessity of again briefly emphasizing the contradiction between indulgence-religion and his own religion. This he did in the four solemn concluding theses (92-95). The true Christian yearns to follow his Master through penalties, death, and hell (94). He does not rely upon the security that the indulgence certificate promises him. He sees the sure way to the kingdom of heaven in present tribulations (95).

In these concluding theses, the basic religious motive from which Luther's protest against indulgences sprang is given unusually clear expression—his opposition to an egoistic religiosity which regards exemption from punishment as the highest good. This egoistic piety he contrasts with ethical piety, which sees the greatest evil, not in punishment, but in guilt, and therefore does not crave exemption from punishment but rather forgiveness of guilt and spiritual improvement. Ethical piety, in order to gain both these spiritual blessings, not only voluntarily endures punishment, but actually yearns for it. The source of the power of this new religion is the Gospel of the glory and grace of God and its strongest motive is not a crude egoistic quest for personal happiness but rather the desire to do the will of God and to do the works of mercy for the brethren (41-51).

All of these ideas were familiar to Luther as early as 1513. He had long since been conscious also of the profound contradiction to the vulgar piety of his time which these ideas implied. Therefore the religious-historical significance of the *Theses* does not consist in the fact that they were the first formulation of a new ideal of piety, but rather in the fact that this new idea of piety was here for the first time used publicly in criticism of the prevailing religion and the prevailing practice of religion. But they are not only a religious-historical document, but also a world-historical document of the first rank. When Luther attacked indulgences he involuntarily—nay, against his will—touched the pope's crown and forced the hierarchy to engage with him in a struggle which was to be the signal for half the world to revolt against Rome.

But on Luther's name day (November 11) in 1517, these far-reaching effects of the *Ninety-five Theses* were not at all discernible. The fact that not a soul reported to attend the disputation that was announced apparently did not disturb him particularly. Nor did the croaking of his jurist colleague, Jerome Schurpff, and the persistent silence of the bishops of Brandenburg and Mainz give him any cause for concern. Yet he would have been glad to know what attitude his friends in Erfurt, Nuremberg, and elsewhere were taking toward these new "paradoxes"; for, as he wrote to Scheurl at the beginning of March, 1518, it was upon their judgment that he wished to base his decision as to whether to suppress the *Ninety-five Theses* or publish them in the regular manner. So, on November 11, he began to send out a few copies of the placard. His friends, however, regarded this sending out of the *Theses* quite differently from what he had intended. They circulated the placard wherever and however they could and called it to the attention of the profit-hungry craft of book printers. Probably before the end of November it was reprinted in Leipzig and Magdeburg. In December it appeared in Nuremberg in a German translation, and in Basel in book form. Thus, quite contrary to his intention, "the *Ninety-five Theses* ran throughout all Germany" before Brother Martin could obtain the judgment of professional people upon them; not, it is true, within "almost fourteen days," but within about fourteen weeks, which in itself was most remarkable, considering the means of communication of that time. In some places they were even publicly posted to give everyone convenient opportunity to read them.

Almost everyone who read them praised and extolled the bold Augustinian. The bishop of Merseburg, Prince Adolph of Anhalt, who was very friendly toward Luther, declared as early as November 27 to Councilor Pflugk of Ducal Saxony that he would be glad if they were posted in a great many places so that the poor people who were to buy the new grace might be warned of Tetzel's fraud. The old Franciscan, Fleck, exclaimed with joy when he found them posted in his monastery at Steinlausig (Müldenstein), near

Bitterfeld, "Ho, ho! there is a man who will do something!"
And the great Nuremberg artist, Albrecht Dürer, when he
had read them, immediately expressed his gratitude by sending to the author, who was quite unknown to him, several
of his woodcut books and etchings. But Dürer was certainly
not the only layman who read them. That is sufficiently
proved by the fact that in Nuremberg, already in December,
it was deemed necessary to translate them into German.

How is this astonishing effect of the *Ninety-five Theses*
even among circles of laymen, who were uneducated in
theology and ordinarily had no interest whatsoever in such
products of scholastic erudition, to be explained? Luther
himself answers: "The whole world was complaining about
indulgences, especially Tetzel's article. And since all the
bishops and doctors kept silent, and nobody was willing to
bell the cat—for the inquisitors of Dominican Order had
frightened the whole world with the terror of the stake, and
Tetzel himself had cornered several priests who had objected
to his preaching—Luther was praised as a doctor because at
last someone had come who dared take a stand in the matter." But this sort of praise was not gratifying to him. Why?
Because in general the *Theses* were looked upon and circulated not merely, as he wished, as disputable statements, but
as established truths. "For," he continued, "I myself did not
know what the indulgences were, and the song threatened
to become too high for my voice." This impression, that the
song was becoming too high for him, was indeed shared by
many readers of the *Theses* who were frankly sympathetic.
This is shown by the statement of the Hamburg priest, Albert
Krantz (died December 7, 1517), "You speak the truth, dear
Brother, but you will accomplish nothing. Go into your cell
and say, 'God have mercy upon me.'"

Even in Wittenberg the response was "at first very weak."
Of the professors, only Carlstadt took Luther's part energetically. But in the Black Cloister there was such great
anxiety and alarm over the clamor that now arose for and

against him that the prior, Ulrich Adam, came to him to implore him not to bring the Order into disgrace. "The other Orders, especially the Dominicans," he lamented, "are already dancing for joy that they are not the only ones in disgrace, but that now the Augustinians, too, must burn." He was probably thinking of the burning of the four unfortunate Dominicans who, with the consent of Pope Julius II, had been condemned to death as alleged blasphemers in the so-called Jetzer case in Bern, 1509.

How the situation was regarded at the electoral court, can, unfortunately, no longer be determined. Spalatin apparently was still not wholly without misgivings at the beginning of 1518. The Elector, as was his custom, veiled himself in silence. The fact that on November 10, after frequent reminders, he finally granted to Luther the promised cloth for a new cowl is, of course, no proof that he was in sympathy with Luther's action. Nor can any similar conclusion be drawn from the fact that he authorized Luther (we do not know when) to invite Tetzel to a debate at Wittenberg, offering him safe-conduct, free entry, and free board and lodging. The absurd gossip that he instigated Luther to take this action out of hostility to the Hohenzollerns, he apparently did not take seriously; for he could take it for granted that it was generally known in Berlin and Mainz as well as in Rome that he did not share Luther's views on indulgences, and should the occasion arise, he could give documentary proof of it by pointing to his constant efforts to obtain new indulgences for the Wittenberg castle church and indulgence privileges for his own personal use.

If even Luther's admirers in general expressed such misgivings concerning the consequences of his attack, one will not be surprised that detractors considered that he was already done for and lost. When the *Theses* were submitted to Tetzel by the bishop of Brandenburg in Berlin, probably still in November, he boasted, "Within three weeks I shall have the heretic thrown into the fire and he will go to heaven in a bath cap" (that is, his ashes would be put into a bath cap and thrown into the water). Equally kindly judgments began to be uttered by increasing numbers of the brethren of Tetzel's Order, the Dominicans who were so powerful because of their connections with the Curia and the House of Hohenzollern and because of their distinguished position in the "sister universities" of Leipzig and Frankfurt on the Oder. Even the old Erfurt Occamists—above all the prince of the Modernists, Jodocus Trutvetter, whom Luther still warmly admired—were now completely finished with Brother Martin, whom they once so highly esteemed, although they did not cry out for the stake.

In view of this conflict of opinions and this, to him, very distressing lack of understanding of the real purpose of the *Theses* which was evident among his friends, Luther felt the urgent necessity of preparing an authentic statement to expound the true meaning of his "paradoxes." About the beginning of February, 1518, he was able to submit these explanations of the *Ninety-five Theses,* as he called them (*Resolutiones disputationum de indulgentiarum virtute*), to his diocesan, Bishop Schulze of Brandenburg, with the request that he ruthlessly strike out everything in them that appeared offensive to him; nay, if he pleased, even throw the whole manuscript into the fire. For "I know that Christ does not need me. He will show His church what is good for her without me. Nothing is so difficult to state as the true teaching of the church, especially when one is so grievous a sinner as I am." He therefore wished everything in the enclosed pages to be regarded merely as provisional, disputable opinions, and not as the definite conclusions of his investigation of the indulgence question.

In the work itself he again took every opportunity to emphasize his absolute submission to the directions of the Holy See. The thesis, "The indulgence commissioners are to be admitted with all reverence" (69), he still allowed to pass without reservation; "for," he wrote, "one must reverently yield to the papal power in all things." But, as Scripture proof for this, he cited not the famous passages concerning the pre-eminence of St. Peter over the other apostles, but rather the passage in Romans 13:1, which is applicable to any kind of authority, "Let every soul be in subjection to the higher powers." Moreover he limited papal power to various external matters. He explicitly excluded the conscience of the believer from this power of the pope. And already he dared to declare frankly and freely that an unjust anathema of the pope can have no effect whatsoever upon the relation of a believer to God, and consequently need not disturb anyone's inner life. True, one must offer resistance to such acts of injustice, but as with any kind of injustice, one must bear them patiently in accord with the command of Christ, "Resist not evil." If this injunction were merely a counsel, as was asserted, and not an absolutely obligatory command, then it would certainly be permissible to oppose the indulgence preachers just as ruthlessly as the Turks. But it is a command, not merely a counsel, and therefore one must submit outwardly to these persons, without, however, in any way approving their speech and actions, for that would be contrary to conscience.

In connection with Thesis 22, Luther incidentally made the very frank statement that "at the time of Gregory the Great the Roman Church did not yet possess sovereign power over all other churches, at least not over the Greek Church." He also fearlessly characterized as an "invention worthy of hell" the famous medieval doctrine of the two swords, which was the basis of the teaching that Christ had entrusted to the pope lordship not only over the church but also over the kingdoms of the world. By the same right, he stated, it could be maintained that the pope had received two keys from Christ, one for the riches of heaven, the so-called "treasure of good works," the other for the riches of earth.

This led Luther to speak of the customary procedure against heretics. It is true, he wrote, that burning at the

stake is very convenient, but it is unquestionably contrary
to the will of the Holy Spirit, for the apostle says explicitly
that there must be sects, and the Gospel says that tares
should be allowed to grow until the harvest. Hence it is not
surprising that he should go on to speak, not of the power
of priests over souls, but only of the service of priests to
souls. He declared positively that Christ did not wish "that
the salvation of mankind should rest in the hands and power
of one man." When the priest absolves a penitent, he functions not as a judge in the place of God; he only declares to
the penitent in a special way the forgiveness promised by
God for the comforting of his conscience. However, this
promise must not be trusted because of the pope or the
priest, for then it could not be relied upon if the priest were
an unworthy man. The promise must be believed simply
because it has come from God. But it must be trusted, for
only he who trusts the promise has true forgiveness, in like
manner as the benefits of Baptism and the Lord's Supper
are received only by those who receive them in faith. The
assertion that the sacraments of the new covenant of themselves justify a man in so far as he does not intentionally
harden himself against their operation is not only false but
heretical. This meant the overthrow of the foundation of
the whole traditional view of the sacraments.

With regard to the sacrament of confession in particular,
Luther rejected here, as he had already done in his lectures
on Hebrews, the traditional custom of requiring of the
penitent a complete enumeration of all his offenses. This,
he stated, not only demands of the penitent the impossible,
but, if he takes the requirement seriously, actually drives him
to despair. Instead of putting him upon the rack in such
a manner and torturing him with the terror of hell and
purgatory, one ought rather to hold before him the benefac-
tions of God and Christ; "then the tears will flow, then he
will begin to hate and despise himself, but without being
driven to despair or falling into the delusion, artificially

fostered in the people by the scholars, that the sinner must always first earn divine forgiveness by his own contrition and outward works of penance." This is the penitence that Christ demands; sacramental penance, ecclesiastical, confessional penance, He did not command. On the contrary, it was first introduced by the pope and the church—at least its third part, the so-called "satisfaction." It is therefore not unalterable and can be reformed at will by the church. Naturally it does not follow that one can observe it or not as one pleases. Respect for the commands and ordinances of the church in such outward matters is just as much a duty as respect for the ordinances of every other authority.

Regarding indulgences in particular, Luther still persisted in his judgment that an indulgence is only a remission of canonical penalties imposed by the priest. It is therefore something of very small value, even of doubtful value, he wrote, for whoever purchases such a remission thereby proves that he has not repented in earnest. On one decisive point in this particular question, however, he already went beyond the *Ninety-five Theses*. The treasure of the church, he said, is Christ alone. There are no merits of the saints, for no saint ever completely fulfilled the commands of God, to say nothing of doing more. We can speak of merit only in reference to Christ. But that merit is not in the dispensation of the church, but in God's alone.

From all these abuses which he had pointed out in the preaching and practice of the church of his day, Luther finally drew a conclusion. *"The Church needs reformation.* This reformation is not, however, the concern of the pope alone, nor the concern of the cardinals; that was plainly shown by the result of the last council [the Fifth Lateran Council of 1512-17]. It is rather the concern of the *whole [Christian] world,* or much more, of God. When it will come *He* alone knows. Meanwhile, it is our task to expose the notorious evil conditions, especially the *servitude* into which the power of the keys has fallen on account of greed for possessions and honor. The Abyss [Antichrist] has already begun his attack and it is not our affair to hold him back."

The *Resolutions* are thus by no means merely an explanation of the *Ninety-five Theses*. They constitute, rather, an independent, reform program of basic importance. The presentation is lively, but is still governed by the desire to come to an agreement with the representatives of the traditional doctrine and practice. It is only in the polemical excursuses against the theses of Tetzel and Wimpina, which were inserted just before printing, that Luther became really coarse and vehement. The document is also highly noteworthy as a scholarly performance. It shows that he had studied with the greatest diligence and success, not only the special literature on the indulgence question, but also canon law, the church fathers, and the chief works on church history. But in its outward plan, despite its numerous quotations from Erasmus' collection of proverbs (*Adagia*), it is still a genuinely scholastic product. Consequently, as he himself admitted, it was hardly pleasant reading for humanistically educated readers.

The bishop of Brandenburg informed Luther, apparently about the end of February, that he was at the time not in a position to examine the manuscript. But, in the meantime, Luther had become so disgusted with his *Theses* and the misunderstanding that they had aroused that he decided to replace and supplant them by a little work in the German language in which he could at the same time warn the people against the false use of indulgences. However, before he had found time to do this, about the middle of March, he received two sharp criticisms of the *Ninety-five Theses*: the counter-theses of Tetzel-Wimpina, and the *Obelisks*, or manuscript glosses, of Dr. Eck of Ingolstadt. The first gave him little offense, but the second was a very disagreeable surprise to him, for it was only in the preceding year that Eck had by correspondence formed a friendship with him through the good offices of Scheurl. In spite of this, Eck now corrected him severely. In a cool, superior tone, Eck treated him as an ignorant, simple-minded, presumptuous, and insolent person. Indeed, he indirectly cast the suspicion that Luther was already a Hussite and a heretic. At first Luther was resolved patiently to swallow this "hellish dose." But his friends prevailed upon him to reply immediately to Eck *privatim*, that is, only by letter. Nevertheless, he considered it best for the present to withhold this reply, the so-called *Asterisks*, and first write the popular tract on indulgences which had been in his mind for several weeks.

This tract appeared before the end of March under the somewhat misleading title, *Sermon on Indulgences and Grace*. It is not a sermon, but a brief summary, in twenty pithy theses, of his study of the indulgence question, in which he had made considerable progress while he was working on the *Resolutions*. The Holy Scriptures, he maintained, require of the sinner only a sincere, genuine repentance, as well as the resolution henceforth to bear the cross of Christ and to do the true works of satisfaction. Such works are, first, all kinds of works which "belong to the soul, such as prayer and the reading, meditating, hearing, and preaching of God's Word"; second, all kinds of work which minister to the mortification of the old Adam; and finally, all sorts of works of love and mercy toward one's neighbor. It is true that God also occasionally inflicts upon the sinner all manner of punishments of a temporal sort, but no man, not even the pope, has the power to remit these punishments. Indulgences are only a remission of canonical penalties. "My will, my prayer, my advice is that no one buy indulgences any more, for it is neither meritorious nor a work of obedience, but, on the contrary, a temptation to throw off due obedience. Whether the poor souls can be released from purgatory by means of indulgences, I do not know, but I do not believe it. Nor has the church as yet decided anything concerning it. In any case, you will be quite safe if you pray for her and work for her in other ways. It bothers me very little that those whose profit is curtailed by these truths revile me as a heretic. Those who behave thus only prove that they are ignorant numbskulls who have never even smelled the Bible, nor ever read the church fathers, and have never understood their own teachers; for if they had, they would know that no one should be called a heretic until he has been heard and convicted of his error."

The tract had scarcely left the press when, to his surprise, Luther was informed that Abbot Valentine of Lehnin wished to speak with him. The prelate delivered to him a very gracious letter from the bishop of Brandenburg, in which he informed him that he had found no error in the *Resolutions* and that they were "good Catholic"; in fact, that he himself thoroughly condemned the indiscreet and presumptuous manner of the new indulgence preacher. Nevertheless, he must beg him to keep silent for a while and not to publish anything new on the indulgence question. The abbot confirmed this instruction verbally, and added that the bishop also wished the recently published *Sermon* to be withdrawn from the market. Brother Martin was so delighted with this altogether unexpected visit and the still less expected amiability of the bishop that he immediately promised everything that was asked of him. On the other hand, this hardly expected complaisance on the part of the professor, who had already been decried for months as a heretic, made such a good impression on the bishop that, before Easter (April 4), he released him from his promise, that is, definitely permitted him to allow the *Sermon* to circulate and to have the *Resolutions* finally put into print. One can only conclude from this that Herr Jerome Schulze did not belong to the intelligentsia of his profession. For with any degree of practical knowledge and attention he must have seen at the first glance at the *Sermon* and the *Resolutions* that Luther no longer stood upon the ground of Catholic doctrine. It must be said, however, that he was primarily a jurist and not a theologian, and probably did not think it necessary to study the two writings thoroughly; perhaps, indeed, he had not read them at all.

Luther was naturally very well pleased with this decision and he now published, apparently in Latin and German at the same time, a public declaration or protestation, in which he expressly acknowledged the *Sermon* and declared that he had not been condemned, either by his university or by his secular and spiritual superiors, but that he had been maliciously defamed as a heretic only by a few insolent and hasty people. He begged these either to show him where he was wrong or to await the judgment of God and His church. "I am not so rash as to prefer my own opinion to all others; but I am also not so foolish as to want to place God's Word beneath the fables of men."

Henceforth the *Sermon* could go unhindered on its way, and it had such immediate success that the purpose which Luther had in view in publishing it, the displacement of the *Theses* from the book market, was actually achieved. Whereas there is not a single extant copy of the first edition of the theses placard, and only three extant copies of two later reprints, there are still extant dozens of copies of the original edition of the *Sermon*, as well as copies of the twelve editions which appeared during the year 1518 in Wittenberg, Leipzig, Augsburg, Nuremberg, and Basel. This is an evidence of the eagerness with which the tract was sought and read, especially in the south, where the towns were numerous.

The *Sermon* was the first of Luther's writings to reach the "people" in south and central Germany. That is to say, it reached those in the towns, and likely to some extent also in the country, who were unfamiliar with Latin. This had the effect of creating a great demand for the other writings which poured from his untiring pen during these weeks, such as the brief exposition of the Ten Commandments, in which he utilized his new religious views for the under standing of this part of the catechism which was so much used during Lent as a mirror for confession; the Latin *Ser-*

mon on Penance, in which he briefly set forth his new view of penance; and the Latin *Sermon* on worthy preparation for the Lord's Supper. The last-named is especially noteworthy because here for the first time he declared that a man is not truly prepared for the Lord's Supper when he thinks himself worthy because he has confessed his mortal sins, but rather when he feels himself altogether unworthy of such a blessing because he is so deeply conscious of his sins and deficiencies and approaches the altar only in humble trust in the promise of God. Luther did not mean that the custom of confessing before going to the Lord's Supper should be abolished; but he was of the opinion that true confession does not begin until after Communion, when man has experienced the goodness of God. He had dictated these same thoughts to his students a short time before in his lectures on the Epistle to the Hebrews. He thus attached the greatest importance to them.

Even at this time, therefore, Luther was striving to make his new view of penance fruitful in the practical, pastoral work of the confessional and to break the way for necessary reforms in this sphere, which appeared to him to be especially in need of reforms. But in the meantime there had begun a great struggle over the cause he represented. To this day it has not reached its end.

CHAPTER XIII

FIRST DENUNCIATIONS IN ROME

It appears that a fairly long time elapsed before Luther's memorial to Archbishop Albrecht of October 31, 1517, reached the hands of the court councilors of Magdeburg in Kalbe on the Saale, for it was not until November 17 that it was opened by them and perhaps immediately forwarded to Albrecht's residence in Aschaffenburg on the Main. There the archbishop laid it before his "councilors and advisers" who were present at the time, about the end of November. The chief article, the *Ninety-five Theses,* he also submitted to the jurists and theologians of the University of Mainz. His advisers recommended that he speedily dispatch the matter to His Papal Holiness, but at the same time prohibit the presumptuous monk from making any further declarations on the indulgence question (*processus inhibitorius*). The first proposal quite suited Albrecht's inclinations. Before December 13 he had already delivered the necessary communications to the Curia. In a letter on December 13 he informed the Magdeburg councilors in Kalbe of this action and at the same time suggested to them that the enclosed *processus inhibitorius,* which had been drawn up in the meantime by his advisers in Aschaffenburg, be "delivered to Luther by Herr Tetzel." He added, however, that he was not at all anxious to burden himself with this affair and incur the enmity of the Augustinian Order. The Magdeburg councilors quite correctly concluded from this that His Grace did not wish to be annoyed any further with the matter, and they therefore contented themselves with putting the documents in the archives. Thus the responsible head of the Mainz indulgence enterprise, as was said in the sixteenth century, wriggled out of his responsibility. He left it to the

Curia to settle this not quite safe affair. What became of
"Herr Tetzel" was immaterial to him.

Albrecht's memorial was forwarded to Rome by the usual
means of communication. It could scarcely have reached
there very much before Christmas. It consisted chiefly of a
composition of the Mainz chancellery in which Luther was
denounced to the pope—not, it is true, for heresy, but for
spreading new doctrines. As documents in support of this
denunciation, there were enclosed (1) "the Article" (what
is meant by this we do not know), (2) the *Ninety-five
Theses,* and (3) the "Treatise," that is, the treatise on indulgences written by Luther before he wrote the *Theses*
and which is still extant. Pope Leo X's leading minister,
Cardinal Julian de Medici, apparently considered it sufficient to have the presumptuous friar warned by the highest authority of the Augustinian Order, and on February 3,
1518, he wrote in this vein to Gabriel della Volta, called
Venetus, the promagistrate of the Order. What Volta did
thereafter we do not know. That he demanded a formal
recantation from Luther through Staupitz and that he required the chapter of the Saxon Congregation at its meeting
in Heidelberg at the end of April, 1518, to surrender the
culprit to Rome is a pure supposition. If he actually did
warn the "presumptuous" brother through Staupitz—and this
has no confirmation whatsoever in any of Luther's own utterances—the warning must have been so mildly expressed that
Luther could not have interpreted it as in any sense an
attempt to make him change his mind.

In the meantime, however, an opponent had long since
entered the lists who was determined to destroy him. This
was John Tetzel. In January, 1518, a chapter of the Saxon
Province of the Dominican Order met at Frankfurt on the
Oder, which was to be opened with the customary disputation. This time the chief role was intended for Tetzel, and
on January 20, in the presence of about three hundred
"fathers," he debated 106 theses, which, as was generally

the procedure in those days, had been prepared for him by a professor of the local university, Dr. Conrad Koch, called Wimpina. Naturally, they were all directed against Luther's *Ninety-five Theses*. But at Frankfurt there was no intention to let the matter rest with this demonstration for the benefit of Brother Tetzel, one of the recognized notables of the Saxon Province. They also discussed at great length the question of how the shameless Wittenberg heretic could be brought to book, and since they were unaware of the measures taken by the archbishop of Mainz, they finally decided formally to denounce Luther in Rome for suspicion of heresy. This denunciation carried far more weight than the denunciation of the archbishop of Mainz. A mere suspicion of heresy was enough to institute canonical proceedings for heresy against anyone, but especially when this denunciation came from the Saxon Dominicans, for the closest confidant of Cardinal Medici, Nicholas von Schönberg, was a Saxon and a Dominican. Moreover, the most influential theologian of the Curia, Cardinal Cajetan, was a member of the Order, and, holding the office of general, he was especially interested and obligated to defend the Order against every libel. How and when this second denunciation reached Rome we do not know. It is certain only that now the Saxon Dominicans were already exultantly proclaiming from their pulpits that Luther would end up at the stake within two weeks or a month. They also sought in every way to bring the University of Wittenberg into disrepute and they did not leave Elector Frederick himself unmolested.

In March Tetzel ventured a new attack. He sent a bookseller from Halle to Wittenberg with hundreds of copies of his Frankfurt theses in order to agitate underhandedly against Luther. But when the poor fellow came to Wittenberg on March 17, the students seized his entire stock and at two o'clock in the afternoon they set up a mock auto-da-fé, at which they burned about eight hundred copies of the theses. Luther was greatly angered by this foolish prank.

He rightly judged that it only made his situation more dangerous. In the meantime, however, Spalatin had already been successful in making such strong representations to the Elector concerning this danger and the harm which the university would suffer from every insult directed against the adherents of "the solid theology," that the Elector had formally taken Luther and Carlstadt under his protection. Nevertheless, Frederick was not at all pleased that, just at this juncture, Luther was about to leave Wittenberg for several weeks to attend the chapter of his Congregation in Heidelberg. How easy it would be for the hostile Dominicans to seize him on the way and by some means or other drag him off to Rome! Spalatin therefore induced the Elector to instruct Staupitz not to delay or detain Luther in Heidelberg, but to send him back to Wittenberg as soon as possible. In addition he provided Luther with a whole series of exceptionally valuable credentials (letters of introduction) addressed to the electoral officials and the princes through whose territories he would pass on the journey to Heidelberg.

CHAPTER XIV

HEIDELBERG DISPUTATION AND BROKEN TIES

On April 11, 1518, Luther left Wittenberg with Brother Leonard Beier as *socius itinerarius,* as the Rule of the Order required. The journey took him first through Bitterfeld to Leipzig, from there through Weissenfels, Saalfeld, Gräfenthal, and Judenbach to Coburg. The wanderers arrived at Coburg, very weary, on the evening of April 15. That same evening Luther informed Spalatin, to the latter's great relief, that no one had molested him on the way. Only in Weissenfels, the local priest, a Wittenberg alumnus, recognized him and kindly entertained him. In Judenbach he had met by chance the electoral councilor, Degenhard Pfeffinger, and induced him to pay the bill of ten groschen apiece for the noon meal, not only for himself but for his two companions. "You know," he added, "that I am glad to make such rich people poorer, especially when they are my friends. The Elector's steward shall surely have to pay for us here too, but I have not yet seen him, because he has gone to the castle. I have fully paid for the sin of coming on foot and, therefore, need no indulgence for it. Nowhere could we find a wagon which would take us along. And so I must continue to render contrition, penance, and satisfaction."

On Misericordias Domini Sunday (April 18) he "finally," as he wrote, reached Würzburg and that evening presented his credentials to the reigning prince, Bishop Lorenz. The prince immediately invited him to his castle, Marienburg, high up over the city. He was so well pleased with Luther that shortly before his death (February, 1519), he wrote to the Elector that he should not allow that devout man, Dr. Martinus, to be taken away, for an injustice was being done to him. He at once promised to have him accompanied to

Heidelberg at his expense. But Luther declined this offer with thanks. He had met several of his brethren, among them John Lang, of Erfurt, in the Augustinian monastery where he had lodged, and with them he could continue the journey by wagon.

On April 21 or 22 he safely reached the Augustinian monastery in Heidelberg, and shortly afterward, on April 25, the chapter of the Congregation was opened according to statute by Staupitz. What Staupitz thought of the "Lutheran alarm" is sufficiently indicated by the fact that he conferred upon Luther the honorable task of presiding over the customary public disputation in the great hall of the monastery with the Wittenberg friar, Leonard Beier, as the respondent, and also of furnishing the necessary theses. Indulgences are nowhere mentioned in these theses. Nor did Luther say a word in them concerning his new views of penance. They treat only of original sin, sin, grace, free will, and faith; in particular, however, of the inability of man to will the good by his own reason and strength. Thus, like the ninety-seven theses of September 4, 1517, they were directed primarily against the Occamists, who were represented in the audience not only in goodly numbers but also with some distinction. Representing the Erfurt Occamists, there appeared his old teacher, Usingen, who had entered the Black Cloister there in 1512. In order to provoke the Occamists, he had also drawn up twelve philosophical theses, in which he directed his attack particularly against the metaphysics of Aristotle and played off Pythagoras, Anaxagoras, Parmenides, and, above all, Plato, against Aristotle. Hence, at this time he apparently felt the necessity of freeing himself altogether from Aristotle in metaphysics. But he never continued these studies later, being satisfied with this single attempt. The Heidelberg professors of theology who participated in the disputation treated him with friendliness and respect, although they were not in agreement with his teachings. Only the fifth and youngest of them, George Schwarz of Löwenstein, could not conceal his annoyance, and consequently only excited general laughter when at one point he cried out angrily, "If the peasants heard this, they would stone you to death."

The younger listeners, however, were actually inspired by the strange Saxon professor. On May 1 the young Alsatian Dominican, Martin Bucer of Schlettstadt, the most gifted of them, wrote to his bosom friend, Beatus Rhenanus: "Though our chief men refuted him with all their might, their wiles were not able to make him move an inch from his propositions. His charm in responding is amazing, his patience in listening is incomparable. His acuteness reminds one of the method of St. Paul. With answers that are as brief as they are acute, drawn from the Holy Scriptures, he overcomes everyone with admiration. On the next day (April 26) I had a confidential conference with him alone and afterward shared his meal with him, which was moderate though seasoned with delicious conversation. Whatever I asked him, he explained to me most lucidly. He is quite in agreement with Erasmus. But he surpasses him in that what Erasmus only insinuates, he teaches openly and freely. Would that I had time to write you more of this. He is the one who put an end to the authority of Scholasticism in Wittenberg and who brought it about that the Greek language, Jerome, Augustine, and Paul are taught there publicly."

Just as deep and powerful was the impression of the Saxon monk upon the two young Swabians, John Brenz and Theodore Billican, who also sought a personal conference with him after the disputation. "As Christ, when the Jews rejected Him, went over to the Gentiles," Luther wrote shortly after to Spalatin in grateful reminiscence of these youths, "so I now confidently hope that the true theology of Christ, which those men who have grown old in their sophistical opinions [the Erfurt Occamists] reject, will pass over to the younger generation." But the students were not the only ones to welcome him in the beautiful town on the Neckar.

The younger brother of Elector Ludwig V, Count Palatine Wolfgang Wilhelm, who had studied in Wittenberg in the summer of 1515, and his former tutor, Jacob Simler, the friend of the famous Jacob Wimpfeling, also received him with great friendliness. The count even invited him, with Staupitz and Lang, to a meal, and then showed them the ornaments of the electoral chapel, the armory, and all the other objects of interest of this "truly royal castle."

It goes without saying that during these days Luther also discussed with the superiors of the Congregation his quarrel with Tetzel and his fellows. When in June he sent to Staupitz his *Resolutions* and a respectful letter to be forwarded to Pope Leo X, it was undoubtedly in pursuance of an agreement which he had reached with Staupitz in Heidelberg. But the chapter did not touch officially upon his affair. The fact that he was relieved of his office as district vicar had nothing whatsoever to do with this affair. It occurred simply because his term of office had expired.

At the beginning of May he traveled homeward again, and this time, on Staupitz' orders, he went by wagon. The Nuremberg brethren took him as far as Würzburg, and from there the Erfurt brethren took him to Erfurt. On the evening of May 8 he sought out his old teacher, Jodocus Trutvetter; but hearing that the old gentleman was not well, he endeavored in a letter which he wrote on May 9 to refute the grave accusations which Trutvetter had raised against him. Nevertheless, he subsequently had a conversation with his teacher, whom he still loved and respected highly, which at least moved Trutvetter to the admission that he could not prove his own position nor refute Luther's. He had already engaged in some warm theologizing with Usingen on the journey from Würzburg to Erfurt, but had succeeded only in leaving the old man pensive and dazed. He, of course, had even less success with men like John Nathin. In order to overcome this opposition, he would gladly have entered into a public disputation in Erfurt also, but he had to forgo this

on account of the three days of fasting and prayer before
Ascension Day. So on May 11 or 12 he separated from his
old teachers with the impression that he had nothing more
to expect from these old men, but must set all his hopes
upon the younger generation. He received still another
fulminating letter from Trutvetter in June, which made any
further intercourse impossible. When the long-ailing old
man died ten months later, on May 9, 1519, Luther felt to
his sorrow that he had unwittingly hastened his death. So
keenly had the old man grieved over the presumptuous and
contemptuous treatment which, in his opinion, Luther had
inflicted upon the scholastic theology! As late as the beginning of 1521, Luther still continued to send occasional greetings to Usingen and Nathin through Lang. But that was no
more than a courteous gesture. In actual fact, he had had
no relations with the Erfurt of his youth since these days in
May (1518). It was therefore hardly a matter of surprise
to him later that Usingen and Nathin, even in their old age,
joined the ranks of his most determined foes.

CHAPTER XV

FINAL RECKONING WITH TETZEL

About May 12, 1518, Luther continued his journey to Eisleben with the Eisleben friars, and from there, on May 14, went on to Wittenberg at their expense. On May 15, he arrived at the Black Cloister, fresher and, as his friends thought, even stronger and fatter (*"habitior et corpulentior"*) than when he had left four weeks before. On the morning of May 16 he again mounted the pulpit of the castle church to preach the Wittenbergers a sermon on the power of excommunication, which was later to play an important part in the proceedings against him. On May 19 he sent a copy of the long-completed *Asterisks* to Eck, who in the meantime had sought to renew friendly relations with him. At the same time he used this opportunity to read the haughty Ingolstadt professor a downright lecture for his double-dealing conduct. Shortly before, on May 9, Carlstadt, whom he had shown Eck's *Obelisks*, had published 406 theses in which he had severely attacked Eck without Luther's knowledge and against his wish. He appreciated that Eck could not suffer this attack in silence and wrote him to this effect; but he begged him, nevertheless, seeing that he had been the first to provoke the Wittenberger, not to treat Carlstadt too harshly. Eck received this letter in good spirit. It now appeared that peace with him had been quite restored.

But Luther was more concerned with two literary works, which he had apparently begun to write before his departure for Heidelberg, than with this still comparatively harmless skirmish between Ingolstadt and Wittenberg. These two works were the Latin revision of his sermons on the Ten Commandments and the second edition of the *Theologia Deutsch*. The former left the press on July 20 and immediately was twice reprinted. The latter appeared on June 4, with the famous preface which has kept the work of this old Frankfurt saint in circulation up to the present time, despite the fact that it is obviously dictated by the effort to play up the "German theologian" as an exponent of the new Wittenberg theology against Tetzel and his like, whereas their theology was in reality much closer to that of the "German theologian" than Luther's. Luther himself, of course, never quite understood this, but as early as 1520 he had already given up his admiration for the "German theologian" and Tauler. From that time onward he never once quoted or recommended either of them.

At the same time Luther was also putting finishing touches on the work which, on Staupitz' advice, he was to present to Pope Leo X as a proof of his orthodoxy and loyalty to the Holy See—the *Resolutions*. On May 30 he was able to send a fair copy, accompanied by a letter to the pope, to Staupitz for forwarding. We still possess one page of the rough draft of this letter written in his own hand, which sheds an interesting light upon the state of his mind at this time. In the draft he writes that he turned to the pope only in order to show the German inquisitors (that is, Tetzel and his fellow-Dominicans) that he was not afraid of them. "I know that man can think of nothing unless it be given to him from above. But least of all can that be said of the pope, of whom it is written: The king's heart is in the hand of the Lord. Therefore, Holy Father, I lay my work at your feet in all confidence. Whatever your decision may be, it will in any case have its origin in Jesus, without whom you cannot propose or speak anything. If you condemn my book to be burned, I will say: As it has pleased the Lord, so it has happened. If you command that it be preserved, I will say: Praise be to God! I lose nothing if it is burned, and I gain nothing if it is not burned. Christ does not need me. He can raise up children from the very stones and destroy mountains in the twinkling of an eye. This, my faith in

my Lord Jesus Christ, is enough for me. May He, the Lord,
preserve you and lead you, not according to your pleasure
or that of any other man, but according to *His* will, which
alone is good and to be praised eternally. Amen."

In the fair copy the long section dealing with the insolent
boasting and threatening of the German inquisitors, primarily Tetzel, with the name and the power of the pope,
has been entirely omitted. However, instead of the declaration that it was immaterial to him what the pope did with
his book, the fair copy now reads: *"For my own protection
I let my book go out under the protection of your name,
Holy Father,* so that all well-meaning readers may know
with what pure intentions I have sought to fathom the nature
of ecclesiastical power and what reverence I hold toward
the power of the keys. If I were as they describe me, the
illustrious Elector Frederick of Saxony certainly would not
suffer such a pestiferous boil in his university, for he is probably the greatest zealot for Catholic truth there is at the present time. Nor would the exceedingly intelligent and very diligent men of this university have tolerated me. Therefore,
Most Holy Father, I cast myself at your feet with all that I
am and possess. Raise me up or slay me, summon me hither
or thither, approve me or reprove me as you please! I will
listen to your voice as the voice of Christ reigning and
speaking in you. If I have deserved death, I shall not refuse
to die. For the earth is the Lord's and the fullness thereof;
blessed be He forever. Amen."

Thus in the fair copy he completely changed the conclusion of the letter. All expressions which were peculiarly in-
dicative of his state of mind during these days he struck out
and substituted phrases expressed in the conventional,
curialistic style. Thus the whole letter, instead of being an
open avowal of his inner independence of all human authorities, has now become a profession of his absolute subjection
to the authority of the pope. Yet he permitted to remain
one sentence which is altogether at odds with the new con-

clusion: "I cannot recant." Can we make him alone responsible for these changes which are so completely contradictory to the convictions which he elsewhere expressed so frankly and freely? No! The reference to the Catholic zeal of the Elector, which is altogether lacking in the first draft, betrays the hand of a courtier who was more familiar with the style of the Curia than was Luther. This courtier can have been none other than his friend Spalatin, who on later occasions was frequently obliged, generally at the command of the Elector, to cast into court language such high official letters and documents before they were forwarded. This is not to say that the Elector already had a hand in the matter in this instance. It is quite possible that Spalatin rendered him this friendly service on his own risk and responsibility.

Apparently on the same day (June 4) on which he delivered the *Resolutions* to Master Grünenberg, who was now constantly busy with the printing of his works, two new manifestoes fluttered into his study. Both of them compelled him to take up his pen again. They were Tetzel's fifty new theses, which openly threatened, not only him, but also the Elector, with the stake and the refutation of the *Sermon on Indulgences and Grace,* which the angry inquisitor had written at the same time. In one or two days he hastily set down on paper a refutation of this refutation, which appeared in print in the second or third week of June under the title, *Freedom of Preaching the Sermon on Papal Indulgences and Grace.* It immediately had such a rapid sale that Grünenberg was obliged to publish it in a second greatly enlarged edition at the beginning of July. In substance it contained hardly anything new. But the tone is altogether different from that of Luther's previous writings. Now for the first time he fought with a peasant's ax and, as he put it, "played" with this enemy, who in his opinion had so exposed himself to ridicule that he was no longer worthy of being taken quite seriously.

At the very beginning of the work Luther wrote that this

"poet" apparently had a superabundance of time and paper, but obviously knew of no better use to make of it than to attack the truth with foul words. "I cast his useless empty insults like paper flowers and dry leaves to the blessed winds, for they have more time for such stuff than I have. I shall deal only with the cornerstones of his house of cards." "When he cites such thousands of scholastic teachers, he puts too high a value on these worthless counters. If he had thought the matter over carefully, he would have found not many more than three, for the others are only yes-men and imitators anyhow." "If it were only me that he mistreated, I would gladly suffer it . . . but it is by no means to be borne when he treats the Scriptures, our consolation, as a sow does a sack of oat-straw." He and his henchmen, wrote Luther, are daily inventing new words for us, *claves excellentiae, claves auctoritatis, claves ministrabiles.* And what for? Ultimately in order to "empty our purses and coffers and, after that, to unlock hell and shut up heaven." "They say that he who buys an indulgence does better than he who gives alms to a poor man in extreme need. God help us, and they call themselves teachers of Christian people! In truth, now we no longer need to be alarmed when we hear how the Turks are desecrating our churches and the cross of Christ. We have in our midst Turks a hundred times more wicked, who are utterly destroying our one and only sanctuary, the Word of God. . . . . If a Christian man is not to help another before he is in extreme need, then Christian love is worth less than the friendship that exists among beasts."

"I do not reject the scholastics entirely, for they have done their best, but only those opinions of theirs which have not been drawn from the Scriptures. And I do it chiefly for the sake of the people, whom they lead, not to things in which they have the support of Scripture and reason, but into the subject of indulgences, where the support is weakest and most wanting." "At last the storm is about my ears and I am called an arch-heretic, heretic, apostate, false teacher,

blasphemer, and so on. . . . When such people, who do not
know the Bible and who understand neither Latin nor German, insult me with such extreme slander, I feel as if a brute
ass were braying at me." "When he offers a club, water, and
fire to prove his doctrine, I, poor brother, cannot forbid him.
Nevertheless, my sincere advice would be that he had better
confine himself shrewdly to wine and the fire that smokes
from a roasting goose, with which he is better acquainted.
. . . Since they are so God-crazy and so bitten with the desire
to burn heretics even for such useless, unheretical causes,
although the subject of indulgences has nothing to do with
faith, salvation, need, or law, forgive me, dear Heavenly
Father, for just once bidding defiance to my Baalites for the
sake of ridiculing all honors which are not thine. Here I
am in Wittenberg, Dr. Martin Luther, Augustinian. If there
is an inquisitor anywhere who thinks he can eat fire and
crack rocks, be it known that here he shall have safe-conduct,
open doors, free board and lodging, according to the promise
of the Elector of Saxony." "When these fellows abuse the
Scriptures and give the lie to God's Word, they call it
improving and honoring Christianity. But when one teaches
that it is not necessary to buy indulgences and that it is not
right to skin poor people out of their money, that is called
slandering the church and the sacrament and scandalizing
Christians. I say this in order that henceforth their language
and the new thieves' lingo may be understood." "His theses,
which he boasts he will defend in Frankfurt on the Oder—the
sun and the moon will be really amazed at the light of their
wisdom—I hold for the most part to be correct, except that
in every place where they say, 'Christians are to be taught,'
they ought to say, 'Indulgence sellers and inquisitors are to
be taught.'" "God help the truth and no one else. Amen!
I am not so bold as to boast that I can fly above the high
trees, but I have no doubt that I can crawl over dry grass."

Thus it may be seen how naturally proverbs, metaphors,
comical comparisons, hyperboles came pouring into his mind

even when he wrote in German. Yet he himself was not altogether at ease while indulging in this "play." He wrote on July 10 to his friend and brother Augustinian, Wenzel Link, at Nuremberg: "In doing this I have followed the advice of my friends too much, and even so I have not satisfied them. I should prefer that the work be not circulated any farther." As a matter of fact, the times had become almost too serious for such playing. On the same July 10, Count Albrecht, of Mansfeld, informed him that he was not under any circumstances to leave the precincts of Wittenberg, for several "magnates had sworn to seize and either hang or drown him." We do not know whether or not there was any truth in the rumor. At all events, Luther himself believed it. But it did not cause him to lose his courage. "The more they threaten," he wrote, "the greater becomes my confidence. Wife, children, fields, house, money, possessions I have not. My fame and my name are already torn to bits. All that is left me is my weak and frail body. If they deprive me of that, too, they will shorten my life by perhaps only an hour or two. But my soul they cannot take from me. I sing with John Reuchlin, 'He who is poor can lose nothing,' etc. I know, too, that he who would proclaim the Word of Christ to the world must, like the apostle, renounce everything and be prepared for death at any time. If that were not the case, it would not be the Word of Christ. It is gained through death, proclaimed and preserved through martyrs, and now, too, it can only be preserved in its purity and handed down to posterity through martyrs!" So he was serious, and yet he felt happy and free, when he learned that Tetzel's threats had not been spoken to the winds.

CHAPTER XVI

BEGINNING OF THE CANONICAL TRIAL

About the time that Luther wrote to Pope Leo X for the first time (May 23-31, 1518), the general chapter of the Dominicans met at Santa Maria sopra Minerva in Rome. The provincial of Saxony, Herman Rab, of Bamberg, who was particularly friendly to Tetzel, attended this meeting. On May 20 the pope had empowered the general of the Order, Cardinal Cajetan, to make twelve of his subordinates doctors of theology, and among the brothers who were honored with this distinction was John Tetzel. As the chapter of the Saxon Province had done in January, so the government of the Order, doubtless at the instigation of Rab, now espoused the cause of Tetzel with as much fanfare as possible.

But Rab was not satisfied. He took advantage of his stay in Rome to see that the charges against Luther were renewed at the Curia. Through the courtiers who belonged to the Order or were friendly toward it, he also tried to induce *Procurator fiscalis* Mario Perusco, the attorney general of the Curia, to get action on these charges. The procurator agreed to proceed. About the middle of June he had the pope authorize him to enter upon such regular proceedings against Luther as were customary in the case of such accusations. At the procurator's request, the chief judge of the Curia, Auditor Girolamo Ghinucci, was entrusted with the preliminary investigation. The formulation of a dogmatic opinion concerning the crimes of which Luther was accused—dangerous doctrine and revolt against papal power —was entrusted to the official expert of the pope on questions of faith, the *magister sacri palatii*, Sylvester Mazzolini da Prierio. Ghinucci was a jurist and consequently not in a position to form an opinion of his own on the questions involved. The *magister palatii*, on the other hand, who was sixty-two years old, had a long theological career behind him. But since he was a Dominican he was not capable of judging impartially the questions laid before him. In his "Opinion" of the *Ninety-five Theses* which, as he boasted, he composed in three days, Prierias did not try at all to enter into the spirit of Luther's thoughts. He simply rejected the *Theses* where they conflicted with popular Thomism and then applied the censures which seemed to him to be necessary: "erroneous," "false," "presumptuous," "heretical." The Thomistic standard on which he based his judgment was his own *Summa de casibus conscientiae*, developed three years before in considerable detail, and with marked dependence upon the *Summa* of his fellow-monk Antoninus of Florence. The church universal, he maintained, is virtually (in its essence) present in the Roman Church, and the Roman Church is represented in the cardinals, but is virtually present in the pope. It follows that the pope is just as infallible as the church universal. And consequently anyone who maintains that the pope cannot do what he actually does do with reference to indulgences is a heretic.

This really finished Luther as far as Prierias was concerned. When, notwithstanding this, Prierias proceeded to discuss the first ninety-two of the *Theses*, one by one, he did so only to establish the degree of objectionableness in Luther's teachings and, at the same time, to cause his own light to shine. For although, as he said, he had become unused to combat, he still had the ambition to demonstrate before all the world that he was intellectually superior to the Wittenberg professor about whom everybody was now talking. So he immediately turned his "Opinion" into a polemical writing, richly interlarded with coarse invectives, and had it printed in Rome that very June under the title *Dialogus*. Strange to say, Ghinucci had no fault to find either with the peculiar form or with the mordant tone of this offi-

cial document. Early in July, therefore, on the basis of this
document, he drew up the so-called "Citation" of Luther.
Drafted in the customary style, the Citation commanded
Luther to appear in Rome personally within sixty days after
receipt in order to defend himself against the offenses of
which he was accused. Ghinucci enclosed a copy of the
Dialogus for the information of the accused. Both documents
were first dispatched to Cardinal Cajetan in Augsburg.
Cajetan thereupon sent them through the Fuggers, with
whom he was living, to the Fugger branch in Leipzig.
Thence they finally reached Wittenberg on August 7.

Luther immediately decided, on the counsel of his jurist
friends who were thoroughly acquainted with legal proceedings, to send a personal messenger to the Elector, who
was then at the Diet of Augsburg. The messenger was to
petition the Elector to secure from the pope, through the
emperor's mediation, a *remissio seu commissio causae suae
ad partes Alemanniae.* In other words, Luther proposed that
he be allowed to vindicate himself in Germany, at a place
above suspicion and before judges above suspicion, as John
Reuchlin had done before. Thereupon he set to work on a
refutation of Prierias' *Dialogus,* which had accompanied the
Citation. In two days he was finished with it. Since Grünenberg already had his hands full of other work which he was
doing for him, Luther sent the manuscript (comprising some
eighty pages when in print), together with the *Dialogus,* to
Leipzig, and had it printed there in the printing office of
Melchior Lotter on Hay Street. The speed with which
Luther worked is astonishing, even when one takes into
account he had now at length fully mastered the subject in
question. The typesetters could not keep up with him any
longer. And for this reason they were a thorn in his flesh
from this time on.

What was Luther's answer to Prierias? "For me the church
is virtually present only in Christ, and it is represented in
the general council." "The pope as well as the general coun-

cil can err, as Nicholas de Tudescho, archbishop of Palermo [died 1445], has established. Only the Holy Scriptures, as St. Augustine stated, are infallible." It should not be supposed from this, Luther continued, that pope and council have actually erred. "Up to this time the Roman Church has never denied the true faith by a formal resolution. It has always asserted the authority of the Bible and of the ancient church fathers, although a good many people in Rome do not believe in the Bible, nor do they pay any attention to it." "If, after a decision has been reached on the question of indulgences [this had not yet occurred in a formal way], I should not respect the decision, I would be a heretic." "Even now I am only taking part in a disputation and am waiting for a council's decree of condemnation."

Even at this time, therefore, Luther did not go beyond what Occam, d'Ailly, and Tudescho had asserted before him. In Luther's mind the statement that "pope and councils can err" had only the significance of a dogmatic theory. To be sure, this is very important for the theologian who inquires after the sources of faith, but it can be a matter of relative indifference to the layman. For Luther, Catholic dogma, in so far as it was really dogma (that is, defined publicly by the formal decree of pope and councils), actually was still identical with the teaching of Christ. But only in so far as it was defined in this way. One is still free to dispute, he said, on such doctrines as have not yet been defined. And all the doctrines which he attacked belonged to this category. Hence, according to his understanding, he had no reason to consider himself a heretic. Moreover, he had a right to reject such a designation with vigor, even if it was used against him by the Curia's official expert on matters of faith.

But at the very time in which Luther was writing these sentences, the conclusion had been reached in Rome that he was guilty of heresy. More than that, Rome was convinced that he had publicly, and in a most offensive fashion,

engaged in the work of a heretic. It had therefore been
decided that he should be hurried as quickly as possible
along the customary path from life to death.

What was it that had happened in the meantime?

CHAPTER XVII

SUMMARY TREATMENT FOR NOTORIOUS HERESY

In the practice of ecclesiastical authorities during the last centuries of the Middle Ages, the ban, like the indulgences, had been converted from a purely penal and disciplinary measure into a financial policy and a means of income. Anyone who failed to pay the tithe promptly, or who failed to pay any other of the numerous church taxes, was banned without mercy, even if he could show that he was unable to pay. If he also let the second date of payment pass without bestirring himself, the ban was extended to include his whole family. That is to say, his wife and children were excluded from the sacraments; in addition to the sacraments, he was himself excluded from all "honorable associations," such as marriages, infant baptisms, funeral feasts, buying, selling, and all other business transactions. And if he died he was thrust into unconsecrated ground like an animal, without bell-ringing or blessing. If this "aggravation" or sharpening of the ban remained without effect, at the next payment date all the places which the banned man frequented were placed under interdict. This meant that the ban was extended to include all his neighbors and fellow-burghers. Ultimately the poor people were forced, as a rule, "to come to terms with the officials in regard to their property or else to run away with their children and become vagrants." The number of persons who had been banned for debts and money was everywhere very large. It always reached its high point in the two harvest months, August and September, when the large tithe was due. Then, to use Luther's phrase, bans flew about by the hundreds like bats.

Just as great a role was now played by ban and interdict in the endless struggles of the spiritual corporations to main-

tain their numerous economic and political privileges. If a
town council, for instance, did not wish to grant such a
corporation (let us say, a monastery or a cathedral or collegiate chapter) the right to import beer and wine free of
duty and the license to retail these alcoholics in the church
buildings, or if a prince or town council dared to arrest and
punish a member of the clerical order who was caught red-
handed in a crime, the church immediately resorted to ban
and interdict. This was done even if the evildoer had only
the so-called "first tonsure" and consequently had not yet
entered clerical orders, and even if the right of the religious
corporations to brew beer and retail liquors had first to be
established by law. Complaints concerning such abuses
comprised the chief subject in the business communications
between the secular and clerical authorities everywhere.
But thus far the attempt to remove them had nowhere
resulted in significant success because the church was not
disposed to renounce its uncommonly effective and very
convenient weapons.

Accordingly, one can understand how the Wittenbergers
pricked up their ears when Luther dared for the first time
(in a sermon on March 14, 1518) "to hang the bell on this
cat," too, and how they turned angrily upon the "game"
which was being played "in which the ban is now invoked
even for trifling causes." But, as in the case of indulgences,
what was the greatest offense to other people—using the ban
for financial ends—interested Luther only in a secondary
way. It seemed to him that the greatest harm in this abuse,
as well as in the other, was that it undermined moral and
religious life. It confused men's consciences by overstrict
punishment of small external transgressions and lax treatment of the gravest moral wrongs, especially when the
accused was a cleric or a well-to-do man. And, above all, it
caused the more earnest and pious people to be beset by
serious scruples and anxieties when they or one of their relatives was unjustly put under the ban. For the belief that

a banned person, if he died under the ban, would incur the loss of eternal bliss was not yet shaken. On the contrary, the church purposely fostered this belief and kept it alive by means of the solemn rites at the publication of the ban, the extinguishing of lights, the ringing of bells, and so on.

A fitting opportunity to enter upon a thorough discussion of the scruples and anxieties caused by such bannings was given to the Reformer by the appointed lesson for Exaudi Sunday, John 15:26 ff., "They shall put you out of the synagogues."[1] In connection with this text, Luther developed his subject from the pulpit of the Wittenberg parish church on May 16. The ban, he declared, always means exclusion only from the outward fellowship of the church, not exclusion from the inner fellowship of believers which rests upon one faith, one love, and one hope. It is not by men that one is placed in this fellowship. Consequently one cannot be thrust out by the will of another man, but only by one's own sin and offense. Resentment over the tyranny of officials, which has frequently led to the murder of such officials, will cease at once when the people learn that these men, despite the abuse of their power, cannot do harm but only good. For to suffer injustice does not harm the soul but always does it good. "If you are unjustly banned for the sake of truth or justice, you may by no means stop doing what causes you to suffer such violence. If, as a consequence, you die without the sacrament, if your corpse is thrust into unconsecrated ground, or even if it is dug out again and cast into the water, happy are you! Blessed is he who dies under such an unjust ban! For inasmuch as he has remained faithful to righteousness, he shall gain the crown of life." This sermon made a tremendous impression, particularly on the jurists and theologians. So it seemed to Luther that the sermon ought to be followed by a public disputation on the same subject. But the bishop of Brandenburg again intervened. On hearing of Luther's intention, he immediately

[1] In German: They shall put you under the ban.

sent a messenger to Wittenberg to request him to postpone the disputation. And since Luther's friends were also in favor of postponement, he submitted.

But several "dreadful spies," emissaries or creatures of the Dominicans, were also sitting under Luther's pulpit on May 16. These men now prepared some theses which twisted his words in a spiteful manner, and they spread these theses wherever and however they could. It was quite by accident that Luther learned of this more than two months later while he was stopping in Dresden with John Lang on business of the Order. He was already looked upon with distrust at the ducal court there, but inasmuch as he was such a famous man, he was invited to preach a sermon on St. James in the castle chapel. He did so on July 25 in the presence of the court, although Duke George himself was in Augsburg at the time. In the evening Luther felt obliged to accept an invitation of the court chaplain, Jerome Emser. On his arrival he found a great number of persons with whom he was not acquainted, among them a zealous Thomist from Leipzig, Magister Weissestadt, with whom he immediately fell into a very lively conversation on Aristotle and Thomas Aquinas. He had no idea that a Dominican from Tetzel's home town, Pirna, was listening to this discussion from behind a door, nor that Emser and his associates had arranged the whole meeting only for the purpose of drawing him out. Only one thing attracted his particular notice. This was that Weissestadt believed that on the basis of the theses (which were alleged to be Luther's) he could jeopardize Luther's life. Soon after his return to the Black Cloister Luther learned that his enemies in Augsburg were also working against him with this forgery. On this account he resolved at once to set down the most important statements in his sermon, as far as he could remember them, and publish them as a pamphlet.

But this time Luther's opponents were quicker than he was. In the last days of July they had already slipped the forged theses, together with a very malicious epigram on the greed of the Curia which purported to have originated with Luther, into the hands of the papal legate, Cajetan, in Augsburg. On August 5 Cajetan then sent the new *corpus delicti* to Rome, together with an imperial letter in which the emperor requested the Curia to ban Brother Martin Luther for teaching so damnably and heretically not only on indulgences, but also on the power of the papal ban, especially because there was reason to fear that with his heresies he would contaminate not only the ignorant people but also the powerful princes. The letter concluded with the assertion that he, the emperor, would not fail to carry out the papal sentence promptly. This dispatch of Cajetan, it can easily be understood, made a very strong impression in Rome. If even the emperor expressed such anxiety, Brother Martin must be far more dangerous than had been thought. Auditor Ghinucci, before whom the forged theses and the forged epigram were placed, could only confirm this view. On the basis of this new material, he declared Luther to be a notorious heretic and recommended to the pope that all the measures which canon law provides for such cases should be applied at once. Leo X agreed to this. He authorized Cajetan on August 23, in a very bulky breve (*Postquam ad aures*), to arrest the new heretic without delay and to guard him carefully until further orders from Rome. Under the same date he asked the Elector of Saxony, in a second breve, to deliver up the "son of perdition" to Cajetan; and in a third breve to the head of the Augustinian Order, Gabriel della Volta, he asked that a brother of the Order, equipped with all necessary authority, be sent to Germany in order to seize the heretic and schismatic Martin, bind him hand and foot, and cast him into prison. Only two days later Volta informed the provincial of the Augustinians in Saxony, Gerhard Hecker, of this breve, and added that he, too, had summoned Martinus to Rome as a rebel of the Order.

With this development Luther's fate seemed to be sealed. Then an incident occurred which immediately induced both the legate and the Curia to play a different tune. On August 27 Elector Frederick definitely refused to subscribe the agreement, laid before the Electors by Emperor Maximilian, concerning the election of his nephew, Charles of Spain, as Roman king. As Cajetan knew, the election of Charles was not at all acceptable to the Curia. But it could only be prevented, as matters now stood, if the Elector adhered to his position. If the legate wanted to do justice to the intentions of the pope, he now had to stake everything on keeping the Elector to his point. He soon had occasion, hardly to his joy, to bring this consideration into play. For a few days later Frederick sent word to him at the Fugger House requesting him to meet Luther in Augsburg, to examine him in a fatherly and not in a judicial way, and then to release him that he might return unhindered to Wittenberg.

What caused the Elector to take this step? To all appearances it was not the papal breve which ordered the surrender of the son of perdition, for it was probably still on its way to Augsburg at that time. Moreover, it was not like the Elector to react so quickly to such an unexpected demand. It was rather Luther's petition of August 8 which caused Frederick to act. For this petition, which sought to make the pope grant a transfer of Luther's case to German territory, had meanwhile been thoroughly considered by the Elector and discussed from all angles with his councilors. The ominous papal breve was probably tricked from the cardinal's secretary later on by Spalatin in the same clandestine way as the other breves, and hence was probably never officially presented by Cajetan. However this may be, Cajetan evidently saw that he was obliged to give in to the wish of the prince and reported to Rome accordingly. There in Rome, meanwhile, on the basis of Cajetan's earlier reports on Frederick's stand in the election question, it had already been agreed that this most influential member in the electoral college must be kept in the best possible humor. For this reason, too, it had been decided, as early as September 3, to confer upon Frederick the highest distinction which the pope had to bestow, the Golden Rose. Consequently, when Cajetan's new dispatches arrived, about September 9 or 10, Rome was ready to comply at once and as far as possible with the wishes of Frederick. Thus the policy of placing secular-political interests above churchly duties and tasks, which had controlled the Curia for centuries, now prevented it from doing in the Lutheran affair what it had itself recognized to be right and absolutely necessary.

On September 11 Pope Leo X had an order sent to Cajetan instructing him carefully to examine Luther in Augsburg, but in such a way as to avoid any disputation, and authorizing him at the same time "to proceed to acquittal or to condemnation, according to the circumstances." About September 20 Cajetan was able to show this new papal breve to the Elector. To be sure, it did not state that Cajetan should dismiss Luther in case the examination which he was to conduct did not turn out satisfactorily, for Frederick had formally assured him "that he would be the first to inflict punishment on Martinus if the latter should be condemned by a verdict of His Holiness in Rome."

Luther had heard nothing at all about the grave danger in which he was. It is true that Staupitz addressed to him a very serious letter from Salzburg on September 14. "As far as I can see, you have only the cross, that is, martyrdom, to expect. Leave Wittenberg, therefore, while there is still time, and come to me so that we might live and die together. It is agreeable to the prince [Archbishop Matthew Lang]." But this letter reached Luther only after he had already been reassured by Spalatin about Cajetan's intentions. Shortly after this, on September 24 or 25, the Elector's order arrived. Luther was to set out for Augsburg at once in order to be examined there by Cajetan.

CHAPTER XVIII

BEFORE CAJETAN IN AUGSBURG

James Vio, of Gaeta, called Cajetan, was one of the very few members of the college of cardinals who were fully conscious of their responsible position and therefore took pains to administer their office conscientiously, to the best of their knowledge, and with a view to the church's welfare. As a member of the Dominican Order, which he had joined at the age of fifteen, he had in his youth become so conversant with the system of Thomas Aquinas that by 1494 he could defend it, and not without success, in a disputation with the renowned humanist, Pico della Mirandola.

Ever since that time Cajetan figured as one of the lights of his Order and rose quickly to its highest posts of honor. When he was only thirty-one years old (1500), he was made procurator general, and the following year he became general. He employed the leisure which his office gave him by composing his famous commentary on the great *Summa* of Thomas Aquinas. In connection with the schismatic Council of Pisa (1511), he was first induced to speak in behalf of the threatened authority of the papacy, and he did so in the manner and spirit of Thomas. It was he, primarily, who prevailed upon Pope Julius II to call the Fifth Lateran Council in opposition to the former anti-papal council. And then, by the fearlessness with which he stood up for Thomas' doctrine of papal infallibility, which was very unpopular at the time, he gave this council its distinctive character. As a reward for this Cajetan was elevated to the cardinalate of San Sisto in connection with the wholesale naming of peers on July 1, 1517, which marked the submission of Leo X to the refractory college of cardinals. He owed his commission as papal legate in Germany, to work for the projected crusade against the Turks, to the fact that Cardinal Farnese had at the last moment refused this rather thankless mission. Cajetan's instructions contained not a word about Luther's affair. When he left Rome at the beginning of June, 1518, this probably did not seem to the Curia to be of sufficient importance to trouble so famous a scholar and cardinal with its settlement. Yet he happened to be the only one of all the men in the Curia who was in some measure a match for Luther.

On December 8, 1517, before he had any knowledge of the *Ninety-five Theses,* Cajetan had finished a treatise on indulgences in which he repeatedly reached conclusions similar to Luther's. Like Luther, he defined an indulgence as a remission of the penances imposed by the father-confessor, and, like Luther, he attacked the view that an indulgence may be procured for the dead without their having confessed and received absolution in the regular way. But he disputed the possibility of an indulgence for the dead just as little as he did the existence of a treasury of good works and the right of the pope to dispense this treasure. So his agreement with Luther did not go far. Nevertheless, the treatise shows that Cajetan was not of the ordinary run of theologians like Tetzel, Wimpina, or Prierias, but possessed the courage and the ambition to form opinions of his own about the problems which occupied his attention.

When he had received the commission to examine Luther, therefore, Cajetan immediately made a diligent study of the writings of the Saxon monk. One fruit of this study appeared in the four little essays which he composed in Augsburg on September 29 and October 2 and 7. In the first, of September 29, he developed against Luther (without mentioning him by name) the argument that inasmuch as indulgences remit penances which have been imposed, they must also cancel penalties in purgatory which correspond to these. In the second essay, of October 2, he maintained, in opposition to Luther, that it is not a sign of imperfection to secure

indulgences. The remission of penalty enables a man to do
even more holy works than before. Indeed, it is even a
meritorious act to procure an indulgence, for, inasmuch as
an indulgence benefits only a person in a state of grace, this
act is a work of infused love and is consequently meritorious.
To make sure, however, it is wise not to omit the works of
penance which have been imposed, despite the indulgence.
Then on October 7, Cajetan wrote two essays on the questions which had been raised by Luther. In the first of these
he conceded that it would be better to give to the poor the
money which was being spent for indulgences. Yet it was
not a sin, he wrote, to omit doing the better for the sake of
a lesser good work. To refuse a poor man alms in order to
apply the money to an indulgence would be a mortal sin
only if the poor man was in extreme need. In the second
essay Cajetan dealt with the doctrine of the treasury of
merits. This doctrine, he held, is more than a "pious opinion."
It is a dogma, defined according to full legal procedure by
Pope Clement VI in the Bull *Unigenitus* of January 27, 1343,
and consequently it must be accepted unconditionally by
everybody. He was certainly not unaware of the fact that
in this he stood alone among theologians. But this did not
hinder him from approaching Luther a few days later with
such a demand for unconditional acceptance.

In this way Cajetan had thoroughly prepared himself, in
his own way, for the coming duel with the "shabby mendicant." He could probably flatter himself with the hope of
a brilliant success in the task (particularly attractive to him
as an old professor) of extinguishing the new light of Wittenberg for the benefit and profit of the church as well as of
his Order, which had been sorely offended in the person
of Tetzel.

Immediately upon receipt of the Elector's letter, that is,
probably as early as September 25, Luther set out in the
company of Brother Leonard Beier, his *socius itinerarius*,
for Weimar, where he was to await more definite instruc-

tions. On his arrival he found that the Elector, who had
left Augsburg on September 22, was already there. On
September 29 he preached to the court in the chapel of the
castle. Then he received from Spalatin a letter of safe-
conduct, some letters of recommendation to notables in
Augsburg, and a full twenty guldens for traveling expenses.
On September 30 he started for Nuremberg and arrived
there in a thoroughly shabby condition about October 4.
He looked about in vain for Christopher Scheurl who, according to the Elector's wish, was to accompany him to Augsburg
as legal adviser. At first he was very depressed in spirit. "I
had the stake before my eyes constantly," he said later.
"'Now you have to die' I told myself." But more than by
his own fate, he was disquieted by the thought, "What a
disgrace I shall be to my dear parents." Moreover, the
brothers in the monasteries in which, after the fashion of
monks, he put up at night, seldom had much consolation
to offer him. In Weimar the provisor of the Franciscans,
John Kästner, said, "Dear doctor, the Italians are learned
men. I fear that you will not be able to stand your ground
against them and that you will then be burned by them."
In Nuremberg several of the brothers of the Black Cloister
at Our Lady's Gate went so far as to advise him to turn back
as quickly as possible. But such faintheartedness always
stirred up in him the finest spirit of courage and trust in God.
"Even in Augsburg," he wrote to Wittenberg from Nuremberg, "even in the midst of His enemies, Christ reigns. May
Christ live and Martinus die . . . . One must become objectionable either to men or to God."

And yet it was not with an altogether light heart that
Luther continued his journey, possibly on October 5, with
the added company of Wenzel Link and wearing Brother
Wenzel's precious new cowl. On the last day's journey he
was overtaken by a severe gastric complaint. Since he could
not walk any farther, he had to hire a wagon for the last
three miles. Entirely worn out in body and spirit, he reached

the Carmelite's House of St. Anna in Augsburg, with whose prior, John Frosch, he had become acquainted in Wittenberg. Through Link he immediately announced his arrival to the cardinal, who was in the Fugger House. But the Saxon councilors, Rühel and Philip von Feilitzsch, who had remained in Augsburg on his account, forbade him to appear on the street until they had procured letters of safe-conduct for him from the emperor and the city council. The imperial councilors actually showed no inclination to provide these until Cajetan explained that they might do what they wished.

Meanwhile the "shabby little friar" could not complain of lack of visitors. All the world wanted to see the new Herostratus who had started such a great conflagration. To satisfy his curiosity, the most famous man of the city, Conrad Peutinger, even invited Luther to dine with him. Cajetan, of course, kept aloof. But one of the distinguished Italians of his retinue, Urban de Serralonga, visited the heretic in the Carmelite House on October 9 and tried to work upon him in "true Italian style." Surely it would be easy, he said, to pronounce the six letters, "Revoco" (I recant)! When Luther objected that he would have to defend his statements under all circumstances, Urban continued: "Dear, dear! Do you want to start a tournament? You have taken the question of indulgences much too seriously. Why not teach something that is not true, as long as untruth brings in a good deal of money? Concerning the power of the pope, of course, one may not dispute. It is so great that the pope can put valid articles of faith out of force by a mere wink. What does the pope care about Germany anyhow?" Finally he remarked, "Do you think that the Elector will take up arms for your sake?" Luther: "By no means." Urban: "But where will that leave you?" Luther: *"Sub caelo"* (under heaven). With this Master Urban felt that it had been indicated that he should make a quick departure.

"The silliness of this middleman restored my confidence not a little," Luther wrote to Spalatin the next day. "Greet my friends in Wittenberg and tell them to be of good courage, whether I return or not. For I have already decided to appeal to a future general council if the legate proceeds against me with force, instead of reason." Then on October 11 Luther addressed a sort of farewell letter to young Philip Melanchthon, who had just assumed his position in Wittenberg and whom Luther loved most tenderly. "Play the man and teach the students the things that are right. I go now, if it is God's will, to be slaughtered as a sacrifice for you and for them. I prefer death to recantation, even if it means— and this would be my greatest sorrow—to lose your blessed society forever." On the same day the imperial safe-conduct arrived. On the morning of October 12, therefore, accompanied by his friends Link and Frosch and three other monks, he was at last able to walk the hard road which led to the Fugger House.

"I had been coached," Luther related later, "on how I should act toward the cardinal," who was surrounded by a great swarm of curious Italians. "First I prostrated myself before him. Then, when he commanded me to arise, I lifted myself only to my knees. Only when he beckoned again did I stand up. Thereupon I asked his pardon for having first waited for the safe-conduct and assured him that I wanted to hear only the truth from him." Cajetan replied with some friendly and courteous words, which a well-mannered Italian always had at his command. But then he explained briefly that he had been commissioned by His Holiness to require three things of Luther. "First, repent your errors and recant them. Second, promise not to teach them again. Third, refrain from all machinations which might disturb the peace of the church." Thereupon Luther asked him to specify his errors. The cardinal called his attention first of all to the fifty-eighth of the *Ninety-five Theses* wherein he had maintained that the treasure of the church is not identical with the merits of Christ and the saints. This opinion, Cajetan continued, is sufficiently refuted by the decretal *Unigenitus*. Then he selected the sentence, from the seventh thesis of the *Resolutions,* which states that it is not the sacrament but faith that justifies. This assertion, he said, is new and false. When Luther replied that he could not yield on this point, Cajetan spoke imperiously: "This you must recant today, whether you wish to or not. Otherwise I shall, on account of this one passage, condemn everything else that you might say!" The Italians who were present accompanied these words "after their fashion" with outbursts of laughter and derision.

With reference to the first point, Luther proceeded to explain that the decretals were no authority for him because they cited the Holy Scriptures improperly and distorted their words. Besides, the decretals only repeated the opinions of Thomas Aquinas. "For this reason I give the Scripture passages, which I cite in the *Theses,* absolute precedence." This went against Cajetan's grain. Although he was not supposed to, and did not wish to, engage in a disputation with the "little brother," he could not refrain from informing him that the pope is above council and Scriptures. As proof for this he cited the condemnation of the Council of Basel by Nicholas V. "You, too, are a Gerondist," Cajetan continued. "All the followers of Gerson are damned just as Gerson himself is." When Luther ventured to remind him that the University of Paris had recently appealed to a future council, Cajetan growled, "The Parisians will have to pay for that!" After this, according to Luther, they began to debate in a confused way about the grace of God. Nothing that Luther proposed was approved by Cajetan. If he cited a Scripture passage, Cajetan burst out in a hearty laugh. Meanwhile he was constantly being hectored: "Recant! Acknowledge your error! This, and nothing but this, is the will of the pope!" Since this kind of talk was getting nowhere,

Luther finally asked for time to reflect and left with his friends.

It can hardly be said that Cajetan adhered strictly to the promises which he had given to Frederick. To be sure, he had begun in a very friendly and fatherly way. But he soon allowed himself to be carried away by his temper. Wenzel Link and John Frosch must have shared this impression, otherwise neither the Saxon councilors, nor the exceedingly timid Dr. Peutinger, nor the very cautious Dr. Staupitz (who had just arrived at St. Anna, to Luther's joy) would have showed any inclination at all to accompany him to the Fugger House on the morning of October 13 for a second audience. Cajetan smiled when he beheld the stately procession. He smiled, too, at the formal declaration (*protestatio*) which Luther proceeded to read in the presence of these witnesses and in which he stated that, inasmuch as he was not convicted or refuted, he could not be forced to recant. He was not conscious, Luther's declaration continued, of having taught anything contrary to the Bible, the church fathers, the decretals, or reason. Yet since he, like all men, could err, he would submit to the judgment of the legitimate church and declare himself ready to hold a public disputation on his statements, be it in Augsburg or elsewhere. If this did not suit Cajetan, he was ready to reply in writing to the objections expressed in the first audience, and to leave the decision regarding his teachings to the universities of Basel, Freiburg, and Louvain and, should these not be sufficient, to Paris as well.

Thereupon the cardinal, like an old professor who cannot stay away from his favorite subject, began again to speak of the decretal *Unigenitus*. Luther replied that he would answer him in writing, that he had already argued enough with him the day before. Cajetan took this remark in bad part. "My son," he said, "I have not argued with you, nor do I want to argue with you now. It is only out of regard for His Serene Highness, Elector Frederick, that I am examining you in a fatherly and gracious way and trying to reconcile you with His Holiness." Nevertheless, when Staupitz also requested him to allow Luther to reply in writing, Cajetan finally granted this request graciously and even dismissed Luther with the words: "I shall be very glad to hear what you have to say and then to settle everything like a father and not like a judge."

As soon as he reached St. Anna, Luther hastily dashed down on paper a detailed defense of the two points which the cardinal had objected to. These notes fill almost three-fourths of a signature in print. With this apology he appeared at the Fugger House for the third time on the morning of October 14, and he was accompanied by the Saxon councilors, Ruhel and Feilitzsch. What had induced the councilors to go with him? It was the impression that Cajetan would not keep his promises, and the intention to remind him of these. As had been expected, Cajetan accepted Luther's script with contemptuous words and gestures, but promised, nevertheless, to send it to Rome. Then he began to thunder "Recant!" again. He expatiated, in a long, impassioned speech, particularly on the decretal *Unigenitus*. Luther tried as many as ten times to interrupt him, but each time he was talked down. Finally Luther also began to talk louder and louder. Once he inadvertently addressed the cardinal with a "you" instead of with "Your Paternity" and was at once sharply reprimanded. "If the decretal actually says that the treasure of the church is the merit of Christ, I will recant," Luther said finally. On this the little man laughed and rubbed his hands with satisfaction. He quickly reached for a book which lay before him and, snorting furiously, read the Bull to the point where it said that Christ (through His suffering) had gained a treasure for the church militant. "This word 'gained,' " Luther cried, "is to be heeded. If Christ has gained a treasure through His merits, this does not mean that His merits are a treasure, but that the treasure consists of that which He earned by His merits, that is, the forgiveness of sin." This put the cardinal in a muddle. In order to hide his confusion, he quickly skipped over to another subject. But Luther pinned him down. He was certainly wanting in deference when he broke out in the words: "Surely Your Highness does not think that we Germans do not know our grammar. To be a treasure is something different from gaining a treasure." Thereupon Cajetan said that he would also refute him from the Bible and began to twit him by saying that the Bible is not free of error. In Matthew 27:9, a passage is ascribed to Zechariah, he said, which actually comes from Jeremiah. But he hardly knew what to do with the Bible. So he came back again to the decretal *Unigenitus*. "Recant!" he said in conclusion, but then he added, "I am authorized by the pope to place you and all your patrons under the ban, and all the places which receive you under interdict." When this threat did not seem to produce any effect either, he rose and said, "Get out, and don't let me see you again, unless you are willing to recant!"

"So his confidence was broken, and while he was crying 'Recant!' once again, I turned to go," Luther wrote to Spalatin on the same day. But Cajetan had just the opposite impression. He said that Luther's confidence had begun to waver. Accordingly he immediately decided to use some other measures to humble him completely. With this in view, after he had eaten (at ten o'clock), he ordered Staupitz and Link to appear before him in the Fugger House. For hours he conferred with the two friars. He tried to persuade Staupitz with many "pretty words" to induce Luther to make a simple recantation, and assured him at the same time that Luther hardly had a better friend. Staupitz replied by saying that he had always urged Luther, and was still urging him, to submit humbly to the dictum of the church, but that he was himself no match for Luther either in learning or in spirit. He, the cardinal, on the other hand, was there as the representative of the pope and was consequently the only one who could deal with the "little brother."

With this calculated bow before the pope's representative, Staupitz cleverly evaded the request in such a way that Cajetan could not even be cross with him for his refusal. But Cajetan would not hear of a resumption of the hearing. "I do not wish to speak to this brother any more," he said, probably with a touch of Neapolitan superstition, "for he has deep-set eyes, and hence curious fancies in his head." He declared himself ready only to draw up the articles which Luther should recant. However, he thought that it would be a good thing not to hurry the matter. The longer the brother was made to wait, he evidently thought, the quicker he would become humble. Immediately on hearing of this, Luther wrote to Spalatin: "I shall not recant a syllable, and I shall have my defense, which I presented today, printed, so that he may be refuted throughout the whole Christian world if he continues to deal with me as outrageously as he has begun. I am also preparing an appeal." And he reported to Wittenberg that "the cardinal may be an able Thomist, but he is no clear Christian thinker, and so he is about as fit to deal with this as an ass is to play a harp."

While Luther was at St. Anna, setting down on paper this scarcely flattering opinion of Cajetan, Brother Link was standing before the little man of power in the Fugger House. Whether he went there of his own accord, or was sent by Staupitz, or was summoned by Cajetan directly, we do not know. Be this as it may, the cardinal evidently believed, when he had dismissed his guest, that he had won the day. He had told Brother Wenzel that he would overlook the question as to whether faith alone justifies, if Luther would only recant what he had asserted concerning the treasure of the church. It was not his intention, he continued quietly, to put Luther under the ban right away; he wished to await further orders from Rome, to which he had already sent Luther's written defense by a fast messenger. Brother Wenzel, he said later, was in entire agreement with his handling of the matter. Thus it seems that Link must have been more conciliatory in the course of this parley than Staupitz had been. One can easily understand, accordingly, why Cajetan believed that he had the cat in the bag and why he said triumphantly to those in his retinue, "This brother [Luther] should have come to market with fresher eggs."

Yet Staupitz was not nearly so much in agreement with Cajetan's handling of the matter as, to all outward appearances at least, Brother Wenzel. It is true that, like Link, he advised Luther to write again to the cardinal in a courteous and humble spirit in order to apologize for the insolent and vehement utterances which he had made against the pope in his writings, to promise that he would be willing to repeat this publicly in all pulpits, and to say that he was resolved to act better in the future. He went so far as to urge Luther to reconsider thoroughly whether his conscience might not allow him to make the required recantation. But he was so indignant at the domineering and violent procedure of Cajetan over against his protégé that he wrote to Elector Frederick on October 15: "The legate from Rome acts, alas, as they all do there. He speaks fair words, but they are all empty and vain. He is intent on making Master Martinus recant. He seeks, by whatever means, to extirpate innocent blood and force recantation. He says that the general of the Augustinian Order has written a letter against Luther and that this is already abroad in the land. Peutinger claims that it is also directed against me. Both of us are to be thrown into prison, and force is to be used against us." So Cajetan had been so imprudent as to divulge something of Gabriel della Volta's warrant of arrest. The papal breve of September 11 had not expressly suspended this warrant, and so it could be carried out at any time. Staupitz did not doubt, therefore, that Cajetan had determined to destroy him, as well as Luther, and he planned to act accordingly.

While the little cardinal was hatching out another essay against Luther in the Fugger House, Staupitz hustled about the whole town to raise a loan for Dr. Martinus, for Luther, he thought, could no longer stay in Germany. He would have to find refuge at once in some place where the arm of the pope could not reach him. Such a place was Paris. But unfortunately Staupitz could not find anyone among his acquaintances in Augsburg who had a sufficient amount of money ready at hand. Nevertheless, he thought it expedient to release Luther from his obedience—that is, to free him formally from all responsibility toward the Order—in order that he might do what he wanted to do without taking the Order into consideration. Then, without taking leave of Cajetan, Staupitz disappeared from Augsburg on October 16 with Brother Wenzel. On the same day, with the knowledge and advice of the two Saxon councilors, Luther deposited in St. Anna before a notary and witnesses, according to proper legal form, an appeal from the pope ill-informed to the pope who should be better-informed (*a papa male informato ad papam melius informandum*). In other words, he rejected the two Roman judges named in the citation of July, Ghinucci and Prierias, on account of bias and deficient knowledge of the matter, and sought a hearing before learned papal commissioners in some safer place than Rome, where even the "best pope," Leo, had barely escaped becoming a victim of assassination during the previous year. Moreover, he was not able to undertake such a long journey at this time, the appeal stated, on account of his weak physical condition.

On October 17 Luther wrote to Cajetan in the tone recommended by Staupitz and Link. This letter exploded the optimistic expectations of the cardinal, for Luther frankly and freely asserted that his conscience would not permit him to recant. He could not and dared not allow himself to be persuaded, he wrote, to speak or do anything against his conscience, whether by command, or by another's advice, or by consideration for another person. Since the news had meanwhile reached the Fugger House that Staupitz and

Link had disappeared from Augsburg without leaving a trace, Cajetan was entirely in the dark, it seems, as to what he should do. So he did what most people do when they are in such a situation and mood. For the time being he did nothing at all. Even when Luther, in a second letter dated October 18, took formal leave of him and announced his approaching departure, not a word was heard from Cajetan. This silence began to make the Saxon councilors and Luther's friends in Augsburg uneasy. So they decided on October 20 to get their protégé out of Augsburg as quickly as possible. When night had fallen, Canon Langenmantel opened a little gate in the city walls, and through this Luther escaped without being recognized. An old city messenger was waiting for Luther outside with a second horse, into the saddle of which he swung himself just as he was, wearing only knee breeches and stockings, without knife, weapon, or spurs. Inasmuch as his horse was unfortunately a very stiff trotter and his companion did not say a word on the way, for years Luther looked back on this ride as a frightful experience. In Monheim, where he made his first stop, he was able to dismount, but not being able to stand up, he fell into a bed of straw like a dead man.

On October 22 Luther rode on to Nuremberg. There he was entertained with the greatest honors by Willibald Pirckheimer, and he made the acquaintance, among others, of the renowned Albrecht Dürer. Before his departure, a letter from Spalatin reached him here, and together with it a copy of the papal breve of August 23, which ordered his immediate arrest. Feeling that he had escaped from a great danger, Luther proceeded, on October 24, to ride northward. About October 26 he met Count Albrecht of Mansfeld at Gräfenthal, not far from Saalfeld. The count laughed not a little at his riding and at once cordially invited him to be his guest. From there the journey turned from the Saale Valley toward Weissenfels and Leipzig. After he had left Leipzig, Luther lost his way, but finally found it again and reached Kemberg safely on the morning of the anniversary of the *Theses*, October 31, and there, since it was Sunday, he immediately read a mass—"so holy was he still at this time." From there he went to Wittenberg, arriving in the course of the afternoon. "I feel so happy and peaceful," he wrote that evening to Spalatin, "that I wonder at the fuss so many great folk are making over my struggles and sufferings." A few days later he had finished a report, supplemented with documents (*Acta Augustana*), of the hearing in Augsburg. Although intended for immediate publication, this report did not appear until the beginning of December. Meanwhile, he had really gone home only in order to take his leave. As soon as the expected Bull of Excommunication arrived, he intended, as Staupitz had advised him, to depart for France. Under no circumstances did he wish to continue to be a burden to his prince.

But in the meantime Cajetan had at last broken his silence.

CHAPTER XIX

FREDERICK THE WISE AT THE CROSSROAD

Shortly after the middle of November, a letter, addressed to the Elector by Cajetan in his own hand on October 25, reached the Elector's residence at Grimma. In it the legate briefly outlined the negotiations at Augsburg, for the failure of which he naturally held Luther alone responsible. In his *Ninety-five Theses,* he continued, Luther had presented his new views *disputative* (that is to say, simply as opinions worthy of discussion), but in his sermons on indulgences and the power of the ban, *affirmative* and *assertive* (that is to say, as an expression of his personal convictions). Inasmuch as the sermons were opposed to the teaching of the Holy See on the one hand, and were notoriously heretical on the other, the Elector, if he did not wish to sacrifice his honor and wanted to heed the voice of his conscience, could not but deliver the "shabby mendicant" (*fraterculus*) to Rome or chase him out of the land. Rome would not delay the further legal prosecution of this pestilential affair, Cajetan concluded.

As early as November 19 the Elector had a copy of this document sent to Luther, together with a note asking him to advance his opinion of it. Luther replied on the same day with a letter which covers more than a signature in print. In it he subjected the assertions and demands of the legate to searching criticism. With extraordinary skill he set forth that he had not been indicted on account of the sermons stigmatized by the legate, but only because of the *Theses,* which were expressly acknowledged by the legate to be not inadmissible. Even more remarkable is the acuteness with which Luther uncovered the weakest point in Cajetan's evidence. This was the assumption that the conception of indulgences attacked by Luther had already been formally accepted and approved by the church. The learned cardinal was himself very well aware of this defect. For this reason he had in the meantime proposed from Augsburg that an official doctrinal declaration on indulgences be decreed in Rome and enclosed a draft of a declaration with his proposal; this declaration (*Cum postquam*) was actually published on November 9. Very impressively, then, Luther explained that Cajetan had not kept the promises he had made to the Elector. On the contrary, he had demanded of the Elector that he deliver Luther up without having made so much as an attempt to designate precisely the errors which he was casting in his teeth, to say nothing of proving that he was heretical. To command the prince to surrender him to Rome meant as much as to command him to commit a murder, Luther wrote. "But in order that no evil may befall Your Excellence on my account, I hereby declare that I am willing to leave your lands to go wherever the God of mercy would have me."

Luther made this statement in all earnest. It is true that on November 23 he tried to induce the Elector, through the university, to ask Rome for a more precise specification of the errors for which he was being reproached in order that he might have an opportunity to know and retract them. But he was not thinking of influencing the university on this occasion—as he might very easily have done—to intercede with the Elector in behalf of his continuance in Wittenberg. On the contrary, he got ready for a journey. On November 25 and 28 he also prepared the lamenting Wittenbergers, from the pulpit of the town church, for his imminent departure. The Elector, who had meanwhile left Grimma for Altenburg, did not allow himself to be heard from. Nor did he say what he thought of Luther's intention to appeal to a future general council after the example of the University of Paris. Only after Luther had taken this step, with the customary formalities in Corpus Christi

Chapel, at three o'clock in the afternoon of November 28, did a letter reach him from Altenburg in which the Elector expressly declared that he approved of Luther's decision.

This, it appeared, definitely decided Luther's future. On the evening of December 1 he invited his friends once again to a farewell dinner in the Black Cloister. In the course of the night he intended to leave the city. While he was sitting at table with his guests, he received a letter from Spalatin, through whom the Elector expressed his surprise that Luther had not gone, and requested him to speed his departure as much as possible. He was more astonished than he was shocked by this communication, as he tells us later. "Father and mother forsake me," he thought to himself, "but the Lord will care for me." But while he was still eating, a second letter came from Altenburg, instructing him, if he had not already left, to remain, because the Elector still had some necessary things to discuss with him. Despite these rather startling reports from Altenburg, his friends, like Luther himself, did not doubt that the Elector would be glad to help him if he could. They advised him, therefore, to give himself up to the prince as a prisoner that very night; then Frederick could write to the legate that he had arrested Martinus and that he was ready to have him appear for a hearing in some safe place.

Forcibly to exile Luther, or even to deliver him to Rome, bound hand and foot—this Frederick certainly never thought of doing. For he did not allow himself to be persuaded that this man, for whom practically all his councilors and his whole university warmly interceded, was a heretic. But he did not believe that he could protect Luther from the consequences of the ban. For this reason it would have pleased him if Luther had not returned to Saxony at all. Nevertheless, it is clear that he experienced a change of heart on November 30. Luther later traced this sudden change back to Frederick's negotiations with the papal nuncio, Miltitz. But Miltitz did not reach Altenburg until December 28. In this form, therefore, the report cannot be exactly correct. It is possible, however, that the electoral councilor, Pfeffinger, who was then entertaining Miltitz, informed Frederick at this time that Miltitz was optimistic about the situation, and that this had the effect of calming the prince. Be that as it may, Frederick thought it necessary, at the beginning of December, to lay before his councilors the question as to whether he should surrender Luther. At that time almost all the councilors were "good Lutherers." After a humorous address by the nobleman Fabian von Feilitzsch, who was particularly esteemed by Luther because of his natural good sense, they declared unanimously against the extradition. Thereupon Frederick decided to refuse Cajetan's demands and directed his chancellor to draw up a memorandum for the cardinal to this effect.

Of course, the question as to whether Luther could remain permanently in Saxony was not now answered. But the situation had cleared up enough for the Elector to direct Spalatin to summon Luther to Lichtenberg Castle, near Pretzsch, where no one could disturb them, and there to lay before Luther the status of affairs. This meeting took place between December 3 and 6. We are not informed as to its details. We know only that Spalatin recommended to Luther, on the authority of the Elector, that he should not be in too much of a hurry to get to France. But Luther, we also know, persisted in his resolution to leave Wittenberg, and so he again asked for permission to publish his *Acta Augustana* and his appeal to a future council. The Elector had not countenanced these publications before. And now, as Spalatin told him right away, the Elector refused once again. Meanwhile, without waiting for the Elector's answer, Luther had the two documents printed on December 8 because, as he wrote to Spalatin December 9, he had to hurry with this, as with all things. The Elector was not a little provoked at this. He had word sent to Luther on December 12 that he would permit the further sale of the *Acta* only if the bad passage in the conclusion which designated the papal breve of August 23 a forgery would be struck out with printer's ink. This was done at once.

On December 18 Frederick finally sent off the document in which he rejected Cajetan's proposals after he had, according to his custom, scrutinized and amended it "perhaps ten, even twenty and more times." He enclosed Luther's letter of November 19, but probably only after he had carefully examined it and improved on it here and there.

This decided Luther's future. For Frederick was one of those slow-moving persons who require a great deal of time to reach a definite conclusion concerning a person or situation but, once it is reached, hardly ever allow themselves to be diverted from the opinion but cling to it with the greatest perseverance. And so from this time on he adhered stead- fastly to Luther although it was often made very difficult for him not only by Luther's enemies but also by Luther himself.

Luther rejoiced greatly over the Elector's message to Cajetan, about which he was informed at once. But even now he did not give up the plan of leaving Wittenberg. "I shall certainly wait for the Bull of Excommunication here," he wrote December 26, "but I hope that they will not act too precipitously in Rome." We do not know how he came by this hope. But his hope was fulfilled.

CHAPTER XX

NEGOTIATIONS WITH MILTITZ

Charles von Miltitz was born about the year 1490 in Rabenau, near Dresden, as the posthumous son of an only moderately endowed family of the lesser nobility of Meissen. Like many in his position, he entered holy orders without having the slightest inclination or inner call. After he had spent several years in Cologne for the purpose of study, he went to Rome, where, through his relationship to the Dominican Nicholas von Schönberg, the powerful confidant of Cardinal Medici, he hoped to make his fortune. For the present he succeeded only in becoming papal notary and titular chamberlain. He had never learned to work, and in his opinion work was not necessary. Nevertheless, he occasionally negotiated the purchase of relics and arranged other small transactions in things devotional for the pious princes of Wettin, in return for which he received commissions. His spirit was not very strong, and his flesh was very weak. But on this account he was excellently suited to be a companion of the dissolute young cardinals who, because of their wicked conduct, were the occasion of much scandal in Rome at that time. In drinking, especially, he could hold his ground with any man.

But Miltitz was not satisfied with this empty kind of life. He longed to do great things in the role of political agent. In this capacity he believed himself capable of accomplishing far more, particularly in his fatherland, than the Italian clerics whom the Curia was accustomed to entrust with such commissions. He was not a little pleased, therefore, when, on September 10, 1518, at the instigation of his good uncle Schönberg, he received from the Holy Father the honorable and (on account of the copious gratuities which would surely fall his way in connection with it) probably very lucrative mission of bearing the Golden Rose to the Elector of Saxony. The fact that the Elector's attitude toward the Lutheran affair was not quite clear caused the Curia to postpone the mission for two more months and then to encumber Miltitz' luggage with a Bull condemning Luther, and a number of other bulls and breves besides, almost all of which were concerned either directly or indirectly with the Lutheran affair. In fixing the "faculties," or privileges, which were granted to him as to every papal nuncio, as a sort of stipend, the Lutheian affair was also taken into consideration. Miltitz was not only to appoint five papal notaries and house prelates, five counts of the Lateran, ten poets laureate, and ten doctors of theology, but he was also to free two persons from the legal disadvantages connected with illegitimate birth and thus make them eligible for higher ecclesiastical offices and benefices. Under consideration here were the two illegitimate scions of Frederick the Wise and Anna Weller, of Molsdorf, for whose welfare the old gentleman, as was very well known in Rome, was most tenderly solicitous. Miltitz was very strictly commanded, nevertheless, to negotiate in the closest agreement with Cajetan, and hence to deposit with the cardinal the Golden Rose and the documents entrusted to him. Cajetan, meanwhile, was directed to deliver the Golden Rose only after the Elector had given evidence of a proper measure of virtue in the Lutheran affair—in other words, only after he had declared himself ready to hand over the "son of perdition" or drive him out of his land.

After everything seemed to have been arranged in the best possible way, the nuncio, who was yearning to do great things, was finally permitted to set out for Augsburg in the middle of November. There he was to discuss everything with Cajetan. But when he arrived in Augsburg, he found that the legate had already followed the emperor to Austria. If Miltitz had been better supplied with funds, this would

not have prevented him from remaining in Augsburg. But
unfortunately his purse was, as usual, quite empty. So it
seemed to him expedient to look about for a place where he
might pass the enforced period of waiting both pleasantly
and without expense. He deposited the Golden Rose and
his large letter-bag with the Fuggers, and then he betook
himself to the Bavarian estate of the electoral councilor,
Degenhard Pfeffinger, whom he had known before. There
he learned to his great surprise what a strong following
Luther had in Germany, and that Elector Frederick would
certainly not be disposed to deliver up the daring man without more ado. If he had been a somewhat more conscientious man, Miltitz would have told himself that under these
circumstances he should by no means go to Saxony without
first coming to an understanding with his superior, Cajetan.
But he had a flexible conscience, and his intellectual horizon
was so limited that he never perceived clearly the consequences of his transactions. Accordingly, when Pfeffinger
journeyed to Saxony in the middle of December, Miltitz
joined him without so much as notifying Cajetan. Ostensibly
he went as a private person. In reality, however, he went in
order to try his luck in high politics, a field which had
remained closed to him up to this time. Even on the way,
he could not keep from boasting of the great number of
weighty bulls and breves he had brought with him from
Rome, or from telling the astonished Nurembergers how
very different the pope's attitude toward the Lutheran affair
was from that of the Dominicans. Tetzel's little motto on the
power of indulgences for the dead, for instance, he said,
had so enraged the Holy Father that he shook in every limb
and cried out, "*O porcaccio!*" (Oh, the filthy fellow!). And
the pope had immediately promoted Prierias, for his *Opinion*,
to the rank of "*un buon rabuffo*" (a common clout). These
anecdotes, which gave him the highly attractive air of a
confidant of His Holiness, initiated into all the secrets of
the papal court, were probably of his own invention, or else

were gleaned by him in one of the many gossip-corners of the Vatican. For there was no place in the world where there was so much gossiping and lying as in Rome. Nevertheless, the anecdotes indicate that he was already brooding over the bold plan of reconciling Luther with the pope and dealing the Dominicans, especially Tetzel, a blow.

Miltitz reached Altenburg with Pfeffinger on December 28 and immediately sought an audience with the Elector. He did not demand that the prince extradite Luther, but that he drive him out of his territory. Otherwise, he implied, nothing would come of the Golden Rose. The Elector immediately refused the demand with the argument, well calculated for the flexible spirit of his auditor, that he could hardly force Luther to go to heretical Bohemia. Thereupon Miltitz came out with his real plan—the idea of reconciling Luther with the pope. Frederick, of course, had no fault to find with this. Before his departure for Lochau (now Annaburg), the Elector, therefore, dispatched a swift messenger to Wittenberg with the command that Luther should set out instantly for Altenburg in order to confer with Miltitz there. Then, to show the Reformer how favorably he was disposed toward him, Miltitz decided to slay the black sheep which in his opinion, was responsible for the whole misfortune. This was Tetzel. Twice in a row he wrote threateningly to Leipzig, directing Tetzel to come to him. But Tetzel answered on December 31: "Martin Luther has made the people so cross with me that I have been warned to be on my guard, for many of Martin's followers have vowed to kill me." This was undoubtedly only a pretext. Tetzel probably surmised what was in the wind and preferred to remain in Leipzig.

Luther, on the other hand, arrived on January 4 or 5. For two days, in the presence of the Elector's councilor, Fabian von Feilitzsch, and probably other members of the electoral court as well, he conferred with Miltitz in Spalatin's house on castle hill. On four things, he wrote to the Elector the

following morning, he had come to agreement with the
nuncio: First, he would let the controversy die out on
condition that the opposition would also keep silent. Second,
he would write a letter to the pope in which he would confess that he had been too vehement and sharp, although
he had never thought of injuring the Roman Church, but
was aiming only at the disgraceful preaching [of indul-
gences]. Third, he would have a note sent out, exhorting
everyone to be obedient to the Roman Church and also
confessing that he had expressed the truth in an all too
heated and, perhaps, untimely fashion. Fourth, according
to the suggestion made by Fabian von Feilitzsch at Spalatin's
instigation, he would commit his case to Archbishop Matthew Lang, of Salzburg, and would accept, as far as he could,
the decision determined upon by the archbishop in common
with other learned and trustworthy men. In case he could
not accept it, he would hold to his appeal to a future
general council. The letter closed with the characteristic
words: "I am willing to do anything, provided I am not
made to renounce anything more, for nothing will come
of the recantation."

On the second day Luther presented to Miltitz a draft
(which we still have) of the letter he had promised to write
to the pope. In it he made an honest effort to fulfill his promise. But he absolutely refused to recant. Of course, such a
letter did not serve the purpose of Miltitz. So he dropped
this point, and gave up the demand of the "note" as well.
Of the four points agreed upon in the first conference, therefore, only two remained, as Luther reported to the Elector
on the same day. First, both parties shall be forbidden to
preach, write, and discuss the matter any further. Second,
"Miltitz will induce the pope to direct a learned bishop to
designate the articles which I am to recant. Then, when I
am informed [convinced] of my error, I am to, and will
gladly, recant the same and not weaken the power and honor
of the Roman Church."

At the conclusion of the conferences Miltitz took the Reformer to dinner with him in the castle. It was probably on this occasion that he told Luther that he had discovered on his journey that only two or three out of every five men in all the inns in which he had stopped supported Rome. He added that Luther's case had made more trouble for the Curia than any other in a hundred years. Consequently the Curia would rather lose ten thousand ducats now than continue the proceedings. These and other similarly palpable flatteries must have been uttered by Miltitz on this occasion. He even went so far as to give Dr. Martinus a kiss. Luther wrote afterward, "I pretended that I did not understand such Italian shams." He regarded this kiss as a "Judas kiss" and the tears which Miltitz had shed during the conference as crocodile tears. But in this he probably did "Herr Carolus" an injustice. Although not yet thirty, Miltitz was a decided drunkard. And drunkards weep easily and are apt to become more demonstrative than other people.

Even if it was not possible for Luther to take this negotiator seriously, inasmuch as he was tired of conflict—a mood in which he found himself after the frightful strain of the preceding five months—he rejoiced in the results which had been attained, especially since he could say that he had conceded absolutely nothing to Miltitz that he could not have conceded for reasons of conscience. But in proposing to silence the opposition, Miltitz had undertaken a responsibility which he could not fulfill, much as he might try. He lacked the judgment, however, to see this. He believed that he had been tremendously successful. This pleasant feeling accompanied him on his journey to Lochau, where he wished to confer further with the Elector. Here he allowed the naming of the arbitrator, who was to continue negotiations with Luther, to be taken out of his hands too. For it was certainly not his own suggestion, but in accordance with the Elector's wish that on January 12 he offered this appointment to Archbishop Richard Greiffenklau, of Trier, who was particularly

intimate with Frederick. At the same time he asked Luther
to suggest several names, whereupon Luther likewise proposed the archbishop of Trier as first choice. Then on the
return journey, Miltitz summoned Tetzel to Leipzig on January 17 and, in the presence of the Fugger agent, he instituted a formal hearing for the old man. It accomplished the
desired result, as he wrote to Pfeffinger soon after, and made
it possible for him, as he claimed, to prefer charges in Rome
against the inquisitor, hitherto so feared, on grounds of
embezzlement and immoral life. We do not know if he ever
actually did this. At all events, Tetzel never got over this
blow. He now disappeared from the scene entirely.

Thereupon Miltitz hastened to South Germany in order
to report at last to Cajetan. He would probably have received
a poor welcome if something had not happened in the meantime to change the situation completely. On January 12
Emperor Maximilian, not yet sixty years old, had suddenly
died in Wels, in Upper Austria. As early as January 23 the
pope had directed Cajetan under all circumstances to prevent the election of a powerful prince, in particular the
election of Charles of Spain, and had at the same time designated the Elector of Saxony, not as the most acceptable to
him, but as probably the most promising candidate to whose
elevation he could consent. From that time on, the election
claimed the whole attention of Leo X, with the result that
he looked upon the Lutheran affair simply as a means of
winning the Elector of Saxony to support his policy. The
undoubtedly very optimistic report which Miltitz gave him
at the end of January or the beginning of February concerning the arbitrary steps he had taken in this matter was, therefore, extraordinarily welcome to the pope under the circumstances. He gave ready credence to the assurance of the
"windy" fellow that Luther had been so obstinate toward
Cajetan only because the latter had too openly espoused the
cause of his fellow-monk Tetzel, and that Luther now
genuinely regretted his errors and was ready to recant them

all. So the pope thought it a master stroke when he sent a breve of his own to Luther on March 29, in which he expressed his fatherly pleasure over the good disposition which had been manifested by him and invited his "beloved son" to set out for Rome at once in order to make, before him, the recantation which he had refused to offer to Cajetan because of an aversion which was understandable. It was probably in April that the breve was handed to the Elector with the remark that the pope would be happy to place the necessary money for the journey at the disposal of his beloved son. But Luther himself never saw it. The Elector probably foresaw that Luther would refuse this papal invitation outright, a thing which would bring in its train new complications with Rome which the Elector wished to avoid, and so he preferred not to show it to Luther at all.

Meanwhile Miltitz waited in Augsburg day after day for some sort of expression of praise or love from His Holiness. But it appeared that he had been entirely forgotten in Rome. He became so uneasy about this in the course of time that, after more than six months, he finally concluded that he should report to his superior, Cardinal Cajetan, whom he had slandered so maliciously behind his back. It appears, however, that even Cajetan was at first taken in by Miltitz, for on the following day, May 3, "Herr Karl" could announce triumphantly to Luther, Spalatin, and the Elector that the cardinal had agreed to admit the archbishop of Trier at least as associate judge in the Lutheran affair, and that he would approve everything that the archbishop did or decreed as a judge in his presence. Accordingly Miltitz must have believed that Luther could at once be invited to Coblenz, where Cajetan was, and that his case could now be settled easily. To this proposal Luther remarked, not inappropriately, "Are these people entirely out of their minds? There is no word at all from Rome, and yet the silly Herr von Miltitz dares to summon me—indeed, to summon me alone, to go without the archbishop of Trier—to invite me to a meeting with Cajetan at that!" Accordingly he brusquely refused Miltitz' summons on May 17. With Cajetan, he added, he did not care to have anything more to do. In fact, he had a mind to register a complaint with the pope and the college of cardinals against this man for the heinous errors he had expressed in Augsburg. Meanwhile Miltitz had already requested the Elector *not* to allow Luther to come to Coblenz. About two weeks later, on May 27, he personally, under Cajetan's orders, delivered to the prince in Weimar instructions to have the new papal decretal on indulgences, drafted by Cajetan, published in Saxony, and at the same time to indicate to Luther that the latter no longer had any reason to postpone the recantation demanded of him inasmuch as he had now been sufficiently informed and instructed. Hence the Elector and his councilors cannot be blamed, either, for not having taken Miltitz seriously. Meanwhile they avoided a break with him, for they could hardly have found a better aid for the procrastinating tactics which they pursued.

During these months the Curia revealed that it was even more deluded than this subordinate agent. On June 21 the Elector was informed in Frankfurt by Miltitz, under orders of the papal legate Orsini, that the pope, on condition that the Elector would conform to his will in the matter of the election, promised, among other things, to confer the red hat on one of Frederick's friends whom he could himself designate. Whom did Rome have in mind? It was Luther! In order to win the Elector for the papal policy in the matter of the election, the Curia was prepared to make Luther a cardinal, and eventually to provide him with a "magnificent archbishopric" as well!

By the time Frederick received this offer, however, its purpose had been frustrated. About June 16 Leo X had reached the conclusion, from the reports of his legates, that the election of Charles of Spain could not be prevented, and so he began hastily to retract his steps and wrote to

Germany that he no longer had any fault to find with this choice. In this way Charles V still became emperor with the assent of the Curia. But one cannot deny that Leo X did all that he could to thwart this elevation, and that he tried to obtain the office of emperor for Luther's defender, the Elector of Saxony, instead of for Charles. If he had accomplished his purpose, the history of the Western world would probably have taken an entirely different course from that which seemed desirable to him. In Germany, at least, the authority of the papacy would probably have been done with forever. Thus the great decisions of history often come to pass contrary to the wish of those leaders to whose advantage they contribute most, and they are brought about by those very persons who later have the strongest reason for wishing that they had not taken place. "Like a horse whose eyes are blinded," nations and their princes also rise and fall, and just when they think they are acting most shrewdly and wisely, "they know least of all what they are doing."

At first Luther adhered "rigidly" to the pact of Altenburg. When, on his journey through Leipzig on January 7, 1519, a coarse refutation by Prierias fell into his hands, he simply had this bungling work reprinted with an ironical recommendation on the title page. At the request of the Elector, he also consented (although Miltitz had given up this demand) to have a "note" printed in February under the caption, "Doctor Martinus Luther's Instruction on Several Articles which are Ascribed and Assigned to him by his Detractors." This writing is concerned with the worship of saints, purgatory, indulgences, church regulations, good works, and obedience toward the Roman Church. Despite his earnest effort to avoid offending those who were weak in the faith, only his treatment of purgatory could have been accepted as wholly correct Catholic doctrine. He admitted that miracles were still performed near the bodies and graves of saints. But these miracles were not effected by the sacred bones, but by God. It is foolishness, he wrote, to call upon the saints as if they had power and strength to do anything. It is God alone who does all things. Accordingly the saints should be called upon as intercessors only to honor God through them, and their help should be sought not only for physical, but above all for spiritual, gifts. The ordinary man does not need to know more about indulgences than that they are not necessary or commanded, and that they are of far less value than all the good works which God has commanded. The regulations of the church—such as fasting, the keeping of holy days, and so on—should, indeed, be observed, but at the same time it should not be forgotten that one can be godly without them, and that while they give a good outward appearance, inwardly they are of no value. It would be a good thing if a council would do away with some of them, for "the many lamps of these regulations have almost blotted the daylight of the divine commandments out of men's eyes." "I have not forbidden good works. I have simply declared that, just as the tree must be good before it can bring forth good fruit, so man must first be made good by God's grace before he can do good. I have rejected only the proud, sure, and free good works."

"The Roman Church," Luther continued, "is undoubtedly esteemed by God more than any other church, for in Rome Peter and Paul, forty-six popes, and many hundred thousands of martyrs have spilled their blood. If conditions in Rome are unfortunately such that they might be better, neither this nor any reason whatsoever can be or become sufficient to justify tearing loose or separating from Rome. On the contrary, the worse the conditions become there, the more one should help and cling to the church, for conditions will not be improved by separation and contempt. . . . Love can do all things, and [striving after] unity is not too hard. That is a poor sort of love and unity which allows itself to be divided by alien sin. As to the extent of the power and sovereignty of the Roman See, let the scholars fight it out, for this has nothing whatever to do with the salvation of souls. Christ did not found His church on external, strikingly visible power or on any other temporal things, but on love, humility, and unity, which are inward. Therefore, be the power as it may, whether great or small, extended over everything or confined only to a part, it should please us and we should be satisfied with it as God apportions it, just as we should also be satisfied with the way in which He apportions other temporal goods, honor, riches, favor, skill, and so on. We should be intent only upon unity, and should take good care not to resist papal commandments."

In a letter to Spalatin on March 5 Luther added by way of explanation: "I have never thought of deserting the pope. I am quite satisfied that he is called the lord of the world, and that he is that. I realize that one must honor and endure the Sultan, too, on account of the power with which he is invested. As long as he does not confuse the Gospel with his decrees, I will not stir as much as a hair, even if he takes everything else away from me. For this reason I am willing to put up with the pact [of Altenburg]." So he kept this agreement loyally. For two full months—which meant a great deal in his case—he "began nothing new and stood still." Only when he had come to the conviction that he could no longer keep the agreement because his opponents had no intention of remaining silent, and only after he had very dutifully signified this to the Elector on March 13, did he begin again to print "new things." To such an extent did he produce new things, in fact, that he had to keep two Leipzig printers busy in addition to Grünenberg. He sent them copy for no fewer than five pieces, some of them quite voluminous, during March and April. These were the three treatises *On the Double Righteousness*, *On the Marriage Estate*, and *On the Contemplation of the Blessed Passion of Christ;* then the *German Exposition of the Lord's Prayer for Simple Laymen* and the first part of his *Studies in the Psalms* (*Operationes in Psalmos*). Then in May he sent to Lotter in

Leipzig his *Commentary on the Epistle to the Galatians* on which he had been working since March 13, and at the same time he had his *Treatise on Prayer in Rogation Week* and his first little polemical writing against Eck printed by Grünenberg. He was now producing so rapidly that not only his typesetters, but also his readers, had difficulty in keeping pace with him.

At the same time he was "constantly growing and making progress." In the *Treatise on the Marriage Estate* Luther asserted for the first time that bringing up children is incomparably better than going on pilgrimages, building churches, endowing masses, and doing such other things as are called good works; indeed, for people who have children this is the most direct way to heaven. In the *Treatise on Prayer in Rogation Week* he expressed his earliest criticism of the shameful doing in connection with processions. If these abuses cannot be removed, he wrote, the processions ought simply to be done away with. In the *Treatise on the Double Righteousness* he first expressed the opinion that the command, "Resist not evil," does not refer to the government. On the contrary, a Christian prince or magistrate can fulfill the common Christian duty of love toward his neighbors only when he uses the power given him by God as energetically as possible in order to keep down evildoers and defend the oppressed. But here Luther was thinking only of the fight against crime, and not of war against external foes. Even the war against the Turks he regarded as wrong, although it was allegedly being waged for the faith.

But most important of all these publications was the *Treatise on the Contemplation of the Blessed Passion of Christ*, which was immediately reprinted in Leipzig, Munich, Basel, Nuremberg, Augsburg, and Strassburg. In it Luther touched for the first time on a problem which especially interested monastics. It is the question whether or not to approve the "wooing of Christ" recommended especially by St. Bernard, which seeks, by methodical submersion in the life and suffering of Christ, to engender in the soul a feeling of the nearness and presence of the soul's Bride, and then to associate with Christ as bride and bridegroom, in a sensuous - supersensuous devotion. Luther answered this question with a flat negative. Anyone, he wrote, who contemplates and reflects on Christ's passion in this way converts the passion into a "not-passion." In other words, he makes it a form of self-gratification. Christ Himself earnestly forbade such compassion when He said to the women who wept as they followed Him, "Weep for yourselves and for your children!" The customary coloring of the passion history by introducing new stories, not recorded in the Bible — for instance, concerning Christ's farewell in Bethany and the grief of his mother — also serves this egocentric purpose. Proper reflection on Christ's passion means to make clear to oneself the "unshakable earnestness of God with regard to sin and sinners" which is revealed therein.

In the *Studies in the Psalms*, which appeared at the same time, Luther expressed himself just as unequivocally with regard to this sort of mysticism, which was cultivated with particular zeal in the nunneries and which was very often accompanied there by pronounced pathological aberrations. The sensual images and comparisons of the Song of Solomon, he declared here, can only be used as a symbol of the fellowship which exists between Christ and the believers if one regards them as the expression of the wholly unsensuous affections of faith, hope, and charity. So later, when in very exceptional cases he used the image of the marriage of the soul with Christ, which was such a favorite in the late Middle Ages, he always gave it a different meaning. Not only did he reject this "bride-mysticism," but he also declared his absolute opposition to the methods of the so-called "speculative mysticism" against which he had occasionally warned his hearers as early as 1516. Thus he now rejected mysticism absolutely. If one asks what induced him to do this, one must answer that it was the recognition of an irreconcilable antithesis between this religious way of thinking and the religion of the Bible. The fact that he occasionally cited Tauler and the German Theologian until the close of 1520, and still employed frequent mystical expressions and images in his *Studies in the Psalms,* does not at all alter this conclusion. For, as we have seen, he never really understood these two old men of God and always gave another meaning to the mystical ideas which he continued to use. Hence no reader could be tempted to understand them in the mystical sense.

As in this first part, so also in the rest of his *Studies in the Psalms (Operationes in Psalmos),* the last number of which he did not finish until he was on the Wartburg in 1521, we notice the great progress which Luther had made since 1515 both as a religious thinker and as an exegete. It is true that Hebrew grammar was, as he put it himself, "not yet fully employed therein." But the Hebrew text was now always taken into consideration, and the Septuagint at least occasionally. The medieval method of fourfold exposition had for the most part disappeared, and the Messianic interpretation of the Psalms had been restricted. In the external plan, too, he had now freed himself entirely from the medieval scheme. To be sure, the interpretation had, as he was himself aware, become very prolix, but the prolixity was hardly wearisome, so overpowering was the enthusiasm with which he sought to interpret the *religious* thoughts of the sacred text for his hearers and readers (for it is this that was always of the first importance to him) in living, fluent Latin which was not enfeebled by the pedantic overrefinements of the humanists.

It cost Luther less time and trouble to convert his lectures on the Epistle to the Galatians, which he had delivered only two years before, into a running commentary. Probably the only matter which was entirely new in this book (which did not appear until the beginning of September) was the interpolation of polemical excurses on scholasticism and on the intolerable greediness, venality, law-making, arrogance, and

tyranny of the Curia. Such passages were not wanting
either, in the *Studies in the Psalms*. That the Antichrist was
ruling the Curia, he was already convinced by March or
April, 1519. Likewise, he knew that popes and councils not
only could err, but actually had erred. Nevertheless, he still
demanded obedience, but no longer blind obedience, to the
pope. "A command of the pope is binding only when it is
in accord with the glory of God." "For the papacy is only
a human, earthly arrangement, not a divine institution, and
its tyranny has now become so unbearable that one must ask
whether our bones are strong enough to endure this condition longer." It was in such terms that the Reformer was
thinking and expressing himself publicly as much as three
months before the Leipzig Disputation. But he was doing
this on the basis of the studies which he had already made
in preparation for the approaching disputation.

CHAPTER XXI

THE ADVANCES OF THE HUMANISTS

On February 14, 1519, the renowned printer, John Froben, of Basel, wrote to Luther: "Six hundred copies [of the edition of your collected works which I have published] have been shipped to France and Spain. They are being bought up in Paris, and read and approved at the Sorbonne. The book-seller Calvus, of Pavia, has taken a considerable number with him to Italy in order to sell them in all the towns there. I have also delivered copies to Brabant and England. I have only ten left in stock. Never before have I had so much luck with a book. The abler a man is, the more he is prejudiced in your favor." What Froben did, Andreas Cratander, Adam Petri, and other Basel printers were also doing. In fact, Petri had already suspended the rest of his business in 1519 in order to devote himself exclusively to Luther's works. This, of course, would never have occurred to him if he had not been able to count on the fact that Luther was now selling better, outside Germany as well as inside, than even the renowned Erasmus of Rotterdam.

Whom did the famous Basel businessmen and their colleagues in the German centers of the art of printing have to thank for this excellent appreciation of the new author? All the evidence points to the students and followers of Erasmus, the humanists. It was these men, who were in particularly close contact with the printing craft, who called the printers' attention to this new, fashionable author and induced them to reprint his writings. And then, when these were available in print, the humanists also recommended them on every hand, and at times even sent them out and scattered them abroad in bales. Hence the view that the attention of the humanists was first called to the Saxon monk after the Leipzig Disputation is nothing more than a fable of scholars.

Long before this, the humanists had established personal connections with Luther. The Nuremberg circle had already formed ties with him in March, 1517. The Heidelbergers drew close to him in the spring, the Baselers not later than the summer, and the Augsburgers in October of 1518. The Leipzigers, Peter Mosellanus and his associates, were also in contact with him since the beginning of 1519. And they early felt the need of preparing the way for friendship between him and their highly esteemed lord and master, the renowned Erasmus. In the spring of 1519 the Reformer finally allowed himself to be prevailed upon, especially through Wolfgang Fabricius Capito, the professor and preacher in Basel, to address a sort of letter of homage to the celebrated man who was then in Louvain. But Erasmus was in no hurry to take the hand which had been extended to him. It was not until May 30 that he replied—pleasantly, courteously, obligingly as ever, but utterly cool. Instead of offering Luther support or friendship, he complained rather affectedly that he had again and again been falsely designated as the author of Luther's works and that this suspicion had hurt the fair name of the arts. Instead of encouraging Luther, Erasmus warned him to be sure to proceed cautiously, discreetly, and gently. But it was enough for the humanists that their illustrious master had answered at all. Indeed, Peter Mosellanus, when Luther showed him the letter in Leipzig at the end of June, was so delighted with this new specimen of Erasmian elegance that, without first asking Luther and the master, he had it printed in July. At first Erasmus was quite beside himself at this. He was only pacified when he saw that the letter caused the decided friends rather than the inveterate opponents of Luther to take offense, for he feared the latter far more than the former.

But his students and friends generally believed at this time that, even if he was not so outspoken and consistent, Erasmus desired fundamentally the same thing as Luther, and consequently that, in espousing Luther's cause, they were simply responding to the wishes and designs which he had concealed up to this time for purely political reasons. Hence they did not notice at all that they had actually run into an entirely different channel. The most talented among them—Melanchthon, Zwingli, Bucer, Oecolampadius—were already more Lutheran than Erasmian at the beginning of 1519, and most of the younger men with humanistic interests subsequently went the same way. The few who remained faithful to the ideas of the aging master, who had hitherto been spoiled beyond measure by youthful adherents, were either old men who no longer had the strength to adjust themselves to new convictions, or else were second or third rate minds who, forced to choose between Rome and Wittenberg, finally decided in favor of Rome.

Inasmuch as the humanists were, for the most part, school teachers, their growing interest in Luther and his cause was not slow in showing itself in the fact that they sent their students to Wittenberg. By December, 1518, the little town resembled a swarming ant-hill. By the following May the student enrollment had increased so rapidly that the neophytes could no longer find quarters either in the *bursae* or in the homes of the burghers, and the university had to consider the erection of a large new lecture hall for "the higher faculties"—in other words, especially for the theological men. The number coming from South Germany was particularly large. But since the summer of 1518, Swiss students were also beginning to put in their appearance in the little town. Then in the Easter season of 1519, Tyrolese, Steiermarkians, Alsatians, and Walloons appeared for the first time, and in the fall Scotchmen and Czechs came too. Even more than in these foreigners, Luther was interested in the older people who had left home and position in order to get to know him. The first man of whom this is reported was Magister Thomas Münzer, of Stolberg. Late in 1518 he gave up his good post in the nunnery of Frohse, near Aschersleben, in order to move to Wittenberg. By the summer of 1519 a large number of such "distinguished" persons were sitting at Luther's feet. Among these were Canon Schleupner of Breslau, Licentiate John Herolt, preacher at St. Sebald's in Nuremberg, and Matthew Hiscold, of Bosau. In a scant year and a half, therefore, this pitiful provincial university had almost overtaken the two largest German universities, Cologne and Leipzig. Indeed, it was feared in Leipzig that Wittenberg would outstrip it.

This upward swing can be accounted for only and alone by Luther. Melanchthon, although he was already lecturing to four hundred, was at this time still a rising star. Of the other professors, only Carlstadt commanded a measure of esteem, but even he was esteemed as a "champion of Luther." All this was very well known at the electoral court, and for this reason even more allowance than before was made for the wishes of "Herr Martinus" in the management of university affairs. The thoroughgoing reform of the arts faculty in the spring of 1518, which gave the humanists preponderance and led subsequently to the calling of Melanchthon and the founding of a regular chair of the Hebrew language, is a characteristic example of this. Also in ecclesiastical matters—for instance, the distribution of the benefices of the Elector's patronage—Martinus was already beginning to be heeded. Occasionally he could even venture now to put in a good word with the Elector for others—as, for example, for Magister Melanchthon, who was very poorly paid and excessively burdened with lectures. For himself the most he asked was a black or a white cowl once in a while, and then only when it was absolutely necessary. For such additional needs as he might have—books and, above all, paper—the nine old guldens (some sixty-five dollars) which the niggardly Elector allowed him for pocket money until 1523—for at that time this item was also canceled by the so-called reformers of the university—were, as a rule at least, sufficient. But he would undoubtedly have been willing to do without this grand allowance if the Elector had given him, in its place, an entirely free hand in the vindication of the truth.

CHAPTER XXII

THE LEIPZIG DISPUTATION

Among the people who sought out Luther in Augsburg during October, 1518, was Professor Eck of Ingolstadt, with whom the Reformer had had the painful exchange of correspondence concerning the *Ninety-five Theses* the preceding spring. Luther's personal conversation with this unquestionably astute and gifted South German was so satisfying that he cast aside all suspicion of this scholar, who was highly esteemed even in humanistic circles, and honestly endeavored also to negotiate an honorable peace between Eck and Carlstadt. This purpose was to be served by the disputation to which Eck had already challenged Carlstadt in August. Luther had discussed the matter with Eck in Augsburg in a friendly manner. They agreed in recommending to Carlstadt as a suitable place either Erfurt or Leipzig. In November Carlstadt accepted this proposal, but left the decision to Eck, whereupon Eck chose Leipzig. On December 4 Eck applied to the Leipzig theological faculty and Duke George of Saxony for permission to hold the disputation. The faculty, however, would have nothing to do with this intended honor, as Luther learned from the rector or the dean in Leipzig on January 7, 1519, when he was on his way from Altenburg to Wittenberg. The diocesan who had jurisdiction in Leipzig, Bishop Adolph of Merseburg, also showed himself altogther disinclined to grant Eck's wishes. Duke George, however, had no objections to them and was gradually able to bring the Leipzig theologians, of whom he had a very low opinion, to the point where, on February 1, they reluctantly submitted to his will. The bishop, however, he was unable to persuade.

Meanwhile, on December 29, Eck had published twelve

theses for the coming Leipzig disputation and sent them to Wittenberg without waiting for the answer of the duke and the Leipzig faculty. The first of these theses was directed against the first of Luther's *Ninety-five Theses*. Nor did the following theses have anything to do with the questions on which he had come to blows with Carlstadt. All of them referred, rather, to utterances of Luther, some of which he repeated in distorted form. There is no doubt that the slippery Swabian was seeking a quarrel with Luther, as he later openly admitted. He saw his opportunity chiefly in the Reformer's incidental remark in the *Resolutions*, "The Roman Church at the time of Gregory did not as yet possess sovereignty over the Greek Church." It was his intention to chastise Luther for this remark in his own twelfth thesis: "It is false to assert that the Roman Church before the time of Sylvester (314-35) had not yet possessed sovereignty over the other churches." It is true, this is not exactly what Luther had said, but it corresponded with his convictions. Luther not only accepted this thesis, therefore, but trumped it by now making the assertion even more pointed. "That the Roman Church is superior to all others is proved only by the utterly worthless papal decrees of the last four hundred years. Against these stands the testimony of the authentic history of eleven hundred years, the text of Holy Scriptures, and the decree of the Council of Nicaea, the holiest of all councils." Is this to be interpreted to mean that the papacy did not arise until the twelfth century? Luther answered later that such a stupid assertion surely could not be attributed to him. He simply meant to say that it was the codification of the decretals after Gregory IX that had made it possible for the popes completely to enforce their claims, especially in Germany.

Why, then, did Luther express himself so strangely, even ambiguously? Because, as was customary in disputations, it was his purpose to set a trap for Eck, who was himself adept at setting traps. He did not think of the impression this radical sounding thesis would make on his admirers as well as his enemies. Indeed, he was highly incensed when Spalatin, probably at the command of the Elector, remonstrated with him concerning it. He wrote near the end of February: "Let my friends think me mad. Like Christ, I, too, must be deserted by everyone. If I go down to destruction, no one will be harmed by it. The Wittenbergers do not need me any longer. Do you think that I am not worthy to suffer martyrdom for this cause? I have always told you that I am ready to get out if I should endanger the Elector by my presence. I have to die some time anyhow."

By this time he had already published the above-mentioned ominous thesis and the eleven other less dangerous sounding ones, along with an open letter to Carlstadt in which he exposed Eck's machinations and announced that now he, too, was under the necessity of debating with Eck in Leipzig. This announcement aroused almost as much of a sensation as the new theses. On February 12 the bishop of Brandenburg, on his visit to Wittenberg, remonstrated with him not to engage in such a hazardous affair. Elector Frederick was evidently of the opinion that, since Eck had not attacked him directly, he was still bound to the agreement at Altenburg. Then, unexpectedly, Eck himself came to his assistance. On February 19 he wrote to Luther that he was definitely counting on his presence in Leipzig, first, because he was the real author of the false teachings for which he had attacked Carlstadt, and, second, because, as was evident to Luther, the theses which he had published on December 29 were not directed against Carlstadt but against him. Luther laid this "triumphant" letter before the Elector on March 13. After this the Elector no longer felt it necessary to keep him gagged, and henceforth let him go as he pleased.

But Luther had committed an error of omission in the open letter to Carlstadt which was to give him trouble for months. Instead of first turning to Dresden and Leipzig to request written permission to hold the disputation, he had forthwith announced, "I will cross swords with Eck in Leipzig." The university acceded to his "humble" petition in March, but the proud and willful duke could not so soon forget Luther's presumption. He informed him on March 4 that he could grant him permission only if Eck expressly wished it. Then Luther wrote to Eck in haste. But it evidently gave Eck a peculiar pleasure to let the impatient monk writhe, for he gave him no answer, even though he was fairly panting to debate with him and had just republished his theses, with one added, under the revealing title, *Theses against Luther to be disputed in Leipzig*. A second letter of Luther's had the same result. Nor could the duke be moved to change his mind even by an appeal to Eck's printed challenge. Thus on June 6, three weeks before the time set by Eck for the beginning of the disputation, Luther did not know whether he would receive permission from the duke, not to mention whether, as "a person entangled in the jurisdiction of His Holiness the Pope," he would receive the necessary safe-conduct. He was determined, nevertheless, to go to Leipzig if necessary without a safe-conduct. But in case he was still to be refused a hearing, he had a surprise up his sleeve for those who were envious and jealous of him, especially the Dominican provincial, Herman Rab, to whom he traced the enigmatic conduct of the duke. This would prove to them that it was not so easy to gag him. The surprise was the *Resolutio Lutheriana super propositione decima tertia de potestate papae*, a written defense of the "odious thirteenth" thesis (originally the twelfth) on the origin of papal primacy, which he had had printed secretly so as to be able to publish it immediately in the event that he was unable to get a hearing in Leipzig.

The work is a brilliant testimony to the speed with which Luther was able to familiarize himself even with problems which were foreign to his nature. However, if it is compared with the antipapal polemics of the last centuries of the

Middle Ages, of which at this time he still had very little
knowledge, it does not at first glance appear to be particularly new or original. His demonstration that the famous
Biblical proofs for the primacy of the pope "did not hold
water," as well as the contention that the New Testament
makes no distinction between presbyters and bishops, and
the passages which he quoted from the church fathers and
the *Historia Tripartita* to prove the nonexistence of primacy
in the history of the church during the first six centuries
are all to be found in this earlier literature. Even the opinion
that Antichrist was reigning in the Curia is to be found long
before Luther among the Cathari, the Waldensians, and the
Wyclifites. All that is new in these polemical sections is,
first, his proof of the gross maltreatment to which the popes
in their decretals subjected the Bible in their effort to sub-
stantiate their claims to sovereignty; second, his contention
that it was not until the time of Emperor Constantine IV
(669-83) that anything like a primacy in the legal sense
arose; and, finally, his establishment of the fact that the
Greek Church, like the other eastern churches, was never
actually under the sovereignty of Rome and still had just as
good a right as the Roman Church to call itself a Christian
Church. Even here, however, he made a contribution that
was positively new, something not thought of by the many
critics of the papacy in the Middle Ages, even by Marsiglio
of Padua and Wyclif. He was the first to declare *publicly:*
"Where the word of God is preached and believed, there is
the church. It is called a kingdom of faith because its King
is invisible, an object of faith. But they [Eck and his fellows]
make of it a realm of visible things in that they give it a
visible head." "But I do not know whether faith can suffer
any other head than Christ."

Thus, in his criticism, Luther began with a conception of
the church that is altogether different from that of all the
other medieval critics and sectarians. For them the church
was the visible ecclesiastical institution, which they still

acknowledged to be identical with the Kingdom of God, no matter how much fault they might have to find with it. In actuality, their opinions differed from those of the popes only in questions of government. Luther was the first to break with this characteristic view held by all of Catholic Christendom. Consequently he no longer knew what to do with the idea of papacy, or even the Catholic idea of the church as such. But, as always, it was very hard for him to throw the old views overboard. He took the greatest pains, therefore, to demonstrate that the existence of the papacy would be quite compatible with his ideas if, in addition to the honorary pre-eminence which was naturally due him as the successor of Peter, the pope would consent to claim nothing more than the rank of a supreme officer of the church according to human law, and hence renounce the *religious* prerogatives hitherto conceded to him.

But even at this time Luther already had the feeling that he would not be able to hold to this recasting of the idea of the papacy, for ever since his encounter with Cajetan he had been unable to rid himself of the terrible thought that the papacy was Antichrist. He had first expressed this thought in a letter to Link on December 11, 1518, but then merely as a suspicion to which he had come, he knew not how, after the completion of his *Acta Augustana*. In the spring of 1519, when he began an intensive study of canon law in preparation for the disputation, this suspicion became such a certainty, in view of the unscrupulous perversions of the Scriptures which the popes resorted to in their decretals, that he was constrained, on March 13, to confide to the uneasy Spalatin, "I speak it in your ear: I know not whether the pope is Antichrist or an apostle of Antichrist." But he did not advocate this publicly until the end of March, in the first part of his *Studies in the Psalms*. Even here it is posed merely as a hypothetical question and not without emphasizing in the strongest terms his personal fidelity to the present possessor of the tiara, Pope Leo X. Was this hypocrisy?

No, it was only a symptom of the peculiar state of his mind at the time. On the one hand, he did not want to see the papacy completely done away under any circumstances; on the other hand, however, he no longer knew how to justify its existence. As always, he reached a clear understanding of the question only through severe struggle. Outwardly, however, no one would have suspected that he was going through these struggles. When, at the beginning of May, the provincial chapter of the Franciscan Observants, provoked by the utterly coarse sermons Thomas Münzer had been preaching since April 26 as an assistant to Franz Günther in Jüterbog, condemned Luther's teachings and denounced him as a heretic to the bishop of Brandenburg, the Reformer rebuked them with such vehemence that at first they did not dare to take any further steps. When the false rumor came to his ears that he had already been burned in effigy in the Campo di Fiore in Rome, he merely wrote (May 30): "Rome burns to destroy me. But I am so cool, I only laugh at her." In fact, he needed but one thing to live by—the certainty that God was gracious and merciful toward him. But even now, particularly in such times of inner tension, he was still under the necessity of struggling again and again to renew this certainty.

Eck arrived in Leipzig on June 21 or 22. He came with excellent recommendations from the Fuggers, whom he had put under great obligations by his celebrated opinion concerning their financial operations which had been contested as usurious. On June 30 he marched with the Leipzig theological faculty in the Corpus Christi procession. The Wittenbergers, traveling in two ordinary open wagons, did not reach Leipzig until some time on June 24. In the first wagon sat Carlstadt with a great stack of heavy books. In the second were Duke Barnim of Pomerania, the then honorary rector of the University of Wittenberg, and Luther and Melanchthon. Nearly two hundred students, armed with spears and halberds, marched along with them. As they were entering Grimma Street, a wheel of the first wagon broke down and Carlstadt toppled out, painfully injuring both his thumbs, to the great satisfaction of the numerous superstitious old women of both sexes among the onlookers. Meanwhile Luther rode on to Hay Street where Melchior Lotter, the bookprinter, who, like many other tradesmen, kept a public wineshop, had prepared quarters for him and his friends.

Upon his arrival Luther learned that a mandate of the bishop of Merseburg, which prohibited the disputation under severe penalty, had just been posted on the church doors. Immediately afterward, however, it was announced that the town council had already had the mandate torn down and had thrown the man who had posted it into prison. The town authorities would certainly not have taken such quick and severe action if they had not been given previous instructions by the duke. For the duke respected the wishes of the bishops only in so far as they suited him. So in this case as well, he had no hesitation whatsoever, a few days afterward, to send the presumptuous mandate back to Bishop Adolph, and accompany it with some very ungracious words, even though it did contain the new papal decree on indulgences. But this was done for Eck's sake, not for the sake of the Wittenbergers, for the attitude of the ruling classes of Leipzig was highly unfavorable toward the Wittenbergers, though the town council had not refused them the customary honorary gift of wine. While Eck was honored in every way—the town council even put at his disposal a horse and groom for his daily rides through Rose Valley and Scheib Grove—the Wittenbergers were deliberately ignored. Only Simon Pistoris, the professor of law, and the physician, Dr. Henry Stromer of Auerbach, dared to associate with them in public and even, on one occasion, to invite them to dinner.

Eck immediately sought in his own way to capitalize on this good will which was so openly shown toward him. When, on June 26, he and Carlstadt were summoned by

Councilor Caesar Pflugk, the ducal commissioner, to appear at the Pleissenburg to make the customary final settlement of the terms of the disputation before a notary and witnesses, Eck suddenly announced that he did not wish to dispute in the German style, as had been agreed upon, but in the Italian style, that is, by free statement and reply; and also that now he must absolutely reject the previously agreed upon publication of the protocol. Why did the old agreement suit him no longer? Because he thought he was superior to Carlstadt and Luther in free argument, while he secretly feared the criticism which might result from publication. On the first point Carlstadt remained inflexible. On the second he finally yielded. Luther was not invited to assent to this arrangement until the next day. At first he positively refused to participate at all in the disputation under such conditions. This was highly displeasing to Eck, who, in the meantime, had procured permission from the duke to allow the Reformer to participate. Luther's Mansfeld countryman, Saxon Councilor Rühel, and also Carlstadt, Amsdorf, Melanchthon, and his friend Lang urgently pleaded with him to yield, if only to give the lie to the malicious rumor that he was now afraid of Eck and was turning tail. He finally allowed himself to be persuaded, and on July 4, shortly before seven in the morning, in the Pleissenburg, he signed the pact which Eck "had forced upon the Wittenbergers contrary to his own letter, seal, and promise." Nevertheless, he expressly declined to accept the pope as a judge of the disputation and reserved his legal right of appeal to a future council.

Before this, the disputation had been opened on the morning of June 27 with the customary great ceremonial. This consisted of the formal welcome of the disputants in the great lecture hall of the university on Ritter Street; a festival mass in St. Thomas' Church with twelve-part singing by the St. Thomas choir under the direction of the cantor, George Rhau; a festival convocation in the magnificent tapestry-hung court room of the Pleissenburg castle, including an almost two-hour Latin address on "The Art and Method of Disputation, especially on Matters Theological," delivered with frightful coughing and croaking by Mosellanus, the professor of poetry, and concluding with the rendition (the audience kneeling) of the hymn *Veni Sancte Spiritus* by the St. Thomas choir and the combined fife corps of the town.

During the first week only Eck and Carlstadt disputed. But neither of them overexerted himself. On June 27 they debated only three hours, from two to five o'clock in the afternoon; on June 28 four hours, from seven to nine and three to five o'clock. On June 29 and 30 and July 2 the battle was suspended entirely on account of the church festivals, and on July 1 they were satisfied with about two hours. The seventy-six burghers in armor and fine weapons who marched out each day with drums beating and trumpets sounding in order to maintain order in the town during the hours when the disputation was going on, had very little to do during this week. On June 29, at the request of Duke Barnim, but greatly to the displeasure of Councilor Caesar Pflugk, Luther preached in the disputation hall on the Gospel for the Day, Matthew 16:13 ff. The sermon treated "the whole subject of the disputation," namely, first, the grace of God and free will and, second, the power of St. Peter. This immediately prompted Eck to preach two counter-sermons against him, on July 2 and 3, before a crowded auditorium in St. Nicholas' Church. Otherwise Luther had peace for a change, and even time to see the limited number of places of interest in that "city of mammon" which was so highly unsympathetic toward him. Sometimes he had some very strange experiences. At St. Paul's, for example, the Dominicans, as soon as they noted his presence, hastily snatched to a place of safety the monstrance containing the sacrament. Those who were still saying mass at the side altars fled in haste into the sacristy with the sacred vessels, "as if the devil were chasing them." However, this did not prevent him, several days later, from writing a friendly letter to his old adversary,

Tetzel, who was prostrated in the same Dominican monastery (St. Paul's) with a severe illness from which he died soon after, on August 11. He consoled him by saying that "he should not distress himself, for the affair had not begun on his account, but the child had an altogether different father." He was thinking, of course, not of the secret relations which were supposed to have existed between him and the devil, but of Archbishop Albrecht of Mainz or the pope.

On July 4, at seven in the morning, he finally climbed into the lecturer's desk, which was embellished with an embroidered picture of St. Martin and which had been set aside for the Wittenbergers. On this morning the great court room was, if possible, even more crowded than on the first day of the disputation. Behind the cathedra, decorated with the picture of St. George and allotted to Eck, the members of the Leipzig theological faculty took their seats, led by their senior, Jerome Dungersheim of Ochsenfurt, who had already exchanged with Luther a great number of very learned letters on the power of the pope. The other faculties were also represented in great numbers. Among the others present were Abbot Valentine of Lehnin, who had been specially sent to Leipzig by the bishop of Brandenburg; the abbots of Pforta, Pegau, and Bosau; and the principal of the monastic school of St. Emmeram in Ratisbon. Other companions of Eck were also present: the Dresden court chaplain, Jerome Emser; the pastors of Görlitz and Annaberg; the former indulgence preacher, Baumgartner; and many other Saxon clerics and monks. Only the Dominicans had intentionally stayed away.

Besides the disputants, the Wittenbergers were represented by Melanchthon, Amsdorf, Eisermann, and Magister Fabricius Fach. Among their friends were Matthew Hiscold, monk of Bosau, Magister Adam Krafft, the Augustinian John Lang of Erfurt, Dr. Auerbach, and perhaps also the electoral councilor, John Rühel, and the electoral chief magistrate, Hans von der Planitz, of Grimma. Even the jaundiced face of Magister Thomas Münzer, who in the meantime had found a refuge in Orlamünde on the Saale, appeared on the Wittenberg side at the beginning of the debate. Among the most distinguished personages, Duke Barnim, who "did not miss a single hour of the disputation," had undoubtedly already made his appearance. Whether Duke George, his son John, and the twelve-year-old Prince George of Anhalt, who was still attending school in Leipzig, were also present, we are not informed. In any case, we are certain of the duke's presence only for the discussion on the afternoon of July 5. Councilor Pflugk functioned as his representative and commissioner, and Francis Richter, the secretary of the university, and John Graumann, called Poliander, the rector of St. Thomas' school, acted as secretaries. In addition to these, about thirty other persons took notes privately. Since Luther and Eck were disputing in the German fashion, the participants had to speak so that the secretaries could write down their speeches word for word. This certainly could not have been very pleasant to listen to. It is, therefore, quite possible that some of the listeners occasionally dozed. But it is undoubtedly a malicious fabrication that the "Leipzig theologians, who always sat near Eck, all slept so peacefully that they generally had to be roused when the disputing was over so that they would not miss their meals and thus lose their power and strength, which they would have to use against the heretic when the council met."

Mosellanus has given a full description of the two chief disputants as they looked to him at the time. He did this in a letter to his friend Pirckheimer on August 3, and in another written five months later to his pupil, Julius Pflugk. He wrote: "Martinus is of medium height, haggard, and so emaciated with care and much study that one can almost count all the bones in his body. Nevertheless, he is still in the vigor of manhood. His voice rings clear and distinct. . . . In his manner and social intercourse he is cultivated and affable, not at all gloomy or arrogant, always in a good humor, in company agreeable, cheerful, and jocose. No matter how hard his opponent threatens him, he is always confident and joyous. . . . Eck is a great, tall fellow, solidly and robustly built. The full, genuinely German voice that resounds from his powerful chest sounds like that of a town-crier or a tragic actor. But it is more harsh than distinct. The euphony of the Latin language, so highly prized by Fabius and Cicero, is never heard in his mode of speech. His mouth and eyes, or rather his whole physiognomy, are such that one would sooner think him a butcher or a common soldier than a theologian. As far as his mind is concerned, he has a phenomenal memory. If he had an equally acute understanding, he would be the image of a perfect man. He lacks quickness of comprehension and acuteness of judgment, qualities without which all the other talents are vain. . . . His gestures are almost theatrical, his actions overbearing; in short, the impression he gives is not at all that of a theologian. He is nothing more than an uncommonly bold, even shameless, sophist."

Exactly! In intellectual capacity Eck was far behind both men with whom he ventured to compete in Leipzig. There is not a single idea in the more than seventy-five writings which he has left behind which had not been expressed before, and generally better, by others. As a writer he did not rise above the average professorial level of his day. His Latin was mediocre, his German less than mediocre. The range of his scholarly interests was not small, but his erudition was never deep, and in Amsdorf's judgment he was not even so thoroughly at home in the traditional scholastic philosophy as he wished to make his hearers believe. Moreover, he knew so little about the Bible, although he had already been an ordinary professor of theology for nine years, that in contrast with the Wittenbergers he laid himself open to the sharpest attacks on this point. The only advantage he had over his colleagues, as not only Mosellanus but all the other observers emphasize, was his extraordinarily good

memory and his quickness at repartee in debate, supported
by a powerful voice and an unusually self-confident disposition. He was, therefore, very fond of debating, especially
in the Latin style, in which he was almost always able to
outstrip his opponent with his good memory and his ready
tongue, and could even occasionally risk an outright sophistical argument and maneuver with citations which were
nowhere written as he quoted them. In Leipzig, to his
annoyance, he now had to dispute in the "German style."
But as early as June 28 he had succeeded at least in gaining
one point—that his opponent would not be permitted to read
his arguments or consult any books which he may have
brought with him, but must rather meet him in a contest
"of memory and gift of gab," as Luther aptly expressed it.
He had no difficulty with Carlstadt in this respect, for, as
the swarthy little man complained, his "memory had completely trickled away" with the blood which he had lost
in the fall from the wagon and the bloodletting afterward
prescribed for him. Consequently Carlstadt was often
unable to follow his adroit opponent, much less answer him
on the spur of the moment. He was always painfully dependent on the notes which he had thought out and written down
at home and then dictated to the secretaries at the disputation in a dull, unpleasant voice. When this was forbidden
him on June 28, upon Eck's insistence, it was "all over with
him." "No more is expected of Carlstadt here," wrote Eck
triumphantly to Ingolstadt on July 1. And even Luther
wrote later, "He is laying up disgrace instead of honor, for
as a disputator he is utterly ruined."

Carlstadt's eclipse made the Leipzigers so much the more
eager to see how the other Wittenberg "monster" would distinguish himself on the platform. The mere fact that the
"rascally viperous fellow" wore a silver ring instead of the
customary gold one seemed suspicious to them; but much
more so the fact that this ring had a capsule in it. "What
is hidden in the capsule?" they whispered. And someone

answered in all seriousness, "The devil!" They were also highly offended when—we do not know whether on this or the following day—Luther brought with him a small bouquet of pinks and, when his opponent began to thunder, smelled them with gusto. In the course of the following weeks, they made out that this bouquet had been a whole wreath of pinks; then they had him wearing this wreath publicly through the city; and finally they spread the story that he had actually had the wreath on his head when he rode out of the city gates.

Nevertheless, when this godforsaken man began to speak, punctually at seven o'clock, they listened to him in profound silence. At the very outset, Luther emphasized that, out of reverence to the pope and the Roman Church, he would gladly have left untouched the question which was to be debated if Eck had not forced him to broach the subject. He then expressed his regret that he saw none of the people in the hall who in recent times had so often pilloried him, publicly and privately, as a heretic. He was referring to Tetzel and his aiders and abetters in the Dominican monastery of St. Paul; thus he was still unaware that Tetzel was lying there in his cell on his deathbed. He then gave the floor to Eck.

The first day passed without incident. However, on the afternoon of the second day (July 5), Eck could no longer restrain himself from pointing out that Luther's view of the primacy of the pope was extraordinarily close to the error of the schismatic Bohemians. Luther immediately repelled this insinuation. At the close of the discussion, however, Eck brought it up again. He remarked sarcastically, "If the Reverend Father is so opposed to the Hussites, why does he not use his excellent talents in writing against them?" Luther again sharply forbade him to insinuate that he was a Hussite. Then, when he had the floor again, about two o'clock in the afternoon, he returned to Eck's slur and declared roundly, "Among the articles of John Huss and the Hussites, there

are many which are genuinely Christian and evangelical and
which the church universal cannot condemn; thus, for example, the sentence, 'There is only *one* universal church.'" These
words fell like a thunderbolt in the hall. Duke George, who
was present on this day, put his arms akimbo, shook his
head, and cursed aloud, "That's the plague!" Eck at once
triumphantly pounced on this heresy, while Luther protested
excitedly. But Eck would not let him go; he sought by all
the rules of the art to ride him farther into the swamp,
charging that he did not even shrink from imputing error to
such a holy and universally recognized council as that of
Constance. Luther interrupted him at once to maintain that
he had had no intention whatever of saying anything against
the Council of Constance, which, in point of fact, was true.
Eck, however, declared that he would prove it from his writings and utterances, and again characterized him as a patron
of the Hussites. Luther interrupted him again and called
this assertion a shameless lie.

On the morning of July 6, Luther began by complaining
that Eck was conducting himself toward him, not as a party
having equal rights, but as a judge, contrary to the disputation agreement. He then continued, "I have not approved
the errors of Huss, but you must prove to me that the articles
which I characterized as Christian are erroneous." At one
o'clock in the afternoon, Eck denied that he had called
Luther a heretic, but that he had merely maintained that his
assertions were favorable to the views of a heretic, especially
those of the Hussites. He did this because, in the meantime,
the ducal commissioner, Pflugk, upon the insistence of von
der Planitz, the chief magistrate, had forbidden the disputants to make such personal remarks. On this afternoon,
Luther had the floor for only a few minutes at the close, for
Eck had intentionally overstepped the time allotted to him
in order to talk him down. Luther merely stated that since
Eck had succeeded in cutting him off, he would express
himself in writing at a later time concerning the articles of

Huss of which he was accused, since by order of Duke
George this question was not to be touched again in the
following days.

Nevertheless, on the morning of July 7, the two disputants
again fell into an agitated discussion of the same question.
Luther then began to treat the question whether the primacy
of the pope was based on divine or human right. Another
incident occurred in the afternoon. Luther maintained that
Eck must first prove that councils cannot err and have never
erred. Eck immediately nailed down this incidental remark.
"Reverend Father," he declared solemnly, when he had the
floor an hour later, "if you believe that a regularly assembled
council has erred and can err, then you are to me a heathen
and a publican. What a heretic is, I need not explain here."
It was not until early on July 8 that Luther answered this
briefly by saying that decrees of councils were not *juris
divini* and, therefore, not authoritative to him. Eck replied
in a threatening manner that the judges of the disputation
would have to decide concerning this declaration, and then
concluded the discussion of the primacy of the pope with
the words, "Would that the Reverend Father might come
to the same insight as did the truly wise representatives of
the Greek Church, who, in Florence, submitted to the pope
as the true vicar of Christ, on November 22, 1439. All this
I leave to the judgment of those whom this matter concerns
and whom it *shall* concern. To God alone the glory." After
a short interval, they entered immediately into a debate concerning purgatory (July 8, 9, and 11, in the mornings). Then
the question of indulgences was given the floor (July 11, in
the morning), and finally the doctrine of penance (July 12,
13, and on the fourteenth from seven to eight o'clock in the
morning). On July 14, at eight o'clock, Carlstadt again came
into action to dispute with Eck for two more days on the
question whether the human will, without divine grace, is
able to work nothing but sin. Then the disputation was
brought quickly to a close because the Elector of Branden-

burg had announced that he intended to visit the duke with a large retinue.

Mosellanus described his impression of Eck's and Luther's manner of disputing, as well as their appearance. "Eck," he wrote, "throws everything together promiscuously and without selection—arguments from reason, Scripture texts, citations from the Fathers — without considering how inept, meaningless, and sophistical is most of what he says. He is concerned only with showing off as much of his knowledge as possible, so as to throw dust in the eyes of the audience, most of whom are incapable of judging, and make them believe that he is superior. In addition, he has an incredible audacity which, however, he covers up with great craftiness. As soon as he sees that he has made a rash statement, he gradually turns the discussion into another channel. Sometimes he embraces the opponent's opinion in somewhat different words, and then, with astounding guile, attributes to his antagonist, in a completely changed form, his own previously held opinions. Luther is extraordinarily learned. Above all, he possesses such an astonishing knowledge of the Bible that he knows almost all of it by heart. He understands enough Greek and Hebrew to be able to give an independent judgment of the value of the translations. He is never at a loss in speaking, such an immense stock of ideas and words does he have at his command. But what most men blame in him is that he is more imprudent and cutting in his criticism than is safe for a man who is going his own way in religious questions or than is decorous for a theologian in any case. This fault he probably shares with all who come late to learning. Carlstadt, however, is even more impetuous."

However, this sharpness in criticism which Mosellanus censured was not so prominent in the disputation. Only a few times, when Eck shouted at him, did the discourteous title, "Lord Ranter," escape Luther's lips. But then Eck honored him with terms like "impatient monk," "heathen,"

and "publican." In general, however, the disputation itself
was conducted with great courtesy. The audience, on the
other hand, often behaved more violently. When, on June
28, Eck prohibited Carlstadt from reading his notes, the
Wittenberg students drew their daggers and set up such an
"insolent clamor" before Eck's quarters that, on June 30, the
town council deemed it necessary to station thirty-four
armed guards in the neighboring houses. The Leipzig students behaved themselves no better than the Wittenbergers.
They wrangled so violently in the taverns that many innkeepers—like the printer Martin Landsberg, in Ritter Street,
posted one of the town council guards with a drawn halberd
in the main room in order to be prepared for the worst. But
when Luther began to dispute, the town had become quiet
again since most of the Wittenberg students had already
departed for lack of money.

Mosellanus declared, "Eck's credit has received a great
blow among us on account of the disputation. Almost everyone here is now more kindly disposed toward Martinus than
before." But he was thinking only of those people with
whom he had intimate contact. Eck undoubtedly made
more of an impression upon the majority of the audience
than did Luther. Even Duke George was altogether pre-
possessed in Eck's favor. This was clearly in evidence even
during the disputation. He presented Eck with a magnificent stag, and Carlstadt at least with a hind, but he intentionally let Luther go away empty-handed. It is true that
he later invited the Reformer to dinner with Eck and Carlstadt, but then he invited Eck again as an extra favor. Though
he was not so discourteous as to refuse Luther's request for an
audience directly, he did consider it fitting to confront him
on this occasion with the unfavorable opinion of his writings
which had been whispered into his ear by his court theologians (especially the chaplain, Emser), and also to reproach
him again with Eck's sneering admonition that if he was so
opposed to them, he ought to write against the Hussites. He,

of course, took Eck's part again when, on July 14, he quar-
reled with Luther over the question whether only the theological faculties of the universities of Paris and Erfurt, which
had been chosen as judges of the debate, or, as Luther
wished, all the faculties together should function as judges.

When the duke's unfavorable decision reached him from
Rochlitz on July 16, Luther probably had already left Leipzig
and set out from Grimma, where he had a conference with
Staupitz and Link. On July 20 he arrived at Wittenberg,
deeply depressed over the whole course of the disputation.
Eck, on the contrary, remained in Leipzig until July 26, in
order to enjoy to the full his supposed victory over the two
Wittenberg "monsters." He understood how to do that very
well, as is shown by his experienced observations on the poor-
ness of the Leipzig beer and on "the voluptuous prostitutes
in this city much given to love." The Leipzigers assisted him
loyally. The town council presented him with a robe and a
Schamlot, an article of clothing made of Angora goat's-hair.
The theological faculty arranged a special disputation in his
honor, in which he sorely harassed and vexed Magister
George Helt, who even at that time smelled somewhat of
Luther. The notables were never tired of inviting him to
table and feting him in other ways. The duke not only paid
his whole account of eighteen guldens at the hostelry, but
also introduced him to his noble visitor, the Elector Joachim
of Brandenburg, thereby giving him an opportunity to
intrigue against Luther and Carlstadt in the presence of the
prince, who was reputed to be unusually learned; and what
was almost more important, in the presence of the bishop of
Brandenburg, who was in the prince's retinue. The bishop
at once requested of him a judgment on the complaint of
the Jüterbog Franciscans. In less than two hours, the ver-
satile doctor delivered this highly inquisitorial document to
the bishop, who was so delighted with it that he paid out
fifteen crowns in gratitude and zealously circulated the work
throughout his diocese.

Having succeeded so well with the Brandenburg sovereigns, Eck decided, on July 23, to try his luck with Elector Frederick, who had just arrived at his castle, Altenburg, which was, for a good rider, within very easy reach of Leipzig. In a letter he movingly reminded Frederick that he had vainly begged him six times for an audience when he was in Augsburg. In conclusion, he admonished the Elector to have Luther's *Resolution on the Thirteenth Thesis concerning the Power of the Pope*, which was printed but not yet published, burned immediately. But the Elector, unfortunately, showed himself to be quite impervious to Eck's admonitions. He merely replied that he had passed on his letter to Luther and Carlstadt. On the same day (July 24) Eck took another step toward the destruction of the Wittenberg "monsters." He solicited the assistance of the Dominican, Jacob van Hoogstraten, against the Wittenbergers. Hoogstraten was the chief inquisitor of western Germany and Luther had already been obliged to defend himself against his attacks by means of a public placard posted on July 13. On July 25 he preached once more against Luther and prepared for the press a polemic against the "grammatist," Melanchthon, who had gained his ill-will by his extremely objective report of the disputation to Oecolampadius. He then left Leipzig on July 26, in the train of the duke, setting out first for Annaberg. From there he departed for Ingolstadt, "in triumph," as he himself put it. He was received by his university as a conquering hero, that is, with a magnificent gift of money.

However, when he went to Augsburg soon afterward for the purpose of putting into print the brilliant testimonials which he had received from the duke and the University of Leipzig, Eck made the surprising discovery that the number of those who believed in his triumph was extraordinarily small. The first reports which he received concerning the feeling toward him sounded very favorable for the most part. But among them was a very pro-Wittenberg pamphlet of

Matthew Hiscold, monk of Bosau, which required immediate refutation. Then the Wittenbergers suddenly began to
flood the market with publications against him. As early as
the beginning of August, Melanchthon dealt him a cutting
blow in return for the polemical treatise of July 25. Eisermann lambasted the Leipzig Magister Rubeus (Pollinger),
who had extravagantly extolled Eck as a new Hector in a
paper teeming with the grossest grammatical errors, with a
satirical panegyric so thoroughgoing that the wretched fellow apparently never again ventured to express himself in
Latin. And Luther had three works against him printed at
the same time, still in August. The first was a new, enlarged
edition of the *Resolution on the Thirteenth Thesis concerning the Power of the Pope;* the second, the *Resolutions concerning the Theses Disputed at Leipzig,* with an exhaustive
report of the disputation; and the third, a sharp retort to
Eck's opinion on the complaint of the Jüterbog monks
(*Contra malignum Eccii judicium*). During the next few
months Carlstadt also published three, in parts enormously
gross, polemics against him.

Even more hazardous to Eck's reputation and fame than
these attacks themselves was the echo that they called forth
in the camp of the hated "grammatists" — that is, of the
humanists. "Luther will perish by his honesty. Eck has left
out the first letter of his name, J (Jeck—fool)." This saying,
ascribed to Erasmus and therefore eagerly hawked about,
best characterizes the attitude that was prevalent among the
closely allied circles of grammarians, not only in Nuremberg,
Augsburg, Strassburg, Schlettstadt, Heidelberg, and Erfurt,
but even in Leipzig itself. Naturally, Eck did not fail to
chastise these odious fellows in the grossly abusive polemics
which he now let loose upon the Wittenbergers. But this
only resulted in their proceeding to attack him themselves.
In December Councilor Spengler, of Nuremberg, published
against him, in the German language, a warm and manly
address in defense of Luther. At the same time, John

Oecolampadius, instigated by the Augsburg canon, Bernard Adelmann, published his *Answer of the Unlearned Canons,* which hit him harder than all the missiles of the Wittenbergers. Another South German poet (Nicholas Gerbel of Strassburg?) exposed him to the curse of ridicule in the fierce satire, *Eccius dedolatus.* In vain he sought to institute, at least in Ingolstadt, a public burning of Luther's writings and these lampoons. In vain he sought by every means to undermine the credit of that "pestilential University of Wittenberg." But, despite Eck's declamations, the influx of students to that miserable hole on the Elbe increased more than ever. From October 1, 1519, to May 1, 1520, two hundred thirty-six new persons matriculated. Among them were not a few of Duke George's subjects, even one of the secretaries of the disputation, the former rector of the Thomas School in Leipzig, John Graumann, called Poliander, who immediately began to use his nimble pen to write down the Reformer's sermons as far as possible word for word.

The hopes which Eck and his patrons set upon the two universities which had been entrusted with the arbitration of the disputation proved to be equally delusive. The Sorbonne of Paris, it is true, accepted the office, but only on condition that the duke furnish each of the twenty-four members of the court of judges appointed by it with a printed copy of the proceedings, and grant a remuneration of from twenty-five to thirty gold crowns. This, of course, was far too expensive for the duke, so he pursued the matter no further in Paris. The Erfurt theologians, however, definitely declined the intended honor on December 29. Thus the whole cleverly maneuvered campaign against the Wittenberg monsters, which had begun with Eck's theses on December 29, 1518, had to be acknowledged as frustrated at the end of 1519. Instead of being weakened, Luther's position was now stronger than ever before. He now had on his side the men who were leaders in the circles of power and culture not only in Germany, but also in the Netherlands

and France, and, what surprised him especially, even in
Bohemia.

Even at this time there was already a great number of
Erasmians in Bohemia who were studying his writings with
enthusiasm. Among them were John Poduska, priest of the
Teyn Church in Prague, and his vicar, Wenzel Rozdalovsky.
When these men learned from the Prague organ-builder,
Jacob, who had visited the Reformer during the disputation
at his quarters in Hay Street, perhaps on July 10, how Christian he judged John Huss to be and how anxious he was to
read something of Huss's, they immediately sent him (on
July 16-17) Huss's book, *On the Church,* and a present of
several knives, and joyfully greeted him as the Saxon Huss.
The letters, however, were apparently opened on the way.
In any case, the Dresden court chaplain, Emser, learned of
the hopes which the Prague Utraquists were now setting
upon Luther and hastened on August 13 to address an
open letter to John Zak, the Catholic diocesan administrator
in Prague, who probably had put him upon this track. In
this letter he hypocritically defended Luther against the
suspicion of being a Hussite or a friend of the Hussites, and
related all sorts of highly curious things concerning Hussite
demonstrations in favor of Luther. Luther did not surmise
the true connection of the thing; nevertheless, he thought it
well to deal the old intriguer a nasty blow with the rude
book, *Postscript to the Emser Goat* (Emser's coat of arms
bore a goat). Not until after this book had appeared did
the messenger from the electoral court reach him on October
3 with the letters and gifts from the two priests of Prague.
At first he apparently did not know what attitude to take
toward the matter. At this time he was by no means in
sympathy with Huss and the Hussites. Moreover, he somewhat distrusted the decidedly Erasmian tone of the two
letters. Nevertheless, he decided to send his collected works
to the two foreigners in return, but he did so with quite
unusual precautions. He himself wrote nothing at all, but

requested Melanchthon to dictate the accompanying letter to the messenger who would take the package to Prague.

The book of Huss's which had been sent to him, probably a copy of the edition from the Anshelm press, he left unread for months. Not until it began to make a stir in Germany—thus about the beginning of March, 1520—did he feel moved to look into it. But just for that reason it now affected him all the more powerfully. "I have been teaching everything that Huss did, without knowing it," he wrote to Spalatin, "and Staupitz, too, has done the same without being aware of it. All of us are Hussites without knowing it, even Paul and Augustine. How terrible are the judgments of God! The evangelical truth has been burned for a hundred years; it is condemned today and no one may confess it!" If he was still determined to write *against* the Bohemians on February 7, from now on Huss and Jerome of Prague were for him martyrs to evangelical truth, and the Hussites members of a communion with whom the Catholics—that is, other Christians—must by all means be reconciled. He was still unaware of the tenacity with which Huss held to the idea of merit. But even when he later learned to know more of this side of Huss, he never gave up the belief that this devout man had been a true evangelical Christian, at least in the last moments before his death, for his last words had been a prayer for the grace of Christ. So completely had his attitude on this point changed after his study of the "scholarly" book, *On the Church*, whose real author, Wyclif, he did not know!

Accordingly the Leipzig disputation undoubtedly meant, on the whole, a severe defeat for Eck and the Dominicans associated with him. Nevertheless, Eck had achieved several partial successes which were to be very important for the further development of the campaign against the Wittenbergers. Above all, he had succeeded in arousing the interest of Jacob van Hoogstraten by the bold pretense that the struggle against Luther was merely a continuation of the struggle against Reuchlin and his colleagues. He thus induced this powerful inquisitor of Cologne to mobilize against the Reformer the two West German universities of Cologne and Louvain, which were amenable to his influence.

On August 30 the Cologne theologians had already condemned eight of Luther's statements drawn from the Basel edition, primarily, however, his view of papal primacy. They demanded therefore, that his works be suppressed and burned. The Louvain theologians did not express themselves until November 7. They said not a word concerning Luther's attack upon the divine right of the papacy, which seemed to Eck and the theologians of Cologne to be his most grievous sin. On this point, a good number of them were of the same opinion as the new heretic. They, therefore, dwelt the more on the statements which they had ferreted out of Luther's writings on indulgences, the ban, and worthy preparation for the Lord's Supper, calling them false, offensive to pious ears, erroneous, and smacking of heresy. In consideration of these statements they, too, passed the sentence: Luther's books are to be suppressed and burned. On December 4 this judgment was espoused by one of the most distinguished and powerful men in the circle of the new emperor, Cardinal Adrian of Utrecht, archbishop of Tortosa in Spain. The judgment thus took on an altogether special significance, as was immediately recognized at the electoral court.

But perhaps even more important was the fact that in Leipzig Eck had succeeded in inciting against Luther both of the nearest neighbors of Electoral Saxony, the Elector of Brandenburg and Duke George of Saxony. We do not possess any records which clearly express the attitude of the court of Berlin at this time. But we can guess it by the attitude of the bishop of Brandenburg, who was formerly so kindly disposed toward Luther. This prelate asserted, as early as September, 1519, that he would never rest until he had delivered Martinus to the flames, like the fagots which he was throwing into the stove. The Dresden court was now even more hostile to him. Emser was incessantly agitating against him there, and he could expect nothing good from the duke, who was studying all his books with Argus eyes.

CHAPTER XXIII

GROWTH OF ACTIVITY AND INNER PROGRESS

Immediately upon his return from Leipzig, Luther resumed the whole range of his pastoral activity which had already cost him much time and energy. The more famous he became, the more frequently clergymen and laymen—now even from a distance—sought his counsel and encouragement in their spiritual problems. But there was hardly anyone who was consulting him more than his territorial lord, Elector Frederick. The journey to Frankfurt and the excitement during the days of the imperial election had so exhausted the prince, who was only in his fifty-sixth year, that for nearly eight months after his return home he lay dangerously ill with violent fever, gout, and kidney-stone colic. At the court it was even believed that he was dying. In order to cheer him in these days of suffering, Luther immediately composed, at Spalatin's behest, a unique letter of consolation, *Tesseradecas,* or *The Fourteen of Consolation.* "The fourteen" were the seven evils and the seven blessings which a Christian should keep before his eyes, instead of the fourteen patron saints, in times of suffering—the seven evils in order to recognize how trifling all human suffering is in comparison with the suffering and death of Christ, and the seven blessings in order to strengthen oneself inwardly with the realization of the inexhaustible grace and goodness of God.

As soon as the Elector had recovered, he asked the Reformer (not only for his own sake, but also in order to take Luther away from the writing of sharp and spiteful polemics) to prepare a large new work, a book of sermons for all the Sundays and Holy Days of the Church Year, but especially for Lent. Luther set to work at once. But he did not make very much progress during the next year and a half. In March, 1521, he submitted to the prince only a small sample in printed form (*Enarrationes epistolarum et evangeliorum, quas postillas vocant*). Not until he was at the Wartburg was he able to take up the work again, this time in German, and to finish at least a considerable portion of it. Nevertheless, he had found time in the latter part of 1519 to prepare a whole series of small devotional writings: a brief prayerbook, extraordinarily effective in style and content, in connection with the seven petitions of the Lord's Prayer; a short explanation of the Lord's Prayer "before and behind" each petition; and five so-called *"sermones"* on preparation for death, repentance, Baptism, the Lord's Supper, and the ban. Besides these, he treated, twice in a row, the economically important problem of taking interest (the short and the long *Treatise on Usury*) and put out continuations of his *Studies in the Psalms (Operationes in Psalmos)*. All told, he published sixteen pieces within six months after the disputation, including the three polemics against Eck and Emser but not including the *Commentary on Galatians*. This commentary had been finished earlier, although it did not appear until September. These comprise some fifty of our average printed signatures today. Hence he delivered about two signatures to the printery every week. In addition, he usually preached two or three times, lectured at least two hours, and continued to conduct occasional disputations with his students.

Luther himself said at this time: "I have a swift hand and a quick memory. When I write, it just flows out; I do not have to press and squeeze." But did not this mass production sometimes affect the quality of his work? As far as the external form of his books is concerned, he was satisfied at this time, at least when he wrote in German, briefly to formulate in the fashion of academic theses the thoughts which seemed important, and then simply to set them down in a numbered series, one after the other. In his polemics, however, he generally followed his opponent's train of thought. Thus he troubled himself very little about the external plan of his writings, and about the elaboration of his ideas even less. As soon as he had clearly grasped a thought, he could formulate it and put it down on paper, no matter whether he was writing in Latin or German. Even citations, metaphors, analogies, and proverbs flowed out of their own accord, especially when "a good, strong anger stirred in my blood." Once he had begun to write, he usually sent the finished sheets to the neighboring printing shops without going over them again, especially if the product was one of such wrath that he intended it to have an immediate effect. And he changed hardly anything in the proof. One may not conclude from this peculiar method of working, however, that he had already ceased, as he once put it, "to bring forth something new." On the contrary, his mind was even more active (*in actu et motu*) at this time than it had been in the quiet years before 1517. But he usually required an external stimulus in order to produce something new. Such stimuli were provided in great abundance by his opponents, but the questions of his friends, of Spalatin in particular, also provided constant incentive, especially in that fruitful period after the disputation. This is manifest, above all, in the treatise on penance, Baptism, and the Lord's Supper, which was written by him at the instigation of Spalatin for Margaret, the widow of the duke of Brunswick-Lüneburg. Likewise was this true of the two treatises on usury, the letter to Spalatin on December 18, the sermon on John 21:22 of December 27, 1519, and the disputation on infused grace which was held in January, 1520.

In the first three of these writings Luther was concerned for the first time with the question of the sacraments as such. What is a sacrament? It is a sign which not only represents but also embodies certain inner, spiritual gifts. These gifts, however, can be truly recognized and appropriated only by the believer. The gift of Baptism is, in the first place, the forgiveness of sins, and in the second place union with God in a gracious and eternal covenant, on the strength of which God does not charge a man with his sin as long as that man is constantly trying and desiring to rid himself of the old Adam. The gift of the Lord's Supper is communion, an inner union with Christ and His members which grows out of faith in His benefits and the forgiveness of sins. The Reformer did not doubt that Christ is truly present in the Lord's Supper. But "how and where, leave that to His care." By this time, he had given up the Catholic doctrine of transubstantiation. With regard to the sacrifice of the mass, he maintained absolute silence, a sure indication that he no longer knew what to do with this center and kernel of the Catholic cultus. As far as the external form of the sacrament is concerned, he declared that it would be a good thing if a general council would decree that the cup, as well as the bread, should be given to all people, and not to the priests alone. In his letter to Spalatin under date of December 18, he further asserted that he acknowledged no sacraments other than these three: penance, Baptism, and the Lord's Supper. "What has been invented concerning the seven sacraments, you will have occasion to hear another time." And in the disputation of February 3, 1520, he added: "The word 'sacrament' is unknown to the Bible. It is an error to designate marriage as a sacrament on the basis of Ephesians 5:31 ff."

Now, in truth, Luther was done with the Catholic conception of sacrament. In the aforementioned letter of December 18, in reply to a question put by Spalatin, he declared: "Clergymen are distinguished from laymen, it appears, only in that the former are charged with the administration of the sacraments and the preaching of the Word of God. Otherwise they are entirely alike. In fact, Peter and John expressly say that all are priests. I wonder how ordination came to be a sacrament." It is evident that the basic ideas later incorporated in his famous works, *To the Christian*

Nobility and *On the Babylonian Captivity,* had already dawned on him in December, 1519.

In the *Treatise on Baptism,* Luther touched publicly for the first time on the "common" question as to whether "the vows of chastity, of the priesthood, and of the clergy" were more and greater than Baptism or the vow which the Christian makes to God in Baptism. His answer was a candid negative. But at this time he would have only the mendicant orders done away with, not monasticism as such. On the contrary, he asserted that monastic life could be used to cultivate, in a particularly vigorous fashion, the mortification of the old Adam which is the purpose of Baptism. Unfortunately, the monks do not think of this, he said, for they see the essence of monastic life in the outward show of work-holiness. So he tried, in keeping with the conservative character of his nature, to remodel this institution, too [in the light of his new views] before rejecting it. But in reality he had already broken with the ideas on which monasticism rested. This is shown by the two treatises on usury and the sermon on John 21, delivered in Kemberg on the Third Christmas Day (December 27, 1519). In the sermon he said: "Everyone should remain in the natural calling to which divine Providence has appointed him. This calling of his is the place in which he can and should serve God and his neighbor. Anyone who neglects the duties of his calling will not be helped at all by fasting, making pilgrimages, telling beads, endowing masses, and such other 'good works' as there may be. First take care of your wife, your children, and the poor, and then make a pilgrimage to Rome, set up candles, endow masses, erect new altar pictures, and the like! Instead of this, you are constantly quarreling with your wife and allow yourself to be deluded by the devil into doing such spectacular good works." He did not mean by this to call "the extra works invented by men" utterly reprehensible, but simply to establish their true worth. But in establishing this, he actually declared them ethically and religiously worthless, while the work of one's calling was alone declared good and holy.

In other respects, too, Luther was now venturing to express ideas which sometimes incorporated very radical demands. In the above treatise, for example, he suggested that henceforth every town care for its own poor, and in the *Treatise on the Lord's Supper* he proposed that the confraternities turn themselves into associations for the voluntary care of the poor. While these suggestions were not altogether new, the energy with which he discussed them made such an impression that they now began to be considered seriously throughout Germany, and a thoroughgoing reformation of the care of the poor was undertaken in Wittenberg as early as 1520. Luther had less success with his ideas concerning the reform of worship. His suggestion regarding the restoration of the cup to the laity caused such offense at the Dresden court that Duke George denounced him to the Elector on December 27 as a secret Hussite. Moreover, Duke George immediately mobilized the bishops of Meissen and Merseburg against the "very Pragueish" *Treatise on the Lord's Supper*. The bishop of Meissen responded by issuing a mandate of his own against the sermon on January 24.

This new quarrel was exceedingly disagreeable to the Elector. He asked Luther to address an immediate pacifying explanation to the archbishop of Mainz, the bishop of Merseburg, and probably several other prelates, and to allow him to examine the explanation before sending it. Luther was ready to do so at once. But the more "stupid than Stolpic note" (Stolpen was the residence of the bishop of Meissen) vexed him so much that he could not help subjecting it to an extremely witty criticism on February 7. Then, without first asking the Elector, he published this criticism, under the title, *Answer to the Note which Appeared under the Seal of the Stolpen Official*. Miltitz nearly split with laughter when the bishop of Meissen read this latest production of Dr.

Martinus to his court in Stolpen on February 16, and the
unfortunate official, Licentiate Christian Betschitz, whom
Luther had prudently chosen, instead of the bishop, as the
butt of his jests acknowledged each new bit of the Reformer's
banter with a furious curse. Duke George himself could not
altogether stifle his laughter when the amused nuncio handed
him the little script in Dresden some days later. But he
immediately reached for his pen and, without any help, composed an answer in his own horrible handwriting to the
"scandalous, injurious hodge-podge," this answer to be published at once in the name of the bishop of Meissen.

It was probably surmised at the Elector's court that something of this kind would happen. At all events, Luther's arbitrary procedure brought down a storm of anger upon his
head. Spalatin had to reproach him very sharply for having
despised good counsel, and for not having taken the wishes
of his friends into consideration. But Spalatin did not gain
anything by this. That he had been more vehement than
he should have been, the Reformer agreed without further
ado. But Spalatin, he said, was not a whit better, as his
letter showed. If every sharp word uttered against manifestly dishonorable opponents were a slander, Christ and
Paul would have to be called slanderers. Nevertheless, on
February 22, Luther brought himself to the point of signing
the letters to the archbishop of Mainz and the bishop of
Merseburg, which he had composed before the note from
Stolpen had arrived and which had meanwhile been thoroughly corrected by Spalatin and the Elector in Lochau; and
he sent these letters to the noble addressees by his own messengers with a request for an immediate response. The two
prelates were apparently surprised beyond measure at
Luther's wholly unexpected readiness to be corrected by
them. The bishop of Merseburg could not keep from impart-
ing a sort of censure in his response, but in the conclusion
he was very friendly and suggested a personal meeting with
Luther. Even more conciliatory and gracious was the

response from Mainz, dated February 26. The bishop of Meissen had been prudent enough not to publish the statement which Duke George had handed to him, and by the beginning of March the episode seemed, to the great relief of the Elector, to have been thoroughly settled.

But Elector Frederick was in no wise satisfied. He had known since December that a new attack was being planned in Rome, not only against Luther, but also against him. He had known, too, since the end of February, that Eck had been summoned to Rome. Therefore, when the condemnation of the Louvain and Cologne theologians, which had been printed some weeks before, reached Saxony in the middle of March, the situation seemed to the Elector so serious that he asked Luther to address an open letter to him with a reiterated proposal of peace to all his opponents. Luther immediately laid this request before his Wittenberg friends. Then, in agreement with their opinion, he refused on the ground that he had already done this often enough of his own accord, but that he could not withdraw from the controversy now—especially while men like Eck were the leading opponents—without denying the Word of God. With that the Elector gave in, as he always did when a stronger will opposed him. But he probably allowed Luther's answer to the Cologne-Louvain condemnation (March 27), which had been finished in the meantime, to pass unhindered only because the Reformer—"to his good fortune," as he himself put it—had overlooked the highly curialistic utterances of the cardinal of Tortosa and had even referred to the cardinal several times with praise. At the same time the news that the esteemed Louvain theologian, Dorpius, had not voted to condemn Luther probably influenced the Elector to take a calmer view of the situation. Certainly this news seemed to confirm the opinion of the Lutherans around him that the Cologne-Louvain condemnation was only an intrigue of the same obscurantists who a few years before had plotted the sensational trial of the pious humanist, John Reuchlin, whom the Elector had also held in high esteem. With this assurance Frederick finally put his mind at rest again.

Yet the Elector was not entirely at ease with regard to the whole matter, because at bottom he did not understand Dr. Martinus. Like an old clucking hen he anxiously watched the daring activity in his hitherto tame university of this strange chick which had been shoved under him by Spalatin. But in this feeling he was quite alone in his land at the time. With the exception of Count Philip Solms, all his councilors were "good Lutherers." His nephew, John Frederick, and his brother, Duke John, could also be so designated. On this account the Reformer had often been urged to place Duke John under personal obligation by means of a favor in the humanistic fashion—by the dedication of a devotional work in the German language, for the duke was said to be "very eager" for such reading matter. Up to this time Luther had always refused, for it did not seem proper to him to "put the Holy Scriptures into the service of any other name than the name of God." Nevertheless, persuaded by Spalatin, he finally decided on March 29 to dedicate to the duke the *Treatise on Good Works* which he had just begun to write. Some days before this he had told his friend: "The promised treatise is developing into a little book; so quickly is it growing under my hands. If this continues, it will, in my opinion, be the best thing that I have published up to now." This expectation came to fulfillment. This treatise became, if not the very best, at least one of the best writings which he gave to mankind.

Before 1517 Luther had occasionally been reproached with forbidding "good works." Now this reproach was echoing from all sides. He therefore felt compelled, as he wrote in the introduction (later deleted) to the treatise, to set forth "in the bluntest and clearest fashion" how good works are to be done and how they are to be recognized. "It must be known in the first place," he began, "that only those works are good works which God has commanded. The first and highest and noblest of all good works is faith." This sounds as "arbitrary and dogmatic" as can be. But here, as always, Luther was offering new wine in old bottles. This at once becomes clear when one asks what faith is. Faith, wrote Luther, is not a work of man. It is a disposition produced by God, or, more correctly, the consciousness of new life which takes root in the soul when it has gained the assurance of God's favor through the glad tidings of God's love in Christ. What man does in response to this disposition or consciousness is good, trifling though it may appear outwardly—even walking, standing, eating, drinking, sleeping, and picking up a straw. On the other hand, what he does not, or cannot, do in response to this disposition is not good, no matter how magnificent and holy it may look outwardly. Thus the prevailing Catholic view was simply reversed by Luther. What one does to win God's favor—as fasting, telling one's beads, making pilgrimages, endowing masses, building churches and monasteries—is not good, but that is good which God himself does indirectly in and through man, by means of the consciousness of new life brought about by faith which He has awakened. Moreover, anyone who has thus received the assurance of God's favor no longer needs any law; he always knows of himself what he should do and what he should not do. An urge, a sure instinct, gives him direction, and always gives him the right direction.

Luther illustrated this with a "crude, fleshly example." "If a husband is certain that he is loved by his wife and is pleasing to her, who teaches him how to behave, what to do, leave undone, say, and think? Confidence alone teaches him all this, and more. There is no distinction in works. He does what is big, important, and consequential just as readily as he does what is small, unimportant, and inconsequential, and that with a joyful, confident, and peaceful heart. But where there is doubt as to the other's love, the seeking after works whereby he can gain her favor begins; he sets to work with a heavy heart and much reluctance, is like a prisoner on the verge of despair, and often loses his mind entirely. So a Christian, who lives in such trust toward God, knows all things, can do all things, dares all things that are to be done, and does all this cheerfully and willingly, not that he may thereby gather a good store of merits and good works, but because he delights in pleasing God. He serves God without looking for a return, satisfied that it pleases Him. On the contrary, anyone who is not at one with God begins to search and to worry as to how he may make amends and move God with many works. He runs to St. James, Rome, here and there, he fasts on this day and on that, he makes confession here and makes confession there, questions this man and that. And yet he does not find peace, and he does all of this with great effort, despair, and aversion in his heart." It is true, wrote Luther, only thoroughly mature Christians can abandon themselves to this inner impulse without any trouble at all. Immature Christians, like children, for example, cannot. Nor can those who are still fleshly minded, for they very easily become indolent and have a tendency to make of this liberty a cloak to hide the flesh. Nor can criminals and evildoers. These still have need of the law; indeed, they have to be held to that which is good and kept from that which is evil by force and compulsion.

In this way the Reformer described faith as the fulfillment of the first of the Ten Commandments. Quite as new and original is what he had to say about the fulfillment of the other commandments. The greatest and most difficult task enjoined by the second command, Luther wrote, is to defend the holy name of God against those who misuse it, "for it is not enough that I praise and honor Him for myself and in myself. I must be willing to heap upon myself the enmity of all men for His sake, to provoke even my father and mother, to oppose the spiritual and secular government, to bring down upon my head the criticism of the rich, the learned, the saints, everything that has value in the world, and thus demonstrate in deed that I love God and His honor above all things." But how can this be demonstrated by deeds? In the first place, said Luther, by opposing all injustice whereby truth and righteousness suffer violence and harm. Save the poor and forsaken from the power of the unrighteous, and help the needy to get his due! "If one cannot prevent injustice and further truth by force, one should at least not sanction injustice, but fearlessly speak out the truth. God wishes that we work with Him, and honors us in that He desires to do His work—to help the poor—with and through us." In the second place, one honors God in deed when one resolutely sets oneself against all abuse of spiritual power—for example, the abuse of the ban by officials, bishops, and popes—no matter whether such abuse is practiced by the highest or the lowest priest, "whether big John or little Nick said it," whether it occurs in God's name or in man's.

The exposition of the third commandment gave Luther an opportunity to demand an appreciable decrease in the number of holidays on the ground that they were used only for idleness, gluttony, carousing, gaming, and other outrages. In connection with the third commandment Luther also proposed a reform of worship. The mass, he wrote, should again become what it once had been—the carrying out of Christ's testament. Moreover, the sermon should be nothing more than the proclamation of this testament, namely, the forgiveness of sins. Then Luther dealt with prayer at great length. As the highest and most important prayer, he designated intercession for all Christendom, for the afflictions of all men, no matter whether friend or foe; and with sharp words he attacked thoughtless babbling from a book (the breviary) or in connection with the rosary. He also offered new rules for fasting and the customary mortifications of the flesh. "If someone should discover that more wantonness arose in his flesh from eating fish than from eating eggs or meat, let him eat meat and not fish. Again, if he discover that his head becomes confused and stupefied and his body and stomach are disordered from fasting, or

if he find no trace of wantonness in his flesh, let him stop
fasting altogether, and let him eat, sleep, and be idle as much
as is necessary for his health, regardless of whether the
church commands these things." At the same time, of course,
everybody should be very careful in his conduct not to step
on the toes of "weak" Christians who still cling to these
external observances in a spirit of bondage. One must always
deal with these as one does with the sick. "On the Last Day
Christ will not ask you what you have done for yourself, but
how much good you have done for others, the least of these.
Among these 'least' of men are numbered those who are
in sin, spiritual poverty, and spiritual bondage."

In the exposition of the fourth commandment Luther proceeded to abuses in the government of the church. The
clerical estate. he said, was more secular than the secular
estate. Rome haJ become a market for benefices and indulgences, and ecclesiastical offices had in a large measure
become the prey of stable boys, muleteers, and even the
"rakes" of the papal court. Some advocated, he said, that a
council remedy this. But up to that time the councils had
not succeeded in doing anything. The best thing would be
for the kings, princes, and cities to begin to put a stop to
the activities of the papal courtiers. They would not thereby
be claiming any power over faith, with which they of course
had nothing to do, but would only be preventing the abuses
and encroachments of papal power. The secular government should set itself just as sharply against luxury in food
and clothing, spreading more and more, and against usurious
financial transactions, and it should also relentlessly suppress
brothels. Obedience to the secular government was, indeed,
a religious duty, for all government is of God. But if a prince
and lord required something of his subjects that was contrary to God's commandment, or prevented them from fulfilling God's commandment, obedience was at an end and
duty was already suspended. Especially was one not in duty
bound to obey a summons to a notoriously unjust war.

The Reformer's treatment of the remaining six commandments was considerably shorter. In connection with the fifth
commandment he declared, among other things, that we
should not pay attention to our own property, honor, or loss,
but that we must parry damage and offense to the honor
of God, of His commandment, and of our neighbor — the
government must do this with the sword, others at least
with words—but in doing so we must always have sympathy and compassion toward those who have deserved
punishment. In the case of the eighth commandment Luther
again strongly emphasized that one must not only tell the
truth but must also oppose the lying and injustice by the
mighty of this world against peasants, herdsmen, stable boys,
and other men of low degree. Why does this so seldom happen? It is because of a lack of faith, for "where there is a
proper confidence in God, there is a bold, defiant, fearless
heart that ventures and defends the truth, though it cost life
or cloak, though it be against pope or king."

This *Treatise on Good Works,* rather than the little *Treatise on Christian Liberty* which was hastily written in one or
two days, deserves to be called "a summary of the Christian
life." Not only is it measurably richer in content, but it also
turned out much better than the more hasty production,
which was never prized very highly by Luther himself and
which has been accorded praise since the eighteenth century
chiefly because of its happy title. Above all, the connection
between faith and works, religion and morality, is set forth
much more clearly and consistently, and is also illustrated
much more aptly (compare the analogy of the husband), in
the *Treatise on Good Works* than in the *Treatise on Christian Liberty.* Nor is the former in any way inferior in style
(compare, for example, the ingenious summary of the chief
thoughts in rhymed sentences: *Wie's einer sich zu Gott ver-
sieht, so ihm geschieht. Wir sind Kinder und doch Sünder*).
In short, despite several remnants of Catholic thought which
had not yet been cast off, this treatise is actually the classical

presentation of the new ideal of piety which Luther had gradually come to embrace.

What is the significance of this new ideal of piety for the history of religion and culture?

In the first place, it overcame the dualism, the intellectualism, and the rigid arbitrariness of medieval ethics. The distinction between profane and holy acts, so characteristic of ancient and again of medieval thought, no longer existed for Luther. In his eyes everything was holy which was done with the right disposition toward God—even walking, standing, sleeping, eating, and whatever else may be done for the nourishment of the body and the common good. On the other hand, everything was unholy which was not done with this attitude, even the works which had hitherto been regarded as specifically holy—praying, fasting, making pilgrimages, saying and endowing masses, building churches and monasteries. Like the dualism between holy and profane, the dualism between common morality and monkish morality was no longer valid for him. To be sure, he recognized different degrees of ethical maturity, but not different ethical ideals. The ideal was the same for all men. Moreover, he no longer held that the source of ethical and unethical conduct is in the intellect, but in the will, and, indeed, in the feelings which determine the will. For this reason the transformation of man's disposition was for him the principal problem of ethics. Finally, he no longer regarded the ethical in terms of an external obedience to a number of commandments imposed on man from without, but, at least in its normal form, in terms of an impulsive expression in one's life of an inclination toward God and what is good. This, together with the overpowering feeling of joy that accompanies assurance of God's favor, grows spontaneously from within.

This fundamental way of looking at things was not in conflict with the fact that Luther based his discussion on the Ten Commandments, nor with the fact that in doing so he regarded these as absolutely binding commandments of God. In his opinion, the commandments were not binding because they had once been given by God to the people of Israel from Mount Sinai, but rather because they agree with the natural moral code which is written in the hearts of all men, and hence they represent a norm native to the human spirit.

Luther's new idea of piety is significant, too, because it overcame the perfectionist morality of antiquity which had survived especially in monasticism. The ethically healthy man, according to Luther, does instinctively "what turns up" without giving the slightest thought to what he might get out of it for himself. He is free of all self-righteousness because he knows that he is and remains a sinner and can never say to himself that he has done all that he ought to have done. But he is equally free of all self-torment, for he knows that "even if we are sinners, we are nevertheless children" and may be sure that God forgives us our trespasses. Consequently he is not forever anxiously taking his pulse to find out if he is really healthy, nor does it ever occur to him to make himself, by a grand show of extra works, healthier and more perfect than he is. Such extra works always have the opposite effect from what they are supposed to have! They do not make a man more perfect. They only drag him down. And this is because they do not spring out of an overflowing love toward his neighbor, but out of an egoistical self-interest.

On one point, however, the *Treatise on Good Works* did not seem to stand on the full height of the Reformation ethic. Nowhere was there any express reference to the ethical significance of vocation. Yet, even if Luther did not happen to use the word "calling" here, he clearly incorporated the ideas which he associated with this term. "What turns up for a man to do" is of course primarily the work which he has to do in his calling. Luther did not mean by this that a man should be so preoccupied with this work that he should look

neither to the right nor to the left. On the contrary, he
expressly declared this abnormal. "No one is so heavily burdened with his work," he said, "that he cannot speak with
God in his heart at the same time." Highly as he esteemed
work in one's calling, Luther never saw in it the real purpose
of human existence. It was simply the opportunity which
Providence gave each individual for the expression of his
faith and his love of his neighbor. Here, too, his ethic was
never worldly, earthly, or even economic. It always had a
purely religious orientation.

In this treatise Luther incidentally alluded to two new
works which he thought of preparing in the immediate
future. One was a work on the mass; the other, the work on
faith. He composed the second of these in great haste during
October and gave it the title, *Treatise on Christian Liberty*.
The first, which grew out of the sermons he preached during
the Easter season, was finished in April, 1520, but was not
given to the public by Grünenberg until August. The very
title (*Treatise on the New Testament, that is, on the Holy
Mass*) indicates what had become for him the chief thing in
the mass: the words, "This is my body, this is the cup of the
new testament in my blood, which is shed for you for the
forgiveness of sins." So the essence of the mass is the gift
which Christ in these words bequeathed to His church. And
this gift is the forgiveness of sins, the seal or notary sign by
which He confirmed or corroborated this provision of His last
will, His own flesh and blood *under* the bread and wine. But
today, wrote Luther, this real meaning of the mass has unfortunately been twisted into the very opposite. From a gift of
God to man it has been made into a gift of man to God, a
sacrifice, even a meritorious work. But is the idea of sacrifice
to be rejected altogether on this account? No. Believers can
actually sacrifice something during the mass. First of all,
they can give or surrender themselves to the will of God and
offer praise and thanksgiving to Him. Furthermore, they can
lay these prayers on Christ, as it were, and allow them to be

offered to God through Him, their heavenly High Priest. But this spiritual sacrifice can also be offered outside of the mass. So it is not an essential part of the sacrament.

But what should become of the souls of the many departed? Luther's answer was to let the customary practice be what it may. We may pray for the poor souls in purgatory, he wrote, but that a soul is released from purgatory by a mere external celebration of the mass cannot be proved either from Scriptures or by reason. If the mass is not designed to help one to believe in Christ's testament, the forgiveness of sins, it should be entirely dispensed with. Endowed masses ought at least to be reduced, the words of institution spoken aloud, and the whole mass liturgy translated for the Germans into their mother tongue. Finally, if the true sacrifice in the mass is prayer, who may make such a sacrifice? All believers, Luther answered, for "faith makes all people priests and priestesses, be they young or old, lords or servants, women or men, scholars or laymen."

Once again we have in a few pages an abundance of new ideas of vast practical consequence. But even more characteristic of Luther than the entirely new and sometimes extraordinarily revolutionary ideas and demands was the desire, which appears so prominent, especially in the treatment of the notion of sacrifice, to retain as much as possible of the old. One may say that Luther did not discard anything which had once been sacred and precious to him until he had tried in every possible way to recast, reinterpret, or, in some form, to save it. He did this not only out of consideration for the weak souls among his hearers and readers who still clung to the old usages and conceptions, but also because he himself was exceedingly reluctant to part with the old.

It was equally characteristic of Luther that in these books intended for the laity he should treat in a purely suggestive way questions concerning which he was not yet entirely clear —the question, for example, regarding the manner of Christ's presence in the Lord's Supper. This accounts for the fact that he occasionally expressed himself much more radically in the pulpit, before his Wittenbergers who were already accustomed to stronger fare, than he did in books on the same subjects. It was simply that he wished primarily to build and not to destroy, to help souls and not to change the existing ecclesiastical arrangements. "I am not daring," he once said. "On the contrary, I am timid about starting anything new." Consequently, he found no pleasure in being a public figure, especially because in the world outside it was easy for him to become indignant—that is, to fall into sin. But his opponents did not permit him to "crawl into his monk's corner, but were constantly compelling him to come forth and defend truth and justice with a defiant and undaunted courage."

CHAPTER XXIV

AGAINST THE FOUNDATIONS OF MEDIEVALISM

Early in May a crude Latin polemic, *On the Apostolic See,* by the Franciscan lector, Augustine of Alfeld, reached Wittenberg from Leipzig. In it everyone who contested the divine right of the papacy was solemnly declared to be "a wrong-headed heretic." Luther did not at first deem it necessary to respond personally to this weak production, so he charged his *famulus,* the Augustinian Francis Lonicer, with the task. On May 13 he provided the young man with the necessary data for this purpose. It was only after Alfeld had also published this "asinine book to poison the minds of poor people" in German, and Luther had become aware, to his astonishment, that this work had made an impression on even such learned men as his juristic colleague, Wolfgang Stähelin, and Provost Dr. Nicholas von Heynitz, in Bautzen, that he himself felt compelled to answer in German the far-famed Leipzig Romanist. He took the opportunity to explain to the laity what Christendom, or the church, really is. In scarcely two weeks (May 17-30) the new book was on paper with the title, *The Papacy at Rome, an Answer to the Celebrated Romanist in Leipzig,* and by June 16 it was off the press.

Hardly had this book gone to the printer when Luther received, probably from Nuremberg, the *Epitome* which had appeared in 1519. This was a summary of the contents of the third book of the voluminous *Answer* which his old opponent, Prierias, had written, particularly against the thirteenth of the Leipzig Theses. Prierias argued here that every decision of the pope in questions of faith and morals is infallible because it comes from God, and hence every such decision is to be received by everybody without opposition, under pain of temporal and eternal death. None of the countless pronouncements of his opponents made such an impression on Luther as this "hellish manifesto" of the official papal expert in matters of faith. One thing, about which he had had intimations even a year and a half before, and about which his doubts had been dissipated by the reading of Lorenzo Valla's work on the forged Donation of Emperor Constantine, had now become a certainty for him. The papacy was the Antichrist! The papacy, and not necessarily the reigning pope, Leo X. For now, as before, Luther spoke of Leo in extraordinarily friendly and sympathetic terms on the ground that he himself was not to blame for the anti-Christian acts of the curia, but was simply the innocent victim of the robbers, heretics, and murderers of souls who were playing the tune in Rome.

Luther expressly rejected as a false and vain fancy the popular notion of Antichrist according to which the Antichrist was represented as a specific, single individual who would appear at the end of time and accomplish every imaginable kind of miraculous deed. This does not mean that Luther simply adopted the conception of the medieval sectarians who had designated the papacy or the Catholic hierarchy as Antichrist. On the contrary, he saw in the Antichrist a demoniacal power which had come to infect the Roman court only gradually in the course of history—that is, only after the time of Gregory the Great, who was still a very godly man—and then, in the course of the centuries, had spread the contagion so thoroughly that "the mystery of iniquity" had now become notorious and had to be exposed. Moreover, for him the principal hallmark of the anti-Christian spirit was not, as for the medieval sectarians, the striving after *earthly* power and *earthly* riches, nor was it the moral depravity of the curia. It was, rather, the popes' claims to divine infallibility by which they actually set themselves above the Holy Scriptures and consequently above God, and the desire (which appeared in their decretals on every hand) to falsify the clear meaning of the Scriptures in order to gain lordship over the *consciences* of men, and then, with deceitful statutes of every kind, to cast the faithful into bondage. Included also was the contention—and this was especially offensive to him—that the pope had the right to release men from oaths, vows, and covenants confirmed by oaths, whenever it pleased him to do so.

Of only secondary importance to Luther were the moral marks of the Antichrist on which Wyclif, Huss, and the Bohemian Brethren had laid the greatest weight—the boundless greed, the desire for earthly power, and (what seemed especially heinous to the Reformer) the pederasty which was now prevalent at the curia. Not until later did he add a further religious characteristic of the Antichrist: the Romanists themselves do not believe what, under pain of death by burning, they teach and command others to believe. He was convinced by 1520 that they were for the most part religious nihilists. His chief proof for this was the fact that the last Lateran Council had deemed it necessary to adopt a formal definition of the immortality of the soul. As a further evidence he cited his own experience in Rome and the extremely frivolous utterances on the power of the pope which he had heard in Augsburg from Master de Serra Longa. As far as his remarks on the prevalence of the sin of Sodom in Rome are concerned, he based these on what he had himself heard in Rome and upon the *eclogues* of Battista Mantuanus. Of course, he never held the opinion that *all* the men at the court were depraved from top to toe. He never doubted that there were learned and godly men even among the cardinals; later he mentioned several pious preachers who, before the recovery of the Gospel, had boldly attacked the prevalent corruption in Rome. But these men, said Luther, were powerless against the robber band of nihilists who were setting the fashion at the curia. "They did not dare so much as to open their mouths unless they were willing to be poisoned immediately or put out of the way in some other fashion."

The significance of these new convictions for the molding of the Reformer's attitudes and actions can hardly be over-estimated. From this time forward he was convinced that the Last Day was at hand. The principal sign given by the Bible had already been fulfilled. The Antichrist had set up his throne in the temple of God. But Luther regarded this with feelings far different from those of medieval Christians. He was not afraid of it. Like the earliest Christians, he longed with his whole heart for the "precious Day of Judgment." But it was no longer possible for him to tolerate the papacy as a human institution (his earlier tolerance had been accompanied by growing reservations), for he now came to the conclusion that the papacy had not come into being like other human governments; on the contrary, it had gradually developed, under demoniacal influences, out of the Roman episcopate, and hence it was basically a devilish institution which had to be resisted by every means, like the devil himself. The fight against the papacy was now a religious duty for Luther, and so it was henceforth conducted by him just as relentlessly as the fight against Satan. It is true that in the notes with which he furnished Prierias' book early in June, which was published some weeks later, he did not venture to draw all the consequences then in the making. Yet he was through with Rome. "Farewell, thou unhappy, lost, sacrilegious city! Let us hand this Babel over to the servants of Mammon, the unbelievers, apostates, pederasts, devotees of Priapus, robbers, simonists, and all the other wild prodigies with which this pantheon of godlessness is filled to the brim. Let it become a dwelling place of dragons, lemures, vampires, and ghosts, and, in keeping with its name, become an everlasting chaos." But this farewell was so painful for him, as he himself said, that at first he could promote the fight against Rome only hypothetically. "*If* the Romanists continue thus in their raving, in my estimation the *emperor,* the *kings,* and the *princes* will simply have to take action against the pest with force of arms and settle the issue with these people, no longer with words but with the sword." "*If* we punish thieves with the gallows, robbers with the sword, and heretics with fire, why do we not turn with force of arms against these teachers of iniquity, these cardinals, these popes, and this whole Roman Sodom which unceasingly lays waste the church? Why do we not wash our hands in their blood?" [1]

But Luther quickly proceeded to action. As early as June 6 or 7 he determined to carry out the ideas which he had expressed in the above sentences. He resolved to prepare a *scheda,* or placard, to summon the emperor and the whole nobility (that is, all the princes and secular rulers of Germany) to make open war upon the tyranny of the Roman curia. When he began to work on it, the placard gradually grew into a book or, as he called it, a letter—*An Open Letter to the Christian Nobility of the German Nation concerning the Reform of the Christian Estate.* The book was in the press by June 23. It appeared at the beginning of August. Eighteen days later, four thousand copies of it had been sold and a number of reprintings were on the press, for not only the nobility but the whole upper class of the nation literally snatched copies out of the hands of the booksellers. Duke George himself, who at once tried to suppress it, was so fascinated by the book that he wrote to Rome: "What is written there is not altogether untrue, nor is it unnecessary that it should be brought to light. If no one ventures to speak of the evils in the church and if everyone must keep silence, the stones will eventually cry out." Of course he did not tell the Reformer that this was his opinion. But other princes did not hesitate to express their gratitude and admiration for the book which had so quickly become famous. At

---

[1] As often in Luther, a citation from the Psalms (Psalm 58:10 in the Vulgate). These words were torn out of their context at that time and were misinterpreted as a summons to murder the pope and the cardinals. Luther protested against this as early as 1520-21 (cf. Weimar edition 6, 585, 620; 7, 645 f.).

the beginning of December Luther showed Spalatin more than thirty such letters of appreciation.

Just before this open letter left the press two new polemical works reached the Reformer. One was written by the Italian Dominican, Isidore Isolani, and the other by the tireless "Leipzig Romanist," Alfeld. Neither seemed to be worth an extensive refutation. Yet Luther did not wish to pass them up without at least a word of criticism. Moreover, the question which had been raised by Alfeld, whether the withdrawal of the cup from the laity can be justified from the Bible, interested Luther. So he decided to answer Alfeld, at least briefly. In order to irritate the generation of vipers even more, he thought it would be good to combine with this reply an investigation of the question of sacraments in general. On August 31 he mentioned the title of the new work—*De captivitate Babylonica ecclesiae*—for the first time and remarked that little of it had as yet been printed. In September he made such rapid progress that the rather thick book came from the press on October 6. But why, despite its size, did he call it only a "prelude"? Because it was intended to be a prelude to the refutation which Rome was still to expect from him. And why did he give it the curious title, *A Prelude on the Babylonian Captivity of the Church*? Because true Christians, who alone are the church, were undergoing the same experiences as the Jews had suffered in the Babylonian Exile. Like the latter, Christians were being robbed of their freedom. But this was simply a consequence of the Antichrist's success in putting the sacraments in chains, which prevented the sacraments from effecting what they were supposed to. This gave Luther his theme. And he proceeded to develop it without undue polemics in a tone of calm discussion.

Properly speaking, Luther began, the Bible recognizes only one sacrament, the word of God, and three sacramental signs, Baptism, penance, and the Lord's Supper. Consequently only these three can with right and authority be designated as sacraments. But they all have been twisted, corrupted, and distorted. The Lord's Supper has been distorted by the Antichrist, in the first place, by withholding the cup from the laity and, in the second place, by demanding that everyone, on pain of death by burning, must believe the absurd doctrine of transubstantiation, instead of allowing everyone to form his own opinion of the presence, affirmed by the Scriptures, of Christ's body and blood in the elements of the Lord's Supper. The worst distortion of the Holy Supper, however, is the transformation of God's gift into a gift which men make to God, into a sacrifice. The Reformer's argument for this is very similar to, although considerably sharper than, that in the *Treatise on the New Testament* which had appeared a short while before.

The Antichrist could do less harm to Baptism. Nevertheless, he succeeded in making the faithful forget entirely on what this sacrament actually depends—the Word of Promise which is spoken during the administration of Baptism, "Whosoever *believeth* and is baptized shall be saved." For Baptism in itself profits nothing and is of no effect, wrote Luther, apart from the faith which trusts this Word. As a result even the faithful unfortunately no longer understand clearly that the blessing of Baptism, because it establishes a covenant and fellowship between man and God, extends throughout the whole life of the Christian, and that in Baptism the Christian has undertaken the obligation of destroying the old Adam in himself with all his sins and vices; but he has in no sense undertaken obligations of a legal or ceremonial nature such as the hierarchy now ventures to impose on him.

As far as penance is concerned, Luther continued, this sacrament has been destroyed and something altogther different has been put in its place. So here the innovations must be removed and the original restored. The four remaining sacraments — confirmation, marriage, ordination, and extreme unction—are unknown to the Bible, he wrote, and must, on this account alone, be roundly rejected. But cannot the church, that is, the communion of true believers, create new sacraments of her own making? She cannot, for the church is not the creator of revelation, but the creature of revelation. She does not stand above, but under, the Word of God to which she owes her existence. Of course she can determine with unerring certainty whether a word, which presumes to be a Word of God, is really of God, for such a word is just as convincing to true Christians as the axioms of mathematics are to the human mind. But no Christian, not even an apostle, can create a new Word of God and new sacraments. Accordingly, if the Epistle of St. James is cited in support of extreme unction, it is not important. Besides, extreme unction is something quite different from the anointing of the sick which is described there. And finally, this letter was probably not written by the Apostle James at all.

In conclusion, the Reformer declared that penance, too, inasmuch as it lacked an essential mark of the sacrament, a material sign, could not properly be called a sacrament. Strictly speaking, therefore, one could speak of only two sacraments, Baptism and the Lord's Supper.

This "prelude" was written in scholarly language. In fact, it is so learned that only scholars can fully understand and appreciate it. But there were such scholars everywhere in the West in Luther's day. While the little book addressed to the nobility was read but little beyond Germany because it was written in German and for Germans, this bright and keen "prelude," opening with an ironical bow to the writer's opponents as to his best teachers, and written in a Latin which was at times somewhat inelegant, resounded like a tocsin throughout the whole western world. As a rule, it first produced a benumbing shock or evoked passionate anger. In Belbuck, near Treptow on the Rega, the Premonstratensian John Bugenhagen, who had hitherto followed Luther cheerfully, threw it on the ground, horrified and angry, after having read it the first time. After he had reread it several times, however, he saw "that the whole world has been blind until now." From that hour he sought to get away from his monastery and go to Wittenberg. But not all the readers of the book were able to overcome their first impression of revulsion in this way. King Henry VIII of England, with the help of his scholars, immediately wrote a reply which appeared the following year under the king's own name, and he remained an enemy of Luther ever after. The emperor's father-confessor, John Glapion, read the *Babylonian Captivity*, too, and he felt, as he said, as if he were being lashed from head to foot, and from that time he could no longer enjoy the books of the Wittenberger. Erasmus was moved to belief that there was no longer any prospect of reconciling Rome and Wittenberg, and although his own thinking on the sacraments was very liberal, he began to draw away from the Saxon agitator, thoroughly disillusioned and alienated.

What was it that so disturbed adherents of the old faith? And what upset even those who were disposed to hold skeptical opinions? It was not the unfavorable remarks about Antichrists and scholastics which occurred here and there in the book. It was rather the fundamental position which Luther took with respect to what a sacrament is. The Catholic Church taught that the mysterious power of salvation which is hidden in the sacraments becomes efficacious in everyone who receives the sacrament. Luther, on the contrary, asserted that it is not the sign, the element, or the sacred formula which effects salvation, but the Word of Promise which accompanies the sign. Not that this Word works automatically; it is efficacious only when it is received in faith. The entire efficacy of the sacrament, therefore, rests upon the faith that trusts this Word. Without such *faith* no one can be saved; without the *sacrament* one can be saved. It is true that Luther was not yet successful, as the contradictory arguments on infant baptism show, in developing this view consistently. Nevertheless, it was clear as a bell that he rejected outright the Catholic doctrine of the sacraments.

But why did Luther reject this doctrine of the sacrament so sharply? Because the primitive notion of the automatic power of sacred forms and formulas, which was inherent in the doctrine, struck him as incompatible with the Christian conception of God and therefore as irreligious. This primitive notion is hidden in all men. For this reason, despite all precautions, it reappears in the higher forms of religion again and again. But it endangers these religions only when it is officially fostered and cultivated, for then it leads inevitably to magical practices of all sorts. The relation of magic to religion is the same as that of evil to good, ugliness to beauty, falsity to truth. Magic is not religion, but the direct opposite. Yet, although it is always counteracting true piety, magic is the constant concomitant of religion. It does not seek, like religion, to make man subject to the will of the Godhead, but it seeks the reverse—to make the Godhead subject and subservient to man's will. This manner of worshiping God was one of the foundations of western culture, and the primitive notion on which it rested formed an essential part of the medieval *Weltanschauung*. Consequently Luther's new teaching turned not only private and public worship, but also the thinking of the people, into entirely different channels. The prevailing order of social and economic life could not long be preserved in the face of Luther's new ideas. The numerous confraternities no longer had any reason to exist. The corporations and guilds had to put their community life on a new basis when the customary mass was abandoned. The majority of the clergy became unemployed and impoverished. The benefices which they occupied, together with the vast accumulations of capital with which the benefices were endowed, were made available for other purposes. In short, when Luther laid hands on the medieval doctrine of the sacraments, he was threatening the very existence of the whole prevailing system of culture.

In this work Luther treated not only the sacraments, but

also the vows which were held to be binding for life. In other words, he attacked monasticism. The Bible, he asserted, knows nothing of such vows. They should, therefore, be annulled by a general edict; at least, their observance should no longer be enforced by the government. "The more I occupy myself with this question, the more I wonder how such force ever came to be applied at all." The duty of fulfilling vows, he declared, is not affected by such compulsion. Duty would continue, even if the government were to leave it to everyone's judgment whether he chose to remain in the monastery or throw off the cowl. Meanwhile Luther confessed that he would have to give this question closer study. So he announced his intention of writing a particular work on this subject. More than a year passed, as a matter of fact, before he could carry out his promise in the famous work *On Monastic Vows* (called *Zehntagebuch* because it was written between November 21 and December 1, 1521). But he had already so thoroughly shaken belief in monasticism's right to existence that discussion of this topic could no longer be stopped. Before Luther had spoken the last word, others proceeded to act, and this made inevitable the break with medieval civilization in this important area too.

Proposals for the reform of marriage laws which Luther included in the section on marriage provoked a similar break with the views and practices of the Middle Ages. In the first place, Luther denied on principle that the church has the right to make laws pertaining to matrimony. He proposed that all the impediments to marriage which had been invented by canonical law should be abolished at one fell stroke. Only the degrees of kinship which were forbidden in the Bible should continue to be prohibited in the future. Just as vigorously, in the second place, did Luther contest the right of the church to try cases involving matrimonial disputes. "Some learned laymen and townspeople are better fitted for this than the popes, bishops, and councils." The contracting of marriage should by all means be made as easy as possible. "I, for my part, abhor divorce so much that, in comparison with it, bigamy seems more tolerable; yet I dare not offer an opinion as to whether the latter is admissible."

Finally, the blunt repudiation of mysticism, which appeared in the section on ordination, was thoroughly anti-medieval too. "Whoever Dionysius the Areopagite may have been," Luther wrote, "he was at all events more of a [Neo-] Platonist than a Christian. One cannot learn to know Christ from him. On the contrary, anyone who knows Christ will lose him if he takes up this author." "I speak from my own experience." We do not know whether Luther was acquainted with the skepticism of Erasmus and of the Italian humanist, Lorenzo Valla (whom he esteemed very highly), with regard to the genuineness of Dionysius' works. But even if he had known something of their opinions, this passage is ever memorable as a particularly brilliant testimony to the keenness and delicacy of his historical and religious perception.

From the first to the last page, therefore, Luther's *Babylonian Captivity* was a challenge to medieval piety and to the whole medieval way of thinking and feeling. Perhaps the modern reader, who has to feel and think his way artificially into the world of the Middle Ages, will not be so clearly conscious of this as of the pronounced conservative vein which also runs through this most radical of Dr. Martinus' writings. To be sure, Luther wrote that it is tyrannical and godless to withhold the cup from the laity. But it would be equally unjust, he declared, if the laity would immediately seize the cup with violent hands, and especially so because this is not at all essential to salvation. He regarded the doctrine that the body and blood of Christ are offered in the Lord's Supper in, with, and under the bread and wine (often called the consubstantiation theory) as far more plausible than the "absurd" transubstantiation theory of Thomas Aquinas. But he by no means wished to force this interpretation, which was more intelligible to him, upon his readers: he simply intended to reassure those who could not believe in a change of substances and who consequently thought themselves heretics. He bluntly called the sacrifice of the mass idolatry; yet he tried to justify the continuance of even the so-called private masses, in which the idea of sacrifice appeared most prominently. He asserted that the more the rite of the Lord's Supper resembles the procedure of the original Last Supper of Christ, the more Christian the celebration. But it did not occur to him, even remotely, to make a law of this and maintain, like the Waldensians and Hussites, that the Lord's Supper is efficacious only when it corresponds exactly with the form of the Last Supper of Christ. Finally, he vigorously disputed the sacramental character of confirmation, ordination, and extreme unction. But he did not conclude from this that these usages should be abolished; he asserted that they might well continue despite their nonsacramental character.

Thus Luther was prepared to make the greatest concessions in such purely ceremonial questions. But it was here that he revealed how very un-Catholic and unmedieval he had become in his thinking and feeling, for form was never a matter of indifference for the Catholic and medieval frame of mind; on the contrary, it was always a matter of the very greatest importance, as, for example, in the treatment of legal questions. Luther wrote in his "prelude": "A wise magistrate will rule better if he follows his nature [that is, his inherent sense of justice] than if he slavishly holds to the written laws. Laws always do harm when they are applied by someone who does not use them in the right way. Thus unwise magistrates do not know how to temper laws according to time and circumstance." When he wrote these words, Luther was abandoning a fundamental medieval attitude, just as he did when he frequently asserted that worship of God does not depend at all on form. The sectarians of the Middle Ages, who have often been called

forerunners of Luther, were still steeped in this formalism
in which one can clearly discern the primitive belief in the
automatic power of correct forms and formulas. It would
have been utterly impossible for a Hussite, for example, to
treat the question of the cup as something altogether unes-
sential to salvation, as Luther did in his "prelude." As late
as 1523, the leader of the Bohemian Brethren, Brother Lucas,
of Prague, was completely at a loss to understand how the
great Wittenberger could decide such questions as the adora-
tion of Christ in the Lord's Supper, not as questions of faith,
but according to the principle, "Free, free it must be, adapted
to the measure of devotion and circumstance." It does not
seem at all strange, when we consider all this, that the
Reformer's conservative position in questions of form made
no impression on the readers of the "prelude" who were of
the old faith. They gathered quite clearly (perhaps even
from these conciliatory utterances) that in the depths of
his soul Luther thought and felt very differently from what
they were accustomed to, and although he warned against
all radical innovations, they believed that it was no longer
possible to reach an understanding with him.

Adherents of the old faith received very similar impressions from the two German works which had appeared a
short time before, *On the Papacy at Rome* and *Open Letter
to the Christian Nobility of the German Nation*.

The whole social, political, and legal thought of the Middle Ages was dominated by the idea that the Christian
nations formed a single outwardly visible society. The members of this society, which was generally called the church,
but at times also the state (*res publica*), were divided into
two classes, clergymen and laymen. Hence society was governed everywhere by two powers, the priesthood and the
kingship, and it was administered by a twofold law, the
ecclesiastical law and the secular law. But this duality which
ran through the whole social organism had to be adjusted
somehow, for the entire universe, as St. Augustine said, is

based on unity; beauty and its perfection rest, both in detail and as a whole, on unity. And so this tendency toward unity also had to be taken into account in the development of all social institutions. One party, therefore, placed the spiritual power under the secular and honored the Christian emperor as the head of the Christian world order. A second and far more numerous group of thinkers and publicists accorded lordship to the spiritual rather than to the secular power, and accordingly ascribed to the pope the dominion of the world. A third group, finally, believed that the problem could be solved by demanding that the secular power submit to the spiritual power in spiritual questions, and by requiring the spiritual power to heed the secular government in secular matters.

Since the end of the thirteenth century, countless attempts had been made to break through the restrictions of these ideas. But none of these attempts had any real success. At the time of Luther's appearance the old view of a single human society called Christendom, with its two estates, its two powers, and its two legal systems, was still dominating the minds of men. Moreover, neither the belief in the necessity of world monarchy nor the conviction that the pope had been called by God to exercise the office of world monarch had by any means disappeared. Even statesmen unhesitatingly acknowledged the successor of Peter as the overlord of the world. They thought it quite in order than in 1493 Castille and Portugal should refer their disputes regarding the newly discovered lands beyond the Atlantic to Pope Alexander VI, and that the pope should, by virtue of his apostolic power and as vicar of Jesus Christ, *present* and *transfer* to the two powers *possession* of these lands.

It was, therefore, something absolutely new to his contemporaries when the Reformer ventured to declare in his work, *On the Papacy at Rome*, that Christianity is *not* an outwardly visible kingdom, but a spiritual community of souls united in faith. This community, he wrote, requires a uniform organization just as little as it requires a visible, human head. It is by nature a spiritual kingdom which is ruled by an invisible king, Christ, by means of the Word of God, which works invisibly. There is *not a single word in the Holy Scriptures* concerning what the Romanists call church, concerning the church in the sense of Catholic ecclesiastical law. Such an external association of nations under the presidency of the pope is not necessary either on spiritual or on secular grounds. The independence of national states— he names France, Hungary, Denmark, and Poland as examples—is not something abnormal, but a thoroughly normal phenomenon. The opinion that monarchy is the only entirely normal form of organization is just as fallacious. The example of the Swiss Confederacy is sufficient to show that a republic in its way is just as normal as a monarchy.

What was the significance of these assertions? They signified the uprooting of the two basic ideas of the medieval conception of society—the *principium unitatis* (principle of unity) and the conception of the *corpus Christianum* (the universal body of humanity, embracing not only Christians, but also heretics, Jews, and heathen). They signified an actual uprooting of these ideas, not simply an attack upon them, which might easily have been warded off! For when Luther demonstrated that the biblical and religious basis, which was absolutely indispensable to them, was thoroughly invalid, he destroyed the foundation on which they rested.

In his *Open Letter to the Christian Nobility,* Luther then laid an ax to the second principal support of that thought-structure which had long been adhered to as an axiom—the doctrine of the two estates, two powers, and two laws. At the very outset he declared that everyone who has come out of the water of baptism is a priest. A special spiritual estate is unknown to the Bible, he wrote, and it is not necessary. The Christian does not need a human mediator to enter into relationship with God; and God, for his part, does not need such mediators to communicate with man. Every Christian is himself able and empowered to proclaim the Word of God. But just because everyone has this right, no individual may put himself forward and exercise this right without the approval and command of the others. The official exercise of this right is to be regarded as a service entrusted to someone by the Christian community, and consequently it can also be withdrawn again. In this respect it is like the office of burgomaster or other offices of shorter or longer tenure. If a clergyman is removed from his office by the community for any cause whatsoever, he once again becomes a peasant or burgher like other people. What distinguishes the clergyman from his fellow-burghers is merely the service which has been entrusted to him, not a special supernatural faculty (*character indelibilis*) which is bestowed in ordination and never again lost. From this it becomes clear that there are not two estates nor are there two powers in Christendom, for power or force may not be used at all in spiritual affairs. Power to compel (*potestas coactiva*) belongs solely to the secular government, and it is to be applied only in temporal affairs. In the last analysis, "as far as spiritual law is concerned, it would be best if it were blotted out from the first to the last letter, or if it were made into a red heap [that is, if it were burned], for it comes not of the good, but of the evil spirit." "Even if there were much good in it, it should nevertheless be abolished, because the pope keeps it hidden in the shrine of his heart [that is, lays claim to the right] to suspend it, not to heed it, and arbitrarily to set himself over the whole world."

After this, what remained of that whole complex of ideas which had formed the basis of the social, political, and legal thought of the western world for nearly a thousand years? Nothing! But here, too, the Reformer poured new wine into old bottles. In his proposals for the reform of Christendom, Luther made use of the familiar notion of the *corpus Christianum* (the universal body of Christian people), the strongest support of which was the canon law which he had

8ROAD TO REFORMATION

so thoroughly condemned. He proceeded to recommend, entirely in agreement with the ideas of his time, that a council be called for the reform of Christendom, and then he set up a program of reform which treated, among "failings of the spiritual realm," many evils which had nothing to do with religion as such. But it was characteristic of him that he almost always used the traditional terms with an entirely different meaning. Who, for instance, was to call the council he desired? And who—if not exclusively, at least chiefly— was to sit in the council and make the decisions? The emperor, the Electors, the princes, the burghers—in short, the secular authorities. What he proposed under the name "council," therefore, was really not a council at all, but a parliament of princes or a diet.

In the section on the right of the secular government to institute reforms, Luther dealt in similar fashion with the famous theory of emergency which had first been developed by the Paris Dominican, John Quidort, in 1302. What did this theory, which was also adduced frequently by the Occamists, originally imply? If the spiritual power failed or was unable to do its duty, according to this theory, the secular power was bound to render assistance in the church's exigency. On the other hand, if the secular power was found wanting in its special sphere of duty, the ecclesiastical power —in the final analysis, the pope—was obliged to proceed to the reform of the critical conditions in the state. Did Luther simply adopt this theory? No, he quietly canceled the second half which referred to the right of the ecclesiastical power (essential for the theory) to institute a reformation of the secular government. Out of the *emergency right* of the government, moreover, he shrewdly made a *duty of love*. And since he placed this duty on the rulers as Christians, he did not derive it from the nature of the state. For by this time he was convinced that the state, as state, had nothing to do with faith or with the proclamation of God's Word. Thus Luther reinterpreted, almost without exception, the notions and theories which he took from tradition. We do not know whether he was always quite conscious of this. At all events this method, which sometimes makes the understanding of his writings difficult for the modern reader, made it unusually easy for his contemporaries to grasp his new ideas and make them their own. Especially did they understand, all and at once, that they no longer needed fear the ecclesiastical power.

But the consequences of these new ideas reached further than any one of them imagined. The so-called medieval unity of culture rested on the complex of views which Luther destroyed at this time. Wherever Luther's ideas penetrated, this unity of culture, which continued only because of the commanding authority of the church, began to totter. Religion, philosophy, science, and art now went their own several ways. Henceforth they developed independently according to their own inherent impulses, and this sometimes caused them to come into conflict with one another. Political and economic life were also gradually freed from ecclesiastical guardianship, even in lands of the old faith. As to whether this development has been a blessing or a curse for humanity, opinions will always differ. But not even those who consider a new cultural "synthesis" possible or desirable will wish that it had not occurred, for on one point there can scarcely be difference of opinion today: the synthesis which the Middle Ages achieved by submission to the *external* authority of the church is not compatible with the modern conception of culture.

Be all this as it may, the fact remains that Luther was the author of the principles which made this development possible, and he also started the development on its way. Four things, especially, stand out as decisive. First, Luther stressed the return of religion to its own proper sphere, the comforting of consciences; second, he committed to the secular power alone the regulation of the whole broad sweep of temporal, earthly life; third, he enabled western peoples, by means of his teaching concerning the religious significance of earthly callings, to apply themselves to their work with a clear conscience; and fourth, he repeatedly emphasized with the greatest vigor that the supersensual world always remains hidden to the intellect, the consequence of which necessarily is that the meaning of life can never be determined by reason alone. It is true that this last insight was lost to view from time to time during the following centuries, but it always emerged triumphantly; in the long run no new cultural "synthesis" could maintain itself if it tried to solve the problem of *Weltanschauung* in terms of reason, that is to say, more or less after the fashion of ancient or medieval rationalism.

Nor did the Reformer himself have the slightest inkling of the far-reaching influence of his new ideas. In his appeal to the secular powers he was simply pursuing an immediately practical purpose—the gathering of all strength for the fight against the tyranny of the Romanists and for the reform of abuses in the ecclesiastical and civil life which seemed intolerable to him. In order to attain this end, he began by picturing in detail all the tricks which the Roman court had invented to get money out of Germany. He owed his knowledge of this subject for the most part to John von der Wyck, later syndic in Bremen, who spent a few days at the beginning of July in the Black Cloister. The practical demands which Luther then outlined were all moderate—more moderate, at least, than one might have expected after the thesis that the papacy is the Antichrist which he had just expounded with such freedom and candor. It is true that he demanded the repeal of annates, reservations, commendations, expectations, and all the countless practices which had arisen since the late Middle Ages and by means of which the pope had seized possession of ecclesiastical benefices. Furthermore, he demanded the suspension of *casus reservati* (cases of conscience and of law which were reserved for the decision of the pope), the elimination of the jurisdiction of pope, bishops, and officials in all secular affairs, the abolition of the pope's secular lordship and of all his suzerain rights over the empire and the kingdom of Sicily, the reduction of the college of cardinals to twelve members, and the reduction of the "vermin and virus at the curia"—that is, the papal court and its bureaucracy—to the absolutely necessary minimum. But he by no means demanded that the papacy and the college of cardinals should be altogether abolished. On the contrary, he held that the pope should remain, but naturally only as spiritual functionary and highest court of appeal for the disputes which archbishops and primates could not settle, and as first and last resort for disputes among archbishops and primates themselves. The college of cardinals should also remain, he wrote, and every cardinal should receive as much as one thousand guldens (some $7,500 to $12,500) in annual salary—a goal which has not been reached today. Luther was equally far from proposing an elimination of bishops, archbishops, and primates. He went so far as to suggest that the German primacy develop into the highest ecclesiastical court for Germany, and that the primate himself (the archbishop of Mainz) be transformed from a mere figurehead into the real head of the national church of Germany. He was even willing to have the cathedral chapters continue as institutions for the care of posthumous sons of the high nobility, on condition that pluralism (the bestowal of several livings on one person) cease.

Far more radical were Luther's proposals for the reform of the lower areas of ecclesiastical organization. Above all, he tried to carry out two fundamental innovations: the abolition of celibacy and the transfer to congregations of the right to elect pastors. Some of his proposals for the reform of worship were also quite radical. In the future all holy days, except Sunday, should be abolished, he wrote, as should all church fairs, pilgrimages, indulgences, and the chapels and shrines in uninhabited places which, with their recently invented saints, had done much harm. The number of endowed masses, masses for the dead, anniversary masses, and mortuary masses should at least be reduced, he proposed; the endowment of new masses should be forbidden, fasting should be made voluntary, and the confraternities should be turned into free associations for the care of the poor. As far as monastic orders were concerned, he recommended that the monasteries of mendicants, with few exceptions, be closed, and that the monks be forbidden to beg, as well as to preach and hear confessions. The rest of the monasteries and foundations should, as far as possible, be turned into schools, and at the same time the so-called perpetual vows should be abolished. Doing away with the interdict and all the other ecclesiastical penalties, which did not appear until the Middle Ages, seemed to him even more necessary. Only the ban should be retained, but it should henceforth be applied strictly in accordance with the prescriptions of the New Testament (Matthew 18:16 ff.). Luther also discussed the Hussite question in great detail. Inasmuch as it was neither unchristian nor heretical to offer the cup to the laity and to refuse obedience to the laws of the pope, he believed that it was now possible to reach an understanding with the Utraquists as well as with the Bohemian Brethren. But if negotiations for peace were to be successful, no cardinal, papal legate, or inquisitor ought under any circumstances to be entrusted with the affair.

Finally, as he had done in the long *Treatise on Usury*, Luther demanded a thoroughgoing reform of the care of the poor. He also called for a good and extensive reform of the universities, and an appreciable increase in the number as well as the reform of the city schools for boys and girls. Above all, he asked that the dominance of Aristotle in the universities be abolished. Only the lectures on Aristotelian logic, rhetoric, and poetics were to continue. In the law faculty the study of canon law should now be done away with entirely, he urged, and in the theological faculty the *Sentences* of Peter Lombard should be abandoned and the

Holy Scriptures made the focus of instruction. In the city schools for boys and girls the Holy Scriptures should also be studied diligently, and thus methodical instruction in religion, a thing which had never before existed, should be introduced.

To the "failings in the spiritual realm" Luther added several in the secular, the removal of which lay particularly close to his heart. As the worst of these failings in the secular realm, he designated traffic in money—that is, the lending of money at interest—a decidedly usurious practice in the impecunious Germany of that day. The Fuggers, for example, whom he particularly mentions, often demanded twenty per cent. Luther also asked for strict laws against luxury in clothing, against excessive eating and drinking, and against the spice trade which was then taking much money out of the country. In conclusion, he repeated a demand which he had expressed before—the complete suppression of the common brothels, the houses maintained by the towns with town money.

This *Open Letter to the Nobility* was not the only manifesto against Rome that appeared in Germany at this time. A great number of similar tracts preceded it. And Luther was acquainted with some of these. The only one that made a strong impression on him, however, was Hutten's dialogue, *Vadiscus*, which had appeared a short time before. What Luther wrote in his *Treatise on Good Works* concerning Roman barter and the activity of the Roman courtiers is essentially an echo from the reading of this book. In the *Open Letter to the Nobility* its influence can no longer be clearly perceived. Nonetheless, there are still various points of resemblance, particularly in the description of the methods of papal finance and the impudence of papal legates. But even in this part of the book Luther revealed that he was always better informed than the Franconian knight, for he had in the meantime been informed by an expert, Dr. von der Wyck, who had precise knowledge of the practices

at the curia. What is more important, Luther was not satisfied, as was Hutten, with a mere description of these sufficiently familiar abuses. Luther immediately gave his criticism of the papal government a practical turn in that he
attacked its roots (the doctrine of the two estates, powers,
and laws) and then set before his readers — this never
occurred to Hutten!—a program of reform which embraced
almost every side of church life and, in the final anlaysis,
was fully constructive in purpose. It is unlikely that he
learned anything from Hutten in drawing up this program.
If, like Hutten, he demanded the abolition of celibacy, he
was only pursuing an idea which he had already expressed
in the spring of 1520 in his answer to the "Stolpic" note. He
had advocated the abolition of mendicant orders before this.
More than of Hutten, these sections of his work are reminiscent of the older reform writings, especially the *Reformation of King Sigismund,* written as early as 1438 but still
widely read in the sixteenth century. Yet, although he mentioned Sigismund frequently, Luther never alluded to the
Reformation, a circumstance which would have been quite
extraordinary had he been familiar with it. The few paral-
lels which appear only demonstrate that he included in his
program grievances and demands which had been current
a long time. But he always formulated these demands much
better and supported them with keener arguments than had
the older publicists, and he also added a large number of
new demands. Moreover—and this deserves emphasis—he
avoided utopian fantasies. The only exception to this rule
is the suggestion, based on inadequate economic discernment, that all taking of interest should be strictly forbidden.
All the rest of his suggestions were practicable, and most
of them were later carried out, even in the lands which
remained Catholic.

This practical vein, which runs through his arguments
despite all their radicalism, does not ultimately explain the
vast success of the tract. Everyone who read it felt at once

that the man speaking here was no ordinary, radical babbler and visionary, but one who knew how to distinguish the possible from the impossible and consequently had something to say to the world. Despite this, Luther would hardly have found such a vast hearing had he not appealed again and again, in words of impassioned wrath, to the patriotic sentiment of his readers. This device, reminiscent of Hutten, has often been referred to as a trick borrowed from Hutten. But Luther had already used this technique in the preface to his *Commentary on Galatians*—and this was written at the end of March, 1519, a year before Hutten sounded his battle cry. There we read: "Those godless windbags — Prierias, Cajetan, and their confederates — abuse us as German bumpkins, simpletons, louts, and barbarians, and make fun of the unbelievable patience with which we allow ourselves to be deceived and plundered by them. For this reason I throw in my lot with the judgment of the German princes who at the last Diet of Augsburg (1518) so correctly distinguished between the Roman Church and the Roman Curia, and refused to give the latter a tenth, twentieth, fiftieth—that is, the very marrow of Germany—for the war allegedly projected against the Turks. Whence, then, do these 'barbarians' and 'louts' suddenly get this discernment, if not from God? I, too, desire to follow the example of these lay theologians." By March, 1519, therefore, Luther was already saying what Hutten did not say until the beginning of the year 1520.

Nor was Luther influenced by Hutten, as it has often been supposed, to appeal to the Christian nobility of the German nation. In the first place, Luther did not have in mind that class of the nobility to which Hutten and his friends belonged, but (chiefly, at least) the high nobility, the territorial lords who were so odious to Hutten. Since the Diet of Augsburg in 1518, Luther believed that he could presuppose the existence among these lords of the same anticurialistic sentiment as that which moved him. In the second place, there is evidence to show that the *Open Letter to the Nobility* was already on the press when Luther received Hutten's first letter of June 4 and the letter of encouragement, dated June 1, from the knight Sylvester of Schaumberg. Since about the middle of March he had known that Sickingen wanted to give him a refuge in one of his castles. But this offer did not seem to make a very great impression on him, else he would hardly—to Hutten's annoyance—have allowed more than six weeks to slip by before replying, on April 30. Unfortunately this reply is no longer extant. But according to Hutten's letter of June 4, it could only have contained a polite refusal.

The *Open Letter to the Nobility* was consequently neither directly nor indirectly suggested by Hutten. It was an entirely independent enterprise of the Reformer. Hence its contents bore an entirely different stamp from that of the Franconian knight's manifesto. It appealed not to the fists of those who had not been called, but to the consciences of those who had been called. It did not advocate war against clericalism, it did not preach revolution, but it simply demanded reform. For this reason it did not begin with the cry, "To arms!" but with detailed evidence to show that the danger cried aloud for the abolition of abuses which were circumscribing and opposing the Gospel. On only one point did Luther chime in with the great knightly publicist, and that was in his hatred for Rome and his love for the "wretched German nation." But Luther's hatred, like his love, was rooted in something different. Here, therefore, where the inner agreement seemd to be closest, we can recognize most clearly what separated and distinguished the Reformer from the unhappy spokesman of the war on clericalism.

If we can give credence to Luther's own account of his great journey to Italy in 1510-11, it was then that he, like Hutten, first became clearly conscious that he was a German. With him, as with Hutten, this national consciousness

first found a predominantly negative expression, in an attitude outspokenly critical toward the idiosyncrasies of the
Italian people, which struck him as being very curious. But
while Hutten immediately aired his annoyance at Italian
manners in outbursts of spoken and written words, Luther
at first fought against this feeling both in himself and in
others. His first utterance on the question of nationalism—
in his lectures on Romans, 1516—was a protest against the
swaggering Teutonism of the humanist poets, of whom Hutten was even then the chief spokesman, and a warning to
his hearers that they should not imitate such unchristian
conduct. One may not conclude from this, however, that
Luther lacked appreciation for the peculiar worth of his own
nationality. When Tetzel and his associates derided his
theology as worthless because it was new and German, he
dispatched them with a flea in their ears by remarking, in
the preface to the second edition of *Ein Theologia Deutsch,*
that this work showed not only that the Wittenberg theology
was old, but also that the German theologians were the best.
And to bring this out forcefully, he now gave this "spiritually
noble" little book of the old Frankfurt mystic the challenging title which has clung to it ever since: *The German
Theology.*

Luther's blood began to boil even more when, some
months later, Prierias pilloried him in the coarsest fashion as
a "leprous son of a - - - - -." In his reply, Luther reproached
"this characteristically Italian temper." Later, in his conferences with Cajetan and in the behavior of Cajetan's
Italian retinue, he got to know "this characteristically Italian
temper" so well that, for him, Italian and haughty, Italian
and brazen-faced, Italian and perfidious, came to be practically synonymous ever after. At the same time he realized
what liberties these Italians believed they could take with
the German people, with what lack of consideration they
believed they could exploit them, and how unceremoniously
they could poke fun at the patience and stupidity of the

German "louts." Coupled henceforth with this personal aversion to the Italian nature was always an indignation at the abuse which the wretched German nation had suffered at the hands of the Romanists along the centuries and which it now had to suffer more than ever before. But this resentment did not turn into uncompromising hatred until the spring of 1520, when Luther realized that the power which was the ultimate cause of all these outrages was not only a foe of the German people but also an enemy of God—the Antichrist. Thus his hatred toward Rome was not rooted primarily, as was Hutten's, in nationalistic but in religious feelings and value-judgments. Luther would hardly have been less vehement if the pope had lived in Mainz instead of Rome and if the "vermin and virus" at the curia had been exclusively Germans. Hutten, on the contrary, like the Italians of today, would probably have looked upon the Holy See as a precious national possession and would have been a vigorous advocate of its continuance.

Like his hatred for Rome, Luther's love for Germany was of an entirely different stamp from that of Hutten and the humanist patriots. The naive notion that Germans were by nature more godly, noble, brave, and loyal—in short, better—than all other peoples, was always remote from him. To be sure, he did write in his *Open Letter to the Nobility,* with manifest dependence on the *Vadiscus,* "The German nation is celebrated in all histories as noble by nature, steadfast, and loyal." But he never thought of extending this praise unreservedly to embrace the Germans of his own time. On the contrary, he always had fault to find with his fellow-Germans. He conceded them only one advantage—a very important one in his eyes—that they were more honest and truthful, and hence of course more gullible, than other peoples.

Luther was as free from political and patriotic ambitions as he was from national pride. He loved his people, not because they seemed more deserving of love than others or because they had some special destiny, but simply because they were his own people. And he served them, not in order to exalt them above others, but because he thought they were more wretched, tormented, and despised than any others and, therefore, were in special need of such service. His feeling for his Fatherland, consequently, was just as natural and unthinking as a child's attachment for its mother or a farmer's love for the soil on which he grew up. And it was just because it was so unthinking, so unaffected, so free from political or national aspirations, that it could never come into conflict with his religious convictions. True, he was frequently assailed by the thought that he was standing alone against the whole world. But he never doubted that he could best serve his people only if he took an open stand for whatever he knew to be true and right, without pussy-footing and without consideration for consequences.

It was only natural that even at that time statesmen should have a different opinion on this subject. Later generations, too, have frequently opined that Luther would have helped his countrymen more if he had been content with the few external reforms for which he would have had the support of the whole Christian nobility of the German nation, and if he had been sufficiently discerning always to set national interest above all other interests, even above religion. But such statesmen and critics have not recognized that even nations do not live by bread alone; that, besides economic goods, nations also need spiritual and moral powers for their existence; and that they languish past help if their leaders, either out of cowardice or else to protect themselves and their adherents, cautiously shun the struggle for truth and righteousness. If religion is consciously or unconsciously misused, as among the Puritans, to justify an economic or imperialistic lust for dominion, it will at first increase the country's power of resistance, it is true, but the blunting of its sense of truth and its feeling for righteousness, which inevitably accompanies this, will bring in its train a lasting

346 ROAD TO REFORMATION

deformation of national character. Not only can this national character not be restored, but, sooner or later, in the close connection between spiritual and economic production, between moral and political achievement, comes a disastrous effect on the nation's material prosperity. For this reason it has been no loss for the German people that Luther lacked the discernment to place national interest above all other interests, and that he always battled for truth and right (as he understood them) with no regard whatever for the possible political consequences of his conduct. For the statesmen around him, of course, this was very inconvenient. For them he was always "much too bold," as Elector Frederick expressed it in Worms on April 18, 1521. But if he had not been so bold, the mighty spiritual movement which he had unfettered would have been annihilated by the storm from Rome which was now bursting over him with its threat of destruction.

CHAPTER XXV

THE PAPAL ANATHEMA

It was a long time before it was discovered in Rome that Miltitz, in vain self-deception, had completely misjudged the true nature of Luther and the Lutheran affair. It was not until November, 1519, that the curia began to become impatient and anxious over the scandalous delay in the proceedings and clearly intimated this to the unscrupulous nuncio. At the same time, Eck, who was generally regarded at the curia as the victor in the Leipzig Disputation, received instructions to appear in Rome and give a personal account of the new heresy to His Holiness. Before proceeding to a resumption of the trial, however, it was desired to make another attempt to prevail upon the Elector to surrender the son of Satan. To this end, Miltitz was to inform Frederick that the pope would not shrink from resorting to the interdict or other penalties if he did not change his attitude in the Lutheran affair. However, the electoral secretary, Rudloff, succeeded in intercepting Miltitz on the way, thus thwarting the desired audience with the Elector. Hence the papal declaration came to Frederick only in a very much softened form, namely, in the form of a letter, overflowing with polite protestations, which the nuncio sent on December 8, 1519. Frederick immediately grasped the seriousness of the situation and submitted the letter to his councilors a day or so following.

All the councilors took Luther's part. Thus they strengthened the Elector in his decision to put off the curia again with an evasive answer. In the memorial which he had drawn up for this purpose, he emphasized, first, that as far as he personally was concerned, he had hitherto made it a point to avoid taking either side in the Lutheran

affair. Second, that not he, but Miltitz, had insisted that
Luther remain in Saxony, on the ground that the matter
might otherwise become, if that were possible, even more
widespread and troublesome. Third, that it was not he, but
Miltitz again, who, as he boasted triumphantly, had induced
Luther at Altenburg to accept the archbishop of Trier as
commissioner or judge in his case. He then described in
detail what not he but Miltitz had done to bring about
Luther's hearing before the archbishop. Hence, the memorial stated, he was not responsible for the fact that the matter
had not proceeded any further than it had. He was therefore
quite unable to understand why his lands should be burdened with the interdict and other penalties. He had always
strictly obeyed all the commands of His Holiness the Pope
which had come to him through Miltitz, and he was ready
to continue as before to prove himself an obedient son
of His Holiness, so far as this was equitable and right.
Thus the memorial vividly reveals how completely the
foolish nuncio had allowed himself to be ensnared by the
"Saxon fox."

But no matter how willing the Elector was "to twist and
turn to keep peace," it was nevertheless very clear in Rome,
from the humble expressions which he used, that he had
no intention of surrendering Luther. Hence Rome now lost
all consideration for Frederick. As early as January 9, 1520,
in a consistory of cardinals presided over by the pope, after
a long, thundering indictment by an Italian curialist, it was
decided to resume the trial against Luther and at the same
time to extend the trial to include his followers and the
Elector. Several weeks elapsed, however, before the pope
put this decision into execution. On February 1 he formed
a commission, consisting of Cardinals Cajetan and Accolti
and the generals and procurators of the mendicant orders
who were present in Rome, to prepare a Bull of condemnation against Luther. Since the legal aspects of the case
had already been settled in substance in the breve of August

23, 1518, it remained only to set forth in detail what was objectionable in Luther's teachings. The commission, however, was not at all inclined to study this material thoroughly. It simply confined itself to the extracts from the Basel edition of Luther's works, which the Dominicans of Cologne and Louvain had mentioned in their *Condemnation*, and then voted upon the statements objected to there, one after another. In this way the commission proceeded with gratifying dispatch.

But to one of the members—Cajetan—it seemed that this tempo was all too lively and that the whole make-up of the commission was not a very happy one. He brought it about that on February 11 the pope appointed to the commission ten more theologians, among them three Dominicans. Thus Cajetan maintained the balance of power in the discussion. The direction in which he threw his influence is shown by the fact that about the middle of March the commission recommended to the pope that only a part of Luther's statements be condemned, but that the others be branded merely as "conducive to scandal," "false," "offensive to pious ears," "seductive," or "opposed to Catholic truth." It was recommended further that, without mentioning Luther by name, this decision be proclaimed in the form of a decretal, and that in a breve the defendant be once more personally exhorted to recant.

At first the pope sanctioned this proposal. He immediately instructed Volta, head of the Augustinians, to make another effort, through the mediation of Staupitz, to induce Luther to recant. But when Volta was writing this admonitory letter (March 15), the man who was seeking to frustrate Cajetan's efforts to institute a decent campaign against the new heretic was already on his way to Rome. That man was Eck. This bitterest of all Luther's enemies succeeded before the end of March in ruining Cajetan's proposals and inducing the pope to appoint a third commission in which *he* was the leader. This commission consisted of only four

persons, Eck, Cajetan, Accolti, and an otherwise unknown
Spaniard, Dr. John. Their orders were simply to draw up a
Bull of condemnation against Luther. Eck's influence reveals
itself primarily in the fact that now the commission scored
against Luther's account, in addition to the teachings
objected to by the Dominicans of Louvain and Cologne and
Cardinal Adrian of Utrecht, a number of new statements
concerning the papacy which were first presented by Eck.
By May 2 the commission had so far advanced that the Ingolstadt professor was able to submit a draft of the Bull to the
pope, who was at his hunting lodge at Magliana, where,
mounted on horseback, he delighted in watching the furious
hunting of wild boar. Accommodating himself to the genius
of the spot, he began with the fine invocation, "Arise, O Lord,
. . . a wild boar seeks to destroy Thy vineyard!"

Not until nearly three weeks later, on May 21, 23, and 25,
was the document thoroughly discussed by the consistory
of cardinals. The sacred college was unanimous concerning
the reprehensibility of the forty-one articles extracted from
Luther's works by the commission. The remaining sections
of the Bull, composed by the jurist Accolti, were also for the
most part allowed to pass without adverse comment. Only
against the statement that the appeal to a general council
was the rankest piece of heresy which Luther had committed was any objection raised by any of the cardinals.
This opposition came from the aged Spaniard, Bernardino
Carvajal, though it was merely a *pro forma* objection. The
only points on which the discussion appears to have spun
itself out to any length were the questions whether all the
heretic's writings should be condemned to the flames, or
only those in which one or another of the forty-one condemned articles appeared; also whether, as Cajetan especially recommended, the exact degree of reprehensibility
should be indicated in the case of each article; and, lastly,
whether the heretic should once more be formally admonished to recant, as Accolti recommended, or, as Pucci pro-

posed, be formally and immediately anathematized. But nothing of any consequence resulted from the discussion. On June 1 the Bull was accepted by the cardinals without alteration, and on June 15 it was drawn up in due form in the papal chancellery and immediately printed.

"Arise, O Lord, . . . arise, Peter, . . . arise, Paul, . . . arise, all ye saints, with the whole universal church. . . ." Thus, passionately and unctuously, the extraordinarily long-winded document opened. Then followed a touching lament that anything so wicked could have occurred among the Germans, those to whom the popes had once given the Roman imperium by reason of their very special affection for them. The document continued with the list of the forty-one condemned articles of Luther, for the most part copied out of the *Condemnation of Cologne and Louvain.* Curiously enough, the Reformer's worst heresies were not mentioned. Why? Because even Eck and Cajetan had not thought it necessary to study those writings which had not appeared until after the Leipzig Disputation, such as the *Commentary on Galatians,* the three treatises on the sacraments, and others. Thus the list included such articles as, "To burn heretics is contrary to the will of the Holy Spirit" and "Secular and spiritual princes would do well if they would put an end to mendicancy," and these were paraded as *heresies.* Many of the statements, because they had been torn from their context, were almost unintelligible, and some were so arbitrarily formulated that Luther was able immediately to assert that he had never taught any such thing. In short, this chief part of the Bull, on which the three commissions had labored for three whole months, was really a wretched piece of work.

The forty-one articles were then condemned indiscriminately, that is, without indication of the special degree of their reprehensibility, and all the faithful, even emperors, kings, and *electors,* etc., were forbidden to believe, teach, defend, or favor them, either publicly or privately. All

Luther's writings in which the forty-one articles were found
— in another place, his writings as a whole — were condemned to be burned and no longer to be printed. Thus the
document was not even purged of gross contradictions
before it was published. Luther himself and his followers
were threatened only with excommunication; that is, even
Luther was granted sixty days' grace in which to recant.
Was this in fact, as the Bull says, "an outburst of the Christian compassion" which filled the pious soul of Leo X? No;
it was nothing more than a legal formality, which could very
well have been dispensed with, since Luther's heresy had
been established beyond question. If Accolti, who was
responsible for the legal texture of the Bull, did not wish in
Luther's case to omit the so-called "evangelical monition,"
this was retained only in order to be able, after the expiration of the period of grace, to make powerful use of the
"stiff-necked obstinacy of the heretic" when it came to meting
out the punishment.

Thus the Bull was not a masterpiece either in content or
in form. But even worse was the fact that before sending
out its decree the curia had neglected to ascertain the effect
such a proclamation would most certainly have in Germany.
No one emphasized this more strongly than Eck, the man
who in reality had played the leading role in the third commission. Three years later he complained that even the most
learned were at a loss to understand why some of the condemned articles were condemned; so harmless and indifferent did they appear. A further defect, he said, was the fact
that the Bull contained absolutely nothing "evangelical and
Pauline." The greatest mistake, however, was that it had
been allowed to go out without the addition of an appendix,
containing a thoroughgoing refutation of Luther's errors
from the Bible, the Church Fathers, and the canons of the
councils. Eck gave the cause for this mistake in a confidential letter which he wrote while he was still in Rome.
"They know little of Luther's errors here," he wrote. This

was actually the case. Even at that time, the curia was very imperfectly informed concerning the Lutheran affair. There had been enough time and opportunity to secure better information but, as is shown by the diary of Paride de Grassi, the papal chief master of ceremonies, the pope and the thirty cardinals who were in Rome at the time had more important things to do than to trouble themselves with this thing. It is hardly an injustice to Leo X to say that he was more interested in the wild boars in the hunting grounds of Magliana than the wild boar which, according to the moving words of the Bull, had invaded the vineyard of the Lord in faraway Germany.

Before the Bull was submitted to the cardinals, it was decided to exert pressure once more upon the Elector by sending him, on May 20, a formal ultimatum through the aged Cardinal Riario and Tetleben, the Mainz agent. The cardinal's letter pointed out in plain terms that the Elector could bring about Luther's recantation, if only he had a mind to. If he did not do so, he had nothing to expect but a disgraceful reproof for his wickedness. What did the Elector do then? He immediately turned over both the letters, which had reached Lochau on July 7, to Luther for reply. Luther advised him to stick to his previous policy; namely, to inform the cardinal that he personally had nothing to do with the whole affair, but that he was ready to induce Luther to surrender himself to a trustworthy tribunal. He added, in reference to an encouraging letter which he had just received from the Franconian knight, Sylvester von Schaumberg, that it perhaps would do no harm if the Elector were to mention casually that there were now people, not only in Bohemia, but even in the heart of Germany, who were determined to defend him, Luther, "in spite of all the thunders" of Rome, if he were driven out of Saxony. Further, the Elector might also tell the cardinal that Luther's teaching had already spread so far in Germany and outside Germany that any attempt to combat it with force instead of the Bible and reason would make of Germany a second Bohemia. It was well known, even in Rome, he wrote, that the Germans have a haughty temper, and therefore even the pope must be careful not to provoke them, especially now when learning and the study of the ancient languages were flourishing among them and even the laity had begun to be wise. Since the curia was so wickedly threatening the Elector, the Reformer suggested that the Elector should not hesitate to answer with similar threats.

In August the Elector did, in fact, venture to send this pill, prepared by Luther, to Tetleben, the Mainz *chargé d'affaires,* though he did sugar-coat it. To the cardinal, however, he continued to play the part of the wholly disinterested neutral, a role which had by this time become with him an agreeable habit. Never, never had he undertaken to defend or advocate Luther's writings or sermons. He had heard, however, that Luther was ready to defend himself on the basis of the Holy Scriptures before impartial, learned judges in an impartial place. He had also heard that his friend, the archbishop of Trier, had been appointed as papal commissioner for this tribunal. Thus he acted as though he personally were merely an onlooker. And yet he himself had maneuvered the whole affair! At the very time that he was writing this to the cardinal, he induced Luther to publish as a placard his "offer" to allow himself to be judged on the basis of Holy Scriptures by an impartial tribunal. At the same time he induced Luther to appeal to the new emperor for protection in a letter which was, of course, scrupulously edited beforehand at the court. For ever since 1519 he had intended taking Luther with him to the diet and had already communicated this to Miltitz, that is, to the curia. If politics consists only in defense against the opposing power's plan of attack, Frederick must unquestionably be counted among the greatest politicians of his time, for scarcely anyone was a match for him in the minor arts of the defensive, especially the art of dissimulation.

In the meantime, however, Rome had already gone over to a formal offensive. On July 17, 1520, the pope had appointed the humanist, Jerome Aleander, his librarian, and Dr. Eck to be his nuncios with the commission to publish and execute the Bull in Germany. Eck was to deliver the chief blow against Luther by publishing the Bull in the Saxon lands, while Aleander was to incite the young emperor against Luther. It is rather surprising that the curia should have risked entrusting such a delicate mission in Germany, especially in Saxony, to such an unpopular personality. It appears that the curia actually plotted to provoke the Germans. In addition, Eck made his case as awkward as possible. He immediately made use of his authority to place other names in the Bull for the purpose of venting his spleen upon several of his personal enemies, such as Bernard Adelmann, Lazarus Spengler, and Willibald Pirckheimer. But, what was even worse, he failed to observe the customary legal forms in the official proclamation of the Bull, thereby giving the secular and spiritual authorities in the Wettin lands an acceptable pretext to prohibit its publication. Thus the action which he had instituted with his customary "shouting, bragging and pomposity" necessarily ended in complete failure.

Only in three places in central and north Germany—Meissen, Merseburg, and Brandenburg—did Eck succeed in carrying out the regular publication of the "holy curse" by means of a public placard. In every other place he was refused admittance. Perhaps most surprising to him was the reception he received on September 29 in Leipzig, the town which had seemed to be so favorably disposed toward him the preceding year. Of course, the town council did not neglect to greet him on his arrival with the customary gift of wine; it even placed the town soldiers at his disposal as couriers for the dissemination of the Bull. The university, however, steadfastly refused to publish it, and in this it was supported not only by the ducal officials, but by the duke himself. Among the student body his presence almost caused a riot. On the following day lampoons were found posted at about ten different places in the town. Presently a ribald song was being sung about Eck in the streets. He thought it best, therefore, to hide himself with all haste within the safe walls of the Dominican monastery of St. Paul. But even there he was harassed with challenging and threatening letters. It is probably not amiss to seek the instigators of these disturbances among the more than fifty Wittenberg students who had come to Leipzig for the Michaelmas Fair, for the Leipzigers, who in general were very well-bred, could hardly have dared such outrages on their own account.

No one derived more satisfaction from the adverse fate of His Holiness' new nuncio than the still undischarged nuncio of 1518, Charles von Miltitz, who had just arrived in Leipzig for the Michaelmas Fair. Miltitz considered it unprecedented that Eck should have published the Bull without first consulting him, and he remonstrated with Eck that the latter had upset all the efforts toward a mutual understanding between Rome and Wittenberg which he had been pursuing for so long with such caution and delicacy. Whether Eck actually swallowed this insult in silence, as Miltitz affirms, may very well be doubted. In any case, the obvious fiasco of the strong man of Ingolstadt had such a refreshing effect upon the sanguine temperament of "Herr Karl" that he now decided to carry out, without delay, the plan which he had concocted several weeks before and which had been approved by Elector Frederick on September 10. His plan was to have a personal conference with Luther for the purpose of again persuading him to write a conciliatory letter to His Holiness. On the same October 3 on which Eck sent the Bull to the University of Wittenberg by one of the Leipzig couriers, Miltitz rode over to Alten-

burg in order to make the necessary arrangements with Herr
Fabian von Feilitzsch, to whom the Elector had referred
him before his departure for western Germany. In accordance with the command of the Elector, Feilitzsch designated
the preceptory of St. Anthony, at Lichtenberg on the Elbe,
about half way between Wittenberg and Leipzig, as the
place for the desired conference. But the preceptor, Wolfgang Reissenbusch, would have nothing to do with this
honor intended for him, fearing that "he, poor devil, would
have to suffer for it somehow." Not until Feilitzsch gave
him permission to stay away from Lichtenberg while the
conference was going on, did he yield. Feilitzsch, however,
apparently did not entirely trust Miltitz. He not only saw
that Luther was accompanied to Lichtenberg by a nobleman and four troopers, but he stationed thirty more troopers
in the vicinity of the preceptory.

At four o'clock in the afternoon of October 11, Luther,
Melanchthon, and an unnamed Augustinian arrived at Lichtenberg in a wagon. Two hours later, Miltitz arrived from
Eilenburg with four horsemen. Perhaps nothing is so characteristic of "Herr Karl's" turn of mind as the fact that he
thought he could still heal the breach between Wittenberg
and Rome with the same trivial tactics that he had used a
year and nine months before. Luther was to write a letter
to the pope and acknowledge that he had never intended to
attack the person of His Holiness, but that he had merely
wished to defend himself from his enemies. The pope was
to put all the blame upon these enemies, especially upon
Eck. Thus "Herr Karl" intended that this time the great
Dr. Eck should play the role of scapegoat, which he made
the unfortunate Tetzel play in 1519. As a token of good
will and the beginning of peace, Luther was to present to
the pope a little book. Both the little book and the letter
must be finished in printed form within twelve days, since
this would give Miltitz time to reach Rome and personally
present the two documents to the pope before the expiration

of the grace stipulated by the Bull. The pope, of course, would be glad "to have an excuse to limit the ban as well as the Bull." In about four months Miltitz would return to Germany with a new breve which would abrogate the Bull, or at least "moderate" it. Moreover, he naturally demanded again that Luther keep silent if his enemies would also keep silence. In short, he merely repeated essentially what he had proposed the previous year in Altenburg. Only two points in his proposals were entirely new: first, the idea, which was probably suggested by Staupitz or Link, that Luther include a personal favor, in the form of one of his writings, along with the letter to the pope; second, the requirement that the letter to the pope be dated September 6 in order that it might not appear as if Eck and his Bull had constrained him to write it. Luther was to date it September 6 because it was on this date that he had promised Staupitz and Link, sent to him by Miltitz for this purpose, to write such a letter.

Luther actually acceded to all these demands. He promised to keep silent if his enemies would do the same. He even agreed to leave unanswered the latest product of that pugnacious Romanist, Alfeld, which had just appeared, but not Eck's polemic against the *Address to the Nobility* which Miltitz had recently sent to the Saxon court. Miltitz was so pleased with Luther that, when the defendant started homeward on the afternoon of October 13, he accompanied him quite a distance on the way to Wittenberg. On the following day he wrote in high elation to the Elector from Eilenburg that now the matter would surely be brought to a happy conclusion and Eck and his followers would have all their trouble for naught. Only two things were still necessary: first, a short letter from His Grace to the pope, with a few friendly words of thanks for the bestowal of the Golden Rose, and, second, money. For without money one cannot travel to Rome, he said, and without gifts—that is, without bribes—it is impossible to accomplish anything there. The

Elector might therefore frequently place his image—that is, the image of his coinage—at his, Miltitz', disposal for the young cardinals who once had been his companions.

While this incorrigibly optimistic diplomat was building these air castles on paper in the Eilenburg castle, Luther had already finished the Latin and the German texts of his letter to the pope and perhaps also the German text of the promised booklet of homage, for he was already quoting several sentences from it in a sermon on October 14. The printing of the three manuscripts, however, dragged on until the end of October; in fact, the Latin edition was not yet in type by the middle of November when the Reformer was no longer in a hurry to publish the work. And the reason for his lack of haste was that, as might have been expected, nothing had come of Miltitz' journey to Rome. Five days before the expiration of the period of grace specified in the Bull, November 21, "Herr Karl" was still sitting at his ease in Erfurt. Whether he had forwarded to Rome the copies of Luther's letter and book, which had been sent to him, we do not know. Apparently he retained them without any scruples whatever and used them in some other way.

The letter to Pope Leo, which had already been composed on October 13, shows clearly how seriously Luther took his obligation to fulfill the Lichtenberg agreement. But it also shows how completely he had broken with the old church. He paid due personal reverence to Leo X, but he declared frankly and candidly, "It is all over with the Roman See; the wrath of God has overtaken it. It is not worthy of the esteem of such as either you or I. Satan ought to be pope, for he certainly reigns in the new Babylon more than do you." Thus speaking, Luther no longer treated the pope as his superior, but as a Christian brother who was in a peculiarly dangerous situation. In conclusion he dedicated the little book, *A Treatise on Christian Liberty*, to the pope as a peace offering; first, in order to show him how he would prefer to employ all his time, if only those godless flatterers of the

Roman See would be satisfied to let him alone; second, because, being poor, he could not show his readiness to serve in any other way; and third, because Pope Leo had no need of any but spiritual gifts.

Concerning the *Treatise on Christian Liberty*, it has already been remarked that the German version was probably written in one or two days, October 13 and 14. The Reformer took far more time in writing the Latin version, and it is therefore far more successful. He himself stated that the real theme of the book is *faith*. Thus we have here the treatise on faith which he had promised and announced the preceding spring. What he wrote in the first part concerning the power and might of faith, is one of the noblest things he ever wrote, even though, properly speaking, he was writing concerning ideas which had long been familiar to him. On the contrary, in the second part, which apparently was very hastily thrown together, he obviously became badly involved at the very outset in the answer to the question of the relation of religion and morality. Hence this second part is far inferior, both as to content and form, to the sections of the *Treatise on Good Works* which treated the same question. More successful and also more characteristic of him were the final words of admonition, added in the Latin edition: To be free does not mean to trample under foot the existing ordinances of the church. For the sake of the weak, who inwardly have not yet gotten away from the old ceremonies, as well as for the sake of the young who cannot do without such external modes of correction, the free Christian must rather be willing, at least for the present, to continue to observe the fasts and similar customs.

If the little book did not turn out to be what it was intended to be, a "summary of the Christian life," or a complete presentation of the new ideal of piety, this cannot be attributed wholly to the fact that since October 15, at the latest, he had been writing two new works which claimed far more of his time and energy. These were a Latin response

to the Bull (*Adversus Execrabilem Antichristi Bullam*) and
a German polemic against Eck's spiteful criticism of the
Address to the Nobility, entitled *Concerning Eck's New Bulls
and Lies*. He called Eck's accusations against him lies. The
Bull, he said, sounded so much like Eck that it may very
well have originated with him, for, try as he would, he could
not understand how the pope would have commissioned
him, of all persons his bitterest enemy, to bring such a document to Saxony. Anyhow, one forgery more or less was of little consequence to the Romanists. As long as he had not seen
with his own eyes the original text and the Bull, with lead,
wax, string, signature, and proviso, he would not yield a
hair's breadth, no matter how much the curialists howled. In
the Latin polemic he again asserted that the Bull was questionable, despite his own belief that it was genuine. But no
matter who wrote it, he continued, there is no doubt that the
author is Antichrist. He will therefore treat it in the future
as the work of Antichrist. He then strongly emphasized the
legal defects of the document and the strange contradiction
that in one place it stated that all his works were condemned to be burned, and in another only those in which
any of the forty-one condemned articles appeared. He then
declared solemnly: "You, Leo X, and you, cardinals, and
everyone else who amounts to anything at the curia: I challenge you and say to your faces, if this Bull has in truth gone
forth in your name and with your knowledge, I warn you,
in virtue of the power which I, like all Christians, have
received through Baptism, to repent and leave off such
Satanic blasphemies, and that right quickly. Unless you
do this, know that I, with all who worship Christ, consider
the See of Rome to be occupied by Satan and to be the
throne of Antichrist, and that I will no longer obey nor
remain united to him, the chief and deadly enemy of Christ.
If you persist in your fury, I condemn you to Satan, together
with this Bull and your decretals for the destruction of your
flesh, in order that your spirit may be saved with us in the

Day of the Lord. In the name of Him whom you persecute, Jesus Christ, our Lord." He then discussed several of the heresies for which he had been condemned. In conclusion he repeated the solemn judgment: "If they condemn me in their sacrilegious heresy, I condemn them in the truth of the Lord."

In the letter which he sent to Spalatin on November 4 along with this vehement manifesto, Luther wrote, "I am also having a German version printed." This German version appeared soon afterward with the title, *Against the Bull of Antichrist*. It was directed to the unlearned laity with the purpose of warning them against the anti-Christian spirit of the Romanists, who were ready to condemn everything that displeased their blind heads. Since he was speaking to the laity, he omitted the solemn condemnatory judgment which he had uttered in the Latin text, for he had no desire to stir up the laity against the clergy. He admonished them, rather, to pray God to turn away His wrath from the clergy and deliver them from the evil spirit which now possessed them. "It is more than enough that we recognize how foolish and furious they have become in the face of the rising truth, whose light is shining even in their faces, so that they see yellow and green and no longer know what they are seeing, hearing, and saying. We must be merciful, not harsh, toward them." In other respects he repeated the ideas of the Latin work only in a general way. In the first pages he still questioned the genuineness of the Bull. In the conclusion, however, he wrote, "If the pope does not recall and condemn the Bull and punish Eck and his henchmen who follow such Bulls, then none can doubt that he is the enemy of God, the persecutor of Christ, the foe of Christianity, and the true Antichrist."

Luther himself characterized his own frame of mind during these days in the following incomparable words: "Be it known to all that no one does me a service by despising that outrageous, heretical, lying Bull, nor can anyone spite me by esteeming it. By God's grace I am free, and this thing shall neither console nor frighten me. I know well where my consolation and my courage abide, and who makes me safe before men as well as devils. I will do what I believe to be right. Everyone will have to stand up and answer for himself at his death and on the Last Day; then, perhaps, my faithful warning will be remembered." The thought of martyrdom had no terror for him. On the contrary, he longed to suffer death for Christ. The numerous encouraging letters, which he now received from all quarters, made no deeper impression upon him even when their authors were princes. He wrote to Spalatin, "You must learn not to put your trust in princes. They will not defend the Word of God; on the contrary, they will rise up against the Lord and His anointed." So he refused to follow even the advice of Elector Frederick, and he would not turn to individuals of princely rank for private advice. On November 17 he renewed his appeal to a future general council. In the same document, published as a placard in both Latin and German, he begged the emperor, electors, counts, princes, knights, towns, and municipalities of the German nation, for the sake of the vindication of the honor of God, the defense of the Christian Church, and the holding of free Christian councils, to support his appellation, to desert the pope, or at least to refrain from enforcing the unchristian Bull until he had been justly summoned, heard, and thoroughly refuted from Holy Scriptures by impartial judges. "But if anyone should despise this my appeal and continue to follow the pope, I consider myself exculpated, for I have besought and troubled their consciences beforehand with this my sincere, brotherly warning, and henceforth I leave him, the pope, and the whole papal crowd to the Last Judgment of God." He thus shrewdly turned his appeal "to a free council" into an appeal to the emperor and the empire. Had he already heard that the Elector intended taking him along to the next diet? No! Or had the Elector induced him to appeal directly to the emperor and the empire in this extremely forcible and impressive way? Again, no! The idea was his own. But the emperor and the empire could no longer shut their ears to his appeal, for all Germany was already listening to his voice as to the voice of a prophet and was awaiting the event which he had so urgently sought in the name of justice and the Word of God.

CHAPTER XXVI

BONFIRE AT THE ELSTER GATE

In the meantime Jerome Aleander, the other special ambassador of the pope, had inaugurated a far more successful campaign in the western part of the empire against this "new Arius and Mohammed." As early as September 28, 1520, he had succeeded at Antwerp in eliciting from the young emperor the order for an edict against the heresy within the boundaries of his hereditary lands in Burgundy. He then managed to bring about the first formal burning of Lutheran books in Louvain on October 8 and in Liége on October 15. In the latter place, thanks to his longstanding relations with the prince-bishop, Aleander was also able to dictate a mandate against "Lutherism." It was not until he arrived in the Rhineland that he, too, began to meet some of the difficulties which had made it absolutely impossible for Eck to carry out his mission. He was able to put up with the fact that the emperor temporarily rejected, for legal reasons, the proposal submitted immediately after his coronation on October 23 that he issue a mandate putting the new heresy under the ban of the empire, since he could reckon with certainty upon the fact that the young monarch and his councilors would do everything in their power to obtain such a law from the German diet.

But the welcome Aleander received in the imperial city of Cologne, which at the time was swarming with princes and other foreigners, was very discouraging. The humanists of the city greeted him with lampoons in which he was cruelly satirized as a son of a Jew, an enemy of the liberal arts, a train-bearer to courtiers, and a protector of sodomites. At the same time there appeared in the city a pamphlet which represented the Bull as being suspiciously like a scribble of the old inquisitor, Hoogstraten, ascribed to the curia, and its acceptance by the University of Louvain as a fraud perpetrated by Aleander. The worst blow, however, was that the Elector of Saxony, who had been staying in the city since September 25, flatly refused to receive him and the Neapolitan, Caracciolo, who was the other nuncio accredited to the imperial court. It was not until November 4, during mass in the Minorite church, that he succeeded in button-holing the prince and compelling him to listen patiently to his demand that Luther's books be burned and Luther himself imprisoned or surrendered to Rome. He brazenly assured the Elector that the emperor and all the princes had already agreed to this proposal. But he received only the curt reply that it was impossible for him to decide such matters out of hand.

The next day the "old fox" made an appointment, not with him, but with that hated man whom Aleander considered the real author of Luther's heresies, his deadly enemy, Eras-mus of Rotterdam, who was also in Cologne at the time. Erasmus himself had been urgently seeking this audience in order to present in person his plan for settling the Lutheran affair. When the Elector asked him for his own opinion of Luther, however, he seemed at first to be unwilling to speak out plainly. But after smacking his lips several times, he suddenly said, "Luther has committed two sins. He has attacked the crown of the pope and the bellies of the monks." Even the Elector, who was looking at the speaker with his customary seriousness and attentiveness, could not repress a smile. Erasmus continued: The real cause of this baiting of Luther is hatred of sound learning and lust for power. The men who are doing it are without exception suspicious persons. (He was referring quite definitely to Aleander, whom he even suspected of having fraudulently made himself a papal nuncio.) The horrible statements of the Bull have aroused all honest, thinking people. Only two universities out of so many have condemned Luther, and have only condemned, not refuted him. He then expressed himself as being especially pleased with Luther's *Offer and Protest,* which the Elector had just had publicly posted in Cologne. Even in the pope's own interest, he said, it is to be desired that Luther be granted his desire to be heard by expert and impartial men. The Elector knew enough Latin to be able to understand what the brilliant little man, declaiming before him, was saying. But Spalatin was obliged to translate into Latin the questions the Elector asked in German, since naturally the great scholar understood no German. Erasmus, however, apparently feared that the prince had not always been able to follow him and, when Spalatin accompanied him back to his quarters at Count Neuenahr's, he immediately sat down and wrote out the leading thoughts of his speech (axioms) on a piece of paper which he then handed to Spalatin as a token of friendly regard.

The Elector not only conferred with Erasmus but also made inquiries whether the emperor had actually promised Aleander to enforce the Bull immediately in the manner suggested by the nuncio. Of course, he found that Aleander had far overstated the case. It was not until the afternoon of November 6 that he notified the two papal ambassadors, through his councilors, that he could not comply with their demands. On the contrary, he reported, he must beg them to abandon the procedure which they had heretofore chosen to follow and instead lend their support toward allowing Luther to be heard, according to his *Offer,* in a safe place before impartial judges. Luther's books, furthermore, were not to be burned until he had been convicted of error. Aleander answered in a long speech, saying that the pope had already troubled himself enough to turn Luther from his errors. Naturally, he would have nothing to do with the arbitration of Luther's case by the archbishop of Trier, to which the Elector had again called attention. This, he said, was already settled, since the delegating judge (the pope) had again taken the matter into his own hands. As far as the rest of the procedure was concerned, it was not incumbent upon him or his colleague to adopt methods other than those prescribed by the Bull. They would therefore continue to burn Luther's books, since this was all that the pope intended.

As far as Luther himself was concerned, he was not at all desirous of "soiling his hands with their blood."

The next day the Elector left Cologne. Immediately upon hearing of his departure, the nuncio decided to make good his words concerning the burning of Luther's books in Cologne. The emperor gave his ready support to the project. But the archbishop, the cathedral chapter, the town council, and even the university refused to take any part whatsoever. Thus the great event took place on the morning of November 12, entirely without the solemn pomp which the church was fond of displaying at such spectacles. Moreover, Aleander was cruelly duped by the clerics to whom he had entrusted the work. Previously, in Louvain, the students had succeeded in palming off upon the hangman a great number of scholastic tomes and old books of sermons, so that in the end the brave fellow unwittingly burned more good Catholic literature than Lutheran books. In Cologne, however, thanks to the clever manipulations of the Lutherans, not a single book of Luther's was burned; only a bundle of waste paper was consigned to the flames. A few days later, in Mainz, Aleander found even less response than in Cologne. Here, on November 28, even the town hangman refused to obey his orders because Luther's books had not yet been legally condemned. The people even threatened to stone him. But on the following day, owing to the intervention of the archbishop, he succeeded in setting up a fine fire, though unfortunately not with Luther's books; for here, too, the students had in the meantime taken charge of the affair and prevailed upon the ignorant grave-digger, who had been hired for the task, to apply the torch to a heap of anti-

Lutheran writings instead of Luther's books. Nevertheless, the nuncio was not mistaken when he declared that the burning of books was more effective than the finest refutations. The trouble it had cost him to put through these two book-burnings no one elsewhere suspected. He himself was completely ignorant of how badly he had been deceived by Luther's followers. From all outward appearances it was evident only that Rome was now beginning to work with a vengeance. This in itself made such an impression upon many people that Aleander thought he could declare triumphantly, "The people are manifestly improving."

Luther presumably did not learn of the *autos-da-fé* in Louvain and Cologne until the end of November. He apparently determined at once to repay the curia in its own coin. When Spalatin visited him in his little cubicle on December 2 or 3, he had already "gathered together the canon law and the decretals to burn them as soon as he heard from credible authority that they had undertaken to burn his books in Leipzig." His visitor informs us that he had also decided to burn the Bull publicly in the pulpit at the first opportunity if his enemies did not mend their abuses. Spalatin reported this at once to the Elector on December 3. Had the Elector any objections to make to Luther's purpose? No; this time he purposely refrained from putting anything in the Reformer's mind, for he himself was extremely wrought up over the book-burning in Cologne, which had taken place shortly after his departure. What it was that moved the Reformer to take action, we do not know.

From all appearances, however, the idea did not occur to Luther until the eve or early morning of December 10. On the morning of December 10, he had Melanchthon post a notice on the door of the parish church inviting "all adherents of the truth of the Gospel to be present at nine o'clock at the Chapel of the Holy Cross outside the walls, where the impious books of papal law and scholastic theology will be burned according to ancient and apostolic usage." Shortly before nine o'cluck he sent Agricola about the town to hunt up a number of these impious works of scholastic theology to be burned with the rest. But none of his colleagues would give him, for this unusual purpose, their copies of either Thomas Aquinas' *Summa* or Duns Scotus' *Commentary on the Sentences*. We can also say with certainty that on the morning of December 10 he still had no intention to burn the Bull, but merely the canon law. It was not until he was preparing for the march to the Elster Gate that he was induced, apparently by Agricola, to take with him a printed copy of the Bull. The place he selected for the "pious spectacle" was the one traditionally used for such ceremonies, the town carrion-pit near the Elbe. [1]

The participants in the ceremony were all professors or students. "A not unknown master of arts," in all probability the above-mentioned John Agricola, heaped up the fagots and lighted them. First he threw into the flames the three large volumes of the Paris, Basel, or Rostock edition of the canon law and the *Summa Angelica* of Angelo de Chiavasso. These folios were followed by about twelve smaller volumes of the writings of Eck and Emser. Then Luther stepped up to the fire, trembling and praying, and cast in another booklet with the words, "*Quoniam tu conturbasti veritatem Dei, conturbet te hodie Dominus in ignem istum!*" (Because thou hast brought down the truth of God, may the Lord today bring thee down unto this fire!) Of those present, perhaps only Agricola, besides himself, knew that this booklet contained the Bull, for the notice which Melanchthon had posted contained not a word concerning the burning of the Bull. Moreover, Luther spoke so quietly that only the professors and students who were standing close to him could understand him and respond with an "Amen." He then returned at once to the town with the other professors. Only the students remained to conclude, with buffooneries and pranks,

---

[1] Therefore *not* the spot now marked with a tablet; the place was situated much closer to the Elbe.

this "pious spectacle," the significance and purpose of which the majority of them hardly understood. Thus the whole ceremony was performed in less than ten minutes and with the simplest formality imaginable, in the presence of only the members of the university. Even the words which Luther spoke, as far as we know the only words which were uttered there at all, were improvised at the moment, possibly suggested by a verse of Psalm 21, which he was discussing in his lectures just at this time. If there were any present who actually expected anything like a spectacle from him, they must have been sadly disappointed. For while he was standing before the pyre he obviously had no thought for the spectators, but only for Him who looked down from above, to whom he prayed in trembling.

Not until the following day at twelve o'clock, when he went into the lecture hall, did the idea occur to him that he owed his hearers a few words of explanation concerning the event of the preceding day. He began his lecture, therefore, with a German address (which was contrary to his custom), in which he pointed out with great earnestness to the group of about four hundred students who filled the hall that now they, too, had only *one* choice, either hell or martyrdom. They would be in danger of the eternal damnation of hell, he said, if they did not find strength to resolve to take up and continue to the last breath the struggle against the anti-Christianity of the papal church, but they would be in peril of martyrdom if they were unable to summon the courage to do this. These words describe the state of mind out of which his deed was born and, at the same time, they reveal the fearful visions that were sweeping through his soul as he stood trembling and praying before the burning pile. He frequently expressed the conviction during these days that the curia would burn all its enemies and that it would have all the kings and princes on its side. He was thus reckoning on martyrdom in all earnestness. But this time the prospect of martyrdom did not have the paralyzing effect that it had on the way to Augsburg (1518); on the contrary, it elevated and stimulated his spirit; for in the meantime he had fought his way through to the conviction that, short of martyrdom, divine truth cannot triumph over this world of unrighteousness. He therefore emphasized again that his conscience had left him no other choice than finally to break with Rome in this way and definitely take upon himself the martyrdom of ceaseless struggle against the Antichrist. In concluding, he stressed the fact that he had not been induced to commit this deed by any sort of worldly motives or tactical considerations, but solely by his desire to preserve as many of his countrymen as possible from eternal destruction.

Hence this address of December 11 is not to be regarded merely as an echo of the event of the preceding day, but as its complement. If he had uttered these words before the burning pile on December 10, even the youngest of the student spectators would have understood that this was not mere play-acting but a deed, and that this deed was his answer to the deadly serious choice which he was now setting before the academic youth: either hell or martyrdom. But was not his own attitude after the event almost arrogant —in fact, such that he could write in humorous fashion to Spalatin about it immediately afterward? We make no mistake if we regard this sudden change of spirits simply as a consequence of the liberating effect that any action, which entails an irrevocable decision imposed by the conscience, has upon the spirit. He was conscious only of having done what he must do in order to keep a clear conscience. It was for this reason that he could later be "more pleased over this deed than over any other deed of my life."

At this time he was working, at the request of the Elector, on an exhaustive apology of the articles condemned by the Bull *Exsurge*, the *Assertio Omnium Articulorum per Bullam Novissimam Damnatorum*, which was to appear at the same time in German under the title, *Ground and Reason for all the Articles Wrongly Condemned by the Roman Bull.* Nevertheless, he felt the necessity of informing the public at once concerning the event of December 10. He did this in the tract entitled *Why the Books of the Pope and His Disciples Were Burned.* The tract makes no mention whatsoever of the burning of the Bull. Nor is this fact mentioned in the official report of the event made by the diocesan, Bishop Schulze of Brandenburg, to the papal nuncio, Aleander. Just as completely silent concerning the burning of the Bull are the foreign ambassadors who refer to the event; the oldest chroniclers of the Reformation, Spalatin, John Kessler, and Cochlaeus; likewise the only German writer who made the event a subject for a polemical tract, Thomas Murner of Strassburg; and even that highly official document, the Edict of Worms of May 8 (26), 1522, which otherwise scrupulously registers all the misdeeds of the Reformer. In the face of this complete silence of so many excellently informed witnesses we would be forced to conclude that the assertion that Luther burned the Bull is nothing more than an old tradition, if we did not have Luther's letter to Spalatin of December 10 and Agricola's report. This remarkable silence proves only that the burning of the Bull was something altogether incidental, not only for Luther himself, but for his contemporaries, over which they were not particularly excited, especially since many of them doubted the genuineness of the Bull.

The *"cosa grande,"* the real event of the day, was for Luther, as for his contemporaries, the burning of the canon law, for this book had far more significance than a single papal Bull. As is aptly suggested by Luther's derisive epithet for it, the "Alcoran of Antichrist," the canon law possessed almost the same authority in the western world that the Talmud had in Judaism or the Koran in Islam. It was the law book of Latin Christendom, invested with religious authority. According to the belief of the time, it was, like the commandments of God, binding upon all Christians *sub gravi,* that is, its nonobservance inevitably entailed the forfeit of eternal salvation. Moreover, it constituted an essential part of the common law recognized by the law of the empire, and thus it had a place among the law books, according to whose instructions the imperial supreme court administered justice. And even though it had long ceased to play as large a part in the administration of justice as did Roman law, general opinion was that in case of conflict canon law took precedence over Roman law, and therefore in the law faculties the canonists always had precedence over the jurists. Thus an attack upon this law was the equivalent, not only of an attack upon the publicly recognized religion, but upon the entire prevailing order of law and society.

This fact was universally recognized at that time. Hence Luther's act made a tremendous impression upon the whole western world. The attitude at the imperial court is reflected in the judgment of the Venetian, Andrew Rosso, "Truly, *una cosa grande,* a prodigious event, the significance of which, considering Martin's large following, cannot be overestimated!" The feeling of the South German humanists is indicated in a New Year's letter of Christopher Scheurl to his friends in Wittenberg, "Everything is resounding with the deeds that have happened among you. Now either the Roman or the Saxon front must flinch." And the furious declamations poured forth by Thomas Murner and the Italian Dominican, Ambrose Catharinus, in their polemical writings against each other are typical of the attitude among the orthodox literati. However, the feeling of astonishment and horror soon gave way to passionate partisanship either for or against this act of Luther. The jurists, for the most part, were of course beside themselves. The old Wittenberg canonist, Henning von Goede, who had previously pretended to be very friendly toward Luther, summed up his opinion in the angry words, "Where did this mangy monk get the arrogance!" His intimate colleague, Jerome Schurpff, though he did not use such trenchant expressions, doubtless

held essentially the same opinion as Goede. Many of the
older humanists took the same attitude toward the affair as
the jurists. Erasmus now considered the breach between
Rome and Wittenberg hopelessly irreparable and abandoned
the tumultuous monk forever. The same change of feeling
toward Luther may be observed in Paul Lange, of Posa;
Kilian Leib, of Rebdorf; Bernard Adelmann, and many
other friends of the "fine arts." At the courts the feeling was
apparently divided. Nevertheless, the number of those who
applauded Luther's act was so great that the emperor
deemed it necessary at the very outset to prohibit any discussion of ecclesiastical law at the Diet of Worms.

Luther, however, when he gave his verdict on the "Alcoran
of Antichrist," was not thinking primarily of this class, but
of the "common people." He wanted to show the people that
they no longer needed to fear the Antichrist or obey his
bailiffs. Did the people understand this? Unquestionably
they did; for now the renewed activity of the hangmen in
the burning of Luther's books, even in middle and north
Germany, no longer made any impression upon the masses
and they frightened nobody away from the reading of these
books, even though the confessors refused absolution to the
disobedient. To the printers and booksellers, however, the
new *autos-da-fé* only meant good business; for the more
severely the authorities dealt with Luther's works, the more
eagerly they were sought after. Even more significant than
the failure of these new book-burnings was another manifestation of the impression made by Luther's act. This was
the mighty agitation that began to seize even the broad
masses during the following weeks and months. If, in the
middle of December, Aleander thought he could assert that
the people were manifestly improving, owing to the book-
burnings, on February 8, 1521 he was reporting to Rome in
consternation, "The whole of Germany is in full revolt; nine-
tenths raise the war cry, 'Luther,' while the watchword of
the other tenth who are indifferent to Luther is: 'Death to

the Roman curia.'" This mighty swelling of anti-Roman
feeling was caused in large measure, if not exclusively, by
the event of December 10. It is hardly probable that what
the common people had heard from Dr. Martinus prior to
this time would have excited them to passion. But the book-
burning at the Elster Gate was an event that worked directly
upon their imagination and was everywhere seen and immediately understood, even by the altogether unlearned who
could neither read nor write. The very thing that affected
this class, however, was that which most offended the educated men of Erasmus' type—the unprecedented boldness
and resoluteness with which the condemned monk and professor dared to hurl defiance in the face of the pope and the
whole hierarchy.

But why did Luther attack the canon law in particular?
Is it possible that he already possessed a clear conception
of the significance of this classical creation of the medieval
spirit for the whole view of the world and society with which
he had unconsciously been in conflict since 1513? No; he
turned against this book only because he saw in it the most
powerful support of that "profane botching of biblical religion" which he was attacking. He saw in it the confusion
of law with religion, of the kingdom of the world with the
Kingdom of God, of politics with the cure of souls, of legal-
ism with piety, and the secularization of religion which is
the necessary consequence of such confusion. All of this he
had long been fighting against, but now it had become absolutely intolerable to him. And why did he burn the *Summa
Angelica* with the canon law? Because for him it served as
a typical example of how far even the cure of souls had been
led astray by this profane botching of religion. In the *Summa
Angelica* the cure of souls was treated entirely as a branch
of ecclesiastical jurisprudence. The pastor was considered
throughout as a judge, and man's whole religious behavior
was viewed as the fulfillment of a number of external legal
duties having no inward relation, and the confessional rep-

resented the competent tribunal for dealing with these legal duties. Even prayer was evaluated as such a duty and thus was for the most part recommended as a *means of punishment*. But Luther singled out the *Summa Angelica* from among the three or four famous *Summae* of this sort (handbooks for confessors) because it probably represented the extreme of this legalistic treatment of ethical and religious questions which is characteristic of all these works.

Another characteristic feature of the whole science of canon law disturbed him even more than this profane botching of biblical religion. This was the attempt in canon law—particularly in the second part, the so-called decretals—to raise the power of the pope to unlimited supremacy. "The sum of this book," he declared, "is that the pope is a god upon earth, above all heavenly and earthly, spiritual and secular powers, and everything belongs to him. None may question what he does." To be sure, no pope had ever uttered the phrase, "Everything belongs to me," but the so-called curialists had no doubt that the pope was lord paramount (in the feudal sense) over all the estates of the world. And in practice the popes had often acted in accordance with this theory, even as late as Luther's time, as is shown by the famous Bull *Inter cetera,* in which Pope Alexander VI *bestowed* upon the Queen of Castile all lands beyond the so-called Azorian line or Line of Demarcation. These curialistic scholars were firmly convinced that the pope was not an ordinary man, but "in some way like a god on earth." As the representative of Christ he stood not only above the angels but above the Mother of God and as such he was entitled, to the same degree as Mary, the angels, and the saints, to religious veneration (*dulia*), though not to worship (*latria*). Indeed, some of them, for example the canonist, Zenzelin de Cassanis, whose gloss Luther found in his edition of the canon law, did not hesitate actually to call the pope *Dominus deus.* This glorification of the pope, which ran through the whole canon law and the glosses appended to it, struck the Reformer as being an encroachment upon God's prerogative of sovereignty, and therefore this whole book of laws seemed to him to be a botch or the Alcoran of Antichrist. Nevertheless, he admitted quite frankly that it contained much that was good, though he added that everything in it was twisted in order to create prejudice and strengthen the pope in his anti-Christian government. Moreover, the good in it was not honestly observed, only the evil and the obnoxious. It must therefore be exterminated entirely, from the first to the last letter.

But he was content to express this demand symbolically by the burning of the anti-Christian law book. He had no intention whatsoever of using force to achieve this end. On the contrary, even though he had received with satisfaction the news of Hutten's plan to seize and capture the papal nuncios, he was thoroughly convinced that "through the Word of God, not by the fist, would the Antichrist be destroyed." When Hutten wrote to him on December 9, proposing a formal alliance and requesting him to influence the Elector to give open patronage or at least silent support to his fantastic plan of revolt, he rejected the proposals unequivocally with the words: "I do not wish to do battle for the Gospel with force and slaughter. The world is overcome by the Word; the church has been preserved till now and will also be reformed by the Word. So even the Antichrist, as he once began his work without force, will also be destroyed without force by the Word."

This trust in the power of the Word seemed at times to be somewhat exaggerated. But Luther could cite his own experience in support of it. He wrote nine months later: "Have I not succeeded in wresting more from the pope, the bishops, the priests, and the monks with my mouth alone, without striking a blow, than have all the emperors, kings, and princes with all their force? Why? Because, as St. Paul says, he (the Antichrist) shall be destroyed out of the mouth of Christ. It is not our work that is now going on in the world, for man alone could not begin or carry such a thing. It is another who is driving the wheel, one whom the papists do not see; therefore they put the blame on us. If the secular authorities proceed to rescue their subjects, in body, possessions, mind, and soul from the abuses that are contrary to the Gospel, naturally no objection can be made to that. But to accomplish this they need not strike and stab. More than enough can be accomplished with a few prohibitions. On the other hand, rebellion is never right, no matter how just the cause. Moreover, the innocent generally suffer more from it than the guilty, and it makes that which it would improve even worse than before."

This faith in the power of the Word was nowhere in evidence at the curia and among its representatives. On the contrary, they had been accustomed, for centuries, even in such struggles of a purely spiritual nature, to rely entirely upon the external means of force and power which were at their command. They now proceeded relentlessly to employ these means against Luther and his followers.

CHAPTER XXVII

AGAINST PRINCIPALITIES AND POWERS

At the time of the Leipzig Disputation, Elector Frederick had intended to take Luther along to the next diet of the empire. It was not his purpose to arrange a hearing for Luther by, or even before, the estates of the empire, for in his opinion this was not within their jurisdiction. What he had in mind was simply to give his friend, the archbishop of Trier, an opportunity to carry out the commission which he had undertaken at the beginning of the year—to settle the Lutheran affair by arbitration—and at the same time to safeguard Luther against all possible attacks from his enemies by having this conference placed under imperial protection.

However, the diet which had been called for St. Martin's Day (November 10), 1519, did not meet. But the Elector did not on this account give up his plan. Shortly after his departure from Cologne, in November, 1520, he addressed a plea to the imperial minister, Chièvres, and to the imperial general, Henry of Nassau, requesting the emperor not to take any steps against Luther for the present, but to allow him, the Elector, to take Luther along to the diet which was to open in Worms on January 6, 1521, in order that the Reformer might be given a hearing before learned, honorable, and impartial judges, in accordance with his own request. Why Frederick had not presented this petition verbally to the authorities of the imperial court while he was still in Cologne, we do not know. Perhaps the reason was his almost morbid shyness and his consequent aversion to verbal negotiations. Chièvres and Nassau apparently considered the petition harmless. At all events, they prevailed upon the youthful emperor, who was still leaning on the advice of others, to tell the Elector (November 28) that he might take Luther to Worms with him; until that time, however, the monk was not to write or print anything against His Holiness the Pope.

Even before this imperial note arrived, news reached the Elector's court that the nuncio had had Luther's books burned in Cologne and Mainz. Frederick did not think that the emperor was directly responsible for this. He felt, nevertheless, that these *autos-da-fé* were personal affronts to him. Although it was not like him to do so, he gave very vigorous expression to his annoyance in a reply to the emperor on December 20. Besides, he withdrew his request with reference to Luther. Meanwhile, there had also been a change of sentiment at the imperial court, which had moved to Worms on November 28. In a confidential conference with the imperial minister, Chièvres, on the night of December 13, and in a session of the German Aulic Council which took place the next day and which was attended by a number of secular princes, Aleander succeeded in stirring up the authorities against Luther. And then he convinced High Chancellor Gattinara, who still clung with particular tenacity to the idea of citing Luther, that there would be no sense in summoning the arch-heretic to Worms unless he first recanted his error. Thereupon the emperor, in a note to the Elector on December 17, withdrew his consent. Luther, he now commanded, should by no means accompany the Elector unless he recanted beforehand. But even then he was not to enter Worms. He was to remain behind in Frankfurt on the Main, in Oppenheim, or in "some other spot around there" and await further orders after the emperor had had an opportunity to discuss his case more fully with the Elector in person. This concession was later used by the Elector to reopen negotiations on Luther's case. But the question whether he should take Luther along to Worms was definitely decided by this note of the emperor. So he had Luther—who on December 21 had told Spalatin that

he would go to Worms even if he was so sick that he had to
be carried there—informed posthaste that nothing had come
of the matter.

While this was going on Aleander achieved two new and
important successes in Worms. On December 29, in the
presence of the emperor, the Joint Council—that is, the representatives of the various imperial lands who were present
at the court—adopted the ordinance against Luther and his
followers which the emperor had already proposed in Aix-
la-Chapelle, but which had later been recast somewhat.
Probably on the same day the emperor charged Aleander
to instruct the two legates, whom he had thought of sending
to meet the Elector, to prepare Frederick for this decision.
But the legation was not formed, because Frederick reached
Worms on January 5. Nor could the edict be published for
the time being because the German chancellor, the Elector
of Mainz, could not be induced to draw it up and sign it.
And finally the emperor, when the Elector took him to task
for his ambiguous position, had to yield and give his troublesome admonisher the "gracious" assurance that "the monk
should be heard and not treated with violence." Frederick
immediately communicated this to the Reformer. The latter
replied on January 25 that he still adhered to his *Offer and
Protest* of the preceding August. Enclosing a copy of it,
Luther declared that he was as ready now as he had been
before to appear in Worms whenever the emperor called
him. But the emperor—or, rather, his tutor and chief minister,
Chièvres, on whom the emperor was still so dependent that
the old man had to sleep with him nights—was not thinking
seriously of keeping this renewed pledge. In fact, in a new
session of the Joint Council held on February 3, he issued a
command that the law which had been drawn up by Aleander should be translated into German and published. Then,
during a pompous reception, on February 6, he did not hesitate to tear up and throw on the floor Luther's *Offer and
Protest* after the Saxon court marshal, Nichel Ende von Stein,

had presented it to him in the name of his lord, Duke John.

Meanwhile, as had become clear even before the official opening of the diet on January 22, the estates of the empire were not nearly so "well-disposed" as the emperor. The nuncio could depend on only the "little red hats"—the cardinals of Mainz, Salzburg, and Sitten—and their adherents, "but there were many other people who wished Martinus well," and even more who manifested extreme hostility toward the curia. "All the German princes," complained the nuncio, "are annoying the emperor by presenting frantic grievances against us." In addition, "every day we are flooded with Lutheran tracts in German and in Latin. No one buys anything else, even at the imperial court. Portraits of Luther, which were recently put up for sale here, were disposed of in a twinkling, so that I could not get one." Aleander also had to suffer personally, as he claimed, from this anti-Roman sentiment of the Germans.

Worse than this was the fact that even the emperor's councilors threatened to emancipate themselves from Aleander and his suggestions. About the beginning of February a conference was held at the residence of High Chancellor Gattinara, who was always going his own way. Here the emperor's father confessor, John Glapion, a French Franciscan who had just been called to the court by Chièvres in 1520, proposed, in the presence of Aleander and Caracciolo, an entirely new method for the settlement of the Lutheran affair. The emperor, Glapion argued, should send several good, learned men to Wittenberg to ask Luther if he was willing to recant. If he did not agree to do this and persisted in his errors even after a second admonition, further action should be taken by the empire against him. But if he recanted, he should be indulgently restored to grace. His books, however, would have to be "sequestrated"—that is, withdrawn from circulation—right away. Aleander and Caracciolo did not deem it necessary to reject these suggestions although they actually amounted to taking the proceedings

against Luther out of their hands and placing them in the
emperor's hands. But Gattinara approved of Glapion's proposals. Nevertheless, the plan of sending an imperial legation to Luther, even if this legation did not directly represent the emperor, was entirely too quixotic. Glapion's goal—
the settlement of the Lutheran affair by a committee of
experts called by the *emperor*—had more chance of being
reached if there were assurance of the Saxon Elector's aid.
As a matter of fact, the Elector had made a somewhat similar suggestion in November, although he did not indicate
that the emperor should select the scholars who were to conduct Luther's hearing. So Glapion dropped the idea of a
legation to Luther.

Instead of this, through the intercession of Count Henry
of Nassau, and not without the knowledge of Gattinara and
probably even of Chièvres, Glapion tried to arrange a personal audience with the Elector about February 7. Of course,
the shy prince could not bring himself to receive him
although his command of French was adequate. And so he
sent his chancellor, Dr. Gregory von Brück, to Glapion. But
Glapion insisted on presenting his plans to Frederick personally. In his first conference with Brück on February 8,
therefore, he tried in every way to arrange a personal audience. When this attempt finally met with failure on February 9, he made an effort to persuade the prince at least to
appoint a higher-ranking negotiator—one of the Elector's
"priviest" councilors, as he expressed it. But Frederick would
not agree to this, so Glapion had to put up with the chancellor, who seemed to him to be too strongly impregnated
with Lutheranism, and he had to confide in him what he
had really intended only for the ear of the "Saxon fox." It is
patent that Glapion desired to convince the Elector that he
was simply concerned about saving Luther and at the same
time reforming the church. It is no longer possible to determine whether this was a tactical move or whether it reflected
his true opinion. The fact that he participated in the session

of the Joint Council on December 29 does not demonstrate that he approved of Aleander's edict. His protest, that "he had not wished to take part in it after that," was not necessarily a lie, even if he was not very particular about the truth at other times. At any rate, his proposal—to have the affair settled by a committee of learned experts appointed by the emperor and to make the recantation as easy as possible for Luther—agrees wholly with his utterances in the conference with Gattinara and the two nuncios (his own report of which we still have). He appears, therefore, to have had honorable intentions. Nor must it be assumed that Glapion was telling a brazen-faced lie when he began his parley with Brück with the statement that he had read Luther's earlier writings with pleasure. For he explained, as soon as he had made this admission, that his delight had now been turned into disgust and dismay by the stupid and consequently (as it appeared to him) thoroughly un-Lutheran book *On the Babylonian Captivity of the Church*. To prove this assertion he immediately quoted to Brück, from memory, several particularly offensive passages of the wicked book. Then, on February 9, he handed Brück a new list of such passages which he had compiled in the meantime. This list, later sent to Wittenberg by Spalatin and furnished with several explanatory notes by Luther about March 19, played no part in the negotiations at Worms.

Nevertheless, Glapion said, every evil can be cured. The harm which had been done by the *Babylonian Captivity* could be mended if Luther would recant this book. But he did not need to recant it directly. He needed only to disavow it—that is, state that it had not been written by him at all. This would surely be believed, for it was exceedingly stupid and not at all like his earlier works. If this did not suit him, Luther could retract it on the ground that he had kicked over the traces in this book simply in order to defend himself from his enemies. Finally, he could also resort to the so-called *insinuatio*—that is, give an orthodox meaning to the offensive passages, according to the directions of the papal nuncios, and then state that this is what he had meant the book to say and that he wanted it to be interpreted only in this way.

When Brück modestly objected that the papal Bull had not been directed against the *Babylonian Captivity* at all, but against those earlier writings of Luther which Glapion praised so highly, the father confessor said blithely that that made no difference whatever. As long as Luther recanted the *Babylonian Captivity* in any one of the ways specified to him, the pope would be ready to listen and would not object to his having another hearing, even on German soil, by unprejudiced experts. Thus he intimated that, under these circumstances, Luther's *Offer and Protest* would be given due consideration. On February 10 he repeated this hint with smirks and confidential nudges. Now at last he came out with the great idea which was the goal of his whole attempt at reconciliation. Ostensibly he agreed wholeheartedly with Luther's *Offer and Protest*. But in actual fact he twisted it into something entirely different. In the first place, proposed Glapion, the court of arbitration requested by Luther and the Elector should be appointed by the emperor. Second, it should be composed of unprejudiced and honorable scholars of acknowledged Catholic convictions (*commendatae doctrinae*). Third, the public should not be admitted to the sessions of the court. Fourth, the court should not convene immediately, but only at a convenient and opportune time in the future. Fifth, until such time both parties must refrain from new actions against each other. Not only must Luther refrain from writing anything new, Glapion proposed, but he must also consent to have all his books which had appeared up to this time "sequestrated" and deposited with some unprejudiced person. On the other hand, the pope and his nuncios must stop burning his books for the time being. And finally, in the sixth place, the Elector himself must approach the emperor with this proposal; in other words, he must leave everything else to the emperor's discretion without first giving Luther a hearing.

Although it was not in keeping with his own wishes and instructions, Aleander would surely have agreed to this plan. But the Elector did not feel that he was in a position to accede to it. He informed Glapion on February 11 that he could not make such proposals to the emperor without Luther's "command." At this refusal "Glapion sighed deeply," Brück reported. "He did what he honestly could do," he said, to save from destruction "the sacred commodity which Luther had almost brought into port." But it was evidently not to be. Thus Glapion himself formally declared that the attempt at reconciliation, which he had allegedly undertaken wholly "without suggestion from the outside," had by this statement of the Elector come to nought.

This failure naturally resulted in making Gattinara and Chièvres more disposed to listen to Aleander again. On the morning following the break-off of negotiations between Brück and Glapion, they asked the nuncio, through the emperor, to speak before the diet in support of his own proposals regarding the Lutheran affair. On February 13 Aleander carried out this suggestion in an address of nearly three hours' duration. The address was not so effective as he imagined because the estates of the empire had difficulty understanding his Latin, which was readily intelligible only to Italian and French ears. He undertook to point out that Luther had plotted to overthrow all government. In his conclusion he emphasized that the burning of heretics and their books was an old and hallowed custom. For the time being, however, he demanded only a law for the suppression of Luther's writings.

Two days later the edict which Aleander had drafted, and which threatened the Reformer and his followers with ban and double ban, came before the diet. But the hope that the Elector, who had not attended the session on February 13, would absent himself from the deliberations was not fulfilled, for the diet delayed a decision so long that Frederick became aware of what was going on. Thus he was still able to make his influence felt both in the assembly of Electors and in the assembly of princes. On February 19 he prevented the diet from adopting the law in the form in which it had been presented. He also succeeded in persuading the diet to ask the emperor, in view of the great agitation among the common people, to summon Luther to Worms and promise him a hearing there before experts. The occasion was not to be used for a debate with Luther, however; he was simply to be asked whether he was disposed to recant the writings and articles which he had written against the Christian church and the Christian faith. The princes of the church, who were responsible for this stipulation, were of course thinking particularly of the statements condemned in the Bull *Exsurge*. If he recanted, he was to be heard further "in the other points and matters" and was to be treated with equity. Among these "other points and matters," according to Aleander, were especially Luther's utterances on the authority of the pope and papal law. If, on the other hand, Luther clung to his errors, the emperor was to publish an edict against him. Finally, the diet took this opportunity to remind the emperor of the *gravamina* (grievances) of the German nation against the curia. The whole resolution patently bore the earmarks of a compromise between the wishes of a minority friendly to Luther and the demands of a majority hostile to him. On the whole, however, it undoubtedly was a crushing defeat for the nuncio and the imperial statesmen who were now associated with him.

In order to adapt Aleander's edict to the will of the diet, the emperor convoked the Joint Council, probably on the same day, February 19. But the Council could not agree on the necessary changes. So an editorial committee was formed, probably on February 20, under the chairmanship of Cardinal Lang. The majority of its members were foreigners, but in the main Lang was given free reign. He undertook to recast the edict in such a way as to make it acceptable both to the estates and to the curia. In his draft he included the summons of Luther, but on the damaging ground that the emperor and empire had agreed upon this measure only to counteract his "memory and fancies" among the common people. He also made the severe regulations against Luther's writings even more severe by extending them to include the writings of Luther's followers as well. In the concluding passage, however, the latter were threatened with severe displeasure and the penalties of ecclesiastical and secular law instead of with the ban and double ban.

Aleander did not approve of this draft, as one can readily understand. The emperor's statesmen also continued to resist the idea of summoning Luther to Worms. Through the emperor they accordingly had the estates sounded out again on March 1 as to where and when Luther was to be summoned. Only when they realized that all further beating about the bush would be of no avail did they persuade their youthful lord to declare himself in fundamental agreement with the summoning of Luther to the diet. Simultaneously, however, they presented Aleander's edict to the estates in the revision of Lang. The diet assented to the emperor's stand regarding Luther, but rejected Aleander's edict without long debate. The emperor simply had to reconcile himself to this decision, and he reconciled himself openly on March 6 when he commissioned the German vice-chancellor, Nicholas Ziegler, to formulate a safe-conduct for Luther.

But perhaps the heretic could still be kept from heeding the diet's summons. It was probably this mental reservation, and not merely the understandable disappointment under which they were laboring, that induced the emperor's councilors to try to unload the calling of Luther on the Elector. And it was for this reason, it appears, that the first draft of the safe-conduct for Luther was given as unfriendly and forbidding a form as possible. The Elector, of course, refused to comply with the request which was put to him, if only out of dread for the responsibility which he would thereby be incurring. What others believed that Chièvres and Gattinara might be plotting is revealed in a remark in the draft of a letter to Luther, dated March 10, which was later stricken out (probably at Frederick's suggestion). "Be sure to keep your eye on what you are about while on your way," we read here, "whether you are making stop-overs, eating and drinking, or whatever else you may be doing." The Lutheran-minded secretary who composed this draft obviously counted seriously on the possibility that the imperialists might try to apprehend or poison Luther on the way. When the imperial councilors recognized that they could accomplish nothing in this way, they finally gave up their resistance altogether and had Ziegler cast the citation as well as the safe-conduct in an inoffensive form. More than this, they even decided, to the indignation of Aleander, to go out of their way to do a special favor and invite the heretic, not through an ordinary mounted messenger, but through an imperial official who was notorious for being very favorably inclined toward Luther. This was the imperial herald, Caspar Sturm, of Oppenheim, called Teutschland. On March 14 or 15 the two documents, predated to March 6, were finally signed by the emperor, and the herald who had been holding himself in readiness for several days set out for Wittenberg on March 16.

Gattinara, who as high chancellor probably played the leading role in the arrangement of these formalities, would hardly have yielded so quickly (contrary to his usual custom) if he had not already been devising a new intrigue with Aleander to scare Luther away from Worms. Following Glapion's proposal in the February conference, he had a sequestration mandate prepared in the German chancellery, which ordered the seizure of all Lutheran books in the name of the emperor and also stated that the diet had made a pro-

nouncement against all innovations in matters of faith and
had summoned Luther to Worms only for recantation. This
mandate, in the preparation of which he had taken a leading
part, Aleander printed at once. But at first he could not get
the emperor to sign it. Only after the diet had given preliminary approval to the emperor's military demands was
Aleander allowed to make the document public. On March
26 it was nailed on the church doors in Worms. On March
27 it was heralded in the town by public proclamation, and
then it was also spread beyond Worms—especially, as it
seems, in Electoral Saxony—by imperial messengers. However, it was heeded but little, even where it was legally published. In Worms itself the sale of Lutheran books went on
unchecked. And its effect on the followers of Luther was
often actually encouraging. If the emperor did not intend
to keep his pledge of safe-conduct for Luther, they said, the
mandate would hardly have given assurance in such clear
words that the emperor would "have him escorted to and
from" Worms. Others, it is true, maintained that it would
be hazardous and wholly unavailing, under these circumstances, for the Reformer to comply with the imperial summons, for a hearing of the kind Luther requested in his *Offer
and Protest*—an examination of his teachings in the light of
the Holy Scriptures—was entirely out of the question according to this announcement. At the imperial court the prevailing conviction seems to have been that the heretic would
now no longer dare to show himself in Worms. So much the
more dejected, in contrast, were the spirits of the guests at
"The Swan," the tavern in which the Saxon Elector had
set up his quarters. In an "opinion" which was probably
requested by Spalatin in the name of the Elector and in
which the various foregoing views were expressed, Chancellor Brück came to this conclusion at the beginning of
April: "I do not know what Martin can do." But then he
added. "I am afraid that he can hardly be given any other
counsel (yet his own counsel is the best) than that he should

come." The words, "I am afraid," clearly reveal Brück's frame of mind; he would have been happy if Martinus himself had reached the decision not to obey the imperial summons.

While the Italian nuncios, in league with the Italian, French, Spanish, and Dutch councilors of the young emperor, who was thoroughly French in training and was at home only in the French language, were plotting this wearisome intrigue in the old Nibelungen town on the Rhine, the bold German who was being marked out for destruction was sitting quietly in his little room, his flying pen producing book after book, letter after letter, sermon after sermon. By the middle of January the Latin edition (*Assertio*) of the great apologetic work against the Bull *Exsurge* which the Elector had asked of him was finished, and by March 2 the German edition (*Grund und Ursach*) was also ready.[1] In the Latin edition he scattered a little salt here and there for the stomachs of the scholars who, he thought, were always very much in need of such stimulation. Such a seasoned passage, for instance, was the assertion which was immediately pounced upon by Aleander and which struck Erasmus like a blow in the face: "Freedom of the will is an empty delusion. Looked at from below, all human activity seems optional and accidental; looked at from above, however, it is seen to be absolutely necessary."

In the German edition Luther did not offer his readers such sharp spices. But so much the more fully did he discuss, at the very outset, the question in which the laity was taking a lively interest: on what grounds he arrogated to himself the right to teach everybody. He answered: "In the first place, I have not pushed myself forward at all. If I could follow my own inclinations, I would always prefer to crawl back into my little corner. But my opponents have drawn me out again and again by craft and violence in order to acquire credit and honor by attacking me. Now that their

[1] Cf. *supra*, pp. 372-73.

game is falling through, my ambition is supposed to be the cause of everything. But, in the second place, even if they were right and I had really set myself up as a teacher, could God not have called and raised me up for this purpose? Do we not read that He usually raised up only *one* prophet from among His people, and never from the upper classes, but generally humble, despised individuals, even common herdsmen? The dear saints, too, always had to preach against sovereigns, kings, princes, priests, and scholars, and risk and lose their necks in doing so. I do not say that I am a prophet. I simply say that they will have to be afraid of this as long as they scorn me and heed themselves. God is wonderful in His ways and judgments. He does not regard great learning and mighty power. If I am not a prophet, I am at least sure of this, that the Word of God is with me, and not with them, for I have the Scriptures on my side while they have only their own teachings. This is what gives me courage; the more they despise and persecute me, the less I fear them. There were many asses in Balaam's time. And yet God spoke only through that one ass of Balaam. But do I not preach a new doctrine? No. I simply say that true Christianity has ceased to exist among those who should have preserved it— the bishops and scholars. But I have no doubt that the truth has always continued to live in some, if only in the souls of children in the cradle. I do not repudiate the Church Fathers. But like all men, they, too, have erred at times. Consequently I believe them only in so far as they can prove their teachings from the Scriptures, which have never erred. The fact that so many big fellows are hostile to me and persecute me simply because I rely on the Scriptures alone, does not terrify me; rather does it comfort and encourage me, for again and again the Bible expressly declares that persecutors and enviers are generally wrong while the persecuted are right, and it refers ever and again to the fact that the majority has always supported falsehood while the few have backed up truth." Nor was Luther alarmed at the peace!' "

Luther, as a matter of fact, noticed nothing of this cry
for "Peace, peace!" He was literally submerged at this time
great unrest and the many storms which resulted from his
appearance. "The truth," he said, "must always be kicking
under a flood of polemical books and letters. To be sure, he
up a rumpus while false teachers constantly cry, 'Peace,
now paid scant attention to this raging and fuming. Henceforth he condescended to reply only to those of his opponents who seemed to amount to something or who seemed
to menace his adherents because of their influence on persons of power and culture. He thought especially of the
Dresden court chaplain, Jerome Emser, as belonging to the
latter group. Consequently he exchanged a large number
of polemical writings with him during these months. The
contents of the first two of these are indicated by their very
titles, *To the Leipzig Goat* and *Reply to the Answer of the
Leipzig Goat*. Only the third, *Answer to the Superchristian,
Superspiritual, and Superlearned Book of Goat Emser*, is of
real importance because here Luther responded to Emser's
attacks by clearly restating and sharply reaffirming his new
teaching on the universal priesthood of all believers. The
teaching of the fourfold sense of the Holy Scriptures, he
wrote, is merely a false delusion. Only the historical, grammatical, literal sense is authoritative. Allegorical interpretation is justified only where the sacred writers make use of
it themselves, as does St. Paul in Galatians 4:22 or Ephesians
5:32. In this third writing Luther also took up the pamphlet
which the Franciscan, Thomas Murner, had in the meantime directed against the *Address to the Nobility*. But it was
impossible for him to take seriously the "bungling tomfool-
ery" and the "unscriptural twittle-twattle" of this "prattling
wordmonger," and so he disposed of the "good Moron"[1] in
short order. He did not even deign to glance at the later
writings of this "frivolous fellow" who would not allow hard-

[1] Luther puns on Murner's name, calling him *Murnarr*.

working and busy people like himself to rest and who simply wished to show that the Rhine would run dry before he would run out of words.

The *Apologia* of the Italian Dominican, Ambrose Catharinus, which came into Luther's hands on March 6 or 7, also appeared to him to be a frightfully dull production. But he finally decided that it was necessary to refute it at some length because it was dedicated to the emperor, who was urged in forceful fashion to take steps against the new heretic; perhaps also because he had learned from Spalatin in the meantime that the pope had the book formally presented to the emperor at Worms in January. By April 1, hence immediately before his departure for Worms, Luther had completed his *Answer,* comprising some eight signatures in print (*Ad librum eximii magistri nostri Ambrosii Catharini defensoris Silvestri Prieriatis acerrimi responsio*). He refused from the outset to discuss the almost countless errors and heresies which the haughty Italian had disdainfully thrown up at him. Luther was content to pick out two points, his teaching on the church and his teaching on the papacy. The church, he asserted, is not limited to definite places and persons or attached to any other physical, visible, and tangible things. Nevertheless, it is always present in the world and in the flesh. But where is it always present? Where the Gospel is preached. Where this is not done, the church does not exist, even if Baptism and the Lord's Supper are there and are administered in an externally proper way. Only the church whose marks are the preaching of the Gospel and the observance of Baptism and the Lord's Supper in accordance with the Gospel, is the church of Christ of which the Bible speaks. The Bible, to be sure, also speaks of the pope's church. But where? Everywhere where it refers to the Antichrist.

This led Luther to discuss these passages at length, particularly Daniel 8, and to interpret them allegorically to the minutest detail. Four things in this interpretation are especially worthy of note. First, he asserted that the Antichrist is not an individual person who will appear at the end of time, but a demoniacal power which has been active within the bosom of Christendom since the fall of the Roman Empire—indeed, since the days of the apostles—and which then, since the seventh century, found its classical embodiment in the papacy. Second, he claimed that "the papacy arose out of, and in, the fallen Roman Empire, and took its place, as history and contemporaneous experience teach." Third, the claim that the Roman Empire was translated to the Germans by Pope Leo III is, wrote Luther, nothing more than a fable employed by the popes to strengthen their power over the world. The Roman Empire was the last world-empire of history. The Holy Roman Empire of the German Nation has never been more than a nominal empire. Fourth, the empire of the pope will not be destroyed, as the Romanists fear, by laymen. On the contrary, it will remain until Christ's second coming, and then it will collapse simply because "the Spirit of God makes all deception manifest. For to make falsehood manifest means to destroy it." Although Luther had maintained as late as June, 1520, that the abolition of the papacy by the secular heads of Christendom was desirable, it was now an article of faith for him that the Antichrist would not be destroyed until the end of time, and then by the Word of God. Accordingly the Antichrist may and can be opposed now only by means of the Word, for Word and Spirit are the only weapons that can accomplish anything against it. For religious reasons alone, therefore, Luther would have nothing to do with a war against the hierarchy in Hutten's sense. But he had an additional reason. Such a war would be nothing but murder, for to wage war on clerics would be the same as waging war on women and children.

In the epilogue of April 1 Luther called his *Responsio* the second part of the "palinode," or retraction, which he had promised the Romanists in the *Babylonian Captivity*.

Thus he related it directly to this most forceful and scholarly of his great attacks on medieval ecclesiasticism, thereby indicating how important he deemed what he discussed here, especially with regard to the Antichrist. As a matter of fact, he never presented this subject more spiritedly and sharply than in this "postlude" to the *Babylonian Captivity* which has been almost entirely forgotten since the seventeenth century despite the fact that it is couched in particularly apt language. It was with the concluding sentences of this work ringing in his ears that he set out for Worms.

When we observe how arrogantly Luther played with his antagonists in these writings, we are apt to conclude that fighting was for him the real essence of life—a boorish style of fighting at that, in which the flail and ax are legitimate weapons. As long as the scuffle lasted, he undoubtedly felt very much at home in it. But when he wiped the dust out of his eyes, he was often seized by a sense of shame and regret. "I am myself aware [that I am too sharp]," he complained on such an occasion. "I am not master of myself. I am carried away by I know not what kind of spirit, and yet I am conscious that I wish no one ill. But my enemies set upon me in so fierce a fashion that I do not pay sufficient attention to Satan. Pray for me, therefore, that I may not think, speak, and write what *they* deserve, but what conforms with God and me." But while "in the thick of the papists' swords, Bulls, and battle cries" he did not forget—not even in this period of the most furious fighting in his life—that he was called not only to wage war, but also, and indeed primarily, to build. Evidence for this is found in the two devotional works which he wrote at this time, the *Advent Postil* in Latin and the *Exposition of the Magnificat,* dedicated to Electoral Prince John Frederick, but of which he could finish only the first four signatures before his departure for Worms. To be sure, he sometimes struck exceedingly martial notes in the *Postil.* But the *Magnificat* was entirely "from the school of the Holy Spirit." It was

thoroughly permeated with the thought, "Oh, taste and see
that the Lord is good: blessed is the man that trusteth in
Him." Besides these, he was still working on his *Studies in
the Psalms,* several additional parts of which he published
at this time, although he had long since lost the joy of working on them. Altogether, during the three months preceding his departure for Worms, he prepared for the press and
published at least fifty signatures of printed matter, keeping
three presses going constantly for his work alone.

Not even in this period of stress, however, did Luther's
activity make him neglect the work of his calling in the pulpit and lecture room. He continued to deliver at least two
sermons and two lectures each week. He had to do the work
of seven men at this time, as he himself complained. But he
was not oppressed by this overabundance of work so much
as by the many transactions and demands of a business
nature which he now had to take care of, and by the numerous visitors who kept him from his work. Thus on January
16, for example, he had to allow himself to be seen and
touched, whether he wanted to or not, by Elector Joachim
of Brandenburg, who was not very kindly disposed toward
him, and by the princes in his escort. Again, on February
3, he had to sacrifice several precious hours to Duke Bogu-
slav X of Pomerania. As a result he no longer had any time
at all for epistolary or personal relations with his friends
although, since the pope had by his ban definitely absolved
him (as he thought) from the regulations of the Order, he
no longer felt obligated to observe the canonical hours. He
was delivered from this "monkey business" and continued
only to wear the garb of the Order and to share its shelter
and table with the other inmates of the Black Cloister.

During this whole time Luther heard little from Worms,
and that little did not disturb him. "Do not pray with your
brothers for me," he wrote to an unnamed head of a monastery on March 24, "but pray for the Word of God, for I am
not concerned about myself [on account of the martyrdom

which certainly awaits me] . . . . Christ will grant me His spirit, which will enable me to scorn the catchpoles of Antichrist as long as I live and to overcome them when I die." It was a painful thing for Luther to see how utterly frail and frightened Staupitz was in the face of the indictment with which he, too, was threatened. He did not conceal from his teacher, whom he had once honored so highly, the indignation he felt at this want of courage to confess his faith. He had a feeling that this onetime "herald of grace and the cross" could not muster the necessary courage to suffer the cross now that the situation was critical. So he actually severed his relations with him when he challenged him, "If you do not wish to follow me, at least let me go! By the grace of Christ I am determined to show the monster his monstrosities openly."

By March 19 at the latest Luther received news from Spalatin concerning the decisions of the diet during the first days of the month. He replied at once. "I shall write to the emperor," he wrote, "that I will not go to Worms if I am only to recant there, for I could do that here just as well as there. But if he should then summon me in order to have me executed and banned on account of this answer, I would be willing to go, for I do not intend to flee in the midst of the battle and leave the Word of God in the lurch." Just one week later, on March 26—the same day that the imperial mandate of sequestration was published in Worms—the emperor's summons, which had been expected for a long time, reached him. To Luther's satisfaction he found that it said nothing at all about recanting. According to the document, the emperor and empire simply wanted to be informed about the teachings and books which had originated with him some time before. Accordingly he was able to obey this summons with a clear conscience. But before doing so, although the imperial safe-conduct allowed him only twenty-one days' grace, he quietly dispatched the projects he had in hand at the time (the *Responsio* to Catharinus, the first parts of the *Magnificat*, and so on). He also continued the regular work of his calling without interruption. On Good Friday, which had not become a holiday at that time, he gave his customary lecture, and on Maundy Thursday and the First and Second Easter Days he preached three times in his accustomed fluent style, without as much as alluding in a single word to the subject which was now the talk of the town in Wittenberg.

It was not until the Tuesday after Easter (April 2) that Luther climbed into goldsmith Christian Döring's little wagon, which was furnished with a "little protecting shed" and which, together with three horses, the Wittenberg town council had placed at his disposal for the long journey. The university had provided him with the necessary traveling money, twenty guldens. Accompanied by Nicholas von Amsdorf, the Pomeranian student Peter von Suaven, and Friar John Petzensteiner, of Nuremberg, as *socius itinerarius*, he started out for Leipzig, and from there he proceeded to Weimar by way of Naumburg. Here the officials of Duke John, who replenished his supply of money for the journey under instruction of their lord, probably showed him the imperial mandate which the Elector had in the meantime hastily dispatched to his brother by one of his councilors. Shortly afterward he also met imperial couriers who had been sent out to post this mandate in all the towns. He tells us later that he was at first very much alarmed by this. The imperial herald, who was genuinely devoted to him, was so dismayed that he asked him whether he wished to continue the journey under these circumstances. It appears that Luther very quickly sized up the situation correctly and concluded that the mandate was simply intended to frighten him away from Worms. So he decided to go on without delay. The imperial herald immediately informed the emperor of this from Erfurt. He added that "wherever he goes, old and young, boys and girls, pour out to meet Dr. Luther, nor can I stop them." In the villages this interest

probably centered on the herald, who, arrayed in the impos-
ing uniform of his office, always preceded the wagon. But
in the towns the people wanted, above all, "to see the wonder man who had been so daring as to set himself against
the pope and the whole world." Some, to be sure, had little
comfort to offer him on the way. "Since there are so many
cardinals and bishops at the diet," they said, "he, too, will
doubtless be burned to a powder in short order, as Huss was
once burned in Constance." In Naumburg a cleric even presented him with a picture of the martyr, Savonarola, to
encourage him. He did not allow himself to be deceived
by such doubtful gifts and talk, however, any more than by
the threats of the imperial mandate. "Even if they kindled
a fire as high as heaven from Wittenberg to Worms," he was
said to have declared, "I would appear in the name of the
Lord, in obedience to the summons, and would walk into
behemoth's mouth, between his great teeth, and confess
Christ."

Like the people, the authorities also showed Luther every
honor, if for no other reason than the distinguished company in which he was traveling. In Leipzig he was simply
presented with the customary gift of wine. But in Naumburg, Burgomaster Gressler immediately invited him to dinner as well. And in Erfurt (April 6) he was formally welcomed as if he were a prince; on the outskirts of the town
the whole university, under the rector's leadership, met him
and then accompanied him with great pomp to his quarters
in the Augustinian monastery. He also had to allow a ban-
quet to be held in his honor, much to his displeasure, and
then, on the following Sunday, April 7, at the "request of
many excellent scholars," he had to preach in the Augustinian church, which was thronged to overflowing. As usual,
he based his sermon on the Gospel for the day, John 20:
19-23, and in connection with this lesson he developed his
principal subject, "How one can become godly and attain
to salvation." In the course of the sermon he let slip many

a denunciation of Aristotle and the scholastics; of unfaithful preachers who tend their congregations as a butcher does lambs on the day before Easter; of priests in general, among three thousand of whom one can hardly find four decent men; of the perversion of divine truth by foolish human laws; and against "all that comes from the pope and is constantly crying, 'Give, give.' " But to those things of which all his listeners were thinking he alluded, at most, in the words: "I know well that one does not care to hear these things. Nevertheless, I shall, and must, speak the truth, even if I lose my head twenty times."

Luther was also invited to ascend the pulpit in Gotha (April 8?) and in Eisenach (April 9?). But after this he had to be more forbearing. He became so ill while he was still in Eisenach that his friends really feared for his life. He himself referred to several afflictions which he had not experienced before. He was probably suffering from the first attack of that treacherous stomach ailment which continued to bother him considerably until late fall. He was bled and given some "precious" water, whereupon he fell asleep. He had recovered sufficiently by the following day to proceed to Berka. But he was still sick when he reached Frankfurt on the Main on Sunday, April 14, two days before the expiration of his safe-conduct. His spirit, meanwhile, did not suffer. "I am coming, my Spalatin," he wrote to Worms on the same day from Wolf Parente's inn, "The Ostrich," on the Corn Marketplace, "although Satan has tried to stop me with more than one sickness. The emperor's mandate, I am convinced, was published simply to frighten me away. But Christ lives, and we shall enter Worms in spite of all the gates of hell and powers in the air."

The "imperialists," as Aleander reported, "were thunderstruck" when Sturm's letter reached Worms about April 13 with the report that "Luther is coming after all, and he is being received everywhere by the people with such enthusiasm that his journey resembles a triumphal march." The emperor immediately commissioned his father confessor to make necessary arrangements with Aleander. Aleander desired, in the first place, to have the "scoundrel" brought into town in as quiet a manner as possible. In the second place, he wished to have him confined in the bishop's palace where the emperor was staying, for no one under suspicion could associate with him there. And in the third place, he wanted to have only one question put to him—whether he was willing to recant. Glapion agreed, and the emperor, with whom he discussed the matter, also approved of these limitations. On the following day, however, Aleander heard that the heretic was to be put up in the Augustinian monastery, under close surveillance, and that it was intended to require of him only a recantation of his theological errors while his attacks on the papacy were to be overlooked. The emperor quickly reassured him. But in reporting this to Rome on April 15, Aleander added dubiously, "If only it turns out this way!"

On the same day Luther left Frankfurt to proceed to Worms. That afternoon in Oppenheim, to his great surprise, he came upon an old acquaintance from the Heidelberg Disputation, the Dominican Martin Bucer, who was now chaplain to Sickingen at the Ebernburg, a few hours distant. The lively little Alsatian urged Luther in every way at his command, and in Hutten's name, to follow him at once to the Ebernburg. For the emperor's father confessor, said Bucer, had something of great importance to discuss with him there in secret. But Luther retorted, "If the emperor's father confessor has something to discuss with me, he may do so in Worms!" He suspected at once that he was only to be held up so that he could no longer reach Worms on time —for his safe-conduct expired April 16—and that proceedings could be started against him as a "disobedient stay-away." And this is exactly what Glapion was aiming at. The fact that Hutten and Sickingen—whom Glapion, in league with the imperial councilor, Armenstorff, had won over to the emperor's side in the course of conferences lasting many hours on April 5 and 6—fell into this trap, and that Hutten even allowed himself to be prevailed upon to see to it personally that this message should be delivered to Luther, is not particularly surprising, for the knightly man of letters was never a good judge of human nature. Glapion, moreover, must have had something unusually engaging about him, for even Bucer, who was far more suspicious by nature, allowed the father confessor to pull the wool over his eyes.

About the same time a letter of Spalatin reached Luther from Worms. His friend wrote that the Elector advised him not to come, for he could not protect him. His case was in a bad way. He had already been condemned. So if things had gone Elector Frederick's way, the Reformer would never have reached Worms. But Luther would not be frightened off by such faintheartedness. "Even if there were as many devils in Worms as there are tiles on the roofs," he wrote back, "I would enter anyway." "I was not afraid," he said later. "I suppose God can make a man that daring. I am not sure that I should now [1540] be so bold."

Tuesday, April 16, at ten o'clock in the morning, while the inhabitants of Worms were eating their midday meal, the trumpet blasts with which the town watchman was wont to announce distinguished visitors resounded from the cathedral tower. Although the people in Worms had become quite accustomed to such occurrences during recent months, they hurried from near and far to Martin's Gate and Kämmerer Street. For that morning news had spread through the town that Dr. Luther was expected by the Saxon lords in the course of the day and that a great company of nobles had ridden out early in the morning along the road to Mainz to meet him. Shortly afterward the powerful figure of Imperial Herald Sturm, which was familiar to all the people, came into sight, and behind him and his servant the little Saxon wagon, under the canopy of which Dr. Martinus himself was seated with the other three, Friar Petzensteiner,

Amsdorf, and Peter Suaven. Following the wagon, on horse, came the young Erfurt professor, Justus Jonas, who had joined Dr. Martinus on the way; and then followed about a hundred men on horse, among them Bernard von Hirschfeld, Hans Schott of Oberwindt, Albrecht Schenk of Lindenau, and other Saxon noblemen who were already familiar to the people of Worms. Since the crowd had grown to about two thousand, the wagon advanced only slowly. When the wagon halted before the House of the Knights of St. John on the right side of Kämmerer Street, a priest threw his arms around Dr. Martinus and touched him three times with his hand as if he had a particularly precious relic before him. But before going into the house, as Aleander's spy claimed, Martinus paused, surveyed the crowd with his "demoniacal" eyes, and said, "God will be with me!"

The population of Worms at this time was at most seven thousand, and it had only two fairly large inns. Consequently the House of the Knights of St. John was so filled from top to bottom that the Reformer had to be content with sleeping space in the room occupied by Hirschfeld and Schott. But he was at least among acquaintances and friends in this "dovecot." And if he felt like it, he could get to "The Swan" quickly. This was the tavern, close by, in which the shy Elector was staying with his retinue, including, aside from Spalatin, his jester, Klaus. As a matter of fact, what happened at the House of the Knights of St. John might well have taken place in a dovecot. After the midday meal, Aleander reported, everybody went to see the arch-heretic. To be sure, "everybody" included only the lesser lights of the diet—counts, barons, knights, and town couriers. The Electors and princes, including Frederick the Wise, purposely held themselves aloof. Only Duke William of Brunswick and the sixteen-year-old Landgrave Philip of Hessia were exceptions to the rule. The latter even sought out the outlaw in his quarters and, among other things, started to discuss the passage of the *Babylonian Captivity* which alluded to divorce on the ground of a husband's impotence. The Reformer was somewhat surprised at this, as we can readily understand, and tried at once to lead the precocious prince away from this subject. Nor did Philip take this amiss. For on his departure he extended his hand loyally and said, "If you are right, Herr Doctor, may God help you!"

"Martinus has of course spoiled everything for the Romanists by coming." In his letter to the curia under date of April 16 Aleander fairly fumed at the fainthearted and even imbecilic imperial councilors who, in his opinion, were to blame for all this mischief because they did not heed his advice. Nevertheless, he was very willing, on the morning of April 17, to confer with the emperor's father confessor, Glapion, about "measures conformable to his wishes." In fact, when "the first hearing turned out not too badly," he pretended, in his daily report to the curia, that he himself had arranged everything in the Imperial Council. He even made it appear as if he had fixed the hour for the appearance before the emperor of the Electors and the rest of the imperial estates. Actually, however, his complaints against the imperialists and his thoroughly erratic assertions regarding the activity of the Saxon Elector clearly reveal that Aleander played a very subordinate part in the events of the next few days. It could hardly have been otherwise, for he was not a participant in the negotiations.

Neither the Elector nor Luther had desired an appearance before the diet. What they had requested was a hearing before unprejudiced experts under the protection of the diet. And this was the proposal of the diet itself on February 19. In the imperial proposition of March 2 and in the citation of March 6, to be sure, such a hearing was no longer mentioned; it was only stated that Luther was to be questioned and heard. Yet the imperial councilors certainly did not intend that the procedure proposed by the diet on February 19 should be precluded. They had not as yet formed any opinion at all with regard to the nature of the hearing.

Hence, if the Elector had intervened energetically at this time, he might have succeeded in securing a method of dealing with the case which would have been more in keeping with his own and Luther's wishes. But as far as we know, he did nothing to accomplish this. As so often, he let the imperial councilors take the initiative in the decision of this question out of his hands. These men had probably agreed among themselves, directly after the receipt of the imperial herald's letter on April 13 or 14, to have Luther brought before the diet. On the other hand, the idea of entrusting the hearing to the Trier official, Dr. John von der Ecken, probably did not occur to them until the session of the Electors which began at two o'clock in the afternoon of April 17. Perhaps this was intended as a courtesy to Elector Frederick, who for more than two years had been urging the settlement of the case in a court of arbitration under the chairmanship of the archbishop of Trier. But it is impossible that Frederick should have suggested the official, for he was an avowed opponent of Luther and was not only living in the same house with Aleander, but was also in heartiest agreement with him. The truth of the matter is that we do not even know whether Frederick attended this session of the Elector's Council, for if his presence on such occasions is not expressly stated, we may never take it for granted, even if the questions which were up for discussion concerned him personally. Hence his intervention in Luther's behalf—which was so immoderately exaggerated by Aleander—was in reality limited, according to the documents and reports we have, to his securing accommodation for the Reformer in the House of the Knights of St. John, to his delegation of Professor Schurpff on the first day and Councilors Thun and Philip von Feilitzsch on the second day to accompany Luther, to his support of Luther's request on April 17 for time to reflect, and finally to his plea, relayed through Spalatin and others, that Luther should not threaten and defy the diet like a new Elias, but should always conduct himself in a courteous, deferential, and humble manner. Accordingly it is no exaggeration to say that Frederick left it to Luther to find his own way out of the net which had been spread for him. But how is it that he could not bring himself to do more for the Reformer? It was because he wanted under all circumstances to keep up the fiction that he was neutral toward both the person and the cause of the Reformer.

It appears that Luther first had a pastoral duty to perform when April 17 dawned. He had to hear the confession of a knight, Hans von Minckwitz, who was lying on his deathbed, and administer the sacrament to him. Then, before ten o'clock, the imperial marshal, Ulrich von Pappenheim, who was also staying at the House of the Knights of St. John, informed him that he was to appear before emperor and realm at four o'clock. So he tried at once to make his outward appearance worthy of the occasion by having an especially large tonsure cut, leaving only a narrow crown of dark, curly hair on his large head. At four o'clock he was conducted by the marshal and herald Sturm to the episcopal palace, not far from the cathedral. They went in a roundabout way, for the streets were so congested with curiosity-seekers that it would have been impossible to get through in any other way. At the palace Luther had to wait for almost two hours. On the way, the faithful herald and other people whom he met had spoken friendly words of encouragement; and he also met such well-wishers and friends when he reached the bishop's palace. But that the well-known captain of foot-soldiers, Frundsberg, was among these friendly spirits, is a legend which first came to light in 1597. Finally, at six o'clock, he was called. Sturm and von Pappenheim led him into the low-ceilinged court chamber in which the diet was meeting. Besides Schurpff, several other Saxon councilors probably accompanied him. For the report of a Spanish councilor of state who was present relates that he appeared with six or seven persons who cleared the way for him in a very discourteous fashion.

From a copper etching of Lucas Cranach, dating from the early months of the year 1521, we can still get a good idea of how Luther looked at this moment. From this etching we gather that he must not have been so frightfully thin and miserable as he seems to have been when Cranach made his earlier etching of the Reformer in 1520. His hollow cheeks and sunken eyes seem to have filled out somewhat. His scrawny neck had become round and solid. Indeed, there was even the suggestion of a double chin now. But more than anything else, the expression on his face had changed. The sickly, drawn look, which is so noticeable in the older etching, had disappeared, and his glance was now frank and bold. Every line in the clear-cut profile, from the projecting eyebrows to the firm, round chin, betrayed strength and determination. But the princes and foreign emissaries who were now staring at him in silence were impressed far more by his large, dark eyes "which flashed and twinkled like stars, so that one could not look straight into them." Of course, the Italians and Spaniards at this solemn session felt that these eyes were "demoniacal." Nor did his mien please the Spaniards in other respects. They missed that dignified sedateness (*sosiego*) which they deemed the most prominent hallmark of good breeding. Aleander, who was not present, even remarked, "The fool entered the hall laughing, and while he was standing before the emperor, he was constantly moving his head this way and that." But Luther could hardly have moved his head thus for the simple reason that he was not standing in an upright position; while he was in the presence of the emperor and the representatives of the empire, he was obliged to stand with his knee lightly bent.

While the thought was running through Luther's head that he was supposed to address the pale youth with the drooping mouth who was seated on the throne (and who

was known to be ill-disposed toward him) as "most gracious
emperor," Dr. Ecken, "a man of very large stature," began
to speak in a loud, sonorous voice, first in Latin and then
in German. "His Imperial Majesty has summoned you, Martin Luther, to find out two things: First, are you willing to
confess that the books which have been circulated under
your name are yours?"—here he pointed to a pile of twenty
books which Aleander had placed at the disposal of the high
assembly as a *corpus delicti*—"and second, are you ready to
renounce these books or part of them?" Aleander claimed
that he had specified what questions should be put. He was
probably correct to this extent, that "the remarkable Dr.
Ecken, who had burned Martin's books in Trier with such
extreme thoroughness," had informed him beforehand as
to what he intended to ask the heretic. Luther, who had
been instructed prior to this by Pappenheim not to argue but
only to answer the questions put to him, was already on the
point of answering the first question in the affirmative when
the suspicious Schurpff suddenly interrupted the deliberations by shouting from Luther's side, "Let the titles be read!"
Thereupon the imperial notary, Siebenbürger (Transsil-
vanus), arose and read the titles. "All of the books were
mine," the Reformer reported later, "but I do not know how
they managed to get them." He had no idea how much effort
it had cost Aleander to gather this little library. Then with
a cheerful expression, speaking first in German, and then in
Latin, "in a very low voice, as if he were frightened or awed,"
but in actuality probably because he did not deem it proper
to shout in this exalted assembly as his friend Schurpff had
done, he declared the books to be his.

As to the second question, inasmuch as it involved faith,
the salvation of souls, and the highest treasure on earth, the
Word of God, Luther requested a respite and time for reflection; for it would be presumptuous and dangerous, he said,
not to deliberate carefully over his answer to such a question, since he could easily, through want of caution, say a

word too much or too little. This request was so fair that the princes and councilors of the emperor—for the emperor himself did not understand a word of the negotiations, but always had to have Ecken's and Luther's speeches translated for him by his councilors—could not refuse to grant it. But the councilors and "little red hats" could not restrain themselves from giving some sort of retort to the heretic at this time. They insisted that he be given only one day for reflection, and that his answer should not be read from a manuscript but spoken freely. Ecken announced this decision to the Reformer. At the same time he declared that Luther must have gathered from the citation that he had been summoned only for recantation. Luther might have replied at once that nothing of the kind was stated in the citation. But at a sign from the emperor he was led away and escorted back to the House of the Knights of St. John by Sturm.

Luther regarded the conduct of the emperor and the diet as very unfair. Of course, he knew very well, even now, that he "could not retract a single letter," as he wrote this same evening to the imperial councilor, Cuspinian, in Vienna. But how much depended on the way in which he formulated, and the arguments on which he based, his negative reply! He probably would have liked to discuss the wording of his statement in detail with his friends, as he was accustomed to do in such cases. But this was hardly possible now, or certainly only to a very limited extent, for only one of his confidential friends, besides Spalatin, was present. This was Amsdorf. But Amsdorf had to keep under cover, for even before his arrival Aleander had threatened that he would not be tolerated in Worms because he had dared to accompany Luther without a safe-conduct. For this reason he never appeared in the conferences at Worms. As far as Spalatin was concerned, he could have helped his friend only in matters of form. And perhaps he did help him at this time by instructing Luther how he should address the emperor and the princes and how he should conduct himself toward them in other respects. But he could not give him any advice with reference to the subject matter itself. Yet Luther hardly felt lonely, for he had long been accustomed, in the critical hours of his life, to rely solely upon God and his conscience. And so, although he had been forbidden to read his reply, he wrote out a careful draft of what he wished to say on the morning of April 18. The single page of this draft which is still extant shows numerous corrections, but the manuscript betrays no trace of agitation.

Shortly after four o'clock Sturm again took Luther by devious ways to the episcopal palace. This time the crowd was even larger than on the preceding day because all the members of the diet, even those who had been unable to get into the small assembly room on April 17, were determined to see and hear him today. Some of them, like the Saxon knight, Starschädel, arrived about ten o'clock in order to be sure to get a place in the large hall of the palace which was designated as the place of meeting for this day. It was six o'clock before the emperor's throne was set up in the hall and the princes began to come down the stairs. Meanwhile it had become so dark before the session was opened that torches had to be lighted. The throng was so great that Luther and the Saxon councilors who accompanied him, Thun and Feilitzsch, had to stand among the princes. For even the princes must stand, unless they were fortunate enough to find room on the stone benches along the walls.

Ecken again opened the meeting with a short Latin and German address. He closed with the same question as on the preceding day. He asked Luther if he was ready to retract all or part of the books which he had confessed the day before to be his. Thereupon Luther, speaking German in a fearless and courageous voice, began by apologizing if he should not give every one of the lords present his appropriate title, or if he should commit a breach of court etiquette in some other way. He confessed once again that he was the author of the books which had been placed before him on the preceding day, but with the qualification, probably suggested by Schurpff, "in case nothing in them has been altered or struck out in a fraudulent fashion." Then he divided his books into three classes: First, there were purely devotional books, in which not even his opponents could find anything offensive. These he could not retract. Then there were polemical books against the papacy. These he could not renounce either, inasmuch as he would thereby open the windows as well as the doors to that papal tyranny under which especially the illustrious German nation had to suffer so much. Finally, there were polemical writings against private persons who had dared to defend papal tyranny and destroy the worship of God as he taught it. Although he had to confess that he had written more vehemently in these books than was becoming to the member of an Order, he could not retract them, for such a retraction would only result in encouraging the spiritual tyrants and in making them treat the people of God with even greater violence than heretofore. Nevertheless, he was very well aware, he said, that he was merely a man and liable to error. As Jesus Christ, who could not err, said to the servant who struck Him when He was before High Priest Annas, "If I have spoken evil, bear witness of the evil," so, declared Luther, he was also willing to be set right by the humblest of servants. So he adjured the emperor, the princes, and everybody by the mercy of God to refute him from the Bible. If he were so refuted, he would at once recant his errors, whatever they might be, and be the first to throw his books into the fire.

Luther believed, as he said, that he had hereby demonstrated that he had duly considered and weighed the dangerous dissensions which had arisen in the world as a result of his teachings, as had been charged against him the day before. Nevertheless, he continued, he was extremely pleased to notice that the Word of God had excited such a controversy and such discord. For Christ said, "I have not come to bring peace, but the sword." "Consequently we should consider how wonderful and terrible God is in His decrees. We should not begin, in our attempt to settle this controversy and dissension, by condemning the Word of God. For that would bring down upon us a flood of unbearable evils, and it would be a very poor beginning for the reign of the young emperor from whom, next to God, so much may be expected. I do not say this because such great lords may need my teaching and warning, but because I dare not evade the duty which I owe to my Germany. I commend myself to Your Majesty and to Your Highnesses with the humble plea that you will not permit my accusers to make me hateful in your eyes without cause." When he had finished, after speaking about ten minutes, he was asked to repeat the whole address in Latin. He did so at once, although he was "very warm on account of the crowd." [1]

Later generations have caught only the crisp "no" in this speech. The original hearers also heard just as clearly its "yes"—the proposal of Luther to allow himself to be set right on the basis of the Holy Scriptures by anyone, no matter how low his station. Consequently the princes, who immediately gathered in a special consultation, had to cudgel their brains to find out what answer to give him. It was quite clear, of course, that the diet could not accede to his offer and permit a disputation on questions which, in the opinion of the ecclesiastical princes who were present, had long since been decided by the church. But it was felt that he could not be condemned outright and that, to make sure, he had to to be asked again if he really wished to persist in

---

[1] The pretty story which was first told by Selnecker in his *Vita Lutheri* in 1590—that Duke Erich of Brunswick, who was very hostile to Luther, had a tankard of Eimbecker beer sent to the Reformer to refresh him—is, of course, a legend. The German diets at this time were not quite so comfortably domestic as that. The story was probably invented by someone who wished to advertise Eimbecker, which was very highly prized at this time, although it could hardly have been transported so far. The same holds for the story of Luther's conversation with the two quarreling Jews (likewise first reported by Selnecker) in connection with which these children of Israel were supposed to have presented him with a bottle of wine.

his "no." So the official was instructed to demand of him another very brief and unambiguous statement.

Thereupon Ecken reopened the proceedings with a moderately long address. He was not sparing in his use of abusive terms, for he obviously intended to break Luther's spirit. He concluded: "Do not expect a disputation on articles of faith which you are obligated to believe unconditionally. Answer straightforwardly and honestly, unambiguously and unreservedly, whether you will retract your books and the errors contained in them or not!" Luther responded to this in Latin: "Inasmuch as Your Majesty and Your Highnesses ask for a plain answer, I shall give one without horns [reservations] or teeth [backbiting]. Unless I am proved to be wrong by the testimony of Scriptures and by evident reasoning—for I cannot trust the decisions of either popes or councils, since it is plain that they have frequently erred and contradicted one another—I am bound in conscience and held fast in the Word of God by those passages of the Holy Scriptures which I have quoted. Therefore, I cannot and will not retract anything, for it is neither safe nor salutary to act against one's conscience." Then he added, speaking in German, "God help me! Amen." [1]

This decided the question on which the diet had sought a further answer. So the princes, who were worn out by the crowds and the heat, started to leave. But Ecken thought that he ought to try his luck again. "Forget about your conscience, Martinus," he began, "for your conscience errs. You will never be able to prove that councils have erred—at least not so far as matters of faith are concerned. In questions of discipline I should have no objection to admitting the possi-

---

[1] The customary conclusion of Luther's sermons; hence a formula, not a phrase consciously used. Cf. Enders, 2, 419. The so-called "Worms dictum" had already appeared in two Wittenberg editions of the year 1521 in the form, "I cannot do otherwise. Here I stand. God help me! Amen." But Luther, who was then at the Wartburg, had nothing to do with these publications. The form which is customary today is found for the first time in the second volume of the Wittenberg edition of his complete works, which appeared after his death in 1546. The authority for his statement is the Latin report, originating with Luther himself and probably written by Jonas, in *Reichstagsakten*, II, 2, 540 ff.

bility of an error." Luther retorted, "I can prove it." But the emperor did not permit him to go on, but signed to the imperial herald to take him away. This caused a great shout to go up, rising above the noise of the general break-up of the meeting, for some of the nobles believed that he was to be put into prison. Luther quieted them, however, by saying, "I am only being escorted." Then they thronged after him in great, jubilant crowds, with arms aloft and hands outspread, as the Germans were accustomed to do at this time in token of victory at tournaments. But the Spanish grooms, who were waiting for their masters below at the entrance, received him with hisses and sneering countenances, and cried after him, "*Al fuego, al fuego!*" (Burn him!) Fortunately the Germans did not understand this "friendly" greeting. Otherwise some swords would probably have slipped out of their sheaths. As it was, the Reformer and his escorts reached the House of the Knights of St. John without mishap. "When he arrived," Sixtus Oelhafen wrote hastily to Nuremberg about nine o'clock that night, "he stretched out his hands, while I and several others were present, and exclaimed with a beaming face, 'I am through! I am through!'"

If things had gone as the young emperor wished, Luther would have been "through" for good. On the morning of April 19 Charles summoned the Electors and many of the princes and asked them what should now be done. As usual, they requested time for deliberation. He replied in French, "Very well! Then I will first let you know what my opinion is." Whereupon he had a manuscript, which he had composed with his own hand, read to them. In it the emperor solemnly declared that he was resolved to stake all his kingdoms and principalities, his friends, his body and blood, his life and soul on the vindication of the Catholic faith and the Roman Church. After hearing Luther the previous day, he said he regretted that he had not proceeded against him long before, and he did not wish to hear him further. He intended to send Luther back at once. He would keep his pledge of a safe-conduct, he said, but on condition that the heretic would not preach or incite an uprising on his return journey. It is possible, even if it cannot be proved, that the drafting of this declaration was Charles' own idea and that he had set it down on paper without any help whatsover from his father confessor. At all events, the manuscript certainly expressed his personal feelings and convictions. That he actually said, when he first caught sight of Luther (as Aleander reported twelve days later), "This man will never make a heretic out of me," is very improbable, for practically all utterances of this kind that were circulated in Rome by the industrious nuncio turned out later to be fictitious. But there is no question that from this time on Charles had a personal aversion to Luther.

That afternoon the Electors deliberated over the emperor's proposition. Aleander reported in one of his dispatches that all six (hence also Frederick) had just decided unanimously to treat Luther as a heretic. But on April 27 he mentioned that the proposal had been signed by only four Electors! It is unnecessary to go to great lengths to prove that Frederick the Wise had no intention of voting against Luther. But neither did it occur to him to take vigorous action in Luther's behalf. It is true, Luther's German and Latin speeches on April 18 pleased him very much as a rhetorical effort. But he thought the Reformer was "much too bold," and for his part he had no desire whatsoever to be bolder than Luther. At this time, as before, he was content simply to vote against the emperor's proposals. But before the estates of the empire had made up their minds with reference to the emperor's opinion, something happened to prevent a speedy settlement of the case. During the night of April 19-20 two placards were posted in Worms. One of them was directed against Luther and probably read: "You are condemned by the pope. You are condemned by the emperor. Frederick will also condemn you and will undoubtedly not keep his promise of safe-conduct. O you fool, Luther! You dare to harp on old errors and do not manage to find anything new!" The other, which was posted on the town hall, ran something like this: "Four hundred nobles have vowed not to abandon the just man, Luther, and to declare their enmity against the princes and Romanists, particularly the archbishop of Mainz. I write poorly, but I intend great destruction. With eight thousand men I mean to fight. Bundschuh, Bundschuh, Bundschuh!"

The archbishop of Mainz was so terrified by this second placard that he immediately sent his brother, Elector Joachim of Brandenburg, to the emperor on the morning of April 20 to ask that he "allow Luther, in the name of the empire and in the presence of several princes, to have another hearing before a number of doctors." The emperor refused outright. Nevertheless, the estates of the empire resolved on the very same day to petition the emperor to have Luther's errors pointed out to him and to seek to have him refuted by three or four honorable persons who were versed in the Holy Scriptures, in order that Luther might not be able to say that his own errors had not been specified and in order that the common people might not conclude from this that he had been condemned without being given so much as a hearing. The emperor replied in writing on April 22 that his opinion was unchanged, but that he would give the estates three days of grace in which to make Luther recant. As for himself, he could not attend these conferences, he wrote, nor would he be represented by one of his councilors. As a result, Glapion, to whom Luther had written directly upon his arrival, had to abandon his intention of having a personal conference with the Reformer.

The diet now made at least an attempt to do justice to Luther's original offer. But from the very start it approached the matter in such a way that it was impossible for Luther to be satisfied. In the first place, almost all the men who were appointed on the committee before which the Reformer was to be given another hearing were avowed opponents of Luther: the Electors of Brandenburg and Trier, Duke George of Saxony, the bishops of Augsburg and Brandenburg, Grand Master Dietrich Cleen of the Teutonic Order, Count George of Wertheim, and two representatives of the cities, Bock from Strassburg and Peutinger from Augsburg. Only two of these nine men, Bock and Peutinger, were not directly prejudiced against Luther. The hearing, in the second place, was put into the hands of the Badensian chancellor, Dr. Jerome Vehus, a jurist, who, it is true, actively espoused a reform of the church in the sense of the *Gravamina* (Grievances) *of the German Nation,* just adopted on April 22, but who had no appreciation for the basic religious views of the Reformer. The fact that Frederick the Wise was not represented on this committee is sufficient to indicate that in this case, too, he deemed discretion the better part of valor. "Were it within my power," he wrote on April 24 to his brother John, who was incessantly urging him to take Luther's part more vigorously, "I should be quite willing to help Martinus secure his rights. . . . My opinion is that he will be driven out and condemned. And anyone who as much as intimates that he wishes him well is deemed a heretic. May it be the Lord's will that it turns out for the best! God will without doubt not forsake justice." The obvious idea of contributing something to this end did not occur to Frederick during these days, however, because he kept his eyes on the emperor, as if hypnotized and did not wish to "burden himself" with him at any price. How different both Luther's and Germany's destiny would have been if this prince had possessed even a tenth of the driving energy and enterprising spirit of his cousin George!

Between two and three o'clock on the afternoon of April 23 Luther, who had been pestered by all sorts of people in the meantime, was summoned by two priests to appear for a new hearing. Shortly before seven o'clock the following morning this hearing was opened by Dr. Vehus in the quar-

ters of the archbishop of Trier in the House of the Teutonic
Order, with Elector Joachim of Brandenburg presiding.
From the outset it bore the stamp, not of a hearing, but of
a friendly conference in which Luther was to be persuaded,
as he himself aptly expressed it, "to unclinch his fist and let
go of the Bible." But he clung, with all deference, to the
principle which he had repeated so often since August, 1519
—that he could yield only to the Bible or evident reasons
This is the way in which Elector Joachim quite correctly
summed up the conference after about two hours of parley.
While the others hastened to the town hall to give their
report to the diet, the archbishop of Trier tried to bring influence to bear upon Luther privately through two other "doctors." One of these was the Frankfurt dean, John Cochlaeus,
who had hurried to Worms as early as April 18 in order to
offer his services to Aleander. The other was Dr. Ecken.
Schurpff and Amsdorf took part in the parley as associates
of Luther. In very lengthy expositions Ecken tried, above
all, to shake Luther's confidence in the Bible. Luther, on
the other hand, claimed the right to criticize the decisions
of councils on the basis of I Corinthians 14:30, "But if a
revelation be made to another sitting by, let the first keep
silence." In the course of the discussion Cochlaeus broke in
all of a sudden to ask, "Has something been revealed to you?"
    Luther: "Yes."
    Cochlaeus: "But before you said just the opposite."
    Luther: "No."
    Cochlaeus: "Who is going to believe that something has
been revealed to you? Where is the miracle, where is the
sign by which you would have to prove this?"
    At this point Schurpff suddenly interrupted him with his
stentorian voice, "Why don't you let Luther finish speaking?"
    But Luther did not discuss Cochlaeus' objection any fur-
ther, for Ecken now turned the conversation back to the
decisions of the Council of Constance. Luther espoused
especially the proposition of Huss which was condemned in

Constance—that the church is the fellowship of the predestined. Once again Cochlaeus interrupted before he had finished speaking, and once again he was called to order by Schurpff. Of course, nothing came of the whole conference. The archbishop arose shortly before ten o'clock with the remark that it was time to eat. He proposed to continue this theological colloquy, which came nearest to meeting the conditions mentioned by Luther in his *Offer and Protest,* during the afternoon. But Cochlaeus and Ecken showed no inclination to continue, probably because they did not feel that they were a match for Luther.

Meanwhile Cochlaeus had a secret message to convey to Luther. He appeared in the House of the Knights of St. John at eleven o'clock, but he met only Amsdorf and Schurpff. He was conversing with these for a while in a very peaceful way when all of a sudden Luther's *socius itinerarius,* Petzensteiner, sprang up and—although he was only a simple lay brother—challenged the dean to a disputation! At this moment Luther entered the room and tried at once to compose the quarrel by means of a homely jest. "My brother," he said, "thinks he is wiser than the rest of us, especially when he has been drinking hard." Everyone laughed, but the friar continued to mutter, especially because Cochlaeus had called him *fratercule,* poor little mendicant. Then Luther sat down with Cochlaeus and talked about all sorts of things in a quiet and friendly fashion. Schurpff tried again and again to inveigle him into a dispute, but Cochlaeus was not in a mood for one. But finally he did start one by asking why Luther had persuaded the people that they had a right to the cup in the Lord's Supper when he admitted that one kind was sufficient. Then someone else introduced the subject of the doctrine of transubstantiation, concerning which Schurpff again insisted on hearing Cochlaeus' opinion. This quizzing, which only brought him ridicule and derision, was very disagreeable to Cochlaeus. So he tried to lead the conversation into a different channel by saying to Luther

abruptly, "If you give up your safe-conduct, I shall be glad
to dispute with you in public." These words caused a veritable tumult to break out in the crowded room. "Indeed, a
pretty inducement!" thundered Schurpff. And the knight,
Vollrat von Watzdorf, crowded in on the impertinent dean
with drawn sword, whereupon the latter immediately withdrew his offer.

After a further exchange of conversation, Cochlaeus finally
confessed that he had not come to dispute but to deliver
a confidential message to Luther. The Reformer went up
into his sleeping chamber with him. But he wished by no
means to be alone with Cochlaeus and insisted on having
at least Brother Petzensteiner there as witness. Cochlaeus
eventually acceded on condition that he would be allowed
to take his nephew along into the chamber. As soon as they
got there, Cochlaeus began. The nuncio had told him the
previous day (April 23), he said, that Luther needed to
recant only those teachings of his which were in acknowledged contradiction to the Catholic faith. As for the remaining controverted points, the emperor and the diet would
commission a number of scholars to examine his books and
remove what was bad. If it would embarrass him, or if he
should be afraid to remain in Saxony, the emperor and the
archbishop of Trier would provide him with a quiet and
safe residence. Aleander's reports to the curia contain no
word of this offer. But this does not prove that Cochlaeus
merely trumped up something for Luther, but only that the
nuncio was not interested in having any hint of this action
leak out in Rome. For we know that Cochlaeus received ten
guldens from him for his efforts and that Caracciolo gave
him a dispensation free of charge. These efforts for which
he was paid could only have been his private mission to
Luther. Thus Aleander's courage, in the face of the diet's
attitude to the *gravamina* as well as to the Lutheran affair,
had sunk to such a low level during these days that he
allowed himself to make the largest conceivable concessions

to "the beast, the monster, the scoundrel." "The monster," however, did not accede to the overtures of Cochlaeus, but went off into an enthusiastic eulogy of the noble intellect of Master Philip Melanchthon, whom he placed high above himself. Finally, Luther said, "I am only one of the very small men of my party. There are others who are far more important and learned. Consequently nothing at all would be gained if I recanted, for the others, who are far superior to me in learning, would certainly not remain silent but would carry on the cause." In bidding farewell he is even said to have shed tears, but he later denied this very vigorously.

In the meantime, Vehus had reported the outcome of his mission to the estates of the empire. Among other things he announced that, according to a statement of Schurpff, Luther was willing to submit his writings to the judgment of the emperor and the diet. This communication, which grew out of a misunderstanding, made such an impression on the estates that they immediately petitioned the emperor to prolong Luther's stay in Worms by two days and then to commission the two jurists who favored reform, Vehus and Peutinger, to negotiate once again with the Reformer. The resulting conference took place in the House of the Knights of St. John on April 25, beginning at six o'clock in the morning. The Saxon side was again represented by Schurpff in the capacity of witness and, at the Elector's special request, by Councilor Thun as well. The misunderstanding caused by Schurpff was soon cleared up. But now Vehus and Peutinger tried all the harder to persuade Luther to submit his writings unreservedly to the judgment of the emperor and the estates. They said that he would not have anything to fear in doing this; the diet would surely act according to its Christian duty and would certainly commit the examination of his books to thoroughly trustworthy persons. But they were unable to give Luther any sort of guarantee for this. At last, after three hours of conversation, he requested time for deliberation. When they returned at one o'clock, he could only tell them that he was unable to take their advice. But they wished to bring about an understanding at any price. So Peutinger immediately proposed that he leave the decision to a future general council. Luther also agreed to this, provided the council would meet soon and the articles which were to be presented there would be specifically announced to him beforehand. If these conditions were fulfilled, Luther said, he would even agree not to defend or otherwise advocate, either by word or pen, the propositions that were declared suspicious, until the council met.

With great rejoicing Vehus and Peutinger immediately reported this to the archbishop of Trier, to whom the diet had entrusted the conduct of the whole case. They did not note that Luther, even with this solution, had no intention under any circumstances of loosening his grip on the Bible. For this reason the archbishop, too, was willing to approve of their proposal and decided to lay the matter before the emperor at once. But he thought it well to make sure first whether Luther was really ready now to submit unreservedly to a council. In order to ascertain this, he again summoned Luther to the House of the Teutonic Order shortly before two o'clock. Luther came at once and gave him a full explanation of the earlier conference. The archbishop, too, tried for a while to persuade the Reformer, at first without a witness, then in the presence of Spalatin, who just happened to come in. He finally asked Luther himself to suggest a method for the settlement of the case. Luther replied that he knew of no better advice than that of Gamaliel in Acts 5:38, 39: "If this counsel or this work be of men, it will come to nought; but if it be of God, ye cannot overthrow it." If his design was not from God, he said, it would certainly be submerged within three, yes, even two, years. The archbishop then asked him what he would do if certain articles were extracted from his writings in order to be submitted to a council.

"Gracious Lord," Luther replied, "if only they do not select just those articles in which the Council of Constance is condemned!"

"I am afraid these will be the very ones," said the archbishop.

"Then I could not keep silent," Luther answered, "nor would I want to—because I am certain of this, that God's Word is condemned in these articles—even if I were to lose my body and my life on account of it, for I cannot depart from the true Word of God."

That settled it. Even the archbishop perceived now that any further conference would be of no avail. So he graciously dismissed Luther and promised, at his request, to obtain for him at once the emperor's permission to leave the city.

Inwardly Luther certainly must have endured far more in these two days than he did during the two hearings on April 17 and 18. It was not difficult for him to defend his position against the obvious malevolence of the emperor and of the majority of the diet. But it was no small matter for him to stand firm against such well-meaning negotiators as Vehus and Peutinger, who were earnestly intent on reaching an understanding, and to ward off all the well-intentioned attempts which they craftily employed to take him unawares. In universal historical significance, too, these conferences, which have fallen into complete oblivion, as far as popular tradition is concerned, undoubtedly surpass the two public hearings on April 17 and 18. This is so, first, because the real decision was reached in them; and second, because it was in them—inasmuch as they were carried on by both sides (including Luther) in an earnest effort to come to an understanding—that it first became very clear that the antithesis between Luther and those of the old faith was not simply one of church politics, but above all one of religion and *Weltanschauung*. And it was this that rendered an understanding between them impossible for all time.

It was about three o'clock when Luther left the archbishop of Trier. Leaving the House of the Teutonic Order in the company of Spalatin, he betook himself first of all to the very ill knight, Hans von Minckwitz. Luther told him in good Saxon dialect, "Tomorrow I shall go away again." Then, around six o'clock, Dr. Ecken appeared at the House of the Knights of St. John with the imperial notary, Siebenbürger, to convey to him in Latin an imperial order. Since all the admonitions of the emperor and the estates of the empire had had no effect on Luther, Ecken reported, there remained but one course for the emperor, and this was to act in his capacity as guardian of the Roman Church and begin to prosecute the heretic. Luther's safe-conduct was to last twenty-one days. During this time he was to return home under his surety, refraining, however, from all preaching, teaching, or writing on the way. Thereupon Luther withdrew for a few minutes, probably in order to speak to his Lord. When he reappeared, he said in Latin, "As it has pleased the Lord, so it has turned out. Blessed be the name of the Lord." Then he expressed his thanks to the emperor and the estates for having so graciously granted him a hearing and also for having kept the promise of a safe-conduct. He had never desired anything else, he said, than a reform according to the word and tenor of the Holy Scriptures. He was prepared to endure everything for the emperor and the empire, even death and the greatest dishonor. But he had always to reserve to himself the freedom to proclaim and testify to the Word of God.

Shortly afterward Elector Frederick, "who did not wish to act contrary to God's Word, but did not care to have himself burdened with the emperor either," had Philip von Feilitzsch and Frederick von Thun inform Luther secretly that he would be "put up" somewhere on the way. We do not know whether it was of his own accord or not that Frederick came upon this idea, which had been mentioned by Luther's friends as early as December, 1518. At all events, he left its execution to his councilors. He did not even wish to know the location that they had selected for putting Luther up. Consequently he could assure the diet with a clear conscience on May 12 that he did not know anything about Luther's apprehension. At first Luther did not like this plan at all. He would rather, he said, have suffered death at the hands of the tyrants, especially at the hands of the furious Duke George. Realizing, however, that he should not ignore the counsel of good people in such matters, he finally acceded.

On the morning of April 26, after the midday meal—at which (as Aleander, who was not present himself, reported to Rome soon after) he was alleged to have toasted "many" slices of bread for himself with his own hands and to have drunk "many" goblets of malmsey—he left the town again, accompanied by his friends in two wagons, but without the imperial herald, and hence without causing a stir. Beyond Martin's Gate he was joined by a band of about twenty horsemen—of course, not troopers of Sickingen, as the uneasy nuncio thought, but Bernard von Hirschfeld and several others of the lords who had gone to meet him on April 16 and who were now escorting him again a short distance along the road toward Mainz.

CHAPTER XXVIII

TO THE REGION OF BIRDS AND AIR

On the evening of April 26 the members of the Wittenberg party safely reached Oppenheim, where they were
rejoined by Sturm, the herald. On April 27 they again spent
the night at "The Ostrich" in Frankfurt on the Main. From
here Luther wrote a humorous letter on his experience at
Worms to the artist, Lucas Cranach. "I thought His Majesty
the Emperor would have brought together some fifty doctors
to refute the monk in argument, but in fact all they said was:
'Are these books yours?' 'Yes!' 'Will you recant?' 'No!'
'Then get out!' O we blind Germans! How childishly we act
and let ourselves be so woefully fooled and mocked by the
Romanists!" On April 28 he went on to Friedberg. Here
he took leave of the imperial herald and sent him back to
Worms with two voluminous letters, one in German to the
imperial estates and one in Latin to the emperor.[1] He perhaps did not dismiss the herald without at least giving him
a hint that he could continue his journey in safety, otherwise
the faithful man would hardly have left him so soon.

On April 29 Luther was in Grünberg and on the thirtieth
on the road to Hersfeld. Some distance outside the city, at
the large milestone, he encountered the abbot's chancellor
and treasurer and soon afterward Abbot Crato himself, who
had ridden out with his horsemen especially to escort him
into the town in state. At the city gates he was formally
welcomed by the town council, and he and his companions
were then handsomely lodged and entertained in the monastery by the abbot. On May 1, at five o'clock in the morning,
he was obliged to yield to Abbot Crato's insistence that he
preach in the monastery church, though he was reluctant to

[1] Original in the Lutherhalle at Wittenberg.

428

do so for fear that his friendly host would suffer for it. In gratitude for this, the abbot accompanied him with his horsemen as far as the "forest" and also saw that he was royally entertained again by his chancellor in Berka. In Eisenach, which he reached on the evening of May 1, the authorities were apparently somewhat reserved, but the people flocked to meet him with joy and urged him to preach from the pulpit of the parish church on the following morning. The priest, however, was very hesitant in giving his consent. He capitulated only after he had established before a notary and witnesses that he had yielded his pulpit to the outlaw under protest. It was here in Eisenach, some time on May 3, that Luther was secretly instructed to turn off from the main highway and continue his journey to Gotha over a less traveled road through Altenstein, Schweina, and Waltershausen. He was perhaps also informed of the approximate time and place of the projected ambush. It was suggested, apparently, that a visit to his relatives in and around Möhra might be given as a pretext for this unexpected detour. He thought it well, however, to let only Amsdorf into the secret and to separate from Schurpff and Suaven at once. While Schurpff and Suaven continued the journey in the Wittenberg wagon on the main highway direct to Gotha, he and Amsdorf and Brother Petzensteiner rode southward in the other wagon to Möhra, where he stayed the night of May 3 with his uncle Heinz in the paternal homestead. The next morning he preached to the peasants in the open air, there being no church in Möhra at that time.

In the afternoon Uncle Heinz and the other Luders of Möhra accompanied him on horseback to the vicinity of Castle Altenstein. Shortly after the Luders had taken leave, Amsdorf saw four or five horsemen "sweep out" of the forest which lined both sides of the road. He immediately called the attention of his companions to this suspicious appearance. In the emergency Luther snatched up his Hebrew Bible and his Greek New Testament. But Brother Petzensteiner, to whom he had previously very wisely said nothing, immediately sprang out of the wagon like a startled rabbit and ran full speed into the bushes. Meanwhile the horsemen had galloped up and were hectoring the driver with drawn crossbows and demanding to know whether he was driving Luther. The driver in his terror confessed at once that he was. Thereupon, while Amsdorf set up a loud shouting, they pulled the Reformer out of the wagon with abusive curses and dragged him down the road toward Brotterode with all speed, so that he had to run along as fast as he could like a dog beside a trotting horse. Not until they were completely out of sight of the wagon did they make themselves known and lift him upon a horse. Then they rode for hours in all directions in order to avoid all the more traveled roads and wipe out their tracks. Luther was thoroughly exhausted when they finally rode over the clanking drawbridge into the court of the Wartburg about eleven o'clock.

Here Luther was given a warm welcome by the knight, Sternberg, and the warden of the castle, Hans von Berlepsch, who had been the chief planner of this bit of "horseplay." They informed him immediately, however, that he would have to change his cowl at once for the knight's attire already laid out for him, and that he must not leave the two rooms[1] which had been prepared for him until his tonsure had grown

[1] Luther states explicitly that he occupied two rooms, sitting room and bedroom, and that the rooms were entered by means of a movable ladder which was taken away at night (*Table Talk* 6, 6816). Not until 1574 does the statement appear that he was lodged in the so-called *Vogtei*, or bailiff's quarters. The room which is exhibited as the Luther Room today, as well as the other rooms in the *Vogtei*, was used as late as the eighteenth century as a jail. Whether it was ever occupied by Luther can no longer be determined. In any case, it was not until the beginning of the nineteenth century that it was furnished as the Luther Room, the expenses defrayed chiefly by Grand Duchess Maria Paulowna. In 1811 the table, which is still the chief article of furnishing, was acquired from one of the Luther houses in Möhra. It was not until later that the two armchairs were placed in the room, one of them coming authentically from Aquileja, the other from Nuremberg. About the same time, the cabinet now hanging on the wall was acquired in Aix-la-Chapelle, and the famous piece of whalebone, which was supposed to have served the Reformer as a footstool, from some other place. The tile stove with the image of the arch-Catholic Elector, Maximilian I of Bavaria (died 1650), which now stands in the corner, had been erected before this time. Finally in 1854 the bed, which came from the inn called "The Boot" at Rudolstadt, was added to the collection. To be sure, it is very old, but neither song nor saga mentions that Luther ever slept in it. When the famous ink spot, which in the year 1706 still decorated the wall behind the stove in the so-called Wittenberg Luther Room, emigrated to the Wartburg, the author does not know. In any case, it is to

and his chin and cheeks were adorned with a regular knight's beard. Fortunately, when he saw the horsemen coming, he had seized his Hebrew Bible and Greek New Testament, so he at least had something to read in his "prison." For he was not permitted to let himself be seen by anyone except Berlepsch and the two noble pages who brought him his meals regularly at ten o'clock in the morning and five in the evening, until the smooth-faced monk had become the curly-headed, black-bearded Junker George, whose strange-

---

be seen in magnificent prominence on a picture as early as 1841. Thus the three portraits by Cranach the Elder, of Melanchthon and Luther's parents, presented by the Grand Duchess Maria Paulowna, are the only authentically genuine articles in the room.

So far as the genuineness of the other so-called Luther Rooms is concerned, the situation is not much better. The so-called ancestral home at Möhra was not erected until 1618, and the birthplace in Eisleben was burned in 1689. Whether Luther was born in the room on the left side of the ground floor, which escaped the flames, and which is exhibited as the room in which he was born, is not known. Only the walls are genuine in the Luther Room exhibited in the house in which he died; the furnishings are as late as the nineteenth century. The so-called *Vaterhaus* in Mansfeld had to be rebuilt in 1805. Only the ground floor of the school in Mansfeld is old, and the Church of St. George was remodeled in 1497 and renovated in 1616. The two Luther houses in Eisenach had nothing whatever to do with either Luther or Ursula von Cotta. Only one old Romanesque column remains of the *Bursa* of St. George in Erfurt. The university building was destroyed in 1510 and was not restored until 1525-50. Even of this reconstruction only the front remains. The Augustinian Church was renovated in 1617; in 1627 it was furnished with galleries and with a new altar wall in 1633; and in 1849-54 it was restored from the ground up. The rest of the old altar and the old pulpit was used for firewood at the time of the Union Parliament. Of the old monastery only the cloister and the chapter house, which was not constructed until 1516-18, still exist. The rest was destroyed by fire on March 6, 1872, including the cell which Luther was alleged to have occupied (page 56 supra). Even the Black Cloister in Wittenberg has not escaped the zeal of the restorer. Since 1844 the main building has been transformed into a sort of castle in Tudor style, especially by the addition of a balcony and an elegant tower and cupola. In the so-called Luther Room, only the masonry is old. The floor, ceiling, paneling, curtain poles, the pegs used for hanging up clothes, the window seat, and the five-storied stove are all restorations. The pine table is doubtless old, but hardly from Luther's legacy. The chapel in which the Reformer preached was destroyed as early as 1542 (cf. p. 82); his "cubicle" was demolished probably shortly after his death (cf. p. 85). The courtyard has taken on an altogether different appearance, through the planting of trees and the erection of the Augusteum and the building connecting the Augusteum with the *Lutherhaus*. The town church appears from the outside on the whole about the same as it did originally, but the inside is completely Gothic. The remains of the pulpit now in the *Lutherhalle* are probably genuine, and also the lectern, but hardly, at least at present reckoning, the sandglass. The castle church, as everybody knows, is completely restored. The tomb in it, however, is genuine and actually contains the bones of Luther. On the Luther oak at the Elster Gate compare the note on page 370.

The genuineness of the so-called Luther relics is equally uncertain. The doctor's ring in the Brunswick Museum probably came from Luther's legacy, but it cannot be identical with the ring that Luther received at his promotion in 1512, for, according to reports of the Leipzig Disputation, that one must have been of silver. All the manuscripts mentioned in the text, however, are unquestionably genuine, and probably also the so-called last cowl of the Reformer, which hangs beside Goethe's sky-blue silk nightgown in the Weimar Library. Nevertheless, it is probably not the very last one which he wore and doffed on October 9, 1524. It appears to be too little worn and must be the *cappa* in which he appeared at the Wartburg on May 4, 1521.

looking features are preserved in Lucas Cranach's famous oil painting of December, 1521.

This is not the place to describe the effect that the report of the surprise attack at Glasbach had upon both friend and foe in Worms and elsewhere in Germany, and how this sudden disappearance of the Reformer affected the subsequent development of the evangelical movement. From this point onward Luther's own life story can be told only in connection with the development of the evangelical movement, for, though Luther's later influence was powerful, after his "imprisonment" his influence was no longer the only influence at work. There were others who worked beside him in a constantly increasing measure, and not seldom also against him, and this always strongly influenced his personal life too. For the most part, therefore, the rest of his life can be viewed only as a part of a larger movement and not as that of an isolated personality. As in the case of his personal life, so also the further development of his views—in so far as there was such development—was from this time forth fundamentally determined by the antagonisms which now began to appear within the evangelical movement. In this respect, too, the moment when the gates of the Wartburg closed behind him for the first time marked an epoch, a decisive turning point in his career. It may be said that now the period of his youth was definitely closed.

But is it not somewhat rash to speak of him as young at this time? After all, he was almost thirty-seven and a half years old. But like most of the great men in the history of religion, he developed exceedingly late. It was not until his thirtieth year—at the age when the average individual as a rule is no longer able to summon up the strength to adapt himself fully and inwardly to new views and new perceptions—that Luther, to use his own words, began to give birth to something new. But this only proves that he must be measured by another standard than that which is applied to the so-called normal person whose career can be summed up in the sentence: He lived, took a wife, and died. To retain his own metaphor, Luther could not give birth until he had conceived, that is, until he had become certain of his God. But when this had occurred, he became, more than any other man of German blood, the exemplification of the truth of the saying, "Where genius and faith meet, miracles occur."

INDEX

INDEX

Abelard, 172

Accolti, 348, 350, 352

Accursius, 33

Adam, Ulrich, 192

Address to the Christian Nobility, 321, 322, 330, 332-46, 358, 361, 394

Adelmann, Bernard, 293, 355, 375

Adolph of Anhalt, bishop of Merseburg, 60, 190, 271, 278, 303, 304

Adrian of Utrecht, 296, 305, 350

Adversus Execrabilem Antichristi Bullam, 361

Aesop, 10

Agricola, John, 184, 370, 373

Ailly, *see* d'Ailly

Aix-la-Chapelle, 382, 430

Albrecht of Mainz, Archbishop, 152, 153, 183, 185, 190, 202 ff., 281, 303 ff.

Albrecht of Mansfeld, Count, 217, 243

Alchemy, 26

Alcoran, *see* Koran

Aleander, Jerome, 355, 365, 366-68, 373, 375, 381-83, 385, 387-91, 402, 403, 405-07, 409-11, 417, 420, 422, 427

Alexander, *see* Villedieu

Alexander III, Pope, 168

Alexander VI, Pope, 68, 174, 175, 331, 377

Alfeld, Augustine of, 317, 322, 358

Alps, 61

Altenburg, 246, 247, 253, 259, 261, 271, 273, 291, 348, 356, 357, 358

Altenstein, 429

Ambrosian liturgy, 75

Amsdorf, Nicholas von, 161, 279, 281, 283, 400, 405, 411, 420, 421, 429, 430

Anabaptist, 113

Anaxagoras, 207

Anhalt, 17, 60

Anna, St., 15, 33

Annaberg, 181, 253, 281, 291

Answer by Prierias, 317

Answer of the Unlearned Canons, 293

Answer to Ambrose Catharinus, 395, 396, 399

Anthony, St., 155, 181

Antichrist, 265, 275, 276, 318, 319, 322, 323, 336, 344, 361, 362, 372, 373, 375, 378, 395, 396

Antichrist, Against the Bull of, 362

Antiqui, 98

Antoninus of Florence, 135, 219

Antwerp, 365

Apennines, 60

Apostolic See, On the, (Alfeld), 317

Appolonia, St., 155

Aquileja, 430

Aquinas, Thomas, 44, 101, 108, 171, 226, 230, 236, 328, 370

Aristotle, 24, 25, 26, 27, 28, 52, 131, 150, 159, 161, 207, 226, 338, 402

Arius, 41, 365

Armenstorff, 403

Arnold, Bartholomew, *see* Usingen

Arnstadt, 29, 42

Arsenius, St., 132

Asceticism, 148

Aschaffenburg, 202

Aschersleben, 269

Assertio Omnium Articulorum, 372, 392

Astrology, vii, 25

Athanasius, 41

Auerbach, 278

Auerbach, Dr., *see* Stromer

Augsburg, 69, 73, 77, 200, 220, 226 ff., 231, 233, 234, 237, 242, 244 ff., 251, 252, 257, 258, 262, 267,

437